Transdisciplinary Feminist R

What is feminist transdisciplinary research? Why is it important? How do we do it? Through 19 contributions from leading international feminist scholars, this book provides new insights into activating transdisciplinary feminist theories, methods and practices in original, creative and exciting ways – ways that make a difference both to what research is and does, and to what counts as knowledge. The contributors draw on their own original research and engage an impressive array of contemporary theorising – including new materialism, decolonialism, critical disability studies, historical analyses, Black, Indigenous and Latina Feminisms, queer feminisms, Womanist Methodologies, trans studies, arts-based research, philosophy, spirituality, science studies and sports studies – to trouble traditional conceptions of research, method and praxis. The authors show how working beyond disciplinary boundaries, and integrating insights from different disciplines to produce new knowledge, can prompt important new transdisciplinarity thinking and activism in relation to ongoing feminist concerns about knowledge, power and gender. In doing so, the book attends to the multiple lineages of feminist theory and practice and seeks to bring these historical differences and intersections into play with current changes, challenges and opportunities in feminism. The book's practically-grounded examples and wide-ranging theoretical orbit are likely to make it an invaluable resource for established scholars and emerging researchers in the social sciences, arts, humanities, education and beyond.

Carol A. Taylor is Professor of Higher Education and Gender, and Director of Research (Department of Education) at the University of Bath. Carol's research focuses on the entangled relations of knowledge–power–gender–space–ethics, and utilises feminist, new materialist and posthumanist theories and methodologies to explore gendered inequalities, spatial practices and staff and students' participation in a range of higher education sites. Her latest co-edited books are *Posthumanism and Higher Education: Reimagining Pedagogy, Practice and Research* (2019, with A. Bayley), and *Gender in Learning and Teaching: Feminist Dialogues across International Boundaries* (2019, with A. Abbas and C. Amade-Escot). Carol is co-editor of the journal *Gender and Education* and serves on the Editorial Boards of *Teaching in Higher Education* and *Critical Studies in Teaching and Learning*. Carol's work is widely published in international journals.

Christina Hughes is Professor of Women and Gender Studies and has worked at the Universities of Warwick, Sheffield Hallam and Kent. She is a Visiting Professor at the University of Coventry. Her research career began with a participant observation study of stepfamilies and has included issues related to employment, career and education. She also has longstanding interests in research methodologies. Her edited books include *Researching Gender* (2013), *Posthuman Research Practices in Education* (2016, with Carol A. Taylor), and *International Perspectives of Learning Gain* (2020, with Malcolm Tight).

Jasmine B. Ulmer, PhD, is Assistant Professor at Wayne State University in Detroit. Within the College of Education, she teaches and directs the doctoral track in qualitative inquiry. Her programme of research develops inclusive inquiry methodologies and pedagogies. She locates her work at the intersection of qualitative inquiry and visual communications, aiming to foster a more diverse, inclusive, peaceful world. Prior to entering post-secondary education, she served as an instructional coach, National Board Certified Teacher, and classroom policy fellow at the United States Department of Education. She has been recognised with the Early Career Award from the measurement and research division of the American Educational Research Association. She has also been a Wayne State University Humanities Center Faculty Fellow and Visiting Scholar at Ghent University in Belgium.

Routledge Research in Gender and Society

81 **Motherhood in Contemporary International Perspective**
Continuity and Change
Edited by Fabienne Portier-Le Cocq

82 **Gender Violence in Ecofeminist Perspective**
Intersections of Animal Oppression, Patriarchy and Domination of the Earth
Gwen Hunnicutt

83 **Reframing Drag**
Beyond Subversion and the Status Quo
Kayte Stokoe

84 **Rape in the Nordic Countries**
Continuity and Change
Edited by Marie Bruvik Heinskou, May-Len Skilbrei and Kari Stefansen

85 **Refracting through Technologies**
Bodies, Medical Technologies and Norms
Ericka Johnson

86 **Young, Disabled and LGBT+**
Voices, Identities and Intersections
Edited by Alex Toft and Anita Franklin

87 **Transdisciplinary Feminist Research**
Innovations in Theory, Method and Practice
Edited by Carol A. Taylor, Christina Hughes and Jasmine B. Ulmer

88 **Identity, Belonging, and Community in Men's Roller Derby**
Dawn Fletcher

For more information about this series, please visit: www.routledge.com/sociology/series/SE0271

Transdisciplinary Feminist Research

Innovations in Theory, Method and Practice

Edited by Carol A. Taylor,
Christina Hughes and
Jasmine B. Ulmer

Routledge
Taylor & Francis Group
LONDON AND NEW YORK

First published 2020
by Routledge
2 Park Square, Milton Park, Abingdon, Oxon OX14 4RN

and by Routledge
605 Third Avenue, New York, NY 10017

First issued in paperback 2022

Routledge is an imprint of the Taylor & Francis Group, an informa business

© 2020 selection and editorial matter, Carol A. Taylor, Christina Hughes, and Jasmine B. Ulmer; individual chapters, the contributors

The right of Carol A. Taylor, Christina Hughes, and Jasmine B. Ulmer to be identified as the authors of the editorial matter, and of the authors for their individual chapters, has been asserted in accordance with sections 77 and 78 of the Copyright, Designs and Patents Act 1988.

All rights reserved. No part of this book may be reprinted or reproduced or utilised in any form or by any electronic, mechanical, or other means, now known or hereafter invented, including photocopying and recording, or in any information storage or retrieval system, without permission in writing from the publishers.

Trademark notice: Product or corporate names may be trademarks or registered trademarks, and are used only for identification and explanation without intent to infringe.

Publisher's Note
The publisher has gone to great lengths to ensure the quality of this reprint but points out that some imperfections in the original copies may be apparent.

British Library Cataloguing-in-Publication Data
A catalogue record for this book is available from the British Library

Library of Congress Cataloging-in-Publication Data
A catalog record has been requested for this book

ISBN: 978-0-367-19004-0 (hbk)
ISBN: 978-0-367-50051-1 (pbk)
ISBN: 978-0-429-19977-6 (ebk)

DOI: 10.4324/9780429199776

Typeset in Times New Roman
by Wearset Ltd, Boldon, Tyne and Wear

Contents

List of figures viii
Acknowledgements ix
Editors x
Contributors xii

1 **Introduction** 1
 CHRISTINA HUGHES

2 **Walking as trans(disciplinary)mattering:
 a speculative musing on acts of feminist indiscipline** 4
 CAROL A. TAYLOR

3 **Critical disability studies and the problem of method** 16
 ADA S. JAARSMA

4 **Historical interludes: the productive uncertainty
 of feminist transdisciplinarity** 29
 ASILIA FRANKLIN-PHIPPS

5 **Powerful dressing: artfully challenging sexism
 in the academy** 43
 LINDA KNIGHT, EMILY GRAY AND MINDY BLAISE

6 **Listening to water: situated dialogues between Black,
 Indigenous and Black-Indigenous feminisms** 59
 FIKILE NXUMALO AND MARLEEN
 TEPEYOLOTL VILLANUEVA

7 The bathroom polemic: addressing the ethical and political significance of transgender informed epistemologies for feminist transdisciplinary inquiry 76
WAYNE MARTINO AND JENNIFER C. INGREY

8 Performance practice and ecofeminism: a diffractive approach for a transdisciplinary pedagogy 90
CARA BERGER

9 Living in the hyphens: between a here, a there, *and* an elsewhere 103
VEENA BALSAWER

10 Caster Semenya: the surveillance of sportswomen's bodies, feminism and transdisciplinary research 116
BELINDA WHEATON, LOUISE MANSFIELD, JAYNE CAUDWELL AND REBECCA WATSON

11 Womanist and Chicana/Latina feminist methodologies: contemplations on the spiritual dimensions of research 124
MICHELLE SALAZAR PÉREZ AND CINTHYA M. SAAVEDRA

12 Hear me roar: sound feminisms and qualitative methodologies 138
WALTER S. GERSHON

13 Inter(r)uptions: reimagining dialogue, justice, and healing 153
ANJANA RAGHAVAN

14 Moving with the folds of time and place: exploring gut reactions in speculative transdisciplinary research with teen girls' in a post-industrial community 168
GABRIELLE IVINSON AND EMMA RENOLD

15 Transition states: chemistry educators engaging with and being challenged by matter, materiality and what may come to be 184
KATHRYN SCANTLEBURY, ANITA HUSSÉNIUS AND CATHERINE MILNE

16 **Embodying critical arts-based research: complicating thought/thot leaders through transdisciplinary discourse** 199
GLORIA J. WILSON

17 **(Un)disciplined: What is the terrain of my thinking?** 212
SUSAN NAOMI NORDSTROM

18 **Sex: a transdisciplinary concept** 224
STELLA SANDFORD

19 **Conclusion: the rusty futures of transdisciplinary feminism** 237
JASMINE B. ULMER

Index 248

Figures

2.1	Sugar cone and label	9
5.1	Power Dressing 1	53
5.2	Power Dressing 2	54
5.3	Power Dressing 3	54
5.4	Power Dressing 4	55
5.5	Power Dressing 5	55
5.6	Power Dressing 6	56
5.7	Power Dressing 7	57
5.8	Power Dressing 8	57
5.9	Power Dressing 9	57
6.1 and 6.2	Water play in a toddler classroom	62
6.3, 6.4, 6.5, 6.6	Black sand–water encounters	65
6.7 and 6.8	Forest–water pipe encounters	68
6.9	Happy water drawing	71
8.1	The central performance space	98
14.1	The syncline	173
14.2	Gastric folds	176
15.1	Snaplog: water and paperclip	191
15.2	Snaplog: planting peas	191
15.3	Snaplog: clay	192
16.1	*(Re)Mixed*	199
19.1	Rust	242

Acknowledgements

Over the years we have taken part in many passionate and provocative dialogues, debates and discussions with feminist colleagues in many different contexts and countries. We give heartfelt thanks to them for sparking and fuelling our (collective) ongoing work to enact feminist praxis in theory, method and practice, and to the authors in this book – our transdisciplinary co-conspirators – whose work across disciplinary borders attests to the energy, generativity and creativity of these endeavours. Such work, in its connections, entanglements and engagements, helps support our (collective) efforts to contest the simplistic and divisive methodolatries of research-as-usual. In doing so, it invents, creates and enacts feminist praxis by linking thinking, knowing, doing and being so that we might better orient ourselves to unpicking, with care and determination, the small and large patriarchal and sexist injustices which deform mainstream knowledge practices. Feminist research burns brightly through our (collective) efforts. Thanks to each other for an energising ride and thanks to the team at Routledge for helping us bring this project to fruition with care and patience.

Carol, Christina and Jasmine
January 2020

Editors

Carol A. Taylor is Professor of Higher Education and Gender, and Director of Research (Department of Education) at the University of Bath. Carol is interested in the entangled relations of knowledge-power-gender-space-ethics, and her research utilizes feminist, new materialist and posthumanist theories and methodologies to explore gendered inequalities, spatial practices and staff and students' participation in a range of higher education sites. Her latest co-edited books are *Posthumanism and Higher Education: Reimagining Pedagogy, Practice and Research* (2019, with A. Bayley), and *Gender in Learning and Teaching: Feminist Dialogues across International Boundaries* (2019, with A. Abbas and C. Amade-Escot). Carol is co-editor of the journal *Gender and Education*, and serves on the Editorial Boards of *Teaching in Higher Education* and *Critical Studies in Teaching and Learning*. Carol's work is widely published in international journals. She is Convener of the Gender and Education Network of the European Educational Research Association, and on the Steering Group of the Educational Congress of Qualitative Inquiry.

Christina Hughes is Professor of Women and Gender and has worked at the Universities of Warwick, Sheffield Hallam and Kent. She is a Visiting Professor at the University of Coventry. Her research career began with a participant observation study of stepfamilies and has included issues related to employment, career and education. She also has longstanding interests in research methodologies. Her edited books include *Researching Gender* (2013), *Posthuman Research Practices in Education* (2016, with Carol A. Taylor), and *International Perspectives of Learning Gain* (2020, with Malcolm Tight).

Jasmine B. Ulmer, PhD, is Assistant Professor at Wayne State University in Detroit. Within the College of Education, she teaches and directs the doctoral track in qualitative inquiry. Her program of research develops inclusive inquiry methodologies and pedagogies. She locates her work at the intersection of qualitative inquiry and visual communications, aiming to foster a more diverse, inclusive, peaceful world. Prior to entering post-secondary education, she served as an instructional coach, National Board Certified

Teacher, and classroom policy fellow at the United States Department of Education. She has been recognized with the Early Career Award from the measurement and research division of the American Educational Research Association. She also been a Wayne State University Humanities Center Faculty Fellow and visiting scholar at Ghent University in Belgium.

Contributors

Veena Balsawer is originally from Mumbai (Bombay), India, but for the last three decades she has lived in Ottawa, Canada. She finally decided to pursue her long-cherished dream and completed a PhD (in Education) at the University of Ottawa. Having been raised by parents who were storytellers, she is interested in stories and storytelling; thus she went in search of women's stories to understand how they negotiate and navigate their hybrid lives. She feels that it is this invisible yarn or thread of stories that binds people together.

Cara Berger is Lecturer in Theatre Studies at the University of Manchester. Her research focuses on feminism and ecology in contemporary theatre and performance. Her writing has been published in *Performance Research*, *Contemporary Theatre Review* and the *Journal of Dramatic Theory and Criticism*. Currently, she is working on a project that re-reads performance works created between the mid-twentieth century and the early twenty-first century through the intersection of feminist and ecological perspectives. She co-convenes the Directing and Dramaturgy working group of the Theatre and Performance Research Association (TaPRA).

Mindy Blaise is Vice Chancellor's Professorial Research Fellow at Edith Cowan University. With Emily Gray and Linda Knight, she co-founded #FEAS (Feminist Educators Against Sexism). In 2010, with Veronica Pacini-Ketchabaw and Affrica Taylor, she formed the Common Worlds Research Collective. Recently she co-founded The Ediths, an ECU group of feminist interdisciplinary researchers currently researching children's waste, water and weather relations. These research collectives are committed to supporting and doing research in collective, ethical and political ways. Mindy conducts collaborative, responsive, embodied and creative research that sets out to challenge sexism and children's relations with place, animals and the world.

Jayne Caudwell is Associate Professor in the Department of Sport and Event Management at Bournemouth University, UK. Her work focuses on gender, sexualities and social justice within sport and leisure cultures. Through her research and academic activism, she has contributed to the development of

LGBTQI equality and inclusion in sport, leisure and physical activity. She is Managing Editor of the journal *Leisure Studies* and was Associate Managing Editor of the *Sociology of Sport Journal* (2014–2017). She is co-editor of *The Palgrave Handbook of Feminism and Sport, Leisure and Physical Education* (2017).

Asilia Franklin-Phipps is Lauder Postdoctoral Fellow at the Teaching and Learning Center at the Graduate Center, City University of New York. She teaches courses at Hunter College, School of Visual Arts and Brooklyn College. In both her teaching and research, Asilia focuses on the production of race and racism, gender and sexuality, pedagogy and arts-based research practices in the context of culture, history and education.

Walter S. Gershon is Associate Professor in the School of Teaching, Learning and Curriculum Studies. He served as Provost Associate Faculty for Diversity, Equity and Inclusion (2014–2017) and is LGBTQ Affiliate Faculty at Kent State University. His scholarship focuses on questions of social justice about how people make sense, the sociocultural contexts that inform their sense-making and the qualitative methods used to study those processes. Although his work most often attends to how marginalised youth negotiate schools and schooling, Walter is also interested in how people of all ages negotiate educational contexts both within and outside of institutions. In addition to peer-reviewed articles, book chapters and guest-edited special issues, Dr Gershon is the author of two recent award-winning books: *Curriculum and Students in Classrooms: Everyday Urban Education in an Era of Standardization* (2017) and *Sound Curriculum: Sonic Studies in Educational Theory, Method, and Practic*e (2017). An edited volume, *Sensuous Curriculum: Politics and the Senses in Education (IAP)*, has also been recently published.

Emily Gray is originally from Walsall, UK, and is Senior Lecturer in Education Studies at RMIT's School of Education. Her interests within both research and teaching are interdisciplinary and include sociology, cultural studies and education. She is particularly interested in questions of gender and sexuality and with how these identity categories are lived and experienced within social institutions. Her key research interests therefore lie with questions related to gender, social justice, student and teacher identity work within educational policy and practice and with wider social justice issues within educational discourse and practice. She is also concerned with popular culture, public pedagogies and audience studies, particularly with online 'fandom' and with media and popular culture as pedagogical tools. Emily is co-founder, with Mindy Blaise and Linda Knight of #FEAS, an international feminist collective committed to developing arts-based interventions into sexism in the academy.

Christina Hughes is Professor of Women and Gender and has worked at the Universities of Warwick, Sheffield Hallam and Kent. She is a Visiting

Professor at the University of Coventry. Her research career began with a participant observation study of stepfamilies and has included issues related to employment, career and education. She also has longstanding interests in research methodologies. Her edited books include *Researching Gender* (2013), *Posthuman Research Practices in Education* (2016, with Carol A. Taylor) and *International Perspectives of Learning Gain* (2020, with Malcolm Tight).

Anita Hussénius is Associate Professor in Chemistry and researcher at the Centre for Gender Research at Uppsala University, Sweden. Her main research interest is gender and feminist perspectives on science and science education. More specifically, her research focuses on issues connected to gender awareness in science and in science teaching. This includes a problematising of the 'science culture', that is, what/how conceptions about the discipline and its practices are implicitly and explicitly communicated in the meeting with students and its consequences for feelings of inclusion/ exclusion.

Jennifer C. Ingrey, PhD, is Adjunct and Assistant Professor in equity and social justice education in the Faculty of Education at the University of Western Ontario, Canada. Her research interests centre around transgender studies, school spaces and gendered subjectivities for young people, as well as writer reflexivity; her teaching interests extend into equity and social justice more broadly to include anti-homonormative, anti-racist, decolonising, anti-classist and disability studies informed curriculum for teacher candidates and graduate students. She teaches in Writing in the English, French, and Writing Department at King's University College where she is also a Writing Specialist. She has a contract with Routledge for an upcoming book entitled, *Re-thinking School Spaces for Transgender, Genderqueer, and Non-Binary Youth: The School Washroom as Heterotopia*. She also co-edited a collection entitled, *Queer Studies and Education: Critical Concepts for the Twenty-First Century* (2016, with Wayne Martino, Nelson Rodriguez and Ed Brockenbrough).

Gabrielle Ivinson Professor of Education and Community at Manchester Metropolitan University. She develops arts-based methods to attune to what lies beyond the spoken word, enabling embodied affects to become visible through multiple media (as sounds, artefacts, dance, movements and films). She co-ordinates the *Creative Margins* network exploring how to make arts accessible to marginalised young people.

Ada S. Jaarsma is Professor of Philosophy in the Department of Humanities at Mount Royal University in Calgary, Canada. Her work examines the intersections of continental philosophy, feminist theory, disability studies and science and technology studies. She is the author of *Kierkegaard after the Genome: Science, Existence and Belief in This World* (2017) and recently co-edited *Dissonant Methods: Undoing Discipline in the Humanities Classroom* (2020).

Linda Knight is an artist and academic who specialises in critical and speculative arts practices and methods. Linda devised 'Inefficient Mapping' as a methodological protocol for conducting fieldwork in projects informed by 'post-theories'. In her role as Associate Professor at RMIT Linda creates transdisciplinary projects across early childhood, creative practice and digital media. Together with Jacina Leong, Linda is part of the Guerrilla Knowledge Unit, an artist collective that curates interface jamming performances between the public and AI technologies. Along with Emily Gray, and Mindy Blaise, Linda is also a founding member of #FEAS. Linda has also been awarded arts research grants and prizes with international reach and impact; this includes works in exhibitions in Australia, the UK, the USA and Canada.

Louise Mansfield is Professor of Sport, Health and Social Sciences and Research Lead for Welfare Health and Wellbeing at Brunel University London. Her research focuses on the relationship between sport, physical activity and public health and she has extensive expertise in partnership and community approaches to physical activity engagement and issues of health, wellbeing, inequality and diversity. She has over 10 years' experience of leading multidisciplinary research projects for local, national and international sport and public health organisations. She is a Managing Editor of *Annals of Leisure Research*, leads the ESRC funded Culture, Sport and Wellbeing Evidence Programme and is known for developing evidence to inform policy and practice. She is co-editor of *The Palgrave Handbook of Feminism and Sport, Leisure and Physical Education* (2017).

Wayne Martino, PhD, is Professor of Equity and Social Justice Education in the Faculty of Education and an affiliate member of the Department of Women's Studies and Feminist Research at the University of Western Ontario, Canada. He is currently Principal Investigator on the SSHRC (Social Sciences, Humanities Research Council of Canada) funded research project entitled: *Supporting Transgender and Gender Diverse Youth in Schools*. His books include: *So what's a boy? Addressing Issues of Masculinity and Schooling* (2003, with Maria Pallotta-Chiarolli); *Gender, Race and the Politics of Role Modelling: The Influence of Male Teachers* (2012, with Goli Rezai-Rashti); *Queer Studies and Education: Critical Concepts for the Twenty-First Century* (2016, with Nelson Rodriguez, Jennifer Ingrey and Ed Brockenbrough); *Queer and Trans Perspectives on Teaching LGBT-Themed Text in Schools* (2018, with Mollie Blackburn and Caroline Clark) and *Investigating Transgender and Gender Expansive Education Research, Policy and Practice* (in press, 2020, with Wendy Cumming-Potvin).

Catherine Milne is Professor of Science Education at New York University. Her research interests include urban science education, socio-cultural elements of teaching and learning science, the role of the history of science in learning science, the development and use of multimedia for teaching and learning science and models of teacher education. She is co-editor-in-chief for the journal *Cultural Studies of Science Education* and co-editor of two book series for Springer Publishers and Brill Publishers.

Susan Naomi Nordstrom is Associate Professor of Educational Research in the Department of Counseling, Educational Psychology and Research at The University of Memphis. She has published on post-qualitative methodologies as well as human and nonhuman relationships in post-qualitative methodologies in leading qualitative research journals.

Fikile Nxumalo is Faculty in the Department of Curriculum, Teaching and Learning at the Ontario Institute for Studies in Education, University of Toronto. Her scholarship focuses on reconceptualising place-based and environmental education within current times of ecological precarity. This scholarship is rooted in perspectives from Indigenous knowledges, Black feminist geographies and critical posthumanist theories. Her research and pedagogical interests are informed by her experiences growing up in eSwatini and working as a pedagogist with children and educators in North American settler colonial contexts. Her latest book, *Decolonizing Place in Early Childhood Education* (2019) examines the entanglements of place, environmental education, childhood, race, and settler colonialism in early learning contexts.

Anjana Raghavan is Senior Lecturer in Sociology in the Department of Psychology, Sociology and Politics, Faculty of Social Sciences and Humanities at Sheffield Hallam University, UK. Her work is located at the interstices of decolonial and queer feminisms, political philosophies and critical theory-practice-performance. She has published work on decolonial spiritual practice, corporeality, cosmopolitanism and women-of-colours feminisms.

Emma Renold's research, inspired by feminist, queer and new materialist posthumanist theory, explores how gender and sexuality come to matter in children and young people's everyday lives across diverse sites, spaces and locales. Here (see www.productivemargins.ac.uk) she has explored the affordances of co-productive, creative and affective methodologies to engage social and political change with young people on gendered and sexual violence, and relationships and sexuality education more widely (see www.agendaonilne.co.uk).

Cinthya M. Saavedra is Associate Professor, Academic Director of the Mexican American Studies Program and Associate Dean for Interdisciplinary Programs and Community Engagement at the University of Texas Rio Grande Valley. Her research centres Chicana/Latina feminist epistemology in the investigation of emergent bilingual, immigrant and borderlands experiences in education. Dr Saavedra's work is published in *Review of Research in Education*, *Equity & Excellence in Education*, *International Journal of Qualitative Studies in Education*, *Language Arts* and *TESOL Quarterly*. She has co-edited special issues in the *Journal of Latino-Latin American Studies* (JOLLAS) and the *Journal of Global Studies of Childhoods*.

Contributors xvii

Michelle Salazar Pérez is interim Associate Dean for Research in the College of Education at New Mexico State University in the United States. She holds the J. Paul Taylor Endowed Professorship and is Associate Professor of early childhood education. Dr Pérez is co-editor of the book *Critical Qualitative Inquiry: Foundations and Futures* (2015), and her work has been published in the journals *Qualitative Inquiry*, *International Review of Qualitative Research*, *Cultural Studies ↔ Critical Methodologies* and *Review of Research in Education*.

Stella Sandford is Professor at the Centre for Research in Modern European Philosophy at Kingston University, London. Her research focusses on philosophies of sex and gender; critical philosophy of race; philosophy and psychoanalytical theory; philosophy of natural history; feminist philosophy and theory; and the application of knowledge from these areas to the critical study of Immanuel Kant. She is the author of *Plato and Sex* (2010), *How to Read Beauvoir* (2006), *The Metaphysics of Love: Gender and Transcendence in Levinas* (2000) and numerous articles and book chapters.

Kathryn Scantlebury is Professor in the Department of Chemistry and Biochemistry at the University of Delaware. Her research interests focus on gender issues in various aspects of science education, including urban education, preservice teacher education, teachers' professional development and academic career paths in academe. Kate is a guest researcher at the Centre for Gender Research at Uppsala University, co-editor of *Gender and Education* and co-editor of two book series for Brill Publishers.

Carol A. Taylor is Professor of Higher Education and Gender and Director of Research (Department of Education) at the University of Bath. Carol's research focuses on the entangled relations of knowledge-power-gender-space-ethics, and utilises feminist, new materialist and posthumanist theories and methodologies to explore gendered inequalities, spatial practices and staff and students' participation in a range of higher education sites. Her latest co-edited books are *Posthumanism and Higher Education: Reimagining Pedagogy, Practice and Research* (2019, with A. Bayley), and *Gender in Learning and Teaching: Feminist Dialogues across International Boundaries* (2019, with A. Abbas and C. Amade-Escot). Carol is co-editor of the journal *Gender and Education*, and serves on the Editorial Boards of *Teaching in Higher Education* and *Critical Studies in Teaching and Learning*. Carol's work is widely published in international journals.

Jasmine B. Ulmer, PhD, is Assistant Professor at Wayne State University in Detroit. Within the College of Education, she teaches and directs the doctoral track in qualitative inquiry. Her programme of research develops inclusive inquiry methodologies and pedagogies. She locates her work at the intersection of qualitative inquiry and visual communications, aiming to foster a more diverse, inclusive, peaceful world. Prior to entering post-secondary education, she served as an instructional coach, National Board Certified

Teacher and classroom policy fellow at the United States Department of Education. She has been recognised with the Early Career Award from the measurement and research division of the American Educational Research Association. She has also been a Wayne State University Humanities Center Faculty Fellow and Visiting Scholar at Ghent University in Belgium.

Marleen Tepeyolotl Villanueva is a PhD student in the Social Justice Education Department at the Ontario Institute for Studies in Education at the University of Toronto, and a former elementary school teacher. She received her master's degree from the University of Texas at Austin's Cultural Studies in Education programme, within the Curriculum and Instruction Department. She is a first-generation student raised in Texas, whose family is from Pame/Chichimeca lands in San Luis Potosí, Mexico and is a member of the Miakan/Garza Band of Coahuiltecan people in Central Texas, as well as a representative for the International Indigenous Youth Council-Texas Chapter.

Rebecca Watson is Reader in the Carnegie School of Sport, Leeds Beckett University, UK. Her research focuses on interrelationships between gender, 'race' and class and informs work on leisure, identities and intersectional approaches across the critical, social analysis of leisure and sport. Beccy is the Academic Lead for the Graduate School at Leeds Beckett. She teaches across undergraduate and postgraduate modules focusing on issues of diversity, equity and inclusion. Beccy was a Managing Editor for the journal *Leisure Studies* between 2007 and 2014. She is co-editor of *The Palgrave Handbook of Feminism and Sport, Leisure and Physical Education* (2017).

Belinda Wheaton is Associate Professor in Sport, Leisure and Wellbeing in the School of Health, University of Waikato, Aotearoa/New Zealand. Her research is rooted in sociologies of sport, leisure and popular culture, underpinned by feminist ethics and politics, and a focus on identity, inclusion and inequality. Belinda is best known for her research on the informal and lifestyle sport cultures which includes a monograph, *The Cultural Politics of Lifestyle Sports* (2013), and three edited collections. She is co-editor of *The Palgrave Handbook of Feminism and Sport, Leisure and Physical Education* (2017) and Managing Editor of *Annals of Leisure Research*.

Gloria J. Wilson, PhD, is currently an Assistant Professor in the School of Art at The University of Arizona. Her ongoing research, teaching and art-making practices examine the intersections of race, gender and participation in arts education and are rooted in critical arts-based and cultural studies approaches. She is published in numerous journals including, among others, *Visual Arts Research*, *Visual Inquiry: Learning & Teaching Art* and *Art/Research International: A Transdisciplinary Journal*.

1 Introduction

Christina Hughes

There is a long history in feminist thought that has been concerned with the shortcomings of disciplinary knowledge. Disciplines cut and chunk human, more-than-human and other-than-human experiences into separate and hierarchised knowledge fields. That such 'disciplining' diminishes our understanding of knowledge as intra-relational, situated and contingent is at the heart of this book. Disciplinarity might create an external façade that the organisation of knowledge is coherent, and even absolute. But it precludes potentially more insightful, creative and intra-active ways of coming to know and, indeed, working towards resolving the many global problems that beset us. And yet many feminists who try to practice our research *with* transdisciplinarity and, in consequence, venture beyond our own disciplinary fields continue to experience how status, power and hierarchy work in terms of who is recognised as a knower and the status of the knowledge we produce.

We as editors of this book along with all of our chapter authors inhabit this landscape: one look at the chapter titles tells us something of the political and affective spaces of the work we do in pushing against the disciplinary powers that seek to constrain our thinking. In the conclusion, Jasmine's metaphor of rust evokes the need to decay, corrupt and decompose disciplinary boundaries. Carol, in Chapter 2, speaks of (and invites) acts of feminist indiscipline. In Chapter 4, Ailsa is concerned with exploring productive uncertainty. Kathryn, Anita and Catherine, in Chapter 15, invoke transition states and Gabrielle and Emma, in Chapter 14, draw on speculative transdisciplinary research. Likewise, becoming (un)disciplined in thinking is core to Susan's exploration in Chapter 18. These chapters offer deliberately provocative challenges which aim at undoing the languages of certainty – as if knowledge could ever be certain. Such undoings take forward long-standing feminist terms of engagement with academic politics; their situated knowledges mark an intent to consciously and systematically disrupt the normative as-is.

Yet there is a strange conundrum in the history of feminist politics and feminist thought which, at one and the same time as emphasising the importance of transdisciplinary knowledge production, has seen disciplines continue to exert their force. The sex–gender binary is one such area. A priori contesting the sex–gender binary should be seen as a political act designed to challenge 'biology is destiny' attitudes and practices. Stella's foundational paper, reprinted as Chapter 18, explores this terrain as she provides a first attempt to construct a transdisciplinary concept of sex. She does this through a close focus on the work of Simone de Beauvoir and illustrates the intra-complexity of language, translation and meaning in producing conceptual understanding.

Stella's chapter draws attention to another phenomenon that has created long-standing struggles in my own career and is echoed in many chapters in this volume. Transdisciplinarity is not the same as multi-disciplinary research where the emphasis is on bringing different individuals from different disciplines *into relation* with one another. It is true that such an approach creates a very interesting ecological field of knowledge. However, ecologies are riven with power and dominance and the question of whose knowledge wins out over whose remains.

We see the implications of this very forcefully in Chapter 10 which focuses on Caster Semenya, the athlete at the centre of controversies on sex testing. As Belinda, Louise Jane and Rebecca indicate, those that legislate for such practices attempt to ignore evidence from different epistemological perspectives. Through their account of cisgender normativity and how it has pitted trans and non-trans women against each other, Wayne and Jennifer, in Chapter 7, also highlight the importance of transcending disciplinary boundaries and logics.

Transdisciplinarity is not, either, the same as inter-disciplinary research where a researcher may draw on more than one discipline or knowledge field but in essence leaves that disciplinary knowledge intact. Transdisciplinarity requires a feminist researcher to be both traveller and novitiate as we have to consistently and repeatedly leave our disciplinary comfort zones and go into unfamiliar knowledge fields often without a map or wayfinder. It requires an inventive willingness, as Linda, Emily and Mindy note in Chapter 5, to break across the disciplinary borders we each might usually rely upon. In this vein, Fikile and Marleen, in Chapter 6, purposefully think with Black, Indigenous and Black-Indigenous feminist theorists and artists, and the potential of multiply situated feminisms alongside everyday early childhood pedagogies; in Chapter 11, Michelle and Cinthya draw on Womanism and Chicana/Latina feminism; and, in Chapter 16, Gloria uses the adjective mixed/*mikst* to summarise how her critical arts-based research consists of different qualities or elements.

For feminists committed to transdisciplinarity such thinking–doing across borders is, as Susan indicates, normal and natural. This is because, as Ada's philosophical interrogation of Critical Disability Studies in Chapter 3 highlights, transdisciplinarity is not understood as a transcendent set of practices. It is a method/ology for bringing disciplinary forms together as emergent and contingent assemblages; *and* an opening towards a reflexive transgression of artificially imposed boundaries; *and* a means of disrupting the fortress model of disciplinarity through enmeshment of theory, positionality, politics and method (Anjana in Chapter 13); and, indeed, as an impossibly entangled antiracist polyphonic cacophony of beingknowinggdoing (Walter in Chapter 12). As Cara's new materialist account of diffraction indicates in Chapter 8, transdisciplinarity produces new concepts to develop new feminist praxis that connects human and other-than-human domains of knowledge. It also encourages ways of writing our work that recognise reciprocity and reciprocal impact, as Jasmine's conclusion indicates and as Veena's poetic renditions (Chapter 9) so movingly enact.

Transdisciplinarity requires not just a rethinking of how knowledge is produced – which is something that feminism is well-versed in. As so much of the work in this book indicates, feminist transdisciplinarity also requires a fundamental shift in the political-ethical questions that are being asked at the heart of knowledge practices. Such new knowledge practices enable us to refuse the 'powerful call' of disciplinary knowledge. They also provoke us to remain alert so that we can resist the normative drag of disciplinary knowledges which repeatedly work to haul us back to the status quo.

The question at the heart of this book is how may we shape affirmative transdisciplinary feminist research praxis? This question is taken up inventively and with feminist passion by our contributors whose work demonstrates their deep commitments to creating new ways of being and doing, learning and teaching, researching and questioning. As they testify, this is not an always altogether comfortable space. But it is an exceedingly generative one as I am sure you will find.

2 Walking as trans(disciplinary) mattering
A speculative musing on acts of feminist indiscipline

Carol A. Taylor

Introduction

This chapter offers a speculative feminist musing on the productive promise of walking as methodological, theoretical and activist feminist indiscipline. It combines an invitation to 'stay with the trouble' (Haraway, 2016) with a transmaterial account of walking (Springgay and Truman, 2017) to indicate how walking as trans(disciplinary)mattering attends to entangled, affective and political materialities which move beyond psychologistic, individually-bodied accounts. The chapter considers what comes to matter (Barad, 2007) when walking is apprehended as a feminist praxis of trans-mattering, and indicates how such an approach might work to contest patriarchal, colonialist, masculinist suppositions. The chapter begins with some definitional work on the conjunction – 'trans(disciplinary)mattering' – which positions walking as a mode of theory–methodology–praxis. This is followed by two instances focusing on walking and whiteness which puts the theory of walking as trans(disciplinary)mattering to work as a productive feminist indisciplinary practice.

Walking as trans(disciplinary)mattering

In what follows, I pursue a line of post/transdisciplinary thinking with Sarah Ahmed, Karen Barad and Kathryn Yuseff, among others, and put walking as trans(disciplinary)mattering to work as a conceptual assemblage, a practical methodological conjunction and a hybrid theoretical politics of location.

I take up 'transdisciplinary' in Sandford's (2015: 160–161) sense as theory and concepts which 'are not necessarily identifiable with any specific disciplinary fields, either in their origin or their application'. Sandford considers both gender and feminism as transdisciplinary in this sense, along with a whole host of fields or studies, including critical race studies, education studies and cultural studies. The transdisciplinary mode I work (walk) towards does not mix or blend disciplines, as in some theoretical martini which accrues disciplinary insights. Rather, it aims to instantiate thinking and praxis as feminist indiscipline which orientates thought in speculative vein to a feminist politics which contests the disciplinary requirement for boundaries, cuts or exclusions in the first place.

In making such an appeal, it speaks into the intimately entwined happening of racism, colonialism and disciplinary thinking.

Sandford (2015) suggests that a number of factors are needed for something to be considered as 'transdisciplinary'. The first is that transdisciplinarity transforms conceptual thinking into a 'historically based [and] materialist' critique (171); the second is that a feminist transdisciplinarity is not a neutral philosophical critique but a politically-inflected act of theoretical and 'practical criticism' (171); and third, that methods which transgress disciplinary boundaries offer a productive means to both unsettle disciplines and to develop a space to think and work within transdisciplinary modes. The figuration of walking as trans(disciplinary) mattering is an attempt to work through these three aspects via two specific research examples.

Walking as a research methodology has gained increasing attention as a means to enact research methodologies which move away from dominant methodologies which privilege speech and human interaction. Pink (2009: 8) sees walking interviews as an alternative methodology for 'understanding, knowing and [producing] knowledge'; Powell (2010: 553) emphasizes walking as multisensory work which 'configures a sense of self in relation to historical, geographical, and localized environments'; and Springgay (2011: 645) calls attention to walking as a foray into 'unrepeatable and fleeing situation[s]'. In addition, walking methodologies present opportunities for research which is emergent, spontaneous and impermanent because walking need not be 'goal-directed in the sense of getting to a preconceived destination' and can be undertaken 'with physically and mentally flexible, free movements' (Jung, 2013: 622). While Jung (2013) promotes the benefits of 'mindful walking', I prefer to move in the direction of walking as an embodied and embedded activity taken up in relation to particular locations, times and geographies.

Thus, I advocate walking as becoming in-tune-with; as slow walking so that one may sense the body's openness and affective immersion in place-scapes; walking as knowing in-walking with mindbody rather than knowledge at a distance based on the cognitive logic of a Cartesian mind/body split. I have referred to this as a mode of 'serendipitous walking' (Taylor and Ulmer, 2019) which is transcorporeal in recognizing that humans and non-humans are enmeshed in material-discursive ways that tell 'stories so far' (Massey, 2005) – stories of power and privilege. Grounded in a processual, post-personal ontology (Massumi, 2014) and as a multi-logical feminist epistemology, serendipitous walking can, I suggest, be a productive endeavour in generating different ways of knowing – and mattering – that are more multiple, complex and discontinuous than the master narratives of White, Western, colonialist patriarchy have allowed.

In this, I agree with Springgay and Truman (2018: 14) who say that 'walking is never neutral', and who urge us to 'cease celebrating the white male flâneur, who strolls leisurely through the city, as the quintessence of what it means to walk' like them, I wish to 'queer walking [by] destabilizing humanism's structuring of human and nonhuman, nature and culture' (14). Thus, walking as trans(disciplinary)mattering is about walking a wavering line – a line that loops, knots, curls, furls and unfurls, a line that knits other lines into it – so as not to re-produce a straight white line. This is walking as errancy; walking governed by a desire to be undisciplined; walking as an orientation toward feminist indiscipline, walking as lack of discipline or control, unwillingness to obey rules; unruly, disorderly; disobedient, ungoverned. Walking as trans(disciplinary)mattering, in refusing to do the work of boundary maintenance, opens a path to a sensing–feeling–knowing activity of speculative indiscipline. In this, it works as a materialist ethico-onto-epistemological endeavour and feminist socio-political praxis.

Walking, envisaged as speculative feminist musing praxis, takes up Haraway's (2016) call to 'stay with the trouble'. The trouble I am interested in is the ongoing work done by Whiteness and how particular activations of research methodology, feminist theory–praxis and human–nonhuman coalitions might help develop 'modest possibilities of partial recuperation and getting on together' (Haraway, 2016: 10). Walking as trans(disciplinary)mattering is a speculative feminist experiment-in-the-making entailing a 'dynamic practice of material engagement with the world' (Barad, 2007: 55) and a suggestive methodology of slow and response-able musing. Speculative musing as a mode of staying with the trouble is, I suggest, a form of contemplating as creating (Deleuze and Guattari, 1994: 212), a praxis in which the *longue durée* of contemplative creation constitutes musing as a political practice (Taylor, 2016) which orients speculation to questions of how to bring forth better entangled futures on a damaged planet (Haraway, 2016). Walking as trans(disciplinary)mattering must, then, be unruly in its orientation to modes of bodily inhabitation which prompt disobedience, ungovernability and a refusal to be subjected to correction or discipline. Asilia Franklin-Phipps (Chapter 4 in this book) interrogates the discipline of history and argues that 'letting go/moving on' is neither possible nor desirable 'when th[e] past has not been let go', and contends that the exploration of 'ugly and painful histories' present opportunities for 'thinking and knowing the present' in different ways. This chapter offers a modest engagement with this profound challenge.

Walking with buildings and sugar: attending to Whiteness

When I was a child I wore glasses and had to go to the Liverpool Children's Eye Hospital every six months for an eye test. It took a whole day: a long trip on the bus, lunch at a restaurant, the appointment and test itself. When it was Dad's turn to take me, we walked slowly around the streets of Liverpool and he read the huge buildings to me. We stopped by the white stone walls, the sky a bright blue sliver with racing grey clouds, wind gusting coldly up off the Mersey, my legs goosepimpled, Dad's eyes crinkled. He held my hand and told me about the merchants whose ships travelled to the coast of West Africa and traded textiles, beads, shells, knives, guns, copper, brass, alcohol, whose crews enslaved Black people in exchange for these goods, and then transported them to the British colonies in the West Indies, Jamaica, Antigua, Grenada, where they sold the slaves onwards to North America, and picked up sugar, cotton, rum and returned to Liverpool. The warmth of his hand as we walked slowly around the city, him telling me about the slave trade triangle, the middle passage, the chains, the deaths, the beatings. Villages unpeopled. Men, women and children labelled, priced and sold as cattle. What grand architecture. What sales. What profit and loss. In all weathers, we walked.

My small girls' body felt it then: Whiteness erects a magnificent façade to hide a rotting heart.

I had no part in the slave trade. But I am White. My working class ancestors and I have not profited from the slave trade like merchants and middle class generations have. But I am White. I am girl, woman, female, my body always othered. But I am White. I am from the North of England, a space ravaged by the geopolitics of post-industrialism so that money can flow to London and the South East. But I am White. I read feminist theory of all kinds looking for kin, for coalitions, for confluences. But I am White.

Those historical injuries did not happen to me but they matter to me.

How, I wonder, can those Liverpool walks provide a route in, a direction, a way of taking my bearings on Whiteness, to face its brutalities and legacies? How can such facing face down that magnificent façade? Holding my smaller hand in his as we walked, my Dad's story was an invitation to look at those Liverpool buildings and refuse that inheritance, refuse the neoclassical colonialist symmetries of a city architecture that held its grandness open to the skies, refuse a system that turns fellow human beings into objects for sale and profit. My Dad left school at 15 but knew that 'white racial domination is enacted moment by moment on individual, interpersonal, cultural and institutional levels' (DiAngelo and Sensoy, 2014: 192–193). Ahmed (2007: 149–150) says, 'Whiteness gains currency by being unnoticed' and that refusing to notice what Whiteness is doing 'allows whiteness to be done'. Ahmed describes Whiteness as 'as an ongoing and unfinished history, which orientates bodies in specific directions, affecting how they "take up" space' (150). Whiteness, she suggests, is real, material and lived; as an orientation it constitutes bodies, their starting points, their directions, and their relations. Drawing on Fanon (1986), she argues that the phenomenal body – the body that feels, senses, knows merely by being a body-in-space – can never simply be a 'neutral' description of a body-at-home (as it appears to be in Husserl or Merleau-Ponty's phenomenology) but is already a body racialized, historicized and, feminists would add, sexualized, aged and dis/abled. The body arrives and the world appears 'as it is', its Whiteness already 'there' in architecture, monuments, statutes, structures, institutions, objects, bodies, relations, habits and practices. This is what White privilege means and does; how it reproduces the normativity that 'is'; how the language of knowing that it writes is inflected by the body.

Whiteness as an inheritance shapes what we come into contact with and conditions our responses. Dad and I craned our necks to look at the details at the top of those buildings, walked across the road to get a better view, passed our palms over the smooth stones, watched the workers going in and out and wondered if they knew that the building they worked in was one of those 'protective pillows of resources and/or benefits' (Fine, 1997: 57) that helped keep the edifice of Whiteness upright. Ahmed (2007) reminds us that Whiteness is not reducible to white skin, it is not an ontological condition, and that asking the question 'what can White people do' is the wrong question because it presumes a return to white agency. Instead, the focus needs to be on power, on developing critique which unpicks the smooth surfaces of power, so that its cracks and instabilities become apparent. Those Liverpool walks with my Dad gave me a glimpse into how the 'institutionalization of whiteness involves work' (Ahmed, 2007: 157): how Whiteness is the work of individuals, a city, a nation; of countries working together in complex socio-economic-political colonial configurations to produce material relations of suffering, destruction and death; and which then produces moves to 'forget' that is what has been done, to erase the complicity of those (in)glorious edifices. Thus, my (ongoing) material and affective entanglement with those buildings is important: their racist work travels into the present and continues to shape bodies, perceptions, psychic (un)knowings, and pride in this city. I am not 'apart' from these matterings.

Which is why these buildings continue to haunt me in tangible ways. As Barad (2010, 2019) points out, hauntings are material; they are not merely subjective memories of a past that has gone. There can be, she says, 'no erasure' of past violences. It is only by 'facing the ghosts, in their materiality and acknowledging injustice' without any empty promises of repair or making amends that we may hear what their 'speaking silence' tells us (Barad, 2010: 264). To 'speak with ghosts', she says:

> Is not to entertain or reconstruct some narrative of the way it was, but to respond, to be responsible, to take responsibility for that which we inherit (from the past and the future), for the entangled relationalities of inheritance that 'we' are, to acknowledge and be responsive to the noncontemporaneity of the present, to put oneself at risk, to risk oneself (which is never one or self), to open oneself up to indeterminacy in moving towards what is to come.... Only in this ongoing responsibility to the entangled other ... is there the possibility of justice-to-come.
>
> (Barad, 2010: 264)

To stay with the trouble those buildings provoked means paying attention to Whiteness – attending to the ongoing work Whiteness does. This means accepting response-ability via orienting my senses towards cultivating a better attentiveness (Haraway, 2016) to how Whiteness works in all manner of small and big ways. This isn't a moral stance. It is, rather, a non-innocent (because I am implicated) ethical endeavour, an effort oriented to learning-with-and-from so that I might in some ways know how to refuse the call, the power, of White authorial power to script history. Walking with those Liverpool buildings offers a means to contest the 'blindness' which produces Whiteness as 'an unracialized identity or location' (DiAngelo, 2011: 59). Pondering those buildings' legacy in the now is, perhaps, an orientation towards helping me develop a little of the 'racial stamina' that DiAngelo (2011: 56) indicates White people lack, due to the 'racial insulation' inculcated by upbringing, culture, and geographies of place.

Many years later. A different city. Walking alone and happening by the Herschel Museum. My footsteps bring me to the following sugar cone and label.

Sugar Cone & Nippers

In the 18th century, sugar came in cones like this one. Sugar cane was crushed and the juices then heated and impurities skimmed off. The remaining liquid was boiled, reduced and then poured into a cone shaped mould, which gave the sugar its unusual shape. This cone of sugar was known as sugar loaf.

Sugar was sold in these loaves and the amount required for a recipe would have to be cut off with sugar nippers, like the ones seen here, then ground down in a pestle and mortar before it was used.

The Herschels would probably have bought sugar that had come to Bath straight from the trading ships docking at Bristol, so it would have been a bit cheaper than in other parts of the country. Sugar was the most important product that came from the colonies in the 18th century and was grown on slave plantations in the West Indies, in places like Jamaica.

At first sugar was so expensive that only the very rich could afford it, but demand was so high that the supply increased and soon even the poorer classes could afford it. During the campaign for the abolition of slavery in England, supporters of the cause boycotted slave produced sugar as a protest.

Figure 2.1 Sugar cone and label.
Source: photo: Carol A. Taylor.

I read the label and muse on the cool abstractions of the writing, its factual explanatory manner, its desire for exculpation. This is the work of Whiteness. If, as Springgay and Truman (2018: 128) assert 'walking-with is an ethical and political response-ability that intimately understands that any step towards a different world is always imbricated in a particular conceptualization of the human' then, as I attend to the 'speaking silence' of those ghosts again, my feminist sympathy for Caroline Herschel – who discovered eight comets and 14 nebulae, yet spent much of her life as her eminent brother's 'assistant', his note-taker and calculator, having been brought to the city of Bath specifically 'to keep house for him' – is conditioned by the entangled race–gender–class relations the label both hints at and hides. It presents another instance (yet another among so many others) of the centring of White subjectivity as an unquestioned shaper of knowledge, narrative and history. This centring hides the work of imperialism, heterosexism and White, Western masculinism behind another cool façade: the object simply 'is', the card simply 'relates' what the object 'is'. This historicizing dissimulation is passed off as a straightforward representation: the card tells the 'truth' (of course it does!). What the card *fails* to adequately tell is that the socio-political relations of racialization grant only some bodies access to the status of 'full human', thereby hiding the dehumanization of Black bodies via slavery. I also notice its quick moves in recuperating the valour of White participation in slavery's abolition (they boycotted sugar!) as yet another iteration of a colonial history that forgets its acts of dispossession, and its 'extraction of personhood' (Yusoff, 2018: 6), its production of nonbeing, for non-White persons

Attending to the sugar cone, in a similar way to attending to those grand Liverpool buildings, brings together Sylvia Wynter's (2003) argument about race as a founding nature–culture category of White, Western modernity with Braidotti's (2013) call for a posthuman affirmative ethics which situates the human within broader ecologies of human–nonhuman relationality. Both Wynter and Braidotti come at the problem of 'Man' from different perspectives but both share the view that White, Western Man, authorizes and institutes practices which situate others as less than human while arrogating to himself a particular mode of being human that is right, proper, rational and legitimate. This enables race to be used as a marker to situate non-White 'others' at a distance from 'full' human being (Snaza, 2019) and positions women, children and the whole of nature as commodities for capture, exploitation and use (Taylor, 2018).

I read in Tibbles (2007, n.p.) that slaves were referred to a 'cargo' or 'pawns'; that between '1700 to 1807, Liverpool was responsible for half the British trade which meant that her ships carried approximately 1.5 million Africans into enslavement, more than a tenth of all Africans who were transported over more than four centuries', that 'at least 40% of Liverpool's wealth at this time derived from slave related activities', and that in 1886 'Liverpool had more millionaires than any other British city outside London'.

Walking attentively, then, helps me, as a White (privileged) body occupying predominantly White space, notice Whiteness. Walking with buildings, ghosts, sugar cones and labels opens a productive mode of agentic dis/orientation, a space oriented to a refusal to be 'recruited' by White habits of thought, by research practices which continue to normalize White epistemes, and by university institutional practices which continue to cohere around Whiteness (albeit with commitments to anti-racist, diversity and decolonizing agendas, themselves shaped by the normalizing episteme of Whiteness). Walking in this way with buildings and sugar involves work of critique which necessarily discomforts, disorients, unsettles, provokes and produces trouble. And it needs to if it is going to work as a tactic which reveals the cracks and fissures in the strategies of White supremacy. Walking attentively can then become, I suggest, an orientation towards considering 'where things can be undone; to locate the point of undoing' (Ahmed, 2007: 165).

Conclusion: walking as feminist indiscipline

The Cambridge dictionary defines indiscipline as follows:

> contumacious
> defiance
> defiant
> disobedient
> insubordinate
> insubordination
> mutinous
> mutinously
> naughty
> rebellious
> rebelliously
> rebelliousness
> refractory
> ungovernable
> unruliness
> unruly
>
> (https://dictionary.cambridge.org/dictionary/english/indiscipline)

In Merriam-Webster it features as follows:

> indiscipline noun
> in·dis·ci·pline |\(ˌ)in-ˈdi-sə-plən\
> Definition of indiscipline:
> lack of discipline
>
> (www.merriam-webster.com/dictionary/indiscipline)

While in Longman's dictionary, this is given:

> in·dis·ci·pline /ɪnˈdɪsɪplɪn/ noun [uncountable] formal
> a lack of control in the behaviour of a group of people, with the result that they behave badly OPP discipline
>
> (www.ldoceonline.com/dictionary/indiscipline)

Blackmore (2014: 178) contends that for feminists, 'research is praxis, in that theory and practice are inter-connected, and that any distinctions between theory/methodology/method are false'. This orientation to research as praxis orients my argument in this chapter that walking as trans-mattering is not simply a method, approach or methodology but, when utilized as a transdisciplinary feminist research practice of attentiveness and response-ability, can be shaped as an ethical practice which places social justice at its heart. The speculative musing undertaken has walked with a theoretical line of thinking which considers race as a material economy (Yusoff, 2018) produced by colonial geo-logics and extractive practices (extracting humanity from some bodies; extracting wealth from the earth) in which benefits for the few (White, Western, male) are appropriated from the violence done to Black bodies, women and children. In this it has brought together some theoretical concepts from the fields of Whiteness and anti-racism, material culture, new material feminism, human geography and what I am tentatively calling object pedagogies (Taylor, 2019), to ponder how bodies and knowledge – and bodies of knowledge – are materially and affectively shaped by landscapes of colonialism which continue to do the work of Whiteness in often unseen ways. My argument is that walking as trans-mattering, carried out with care-full attentiveness, helps us see the work of Whiteness; that our contact with the many buildings and mundane objects our bodies come into contact with can (and must) open Whiteness to interrogation and critique; and that such walking can (and must) also constitute a praxis of feminist indiscipline as a critical dis/orientation which chips away at the edifice of Whiteness, revealing it, as many Black scholars have pointed out, as the racist façade it is.

Barad's (2007: 49) well-known statement that 'knowing does not come from standing at a distance and representing but rather from a direct material engagement with the world' and Jackson and Mazzei's (2012: 116) contention that knowledge is a 'practice of knowing in being' are central to my claims in this chapter for walking as trans-mattering, for walking as a transdisciplinary feminist research-praxis which can open critique of the power of Whiteness. Walking with buildings and sugar indicates the emergent and embodied factors in noticing and coming to know what/whose knowledge matters and brings to the fore our ontological, epistemological and ethical responsibilities as producers of knowledge. The mattering of knowledge is not a neutral matter: what/whose versions of history come to matter more is of profound consequence, particularly for those whose bodies, lives and futures matter less under the aegis of White, western, colonial, masculinist humanism. Rudolph, Sriprakash and Gerrard (2018) show that colonialist logics – in particular the production of hierarchies of race – and disciplinary knowledge formations are deeply intertwined. They point out that Young's (2008) concept of 'powerful knowledge', with its critique of 'standpoint epistemologies', its argument 'that some knowledge offers an objectively better basis for understanding the world than others', and its contention that knowledge equality should be about ensuring that all students have access to the 'powerful', specialized knowledge that is 'produced and legitimised by disciplinary communities, usually within universities' (Rudolph Sriprakash and Gerrard, 2018: 23), is, in effect, a technology which continues to lock White epistemes in place.

As many feminists will know, Haraway (1988) argued this very point a good while ago: that the spaceless, timeless, universalist presumptions of 'objectivity' which underpin science and malestream knowledge is a 'deadly fantasy'. Haraway's (1988: 581) words are worth quoting at length because of their resonance today:

> I would like to insist on the embodied nature of all vision and so reclaim the sensory system that has been used to signify a leap out of the marked body and into a conquering gaze from nowhere. This is the gaze that mythically inscribes all the marked bodies, that makes the un-marked category claim the power to see and not be seen, to represent while escaping representation. This gaze signifies the unmarked positions of Man and White, one of the many nasty tones of the word 'objectivity' to feminist ears in scientific and technological, late-industrial, militarized, racist, and male-dominant societies, that is, here, in the belly of the monster, in the United States in the late 1980s.

And so, in place of binaries, universals and objectivity, she proposes the power of 'situated knowledges', that is, embodied, specific, particular, non-innocent, responsible, non-transcendent knowledge. The partial perspective of situated knowledge – a lesson Haraway says she learned in part while walking her dog and wondering about their very different human–nonhuman sensory apparatuses – 'allows us to become answerable for what we learn how to see' (Haraway, 1988: 583).

The answerability of seeing – and from that the answerability of what we speak, say, do – is the political-ethical question at the heart of knowledge practices. This chapter suggests that walking with buildings and objects offers a mundane but important transdisciplinary feminist instance in how we might enact, embody and embed, ways of situated knowledge-ing that counter the 'deadly fantasy' that continues to centre the ongoing work of masculinity, Whiteness and colonialism. Such work dislocates knowledge from disciplines so that we might refuse their 'powerful call' – a call to incorporation, containment and domestication – to discipline ourselves in their service. Walking as feminist indiscipline thereby activates a conceptual unruliness alive with movement and change. As a feminist praxis, walking as indiscipline suggests there is scope to orient our bodies, wherever they find themselves, towards contact with mutinous potential, with rebellious energy, with an ungovernable unruliness. Such a transdisciplinary orientation can then urge us to 'keep open the force of the [feminist] critique' (Ahmed, 2007: 165).

References

Ahmed, S. (2007). A phenomenology of whiteness. *Feminist Theory*, 8(2), 149–168.
Barad, K. (2007). *Meeting the Universe Halfway: Quantum Physics and the Entanglement of Matter and Meaning.* London: Duke University Press.

Barad, K. (2010). Quantum entanglements and hauntological relations of inheritance: Dis/continuities, spacetime enfoldings, and justice-to-come. *Derrida Today*, 3(2), 240–268.

Barad, K. (2019). After the end of the world: Entangled nuclear colonialisms, matters of force, and the material force of justice. *Theory and Event*, 22(3), 524–550.

Blackmore, J. (2014). Within/against: Feminist theory as praxis in higher education research. In M. Tight and R. Jeroen (Eds.), *Theory and Method in Higher Education Research*. (pp. 175–198). London: SRHE. Published online: August 20, 2014.

Braidotti, R. (2013). *The Posthuman*. Cambridge: Polity.

Deleuze, G. and Guattari, F. (1994). *What is Philosophy?* New York, NY: Columbia University Press.

DiAngelo, R. (2011). White fragility. *International Journal of Critical Pedagogy*, 3(3), 54–70.

DiAngelo, R. and Sensoy, Ö. (2014). Calling in: Strategies for cultivating humility and critical thinking in antiracism education. *Understanding and Dismantling Privilege*, IV(2), 191–203.

Fanon, F. (1986). *Black Skin, White Masks*. London: Pluto Press.

Fine, M. (1997). Witnessing whiteness. In M. Fine, L. Weis, C. Powell, and L. Wong, (Eds.), *Off White: Readings on Race, Power, and Society* (pp. 57–65). New York, NY: Routledge.

Haraway, D. (1988). Situated knowledges: The science question in feminism and the privilege of partial perspective. *Feminist Studies*, 14(3), 575–599.

Haraway, D. (2016). *Staying with the Trouble*. Durham, NC: Duke University Press.

Jackson, A. J. and Mazzei, A. (2012). *Thinking with Theory in Qualitative Research*. Oxon: Routledge.

Jung, Y. (2013). Mindful walking: The serendipitous journey of community-based ethnography. *Qualitative Inquiry*, 20(5): 621–627.

Massey, D. (2005). *For Space*. London: Sage.

Massumi, B. (2014). *What Animals Teach Us About Politics*. Durham, NC: Duke University Press.

Pink, S. (2009). *Doing Sensory Ethnography*. Thousand Oaks, CA: Sage.

Powell, K. (2010). Making sense of place: Mapping as a multisensory research method. *Qualitative Inquiry*, 16(7), 539–555.

Rudolph, S., Sriprakash, A. and Gerrard, J. (2018). Knowledge and racial violence: the shine and shadow of 'powerful knowledge'. *Ethics and Education*, 13(1), 22–38.

Sandford, S. (2015). Contradiction of terms: Feminist theory, philosophy and transdisciplinarity. *Theory, Culture & Society*, 32(5–6), 159–182.

Snaza, N. (2019). Curriculum against the state: Sylvia Wynter, the human, and futures of curriculum studies. *Curriculum Inquiry*, doi: 10.1080/03626784.2018.1546540

Springgay, S. (2011). 'The Chinatown foray' as sensational pedagogy. *Curriculum Inquiry*, 41(5), 636–656.

Springgay, S. and Truman, S. E. (2017). A transmaterial approach to walking methodologies. *Body and Society*, 23(4): 27–58.

Springgay, S. and Truman, S. E. (2018). *Walking Methodologies in a More-than-Human World: Walking Lab*. Abingdon: Routledge.

Taylor, C. A. (2016). Close encounters of a critical kind: A diffractive musing in/between new material feminism and object-oriented ontology. *Cultural Studies<=>Critical Methodologies*, 16(2), 201–212.

Taylor, C. A. (2018). 'Each intra-action matters': Towards a posthuman ethics for enlarging response-ability in higher education pedagogic practice-ings. In M. Zemblyas (Ed.),

Socially Just Pedagogies in Higher Education (pp. 81–96). London: Bloomsbury Publishers.

Taylor, C. A. (2019). *Object Pedagogies: Material Feminist Encounters and Possibilities for a New Ecology of/for Higher Education.* Conference presentation at the European Conference of educational Research, Hamburg, September 6, 2019.

Taylor, C. and Ulmer, J. B. (2019 f.c.). Posthuman methodologies *for* post-Industrial cities: A situated, speculative and somatechnic venture. *Somatechnics.*

Tibbles, A. (2007). *Liverpool and the Slave Trade.* Presentation at Gresham College, March 19, 2007.

Young, M. (2008). *Bringing Knowledge Back in: From Social Constructivism to Social Realism in the Sociology of Education.* London: Routledge.

Wynter, S. (2003). Unsettling the coloniality of being/power/truth/freedom: Towards the human, after man, its overrepresentation – An argument. *CR: The New Centennial Review*, 3(3), 257–337.

Yusoff, K. (2018). *A Billion Black Anthropocenes or None.* Minneapolis, MN: The University of Minnesota Press.

3 Critical disability studies and the problem of method
Ada S. Jaarsma

Introduction

'[W]e are not "solving problems"; we are finding ways to move' (Price, 2011: 101). This description by Margaret Price exemplifies the import of Critical Disability Studies and one of its key concerns: accessibility. Rather than relying on an arc of activity in which pre-determined questions solicit responses to those questions, Price's account locates the work of research in a search for new ways of understanding and relating to access. The logic of 'solving problems,' Price explains, gives way to a shared, emergent project. Price's use of the collective 'we' indicates that this project is collaborative and undertaken together, rather than individual and undertaken alone. This 'we' is open-ended, part of the problem of access that has yet to be fully discovered. As Robert McRuer (2006: 207) asks in a foundational text in Critical Disability Studies, 'What might it mean to shape worlds capable of welcoming the disability to come?'

While it tends to be described as 'interdisciplinary' (Yoshizaki-Gibbons, 2018: 151), this chapter considers Critical Disability Studies as transdisciplinary, for three reasons that, taken together, demonstrate its significance for feminist scholars. First, its emphasis on an open-ended 'we' asks us to inhabit methods in ways that undo the grip of knowledge-in-advance. In a recent essay on neurodiversity and pedagogy, Erin Manning (2018: n.p.) points out that, 'every classroom that knows in advance what knowledge looks and sounds like is working to a norm.' This implicates us, as academics, in our own spaces and disciplinary homes. Invoking terminology from Gilles Deleuze (1994: 197), we could say that the work of Critical Disability Studies *problematizes*. Put otherwise, this work attunes us to problems in ways that compel creative rather than pre-determined responses; it prompts us to engage with the conditions by which problems emerge (Koopman, 2016; Mader, 2017), instead of relying on disciplines to supply us with ready-made problems and methods for resolution. Consequently, I argue in the first section that Critical Disability Studies asks us to scrutinize disciplinary methods as design elements that constrain and afford: *that there are* divergent disciplines, on this account, is an insight that draws us into the problem of access.

Second, I turn to transdisciplinarity as a way to respond to this problem in emergent ways. Using Deleuze, I suggest that transdisciplinarity reflects *immanent* or situated, rather than *transcendent* or pre-set, practices. A key insight of Critical Disability Studies is that access cannot be restricted to knowledge-in-advance: as if retrofitting existing designs or spaces is sufficient for undoing barriers and opening up exclusions. Rather, there is a dynamism to the method, such that flexibility and ongoing revision are integrated into the architecture, relations and research practices. This dynamism gives rise to the creation of locutions that express complex, non-linear ways of thinking and knowing. Price (2015), for example, deploys words like 'bodymind' that resist binary distinctions between body and mind, biology and society. Likewise, Alison Kafer's (2013) phrase 'the curative imaginary' provides disability scholars with a concept by which to identify the entangled array of biomedical, biopolitical and neoliberal forms that restrict, even deny, access.

These curative forms are at work in our universities, often extending to disciplinary methods. Rather than invoking some kind of 'meta-theory' (Mol, 2014: 108) or 'convergentist' account of methods (Halley, 2006: 81), transdisciplinarity responds to problems in ways that bring disciplinary forms together, as contingent assemblages, to displace 'curative' or ableist methods with ones that expand access. (Citations thus far in this chapter, for example, bring Rhetoric, Literary Studies, Anthropology and Philosophy together with interdisciplinary fields like Feminist Studies and Science and Technology Studies). Disciplines are important, proffering divergent ways to account for an 'irreducibly pluralistic' world (Kramnick, 2018: 21). 'Trans'-disciplinarity, in turn, proffers a way to traverse disciplines, utilizing affordances that differing disciplines provide (Jaarsma and Dobson, 2020). Access, Kelly Fritsch (2016) argues, is a boundary-negotiating practice (see also Hamraie and Fritsch, 2019); so too is transdisciplinarity.

Third, I consider how transdisciplinarity, understood as a provisional assemblage, contributes to the search for 'ways to move.' Rather than 'solving problems' that disciplines put forward, transdisciplinary methods proffer a kind of friction that can ease, perhaps redress, exclusions that disciplines produce. In my own discipline of Philosophy, for example, practices of peer review reflect stringent norms about what does and does not 'count' as philosophy, giving rise to a 'monochromatic profile' (Dotson, 2011: 403) that is 'relentlessly white and male' (Wilson, 2017: 859). Rocío Zambrana (2019) argues that peer review practices facilitate feedback loops that keep such exclusions intact (only 2% of the 50 'top-cited' authors in the *Stanford Encyclopedia of Philosophy* are women, Zambrana points out). Transdisciplinarity puts pressure on fidelity to disciplinary methods, thereby undoing closed loops by which the 'we' is produced.

In this chapter, then, I explore recent work in Critical Disability Studies that animates the problem of false problems, reinforced by disciplinary obedience, by invoking transdisciplinary logics and thereby produce new, methodologically pluralistic problematizations. At stake is the nature of 'the problem' that prompts and sustains feminist research methods. A false problem keeps disciplinary methods and inherited logics intact; problematizing, in contrast, draws researchers into a kind of responsiveness that generates the search for new methods, as we accede, actively, to a research problem. This latter kind of problem compels responsive engagement, so much so that 'responsiveness can operate as a measure by which we gauge the ethical adequacy of our practices' (Gilson, 2014b: 98).

The false problem of cure and disciplinary fidelity

'During my second week as a new faculty member,' Melanie Yergeau (2013: n.p.) writes at the beginning of a pivotal essay in Critical Disability Studies, 'I was involuntarily committed to the psych ward at the university hospital.' Yergeau's next lines qualify this tale, implicating us as readers in the workings of curative biomedicine: 'I would say that I make this statement against my better judgement, but such a sentiment presupposes that I *have* better judgement. (Which, according to my ex-doctors, I don't)' (2013).

In this brief but striking passage, Yergeau underscores the point that methods adhere, all too often, to false problems. To be involuntarily committed, Yergeau implies, is to be hailed as what Yergeau (2018: 31) describes elsewhere as 'a problemed and involuntary body.' To be cast *as* a problem is to be identified as other-than-the-norm, and this 'problemed' status explains the initial action in Yergeau's story: positioned *as* the problem, Yergeau receives an onslaught of interventions by those who are authorized to diagnose, adjudicate and medicate. Critical Disability scholarship is replete with stories of such asymmetry: to be 'problemed' is to bear the impact of others' presumptions about pain, suffering and the levels of function required for a good quality of life (Kafer, 2013; Hall, 2015; Pipzna-Samarasinha, 2018). When granted sole explanatory power, disciplines risk this asymmetry as well.

A problem that hails a definite solution is better described as a 'false problem.' As Deleuze (1994: 158) explains, 'we are led to believe that problems are given ready-made, and that they disappear in the responses or the solution.' In the case of disability studies, and Yergeau's story more specifically, this seeming solution entails the unitary terms of pathology, diagnosis and imperatives of medical cure (Silvers, 2016; Clare, 2017; McRuer, 2018). Indeed, this orientation towards 'solutions' is, like cures, at the heart of biomedicine in which there is always the 'promise' of cure, if not today then someday in the future (Kafer, 2013: 54).

Several years ago, immersed in research on placebo and nocebo effects, I became preoccupied by how we express curative sensibilities in institutional spaces. While we might get 'better,' as patients, when we visit the doctor's office (because the doctor's white coat conveys promises of efficacious treatment) or experience negative side effects upon receiving a sugar pill (because those effects were predicted persuasively), we also hail placebo and nocebo effects from our students when we inhabit teaching designs in ways that lay claim to authority. I had no choice, in this research, but to expand my own methods in transdisciplinary ways when I realized the extent to which disciplinary fidelity (in my case, to Philosophy) yields classroom dynamics that deny, and crucially depend upon, affordances that I was wanting to flag and resist. A certain 'god trick,' prevalent in Philosophy classrooms, animates material in seemingly disembodied or universal ways; this 'trick' can be rendered recognizable as reliant on design choices – but only when other disciplines contribute to such analysis (Jaarsma, 2017: 162; see also Berkhout and Jaarsma, 2018). Through 'god trick' pedagogies, instructors in Philosophy become 'omniscient and unlocatable, and therefore shielded from any countergaze' (Price, 2011: 35). By making use of philosophical tropes (like using examples 'that they expect their [students] to know about already' (Mol, 2008: 32)), instructors perform the discipline in ways that block many students from accessing or enacting key methods themselves. My work led me to suspect that students who are barred from learning, through exclusionary designs, also experience nocebo effects, such that test-taking or other classroom activities become fraught with negative side effects (Jaarsma, 2017). Such scenarios cannot be identified when the discipline provides sole resources for explanation. As Joy Brennan (2019) explains, while Philosophy tends to cast itself as universal (deploying 'god tricks' in classrooms), it conflates universality with Western paradigms. There are few degrees of freedom, from within disciplinary membership itself, for affirming other paradigms. 'Access' to Philosophy becomes a matter of submitting to already established conditions, accommodating oneself to pre-set (or 'transcendent') assumptions rather than emergent (or 'immanent') actualities.

To be a problem, according to the false problem of access, is thereby to take on the problem of access. Mel Chen shares an anecdote that exemplifies this dynamic. Positioned as the problemed bodymind in a space where someone is smoking, Chen might say something like 'I can't do the smoke,' as a way not to implicate the smoker. 'Yet the individuated property-assignation of "I am highly sensitive,"' Chen (2011: 274) points out, 'furthers the fiction of my dependence to others' independence. The question then becomes which bodies can bear the fiction of independence and uninterruptability.' The problem of access remains fully intact, in such scenarios, just as it does when disciplinary norms set the conditions by which inclusion can occur. The 'god trick' at play in Philosophy classrooms, for example, is achievable only by those whose bodyminds exemplify the template of 'professional philosopher:' this person 'believes his motivation is entirely free of all particularism,' that good philosophizing occurs 'from a perspective without a standpoint' because it upholds truth as *unchanging and the same for all epistemic subjects*' (Peña-Guzmán and Spera, 2017: 918–920). Philosophers who align with the disciplinary template are racialized as white and cis-privileged as male (Dotson, 2018), able to inhabit methods in ways that cast *others*, those with standpoints and dependencies, as the problem (Mitra, 2018).

Disability scholars note two effects, in particular, of such false problems. First, 'problemed' bodyminds are marked for exclusion. Even in contexts where access is upheld as ethical ideal or legal mandate and inclusion is named as an objective to achieve, compliance to such mandates relies upon locating and managing 'excludable types' (Titchkosky, 2011: 90). Disability scholars like Tanya Titchkosky and Margaret Price identify this as the 'paradox of inclusion:' to affirm inclusion within the logics of the false problem is to underscore, not subvert, the 'radical lack of access' (Titchkosky, 2011: 77). While this paradox of inclusion is at play in principles and practices of accommodation, it is sometimes exemplified by actual design elements. Price (2017: 158) points out, for example, that purportedly 'accessible' entrances are often reachable solely by inaccessible pathways or via heavy doors that lack automatic openers (see Fritsch, 2013).

In these ways, accommodation undercuts, rather than fosters, solidarity: as part of a neoliberal system, only specific kinds of bodies are 'hailed by institutions to represent the professed progress made by liberal rights-bearing subjects' (Puar, 2017: xviii). This is not an open and inclusive understanding of justice, upheld for example by disability justice activists, but rather a biopolitical paradigm that upholds 'rights' as an individualizing and exclusive opportunity for some.

This fiction of one persons' problemed particularity and others' presumed universality leads to the second effect of the false problem: capacity becomes legible through an objectification of deficit (Goodley, 2018). Alison Kafer's close reading of a set of billboards that serve as Public Service Announcements demonstrates how this works. Billboards depict a range of disabled individuals who are excelling, progressing or otherwise demarcated as worthy of inclusion by the broader public. But it is the viewers of these billboards, Kafer (2013: 93, italics mine) explains, who receive a formative message about themselves: '*Their problems* are huge – paralysis, blindness, amputation – and *mine* are small because I'm not disabled.' The seeming focus on disability, in other words, is better understood as 'negations of ableness' (Overboe, 2009: 243).

In this way, the false problem reflects highly influential messages about the contours, capacities and movements of unproblemed or abled bodyminds. This is an important point in Critical Disability Studies: the wide-ranging significance of the unmarked or normate bodymind (Garland-Thomson, 1997; Hamraie, 2012). This template guides the designs of architectural spaces, as well as the practices that seek to mitigate barriers through accommodations. But such interventions, prescribed by the 'problemed' status of disabled bodyminds, shore up the normative status of ability. This is part of the definition of ableism, scrutinized and theorized across Critical Disability Studies. Ableism refers to 'the ideology of ability' (Siebers, 2008: 8) that dictates that 'life without disability is preferable to life with disability' (Hamraie, 2016: 288). According to this ideology, eliminating disability is understood as common sense, authorizing 'compulsory able-bodiedness' to such an extent that ableism works as a kind of exclusionary interpretative frame (Jenkins, 2016: 212). Taken to its extreme, curative practices reflect eugenic commitments (Garland-Thomson, 2012). On these terms, the false problem of access results in violence and harm against many forms of diversity.

How might access be understood differently, beyond 'mere inclusion alongside able-bodied people' (Mitchell and Snyder, 2017: 554)? As Kafer (2013: 102) points out, 'it is not enough to simply insert new billboards in the place of old ones.' The next section affirms transdisciplinarity as a way to relate differently to access. Amending a query posed by Annemarie Mol (2011: 111), one transposed from the work of Marilyn Strathern (1980), we might ask: 'What promises are contained in other languages [and disciplines]?' To recognize that there is more than one language is to resist the monochromatic profile of a non-pluralistic world (Mol, 2014). To reach out towards the promises contained in other languages and disciplines is to lay claim to a logic that works differently from pre-set templates. I describe this logic in what follows.

Intuiting the virtual through transdisciplinary pluralism

This section takes up another insight from Melanie Yergeau, exemplified by the marvelously arch qualification cited above. 'I would say that I make this statement against my better judgement,' Yergeau (2013) explains about being moved, non-consensually, to the psych ward, 'but such a sentiment presupposes that I *have* better judgement. (Which, according to my ex-doctors, I don't).' The latter claim, written parenthetically, performs a different relationship to problems than that of Yergeau's now-former doctors. Whereas the doctors diagnose Yergeau as an autistic problem to be managed through psychiatric treatment, Yergeau resists the terms of the false problem. Highlighting tensions between the ex-doctors' expectations (that Yergeau lack the capacity for judgement) and Yergeau's own essay (which deploys a range of judgements, including that of the ex-doctors), Yergeau exemplifies an approach to problems that is productive, open-ended and emergent.

In a more recent essay, Yergeau (2018: 210) articulates this productivity in a more explicit way: 'I am not claiming wrongness or errancy, but rather possibilities and potentialities.' Yergeau's work models an alternative to the problem/solution dyad. By invoking 'possibilities and potentialities' apart from the logic of the false problem, Yergeau demonstrates how we might relate to potentiality without restricting the possible to what already exists. Recent feminist philosophical work on Deleuze provides a helpful way to understand this alternative logic. Deleuze proffers a concept of potentiality that exceeds the actual: this concept is *virtuality*. This concept expands the relations between what exists and what is possible to include the virtual, or the unactualized. There is no real difference between the possible and the real if 'possibilities' are only retroactively posited, mirroring what is understood to already exist (Gilson, 2014a: 135). If there is no virtual, then our imaginations and practices are limited entirely to 'a retrojection of the real onto an imagined past of the same sort' (Mader, 2011: 112). Put otherwise, if there is no virtual, then there is only the template, or the normate, a 'mirage' in which the possible is projected backwards (Deleuze, 1988: 20), based on what is presumed to be the existing slate of options.

Virtuality refers to the kind of possibility that Mary Beth Mader (2011: 21) describes as 'necessarily excessive.' This is a wonderfully useful phrase, especially in the context of discussions about access. Consider the tendency to make use of methods without noting the different logics or structures at play within them. In Philosophy, in North America, for example, it is rare to find work that addresses the fact that Anglo-English is not only the default grammatical structure of our research but also a specific linguistic and cultural structure, with epistemic values and presumptions (Wierzbicka, 2013; and see Bettcher and Goulimari, 2017 for an excellent and rare counter-example). We do not exhaust all potentialities of semantic expression when we speak, write or communicate in the many divergent ways that expression takes place. When we take care to note the structures at play in our methods, such as the grammar of our linguistic scripts, we can notice what is and is not expressed within these structures – and we open up the great array of possibilities that could, in fact, be expressed. There is no outside of design, or grammar, or language, and yet '[t]he best way to "intuit" the virtual is to inhabit it' (Kockleman, 2017: 131). Disability studies is replete with examples of inhabiting the virtual.

Access is, in part, a problem of structure. When we take the virtual into account, structures can be understood as excessive systems (Mader, 2011). Virtuality, understood as necessarily excessive, is always available to us as thinkers and practitioners: all structures contain unrealized or 'unactualized' relations. In this way, the virtual acts as 'a reservoir of potential' for the creation of change (Gilson, 2014a: 135) – precisely because what is possible is 'to create the possible' (Zourabichvili, 2017: 215). To create possibilities: this is how I understand the import of transdisciplinarity. Drawing attention to structures, including grammar, intensifies our attunement to the specific workings of our own designs and embedded scenarios. Rather than appealing to 'universals' that transcend the flux of circumstance, we are tasked, then, with working in and through the problems that grip us. The distinction that I name above, between emergent and pre-set methods, is useful here. As Ann Burlein (2005: 28) puts it, reading a passage in Deleuze's *Difference and Repetition* (1994), 'the problem (as transcendental rather than transcendent) is not supplemental to its various cases of solutions but immanent.' Describing the problem that animates feminist and disability work as 'transcendental' and emergent, rather than transcendent and pre-set, foregrounds the importance of the very conditions of possibility *of* methods. These conditions include a range of barriers that need to be confronted, but also the array of relations and practices that are yet to be created – relations that become more possible, when disciplines 'cross contaminate' (Mitra, 2018: 76) in provisional ways.

Hailing our attention to conditions of possibility, the problem of access requires us to attend to the genealogies of our disciplines and of our own movements in the world. As Sara Ahmed (2017: 109) points out, 'access can be the formal requirements you might need to enter a world. But accessibility and inaccessibility are also a result of histories that congeal as habits or shared routines.' The very ways in which 'access' gives rise to delimited responses, like accommodation, extend and in turn produce salient dynamics of our environments. Much too often, Price (2017: 156) explains, 'we use the term *inclusivity* as if we could take up its good parts without also confronting the historical and present-day practices of violent exclusion that make its emphasis necessary in the first place.' As disability scholars David T. Mitchell and Sharon L. Snyder (2017: 553) argue, 'we are not only affected by the places we inhabit, but we also leave our imprint on these locations.'

Rather than an outcome that can be 'definitively identified in advance' (Price, 2017: 164), access can be understood productively as a problem, one in which possibilities emerge *as* part of methods themselves. Restricting access to 'accommodation,' on these terms, misses entirely the conditions of possibility for change. As Anne-Marie Womack (2017: 496) explains, 'Because accommodation is defined as an adaptation or adjustment, it presupposes an antecedent. In other words, with accommodation, there is an earlier version, a baseline that has changed.' A baseline is a template, deduced from what already exists. Whereas retrofits send the message 'that disability is an unforeseen and uninvited presence' (Dolmage, 2017b: 108), more emergent approaches to access seek 'to provide space for what disability is and, more so, might become' (Dolmage and Hopgood, 2015: 565; see also Tremain, 2013 and Dolmage, 2017a).

Emergent approaches deploy logics and argumentation that are abductive, rather than deductive. As Colin Koopman explains (2016: 98), such methods can be described as experimentation, in which 'problems do not already contain within them (as if deductively) the responses that would constitute a determination, but rather these responses must be contingently elaborated (as if abductively) on the basis of the problematic conditions.' This kind of experimentation works to elicit new possibilities: McRuer (2018: 21) explains, 'Describing something like culture as "crip" remakes the substance in question,' such that it cannot be known in advance. Along similar lines, Stella Stanford explains that transdisciplinary methods cannot be traced back to disciplinary ones, precisely because they emerge, immanently, in response to problems (2015).

The promise of transdisciplinarity

This last section examines a third insight at play in Yergeau's work, exemplified beautifully by Yergeau's (2013) declaration: 'I am the ultimate unreliable narrator.' On one reading, this claim acknowledges what it means to be cast as a problem by biomedicine. To be diagnosed with autism, Yergeau (2018: 210) explains, is to be understood as lacking

> a theory of mind. We lack symbolic capacity and empathy. We lack tact and we lack a concept of gender, and with it a concept of self. I could keep going on all things lack because our lackluster lack list grows daily.

Yergeau (2018: 210) gives space to this lackluster lack list, pointing out, 'in avoiding the eyes of others, I am indeed missing out on things. In this regard, researchers are right: there is much that I do not learn or experience when I avert my eyes.'

On another reading, of course, this unreliable narration performs incisive and productive work. Yergeau (2018: 211) continues,

> And yet – there is much that I do learn, do experience, do feel and intimate and express and attract and repel. I might not know or recognize your face, but I know your scent, what you wore last Thursday, the exact date on which we met, the rhythm of your pace, the resting cut of your hair against your shoulder, the pulsing force field of the space between our bodies. There are intimacies and knowledges that exceed the eye-to-eye, that exceed the I-to-I.

This passage is a generous one, inviting the reader into the play of sensorial experiences that include forms of cognition and learning that fall outside of the ex-doctors' list of diagnosable problems.

By juxtaposing such divergent readings, Yergeau's passage exemplifies the friction that emerges when differing methods of reading come together. Self-identified as an 'unreliable' and disabled narrator, Yergeau creates the conditions for producing 'counter-diagnostic effects' (Price, 2011: 190) and 'counter-eugenic' relations and spaces (Garland-Thomson, 2012: 341). The need for counter-diagnosis is pressing, given the ways in which institutions and disciplines, oriented around the false problem, exclude divergent forms of knowledge. As Yergeau (2013, italics in original) points out, 'an autistic person cannot experience systemic violence *unless a non-autistic person validates those claims.*' To problematize, rather than subtend, false problems is to collaborate in supporting disabled people and community in varied and open-ended ways (Hamraie, 2017). It's also to insist that methods not be subsumed by one or another discipline: to allow differences, including disciplinary ones, to 'remain incommensurate' (Jaarsma, 2017: 213).

There are several ramifications of this affirmation of problematization. First, the 'we' of research communities is open-ended, extending across disciplinary methods and memberships. As Price (2017: 164, italics in original) emphasizes, we need to think hard about 'what it means to gather in spaces *together but radically not together*' because spaces do not yield the same kinds of problems for every person. This means that the 'we' that emerges out of disability work reflects cross-disability solidarity (Berne, 2015). This 'we' is divergent and diverse. Leah Lakschmi Piepzna-Samaransinha (2018: 147), for example, describes care in this context as a kind of permaculture, rather than monoculture: 'It can become an ongoing responsive ecosystem, where what is grown responds to need.' In contrast to a world with solely one language or discipline, a world that supports permaculture is one that solicits transdisciplinary pluralism.

The verb 'respond' is instructive here, and it gets to the second ramification: methods that problematize are methods that grip, hail, implicate and render us responsive *as* researchers. Unlike the false problem, there is no ready-made schema by which to recognize problems, and no *a priori* form by which to pose a problem (Zourabichvili, 2012). What compels our work, as Isabelle Stengers

(Savransky, 2018: 5) explains in an interview with Martin Savransky, is 'the problematic situation whose gripping drama takes hold of you, forcing you to think.' This is what Deleuze (1994: 197) is affirming when he explains, 'Problems emanate from the imperatives of adventure or from events which appear in the form of questions.' Along similar lines, in his discussion of 'problematization' as an effective mode of inquiry, Michel Foucault is clear that problematizing methods are productive, emergent and immanent *to* the very inquiry itself. So much so that, as he puts it, 'the "we" must not be previous to the question; it can only be the result – and the necessarily temporary result – of the question as it is posed in the new terms in which one formulates it' (Foucault, 1997: 114).

The third ramification concerns access. Making use of methods that attend to ongoing and open questioning (Kafer, 2013: 18), Critical Disability Studies puts forward 'access' as a problematizing question: in Price's (2011: 125) helpful terminology, this might be better described as 'access-as-practice.' This practice reflects the fact that barriers and forms of access arise in context, 'shifting as the circumstances and bodyminds of/in a space shift' (Price, 2017: 160), a process that is collaborative, intersectional and multi-modal (Hamraie, 2018).

Whereas access, cast as accommodation to pre-existing structures, reinscribes individuals as problems, 'access intimacy' is the outcome of collective problematizing (Mingus, 2011). Price and Kerschbaum, disability scholars whose work I follow closely in this chapter, look to activist and theorist Mia Mingus's principle of creating collective access: moving together, but also staying together, such that access becomes irreducibly collective. The refrain of such practices is: 'If you can't go, I don't want to go' (Mingus, 2010). This 'we' reflects a kind of responsive interdependence, practiced in relation to the flux of environs, relations and bodyminds. While it challenges us to let go of fidelity to our own disciplines, it invites us into solidarity with others, achievable through the 'blasphemous interventions' of creative, feminist work (Kafer, 2013: 106; cited in Hamraie and Fritsch 2019, 16). What promises are contained in such interventions?

References

Ahmed, S. (2017). *Living a Feminist Life*. Durham, NC: Duke University Press.
Berkhout, S. G. and Jaarsma, A. (2018). Trafficking in cure and harm: Placebos, nocebos and the curative imaginary. *Disability Studies Quarterly*, 38(4), doi: 10.18061/dsq.v38i4.6369
Berne, P. (2015). Disability justice – a working draft. *Sins Invalid: An Unshamed Claim to Beauty in the Face of Invisibility*. Posted June 10, 2015. http://sinsinvalid.org/blog/disability-justice-a-working-draft-by-patty-berne. Accessed September 5, 2018.
Bettcher, T. and Goulimari, P. (2017). Theorizing closeness: A trans feminist conversation. *Angelaki*, 22(1), 49–60.
Brennan, J. (2019). On disciplines and not-knowing: A reply to Agnes Callard. *The Immanent Frame: Secularism, Religion and the Public Sphere*. https://tif.ssrc.org/2019/04/19/on-disciplines-and-nonknowing/. Accessed April 19, 2019.
Burlein, A. (2005). The productive power of ambiguity: Rethinking homosexuality through the virtual and developmental systems theory. *Hypatia*, 20(1), 21–53.

Chen, M. Y. (2011). Toxic animacies, inanimate affections. *GLQ*, 17(2–3), 265–286.

Clare, E. (2017). *Brilliant Imperfection: Grappling with Cure*. Durham, NC: Duke University Press.

Deleuze, G. (1988). *Bergsonism*. Trans. H. Tomlinson and B. Habberjam. New York, NY: Zone Books.

Deleuze, G. (1994). *Difference and Repetition*. Trans. P. Patton. New York, NY: Columbia University Press.

Dolmage, J. T. (2017a). *Academic Ableism: Disability and Higher Education*. Ann Arbor, MI: University of Michigan Press.

Dolmage, J. T. (2017b). From steep steps to retrofit to universal design, from collapse to austerity. In J. Boys (Ed.), *Disability, Space, Architecture: A Reader* (pp. 102–113). New York, NY: Routledge.

Dolmage, J. and Hopgood, A. P. (2015). An afterword: Thinking through care. *Pedagogy*, 15(3), 559–567.

Dotson, K. (2011). Concrete flowers: Contemplating the profession of philosophy. *Hypatia*, 26(2), 403–409.

Dotson, K. (2018). On intellectual diversity and differences that may not make a difference. *Ethics and Education*, 13(1), 123–140.

Foucault, M. (1997). Polemics, politics and problematizations: An interview with Michel Foucault. In P Rabinow (Ed.), *Ethics: Subjectivity and Truth* (pp. 111–133). New York, NY: The New Press.

Fritsch, K. (2013). The neoliberal circulation of affects: Happiness, accessibility and the capacitation of disability as wheelchair. *Health, Culture and Society*, 5(1), 135–149.

Fritsch, K. (2016). Accessible. In K. Fritsch et al. (Eds.), *Keywords for Radicals: The Contested Vocabulary of Late-Capitalist Struggle* (pp. 23–28). Chico, CA: A. K. Press.

Garland-Thomson, R. (1997). *Extraordinary Bodies: Figuring Physical Disability in American Culture and Literature*. New York, NY: Columbia University Press.

Garland-Thomson, R. (2012). The case for conserving disability. *Bioethical Inquiry*, 9, 339–355.

Gilson, E. C. (2014a). *The Ethics of Vulnerability: A Feminist Analysis of Social Life and Practice*. New York, NY: Routledge.

Gilson, E. C. (2014b). Ethics and the ontology of freedom: Problematization and responsiveness in Foucault and Deleuze. *Foucault Studies*, 18, 76–98.

Goodley, D. (2018). Understanding disability: Biopsychology, biopolitics and an in-between-all politics. *Adapted Physical Activity Quarterly*, 35, 308–319.

Hall, K. Q. (2015). New conversations in feminist disability studies: Feminism, philosophy, and borders. *Hypatia*, 30(1), 1–12.

Halley, J. (2006). *Split Decisions: How and Why to Take a Break from Feminism*. Princeton, NJ: Princeton University Press.

Hamraie, A. (2012). Universal design research as a new materialist practice. *Disability Studies Quarterly*, 32(4).

Hamraie, A. (2016). Universal design and the problem of 'post-disability' ideology. *Design and Culture*, 8(3), 285–309.

Hamraie, A. (2017). Enlivened city: Inclusive design, biopolitics and the philosophy of liveability. *Built Environment*, 44(1), 77–104.

Hamraie, A. (2018). Mapping access: Digital humanities, disability justice, and sociospatial practice. *American Quarterly*, 70(3), 455–482.

Hamraie, A and Fritsch, K. (2019). Crip technoscience manifesto. *Catalyst: Feminism, Theory, Technoscience*, 5(1), 1–34.

Jaarsma, A. S. (2017). *Kierkegaard after the Genome: Science, Existence and Belief in This World*. New York, NY: Palgrave Macmillan.

Jaarsma, A. S. and Dobson, K. (Eds.) (2020). *Dissonant Methods: Undoing Discipline in the Humanities Classroom*. Edmonton: University of Alberta Press.

Jenkins, S. C. (2016). Defining morally considerable life: Towards a feminist disability ethics. In H. Sharp and C. Taylor (Eds.), *Feminist Philosophies of Life* (pp. 199–216). Kingston: McGill-Queen's University Press.

Kafer, A. (2013). *Feminist, Queer, Crip*. Bloomington: Indiana University Press.

Kockelman, P. (2017). *The Art of Interpretation in the Age of Computation*. Oxford: Oxford University Press.

Koopman, C. (2016). Critical problematization in Foucault and Deleuze: The force of critique without judgement. In N. Morar, T. Naill and D. W. Smith (Eds.), *Between Deleuze and Foucault*. (pp. 887–119). Edinburgh: Edinburgh University Press.

Kramnick, J. (2018). *Paper Minds: Literature and the Ecology of Consciousness*. Chicago, IL: University of Chicago Press.

Mader, M. B. (2011). *Sleights of Reason: Norm, Bisexuality, Development*. Albany, NY: SUNY Press.

Mader, M. B. (2017). The Genealogy of Abstractive Practices. *The Southern Journal of Philosophy*, 55, 86–97.

Manning, E. (2018). Histories of Violence: Neurodiversity and the policing of the norm. *LA Review of Books*. https://lareviewofbooks.org/article/histories-of-violence-neurodiversity-and-the-policing-of-the-norm/#! Accessed January 5, 2018.

McRuer, R. (2006). *Crip Theory: Cultural Signs of Queerness and Disability*. New York, NY: New York University Press.

McRuer, R. (2018). *Crip Times: Disability, Globalization, and Resistance*. New York, NY: New York University Press.

Mingus, M. (2010). Reflections on an opening: Disability justice and creating collective access in Detroit. *Leaving Evidence*, August 23, 2010. https://leavingevidence.wordpress.com/2010/08/23/reflections-on-an-opening-disability-justice-and-creating-collective-access-in-detroit/. Accessed October 2, 2018.

Mingus, M. (2011). Access intimacy: The missing link. *Leaving Evidence*. May 5, 2011. https://leavingevidence.wordpress.com/2011/05/05/access-intimacy-the-missing-link/. Accessed October 2, 2018.

Mitchell, D. T. and Snyder, S. L. (2017). Precarity and cross-species identification: Autism, the critique of normative cognition and nonspeciesism. In S. J. Ray and J. Sibara (Eds.), *Disability Studies and the Environmental Humanities: Toward an Eco-Crip Theory* (pp. 553–572). Lincoln: University of Nebraska Press.

Mitra, N. (2018). Disciplinary matters in the *Hypatia* controversy. *Atlantis Journal*, 39(2), 74–85.

Mol, A. (2008). 'I eat an Apple': On theorizing subjectivities. *Subjectivities*, 22, 28–37.

Mol, A. (2011). One, two, three: Cutting, counting, and eating. *Common Knowledge*, 17(1), 111–116.

Mol, A. (2014). Language trails: 'Lekker' and its pleasures. *Theory Culture and Society*, 31(2/3), 93–119.

Overboe, J. (2009). Affirming an impersonal life: A different register for disability studies. *Journal of Literary and Cultural Disability Studies*, 3(3), 241–256.

Peña-Guzmán, D. M. and Spera, R. (2017). The philosophical personality. *Hypatia*, 32(4), 911–927.

Pipzna-Samarasinha, L. L. (2018). *Care Work: Dreaming Disability Justice*. Vancouver: Arsenal Pulp Press.

Price, M. (2011). *Mad at School: Rhetorics of Mental Disability and Academic Life*. Ann Arbor, MI: University of Michigan Press.

Price, M. (2015). The bodymind problem and the possibilities of pain. *Hypatia*, 30(1), 268–284.

Price, M. (2017). Un/shared space: The dilemma of inclusive architecture. In J. Boys (Ed.), *Disability, Space, Architecture: A Reader* (pp. 155–172). New York, NY: Routledge.

Puar, J. K. (2017). *The Right to Maim: Debility, Capacity, Disability*. Durham, NC: Duke University Press.

Sandford, S. (2015). Contradiction of terms: Feminist theory, philosophy and transdisciplinarity. *Theory, Culture and Society* 32 (5–6), 159–182.

Savransky, M. (2018). Isabelle Stengers and the dramatization of philosophy. *SubStance*, 145(47), 3–16.

Siebers, T. (2008). *Disability Theory*. Ann Arbor, MI: University of Michigan Press.

Silvers, A. (2016). Philosophy and disability: What should philosophy do? *Res Philosophica*, 93(4), 843–863.

Strathern, M. (1980). No nature, no culture: The Hagen case. In C. P. MacCormack and M. Strathern (Eds.), *Nature, Culture, and Gender* (pp. 174–222). Cambridge: Cambridge University Press.

Titchkosky, T. (2011). *The Question of Access: Disability, Space, Meaning*. Toronto: University of Toronto Press.

Tremain, S. (2013). Introducing feminist philosophy of disability. *Disability Studies Quarterly*, 33(4). Retrieved from http://dsq-sds.org/article/view/3877/3402

Wierzbicka, A. (2013). *Imprisoned in English: The Hazards of English as a Default Language*. Oxford: Oxford University Press.

Wilson, Y. (2017). How might we address the factors that contribute to the scarcity of philosophers who are women and/or of colour? *Hypatia*, 32(4), 853–861.

Womack, A-M. (2017). Teaching is accommodation: Universally designing composition classrooms and syllabi. *CCC*, 68(3), 494–525.

Yergeau, M. (2013). Clinically significant disturbance: On theorists who theorize theory of mind. *Disability Studies Quarterly*, 33(4), doi: http://dsq-sds.org/article/view/3876/3405

Yergeau, M. (2018). *Authoring Autism: On Rhetoric and Neurological Queerness*. Durham, NC: Duke University Press.

Yoshizaki-Gibbons, H. M. (2018). Critical disability studies. In T. Heller et al. (Ed.), *Disability in American Life: An Encyclopedia of Concepts, Policies and Controversies* (pp. 149–153). Goleta, CA: ABC-CLIO.

Zambrana, R. (2019). On peer review, *The Abusable Past*. www.radicalhistoryreview.org/abusablepast/?p=3016. Accessed June 11, 2019.

Zourabichvili, F. (2012). *Deleuze: A Philosophy of the Event Together with 'The Vocabulary of Deleuze.'* G. Lambert and D. W. Smith (Ed.), Trans. K. Aarons. Edinburgh: Edinburgh University Press.

Zourabichvili, F. (2017). Deleuze and the possible: On involuntarism in politics. Trans. K. Aarons and C. Doyle, *Theory and Event*, 20(1), 152–171, 286–287.

4 Historical interludes

The productive uncertainty of feminist transdisciplinarity

Asilia Franklin-Phipps

Introduction: the necessary work of refusing to let go

At the beginning of Octavia Butler's speculative fiction novel *Kindred*, Dana, a Black woman, has just had her arm amputated. The amputation came after the arm was crushed as she returned from hundreds of years in the past. Dana's white husband Kevin is confused by both her disappearance and, later, her sudden reappearance. He is overwhelmed with the events, particularly because at this point in the novel he knows exactly where she has returned from. Both Dana and her husband are uncertain about how she has lost her arm and do not spend much time investigating or mourning the loss. The loss is yet another that Dana must learn to live with. As Dana tries to make sense of her feelings, she describes herself pulling away from her last and final experience traveling to the past, and then later, returning. Working hard to be a supportive partner, Kevin says, 'just let yourself pull away from it.... That sounds like the best thing you can do, whether it was real or not. Let go of it' (Butler, 1979: 17). *Whether or not it was real or not....*

The realness of Dana's experience might not be the primary issue, but rather the effect of such an experience. At one obvious level Kevin knows it was real, at least real enough that Dana has lost her arm, and is engaging in wishful thinking, disengaging and distancing himself from that which he cannot understand. Kevin does what he knows how to do – questions a time-traveling experience that does not fit into his rational and logical worldview. But on some level, Kevin knows in his body that there will be no letting it go because he was there too. He knows that he will also be unable to let it go. I use Kevin's words here because they echo so much of the conversation in the present about ugly racial histories and how they are knotted and conjoined with gender (Perry, 2018), sexuality (Ferguson, 2003; Spillers, 1987) and labor extraction. Donna Haraway (2016: 13) writes, 'like all offspring of colonizing and imperial histories, I – we – have to relearn how to conjugate worlds with partial connections and not universals and particulars.' It is important to note, that we all do not need to do this in the same way or to the same degree (Hartman, 2007). Well-meaning, white, educated and otherwise thoughtful people wonder why some of us cannot just 'let it go' and move on in order to focus on the present and look toward the future.

This is a notion of time as three sections of a sheet cake: past, present and future. When people ask/insist/beg/discipline others to let *it* go, they are often requesting others to let go of that which does not make sense to them, cannot be processed or integrated into their perspective or knowledge of the world, is too grotesque, too revealing or hurts too badly.

The irony is that those people, like Kevin, have also not let it go either. Those benefiting most from 'histories that hurt' (Ahmed, 2010: 50) and the ongoing trauma of those histories are often the most invested and attached to a studied holding onto social hierarchies that continue to do harm and produce a continuum of humanity (Wynter, 2003). It is white supremacy, patriarchy and homophobia that puts those experiencing the most harm on the defensive. From this view, it is the people in the groups still experiencing the harm are the ones who are unreasonably and morosely hanging onto past wrongs. In this way letting go becomes about language and compliance – a disciplining that seems to erase or mute the past in favor of the present – purging ghosts as though they had not terrorized the entire family for hundreds of years. In a cultural context that is white supremacist and patriarchal, extractive and predatory, knowledge and the reproduction of knowledge most coherent to that system is the most legible and legitimate. This suppresses and/or makes irrelevant other ways of knowing/being/imagining/discovering. Sara Ahmed writes about letting go, what she calls *moving on*, and suggests the impossibility of this well-worn and widely circulated phrase, often directed at those who are in no position to let anything go or move on in that way that is suggested:

> A concern with histories that hurt is not then a backward orientation: to move on, you must make this return. If anything, we might want to reread melancholic subjects, the ones who refuse to let go of suffering, who are even prepared to kill some forms of joy, as an alternative model of the social good.
>
> (Ahmed, 2010: 50)

While Ahmed does imagine a kind of moving on, this cannot happen without 'rereading melancholic subjects,' who are those most often begged to let go and disciplined when they are unable or refuse to do so. Ahmed is, instead, invested in the kind of world that takes the knowledge of melancholic subjects seriously in order to re-engage the present and future world. I would assert that nothing kills joy like epistemological forays into the topic of chattel slavery. Even so, I follow Ahmed, in thinking that those most unwilling to 'let go' are correct and creative, in their insistence, because those ghosts are always all around all of us. These ghosts haunt all of us differently – some lose limbs as Dana did, while others might just lose peace of mind as Kevin did. This is both historical and ongoing (Sharpe, 2016).

In thinking research, this history cannot be disarticulated from what we know as researchers and how we are able to know. The persons who are positioned best to determine what counts as knowledge and who counts as knowers, are often those who have historically been produced and epistemologically legitimated as persons, not those produced as nonpersons (Perry, 2018) or melancholic subjects. The cultural inattention to history as it relates to the present serves confusion and unease about the persistence of violent social hierarchies. When the dominant narrative of an ongoing march toward social justice (also called progress) in the U.S. is undermined and disrupted by such events as Ferguson, Charlottesville or the election of Donald Trump, there is widespread consternation. This is the result of an impoverished imagination that has not taken melancholic subjects seriously as knowers. In cultures oriented to privileging white, masculinist, colonial epistemologies this severely limits how some are able to imagine the world.

But what does it mean to transgress disciplinary boundaries and make a temporary home in a field where you do not belong? Further, how do disciplinary regimes of the institution discourage and make difficult such attempts? What counts as scholarship when we unfix from disciplinary norms and expectations to carve creative spaces for becoming astonished by the knowledge that one is not required to know? These are important and necessary questions that require attention if we want to begin to take melancholic subjects' knowledges and ways of knowing seriously. Such questions also prompt difficult engagements, as Christina Sharpe (2016: 13) writes, 'despite knowing otherwise, we are often disciplined into thinking through and along lines that reinscribe our own alienation, reinforcing and reproducing what Sylvia Wynter calls our "narratively condemned status." We must become undisciplined.' Sharpe, Wynter and Morrison (and many others) consider how slavery has constrained the ability to know/see/imagine particular kinds of people – racialized and otherwise. These theorists do so from different angles – Sharpe (2016) rethinks the violence of the present as it connects to the past, Wynter (2003) examines the category of the human, while Morrison (1993) explores canonical American literature, tracking the agency of absence. Taken together, something new becomes possible and that newness is more complex than a more thorough or complete context. It models a praxis predicated on an ongoing, transdisciplinary attention to the past, across philosophy, literature, film, culture and sociopolitical events.

Transdisciplinarity is a praxis of going beyond collaboration, but is an openness to travel – time, for example – in order to move across fields of knowledge in ways that transform approaches to knowledge production and representation to imagine what else might count as worth knowing – in this case putting on disciplinary suits that do not fit, nor were ever meant to. In other words, becoming uncomfortable in other disciplines that overlap and undergird topics under study and consideration. There are many ways to think the present in terms of the past, both recent and distant. For my purposes I want to think with transatlantic slavery and the 'long disaster … still unfolding' (Sharpe, 2016: 6) to imagine an approach to thinking and imagining feminist research that engages that history through art, literature, film, and other Black artistic expression, a history that produced gendered subjectivity in particularly monstrous and grotesque racial ways. To know, beginning with collective and embodied knowledge of melancholic subjects, researchers must become undisciplined. Sharpe (2016: 50) writes, 'The question for theory is how to live in the wake of slavery, in slavery's afterlives, the afterlife of property, how, in short, to inhabit and rupture this episteme with their, with our, knowable lives.'

In rereading *Kindred*, and thinking about transdisciplinary feminist methodology, I am reminded of travel – across time and space, distant and near – and the way that we move through life noticing and *not* noticing the residue and traces left by the past. Traveling with the past and tracking back and forth, with dizzying speed. This research practice is one that travels across, *through* and *with* texts across multiple disciplines that have weighed in on how bodies are positioned in relation to a vulnerability to violence both in past and present iterations. In my case, this has meant doing research that follows lines of inquiry wherever they lead – literature, literary studies, Black studies, science fiction, science studies, cultural studies, history and even pop culture. This is not an exhaustive list, but it requires a willingness to look where looking is invited and required. Such looking instantiates a layered, even kaleidoscopic, view of topics that are fluid, complex, and shifting. To think through complex topics like race and gender, there must be ongoing but always hesitant searching across disciplines – with different stakes, methodologies and perspectives – never at home because being at home is only an illusion. This also has the effect of better collaboration and communication across disciplinary homes and temporary residencies.

This chapter, then, articulates how letting go/moving on is not possible, nor is it a desirable orientation, because even when we, particularly in fields that do not require history do not say, reference or engage this history in our research work, this past has not been let go. Further, what are the creative implications for thinking and imagining research that, not only, refuses to let it go or move on – even the very worst of the past – but finds occasion to engage, collect and explore ugly and painful histories for their potential in thinking and knowing the present? Finally, what happens when researchers intentionally approaching research through a praxis of becoming undisciplined in order to traverse paths across the perspectives and knowledge absent from the archives (Campt, 2017)? How might this happen across disciplinary bounds in order to better facilitate new approaches to scholarship that cannot be anticipated or imagined ahead of time?

Suspending and refusing certainty: knowing/feeling across time

In *Kindred*, both Kevin and Dana travel from 1973 to the year 1817. How she does this is never explained, but when she is in the 1800s, she remains Black and is therefore a slave. Because of this Dana is vulnerable to all of the monstrous treatments of enslaved people, and the very particular treatment of enslaved women and girls – beatings, ongoing and repeated rape, untreated illness and the lived effects of 'ontological negation' (Sharpe, 2016: 14) – that produced and reproduced gender and race that continue today. On one of her trips, Kevin travels with her and experiences the same historical space and time. Instead of feeling the unrelenting terror that Dana feels, Kevin is able to adjust and adapt to the past because he is a white man. He fits better than Dana in both the 1800s and the 1970s. For Dana, those years matter significantly in her life chances – this is both racial and gendered, historical and ongoing. Ahmed (2007: 156) writes:

> To be orientated, or to be at home in the world, is also to feel a certain comfort: We might only notice comfort as an affect when we lose it, when we become uncomfortable.

While it would be too strong an assertion to suggest that Kevin is comfortable in the 1800s, it is important to emphasize that degree does matter, and Kevin is able to become much more comfortable in the time and space of extreme racial violence. He can find some comfort in this space and therefore, cannot know the place the way that Dana does. His perspective is blurred by his access to relative comfort, which is why he is able to suggest that letting go could ever be possible. In this world, he is regarded as a full person, while Dana must straddle degrees of personhood in both the past and the present (Wynter, 2003; Perry, 2018). By the end, she has lost a part of herself to that past – her arm yes, but much more than that. This is not to say that Kevin does not suffer, but again, degree matters (Perry, 2018). *Kindred* concludes with Dana and Kevin traveling to the planation they experienced both together, but also very different from one another. While Dana will never be able to 'move on' she can figure out ways to live with slavery in a way that Sharpe says that all Black people must do. This living *with* is aided by learning as much as she can about that past – by doing research.

This history, if not left in the past or consciously forgotten, reconfigures what we can know about raced and gendered personhood, even when our work is not directly concerned with the effects of slavery. Knowing the past gives new angles to the present, allows a space for mourning, and makes moving on more possible. Moving on and knowing the past are related. *Kindred* is an encounter with fiction that engages the *present-ness* of slavery, the afterlife of slavery (Hartman, 2007), and in the wake of transatlantic slavery (Sharpe, 2016).

Throughout the novel Dana is 'called' (by a force that is not clear) from her relatively comfortable life in 1976 as a writer to a historical period when her ancestors were enslaved by white people. In this time period, she is tasked with saving a white child from death, as her own existence is linked to his survival. It is important to note that even in 1976 she is vulnerable to the effects of history. She is called by her white ancestor, who requires her help staying alive so that Dana can be alive in the future. From the beginning, her life is tied to white patriarchy in a way that she cannot disentangle. The first time, Dana saves a young white child drowning in a river, she returns home in seconds. Each time she returns, she is changed by the experience – emotionally, psychologically, but also physically – history leaves her with literal bruises, cuts and crushed limbs.

She ages. I read in it the ongoing traces left in and on our bodies and our world of the past. I am not saying anything novel, few people deny the importance of history, but saying is not the same as doing. Thinking with history is not only knowing history but developing a praxis for paying attention to how history frames our present-day knowing in a context where this is not required in many disciplines.

Many have discussed Butler's work in terms of its literary and cultural value (Thaler, 2014; Brown, 2017), so I will not do that here. Instead, I am interested in the effects of encounters with such texts – texts that in many fields (like mine) do not often count as research, data or evidence – but are much more likely to linger, encouraging continued investigation or new ways of sensing the world. How does history – both recent and distant – shift how inquiry projects in the present can be thought, imagined, and undertaken? How can researchers, who are not historians, become sensitized to the ongoing effects of history on bodies, spaces and knowledge? How does this change the kind of research that is possible? And how might transdisciplinary feminist methods be an invitation to notice and think with texts and cultural artifacts that are positioned on the margins, particularly those that travel with the past in meaningful ways?

Inspired by Octavia Butler's work, I wonder how we can better travel with this history as researchers interested in imagining another world – not in order to resolve, as there is no resolution, but instead to engage in creative ways that make other imaginings of gender, personhood, freedom and subjectivity better connected with how those things are differently known and embodied across time. Butler's fictional work and other feminist writers like Nalo Hopkinson and Jewelle Gomez give readers practice in unsticking from any notion that gender could ever not be raced and historical, that the concept of freedom or subjectivity could be stable or contained and that the past could remain in the past.

The historical productions of subjectivity through gender and race provide an important context for imagining transdisciplinary feminist research projects concerned with present issues, problems and concerns that are tied to the past. This is not a call for all researchers to become historians; instead, it is an exploration of what a greater attention to history or time-traveling might do for work concerned with imaging less deadly futures (Haraway, 2016). This is an invitation to think about engaging the past in ways that help us avoid reproducing absences, doubling-down on silences and moving forward without accounting for the ways that gender is felt, known and experienced in ways that are always already historical. Christina Sharpe (2016: 18) calls this 'wake-work,' which she describes as, 'a mode of inhabiting and rupturing the episteme with our known lived and un/imaginable lives. With that analytic we might imagine otherwise from what we know now in the wake of slavery.' This is an approach to knowing that is always a kind of unknowing too.

In what follows, I explore and instantiate how theorizations that activate nomadic subjectivity and wake-work produce space to think about research methodology as travel across space and time, as always entangled in histories and hierarchies of race and gender, as a productive means of becoming newly sensitized to the effects of difference across bodies, human and non-human (Wynter, 2003), entangled in both past, present and future. I write this 'now' in a particularly urgent socio-cultural moment that requires better ways to engage these differences. From this work, I imagine an approach to research that intentionally stages affective encounters with artistic expression concerned with 'histories that hurt' (Ahmed, 2010: 51) as an alternative path to thinking and knowing in research and inquiry projects.

Nomadic subjectivity in the wake

To better imagine the practical implications of theoretical commitments to transdisciplinarity, I am drawn to Rosi Braidotti's (1994) figuration of the nomadic subject, thought alongside and through Christina Sharpe's (2016) theorization of the wake. The distinctions between these two are important – forced migration of slavery and the nomadism that Braidotti describes are differences with important distinctions. But in thinking nomadic subjectivity in/of the wake in relation to how history produces subjectivity is currently useful. Braidotti imagines an ontological and epistemological approach to moving in the world, as Sharpe does, although both offer different ways to do this, ways which are complementary but may, at times, be in tension. Importantly, they both offer a praxis that is new and necessarily creates new knowledge about the world. The complexity of the world requires this kind of working in dissonance and tension – and such work is entirely in keeping with feminist transdisciplinary endeavours.

I accept the premise that we are always already in the wake, even when this goes unacknowledged. From here, we are all tasked with imagining other ways of being of thinking/imagining/knowing in that wake. Braidotti's figuration of the nomadic subject is a fiction, a fiction that, like Octavia Butler's fictional work, enable creativity and rethinking the taken-for-granted. According to Braidotti (1994: 26):

> The nomadic subject is a myth, or a political fiction, that allows me to think through and move across established categories and levels of experience: blurring the boundaries without burning bridges. Implicit in my choice is this figuration he belief in the potency and relevance of the imagination, of myth making, as a new way to step out of the political and intellectual stasis of our times. Political fictions may be more effective, here and now, than rhetorical systems.

These blurred boundaries might become further disrupted by re-membering that which is so easy to forget: the production of an economic structure, culture and society through the bodies of Black women, now largely absented from the record. Through a violent and brutal physical, psychic and emotional labor of bearing children who would then be stolen and sold to labor, this history continues to position Black women in particular ways that cohere with the positioning of Black women during slavery – an ontological negation that is both gendered and raced. This history requires a rethinking of motherhood, labor, subjectivity, family, alongside the entanglement of race and gender. Doing this necessarily facilitates new theories, creative approaches to knowledge, and even new ways to dream that are knotted to pasts and presents that produced them – denaturalizing them and destabilizing them. The work for transdisciplinary feminist methodology is to better think subjectivity as raced, gendered and historical, even when engaged in knowledge projects not directly concerned with those things. This requires moving in relation to new and old knowledge, new and old imaginaries, to think, create and know anew, but – and this is crucial – to do this in relation to a particular history that we are never outside of, although beyond disciplinary norms, that we rarely acknowledge or meaningfully work. This enjoins us to take up the missed opportunity to do the kind of research work that better reflects the complexity of living and dying in this world (Haraway, 2016).

The agency of absence

What does absence do? The ongoing epistemological violence of absenting and/or pathologizing particular knowledges, languages, cultures, experiences and perspectives from dominant discourse has been integral to upholding racial hierarchies. There are many examples of this in scholarly work, but also in artistic expression. In *Playing in the Dark*, Toni Morrison (1993) explores one aspect of cultural disappearing/absenting, by thinking through American canonical literature to discuss the white imaginary and the agency of absence, describing the work of writers as 'imagining others' and 'project[ing] consciously into the danger zones of such others' (4). While Morrison does not say what those danger zones are, I imagine that those danger zones are all the ways that a writer might get those others wrong (or too right). Morrison continues,

> I am interested in what prompts and makes possible this process of entering what one is estranged from – and in what disables the foray, for purposes of fiction, into the corners of the consciousness held off and away from the reach of the writer's imagination.
>
> (4)

Morrison considers the exclusion of what she calls Africanist presence, or American Africanism, in American literature. This refers to what blackness has come to signify, 'as well as the entire range of views, assumptions, readings, and misreadings that accompany Eurocentric learning about these people' (7).

This exclusion is agential, producing unanticipated and ongoing effects and affects that disrupt the literary work, disallowing it to proceed because it does not engage the reality of whiteness and its dependence on the production and reproduction of blackness as other, in what Morrison calls the 'parasitical nature of white freedom' (57), which insists on the relationship between American freedom and the taking of freedom of other peoples. This entanglement makes the absenting of Black people conspicuous to the point of disrupting the narrative, revealing important insights about the production of whiteness. How might transdisciplinary research resist the reproduction of those familiar silences by thinking with historical productions of subjectivity, rather than fantasizing that subjectivity can be thought separate and apart from gender and racial hierarchies?

Becoming polyglot: transdisciplinary unlearning in the wake

There is something about proceeding with caution, while recognizing that the spaces where we are most comfortable to assert knowledge might not be the places we ought to be or are most needed. Braidotti writes, 'all knowledge is situated, that is to say partial; we are all stuttering for words, even when we speak "fluently"' (1994: 14). This stuttering can be a place to practice becoming undisciplined. 'We must become undisciplined. The work we do requires new modes and methods of research and teaching; new ways of entering and leaving the archives of slavery' (Sharpe, 2016: 13). Following both assertions, I wonder how we can speak in ways when we do not yet know what to say in order to know anew? How do we 'travel' across spaces, exploring in ways that we cannot help but to know differently, even when we do not want to? Braidotti speaks to some of these questions:

> I think that one of the ways in which feminists could visualize this multi-differentiated and situated perspective, is through the image of the multiple literacies, that is, a sort of collective becoming polyglot. Feminists need to become fluent in a variety of styles and disciplinary angles and in many different dialects, jargons, languages, thereby relinquishing the image of sisterhood in the sense of a global similarity of all women *qua* second sex in favor of the recognition of the complexity of the semiotic and material conditions in which women operate.
>
> (Braidotti, 1994: 36)

Braidotti and Sharpe invite the creation of new ways of working that are not yet established. Both are concerned with a new method for thinking and doing. For my thinking, they both provide new concepts and models of how those concepts might be put to use but leave room for creative interpretation. While their work and approach are very different, I am interested in how both Braidotti and Sharpe talk about movement – Braidotti, mostly voluntary movement and Sharpe, brutally forced movement – and the way that mobility implicates imagination and consciousness in ways heavy with creative potential. This resonates with Butler's *Kindred* but also with Morrison's points: The pasts shaped how we are able to know, the angles and orientation from which we enter and leave the room (Ahmed, 2007). This cleaving of past and present reflects a desire to re-know the present through creative approaches to knowledge. Their work informs my interest in how we imagine ways of knowing that past, in excess of the fictions of the archive, but not only that. I am also interested in the ways we recognize the many manifestations of that fiction and that excess, that past not yet past, in the present (Sharpe, 2016: 13) and what comes to matter in the production and creation of knowledge.

Sharpe further emphasis the both/and of wake-work, saying 'to be in the wake is to occupy and to be occupied by the continuous and changing present of slavery's as yet unresolved unfolding. *To be* "in" the wake, to occupy that grammar, the infinite, might provide another way of theorizing' (Sharpe, 2016: 14). Another way of theorizing is also what Braidotti is after. 'Writing in this mode is about disengaging the sedentary nature of words, destabilizing commonsensical meanings, deconstructing established forms of consciousness' she says (Braidotti, 1994: 15). Commonsensical meanings and established forms of consciousness are those that cohere with patriarchy and white-supremacy, always in the wake of slavery. Transdisciplinary research is an invitation to work in new and different ways that bust out of the constructed and surveilled borders of scholarship.

If uncertainty were less maligned and embraced, we might think and do research that moves us further away from the kinds of *knowing* that is familiar and most recognizable in institutional spaces tasked with knowledge production, rather than avoiding this space. Research might be imagined as an ongoing unlearning, rather than the hoarding and accumulation of knowledge. This frame might invite researchers to cross the borders of the disciplines where they have been trained, stray from the texts that are most familiar, written in languages that are difficult to understand. As Braidotti (1994: 39) usefully writes, 'nomadic feminist thinkers already have a foot in the next century, while keeping in sight the very past from which they are struggling to emerge.'

Becoming traveler, becoming transdisciplinary feminist researcher, becoming-nomadic

Who do/can we become when we travel, crossing borders imagined and otherwise? Do we travel light or are we burdened with baggage, weighing us down so that we choose alternate routes? Who might we become when we read in languages we do not yet know (or cannot ever know), visit places we've never been, and speak to people who we might otherwise avoid? Some journeys are voluntary, while others are not, and the motivation for travel impacts how one undertakes the trip. And *how* we arrive is sometimes just as an important as the journey. Are we welcomed or scorned? We can be fearful and uncertain when we arrive in a place that we have never been, not knowing how to move, speak or act. How do we approach new people and sensations? How do we think with new ways of knowing and being, in this new place? Do we cluster around the spaces that remind us most of home, doing much of what we might do or say if we were at home? Or do we venture forward, confused and uncertain, hands stretched outward in the dark?

This is what research often feels likes to me. Before beginning, particularly as a newer scholar, I read all of the travel guides, reviews, recommendations and ask for advice from those who have been 'there' before. This is never sufficient, and I still feel that I am groping in the dark. This groping, though, sensitizes me in ways that I do not think are all bad. I am attuned to the unpredictability of learning with and through the work of others, in the world around me, open to discovering paths that I had previously been unable to imagine.

Despite so much discouragement to do otherwise – ever expanding neoliberal production norms, the physical geography of institutions and never having enough time – we might aspire to imagine research in the way that I describe here. By this I mean thinking research as a creative moving with and around knowledge, experience and subjectivity, but always holding those things loosely, open to shifting in response to unexpected encounters with events, art exhibits, conversations, lectures, texts, songs and the work of others. This seems like it might take more time than we have to discover and know in ways that can influence better, less deadly, experiences in the world. I might counter this, though, with the argument that the urgency of the current times require very different imagining of research and a creative *letting go*, not of the past, but instead of the dominant and disciplining narratives of science that have not served the current moment in the ways that we might have hoped.

Thinking broadly and experimentally with the concept of travel, conceived broadly as movement through space and time, I am interested in how this metaphor challenges some of the ways that research is imagined. Travel is ongoing, as we are always moving through the world in both tiny and significant ways. We do not think of this as research, but it can be. It can be gathering 'data' (Koro-Ljungberg and MacLure, 2013; Koro-Ljungberg, 2013), but more importantly, it can be the ongoing work of developing sensitivity to sensing anew in the world where so much goes unnoticed.

One of the things that has served me as an emerging scholar is what I will call productive uncertainty. Uncertainty is often stigmatized in spaces where knowledge is produced, created and circulated. Being uncertain, admitting hesitancy, can be used against you, particularly, when uncertainty is always gendered, raced, classed, surveilled and disciplined. I attempt to resist that norm in order to alternatively imagine uncertainty as a potential space for anxious curiosity and a sensing the world in ways that serve research more productively. Uncertainty is a close relative to *not* knowing what you are doing. I reject this characterization, but my personal rejection does not mean that I am not also subjected to the discipline of these norms and definitions. I also recognize the risk of admitting this in a text that may be read by others. Even so, I do not regard uncertainty as *not* knowing; instead it is a different orientation to knowledge and knowledge projects. This *not* knowing/uncertainty puts me on high alert – noticing and thinking and rummaging through texts and collecting artifacts across disciplines and fields in order to know better and become less uncertain. One of the ways that helps me think about this as an ongoing process is to think in terms of travel.

Becoming transdisciplinary traveler means I must/will consider the implications of the past on research thinking and doing, on subjectivity in the tangle of raced and gendered bodies and on how to do research that take seriously the specters, legacies, and present absences in the world. Braidotti (1994: 25) says:

> The nomadic tense is the imperfect: it is active, continuous; the nomadic trajectory is controlled speed. The nomadic style is about transitions and passages without predetermined destinations or lost homelands. The nomad's relationship to earth is one of transitory attachment and cyclical frequentation; the antithesis of the farmer, the nomad gathers, reaps, and exchanges but does not exploit.

Research is slippery. This is true for all research but feels particularly so in the kind I do which struggles against the borders of disciplines and desires to work in ways that make room for the unexpected, unpredictable, and uncertain. The nomadic tense allows for this, even requires it. The desire to work across literatures and disciplines produces research as even more perplexing and slippery. How and what does and can research become when I am thinking across literature, film, digital media and historical text to produce temporary feminist research creations (Koro-Ljungberg, 2012). Temporary, because research should always be in flux, and must remain open to new insights that allow us to momentarily anchor so that we may think, do and imagine better. Thus, in this chapter, I travel with Black feminist theory, academic writing on the transatlantic slave trade, and Black speculative fiction to wonder about how this collaging of divergent and overlapping texts prepares feminist researchers to notice that which we are over prepared to ignore. I wonder, theorize and speculate in this entanglement of texts and theories at the edges of research, just as I also think through the practical problems that persist in the resistance to gender, sexuality, and racial violence.

Imagining research as onto-epistemological traveling pulls in researchers, the field, participants, artifacts and archives all of whom/which travel together to notice, think, experience and imagine anew. Such onto-epistemological traveling supports the creation of new kinds of knowledge that move toward disrupting the gendered and racial dichotomies as they intersect with other social hierarchies to disallow bodies that have not achieved the status of human to access life in the same way (Wynter, 2003). Thus, onto-epistemological traveling nurtures resistance, giving us more generous bulwarks to reject racial and gendered inferiority, and helping us recognize that a world that is not 'given' can lead to all sorts of policy changes or cultural shifts.

Concluding: new ways of knowing: the practice of 'as if' as nomadic resistance

In concluding, I return to the work of Octavia Butler. I do so because Butler engages much of what I have been concerned with in this chapter – moving across knowledge, time and space, being in/with/of the wake of the transatlantic slave trade to rethink subjectivity as both raced and gendered, becoming with the past in gendered and raced ways, being connected, but not bound to the past. Braidotti (1994: 6) says 'the practice of "as if" is a technique of strategic re-location in order to rescue what we need of the past in order to trace paths of transformation of our lives here and now.' Octavia Butler offers some clues to how to do this, even though I do not know if Braidotti ever read *Kindred*, in which a Black women protagonist negotiates and adapts to the embodied degrees of gendered and raced subjectivity across time – and I am not sure it even matters if Braidotti did read it. What matters for the practice of 'as if' is that our past gives us new ways of knowing the present. Such knowing by one who newly remembers and knows the wake (Sharpe, 2016) can be seen as a form of nomadism that, specifically, resists 'settling into socially coded modes of thought and behavior' (Braidotti, 1994: 5). In my own attempts to deploy transdisciplinary nomadic thinking in the wake, it is important to remember that 'not all nomads are world travelers; some of the greatest trips can take place without physically moving from one's habitat. It is the subversion of set conventions that defines the nomadic state, not the literal act of traveling' (Braidotti, 1994: 5).

References

Ahmed, S. (2007). A phenomenology of whiteness. *Feminist Theory*, 8(2), 149–168.

Ahmed, S. (2010). Happy objects. In M. Gregg and G. Seigworth (Eds.), *The Affect Theory Reader* (pp. 29–51). Durham, NC: Duke University Press.

Braidotti, R. (1994). *Nomadic Subjects: Embodiment and Sexual Difference in Contemporary Feminist Theory*. New York, NY: Columbia University Press.

Butler, O. (1979). *Kindred*. Boston, MA: Beacon Press.

Brown, A. (2017). *Emergent Strategy: Shaping Change, Changing Worlds*. Chico: AK Press.

Campt, T. (2017). *Listening to Images*. Durham, NC: Duke University Press.

Ferguson, R. (2003). *Aberrations in Black: Toward a Queer of Color Critique*. University of Minnesota Press. Minneapolis, MN: Minnesota University Press.

Hartman, S. (2007). *Lose Your Mother: A Journey Along the Atlantic Slave Route*. New York, NY: Farrar, Straus and Giroux.

Haraway, D. (2016). *Staying with the Trouble: Making Kin in the Chthulucene*. Durham, NC: Duke University Press.

Koro-Ljungberg, M. (2013). 'Data' As vital illusion. *Cultural Studies ↔ Critical Methodologies*, 13(4), 274–278.

Koro-Ljungberg, M. and MacLure, M. (2013). Provocations, re-un-visions, death, and other possibilities of 'data.' *Cultural Studies ↔ Critical Methodologies*, 13(4), 219–222.

Morrison, T. (1993). *Playing in the Dark: Whiteness and the Literary Imagination*. New York, NY: Vintage Books.

Perry, I. (2018). *Vexy Thing: On Gender and Liberation*. Durham, NC: Duke University Press.

Sharpe, C. (2016). *In the Wake: On Blackness and Being*. Durham, NC: Duke University Press.

Spillers, H. (1987). Mama's baby, papa's maybe: An American grammar book. *Diacritics*, 17(2), 64–81.
Thaler, I. (2014). *Black Atlantic Speculative Fictions: Octavia E. Butler, Jewelle Gomez, and Nalo Hopkinson*. London: Routledge.
Wynter, S. (2003). Unsettling the coloniality of being/power/truth/freedom: Towards the human, after man, its overrepresentation-an argument. *CR: The New Centennial Review*, 3(3), 257–337.

5 Powerful dressing

Artfully challenging sexism in the academy

Linda Knight, Emily Gray and Mindy Blaise

Introduction

#FEAS – Feminist Educators Against Sexism – is a feminist research collective that uses humour, performance and arts interventions to address sexism in the academic workplace. We write this chapter as the three founding members of #FEAS which is now a collective of over 800 people from across the globe. Our work deals with the experiences of women academics, professional staff, researchers, higher degree students and others in the university context. Although we use the term woman in this chapter and elsewhere, we are careful to pay attention to the intersections of the broad category of 'women' with the other markers of identity that impact upon sexism: race, sexuality, gender identity, class and disability. Our research aims are aligned with the core feminist values of investigating and calling out 'systemic gender disparities, women's "experience", hierarchies between the researcher and research participant, emancipation and social change' (Gunaratnam and Hamilton, 2017: 1) and our particular focus is on those working in Higher Education.

The purpose of #FEAS is twofold. First, we aim to contribute to the existing corpus of feminist research and gender studies in ways that intersect with and complement that work. Second, our arts interventions serve to function within academic and other spaces as feminist activism, challenging everyday and structural sexism within the academy as it affects women employees. We present #FEAS here as a feminist transdisciplinary project and reference Tuija Pulkkinen's (2015: 183) suggestion that transdisciplinarity is an 'intervention which reaches beyond the concepts of accountability, innovation and corporate management'. Our collective processes are transdisciplinary because the ideas, practices, strategies and methods break across disciplinary borders of the situated knowledges and expertise we each might usually rely upon. This is not a chaotic process, however: our habit of using an eclectic approach demonstrates what Pulkkinen identifies as a 'transdisciplinary discipline' (2015: 184), or a paradoxical form of transdisciplinarity that habitually emerges via a rejection of instrumental, disciplinary conservatism. Each #FEAS project emerges from different border-breaking configurations of participants, knowledges, practices and agendas and this reflects the particular ways transdisciplinary gender studies maintain 'an identity based on non-identity' (Pulkkinen, 2015: 184). We do not work to a stable process or sequence; each #FEAS transdisciplinary feminist project has a different construction; however, what is constant is that each project is irreverent, humorous, creative – and deadly serious about raising awareness of the working lives of a broad range of academic women. We are influenced by other feminist artist collectives such as the Guerrilla Girls, Pussy Riot and The Five Mujeres who consistently draw on different practices and tactics to generate interventions that are paradoxically identifiable by being so unpredictable. Our transdisciplinary approach is a powerful feminist method for activism that is driven by an 'essentially critical and politicizing impulse; or in other words, on intervention' (Pulkkinen, 2015: 185).

This chapter focuses on one particular #FEAS project: 'Power Dressing', a transdisciplinary feminist intervention that subverts the sexism entrenched in professional appearance and dressing through the interplay of an extravagant power jacket worn by diversely identifying feminists who might otherwise reject wearing a normalizing, feminizing object of signification.

The account of our #FEAS Power Dressing project is presented as a case study of how a transdisciplinary approach offered rich ways to create interventionist feminist commentary on the politics of dress and clothing in the workplace and to illustrate the value of transdisciplinary feminist research in creating interventions that are not so fixed on 'the creation of new knowledge *about* gender' (Pulkkinen, 2015: 192, original emphasis) as rather challenging 'prevailing ideas' (Pulkkinen, 2015: 192) about the working conditions and diverse experiences of women in the academy.

We are hopeful that our description of Power Dressing provides some ideas and starting points for other feminist projects that want to break borders across disciplines and practices in the creation of activist work.

How dress codes uphold sexism in the academy

Workplaces often require, or request, employees adhere to dress codes appropriate to the job. Dress requirements can be strictly imposed through uniforms and safety wear. However, in jobs without these requirements, such as higher education, there are often implied expectations of how the institution is represented through the appearance and presentation of its workforce. Implied dress codes put particular pressure on women (Casanova, 2015) to figure out what is appropriate clothing that is comfortable and professional (Woodward, 2007). Women face more pressure than men in dressing appropriately because women continue to be in the minority in many professions, especially in business which has 'historically been the domain of men' (Entwistle, 2015: 188).

Sociologist Erynn Masi de Casanova (2015) researched dress codes and masculinity in the business workplace. Through her interviews with men working in the United States corporate sector Casanova theorizes the difficulty women face in dressing 'right' are because they must negotiate the conflicting pressures of style and conformity in a work environment that is still regarded as a man's space. Many of the men Casanova interviewed told accounts of women colleagues being spoken to by their seniors or spoken about by their colleagues because their clothing choices were deemed inappropriate. This did not seem to be a common experience for the men interviewed. The interviewees asserted what is appropriate based on their own clothing choices and habits. The responses provided by the interview participants imply that women are not the natural inhabitants of the workspace because the judgements about women's clothing choices emerged from prejudiced thinking about women just being present in the workplace.

The policing of clothing means that dressing becomes a form of extra labour for women trying to second guess what to wear in the 'absence of definitive demarcations of acceptability for women's attire' (Casanova, 2015: 134), unlike the clear codes in the formal and smart-casual of men's clothing. Women's dress decisions work as an identifier, whereas men blend in more easily. The sharp attention to what women wear in the workplace adds to a general consensus that 'women are seen as bodies out of place' (Casanova, 2015: 134), and a belief that men are the natural inhabitants of the workplace and women are not. All the baseline assumptions and problems around women's appearance and dress emanate from this belief of natural belonging. Casanova (2015: 132) reports, for example, that when talking about clothing appropriateness the men she interviewed referred to people but 'it became apparent they often meant only women'. The judgements the men made about what the women wore upholds a conception that put 'men as the default, normal workers and women as potentially trouble-making interlopers' (Casanova, 2015: 132).

One reason why women's work dress is noticed and flags women as 'other' in the workplace is the regard for women's bodies, as (hetero)sexualized bodies. Joanne Entwistle (2015: 190) states that 'the "rules" or conventions of dressing the female body for work demonstrate how it is routinely associated with sexuality and how women, as objects of the male gaze, need to "manage" their bodies to avoid associations with sexuality'. A participant interviewed by Casanova (2015: 132) suggested that:

> Women in male-dominated environments ... could wield their attractiveness (and their ability to be a sex object for straight men) as a strategy for success. However, the flip side of that coin, he points out, is that this status as a sex object – especially when highlighted by particular forms of dress – could also disadvantage women or weaken their position in the organization.

Attempting to strike that precarious and already-determined balance between one form of sexual objectification and another prevents women from working on a 'level playing field' to men. Furthermore, this extra labour that women undertake when trying to strike that balance is increased for any women who do not fit a white, able-bodied, cis-heterosexual subjectified norm. Women from diverse cultural and ethnic backgrounds, and same-sex attracted and gender diverse women, are tasked with additional work to assert their equal status in a workplace that might have already decided their status.

In a general workplace context, the terms that are used to describe women's workplace clothing are affective, emerging through style and fashion discourses. The men in Casanova's (2015) study commonly used fashion terminology as a way to assert the differences between men's and women's dress, rather than recognizing that difference is brought on by gender or sex discrimination. To use a fashion discourse effectively neutralizes or shrouds any kind of discriminatory element. Referring to how women dress as 'fashion' also permits the idea that women dress to seek the appraisal of others; to 'please or to solicit compliments' (Casanova, 2015: 124). Using the term 'fashion' to describe women's ways of dressing at work also enables men to draw on stereotypes of female knowledge/ male ignorance about clothing, tied to conventional social attitudes about how much men and women care about how they look. This convention surfaced in the ways Casanova's (2015) participants spoke about their colleagues as having superior knowledge of fashion, and that it was an interest in fashion, rather than the women's negotiation of unequal dress rules, that directed their professional clothing choices. Seeing women's work clothing as fashion is not only a belief held by men in the corporate sector, such beliefs can surface in different workplaces, including the university.

Women are victims of a paradoxical pressure in terms of their dress (Mavin and Grandy, 2016). Men assert a form of masculinity in declaring how little they know about the world of fashion (not just women's but all fashion) while asserting and upholding strict normalizing codes of what is acceptable – and what is definitely unacceptable for women to wear at work. Casanova (2015: 127) tells how:

> Most participants easily answered my question of what men in their company wore to work. But many appeared flummoxed when I asked what the equivalent of that male work dress was for women, when I enquired as to what women wore to the office.

These same participants could, however, clearly articulate in detail what wouldn't be acceptable for a woman to wear to the office. The men could describe items of clothing that revealed too much or too little of the body, or that was symbolic of other events where it would be OK for a woman to be more obviously a sexual object (such as in a nightclub or bar). The responses exemplify how men can find women's fashion mysterious while also having enough knowledge of dress to assert strict guidelines based on their insider knowledge of suitable business attire.

The dress code expectations placed on women co-workers to appear simultaneously alluring and seriously professional, by men who profess bafflement as well as expertise in those dress codes, presents an impossible paradox for women to somehow successfully navigate these pre-asserted distinct/indistinct rules, and it is this impossible paradox that the Power Dressing project comments on. The ubiquitous business suit, or smart-casual sports jacket and pants, means that no matter what a woman chooses to wear, it stands out as different. Men know this, declaring that 'being a guy, it's pretty hard to screw [work attire] up' (Casanova, 2015: 134). As Casanova (2015: 128) asserts, a paradoxical pressure emerges from a belief that 'dress is a distinctly gendered practice … fashion as a feminine area and work as a masculine area'. Although men's work attire is managed through social codes 'those codes symbolize a notion of professionalism rather than cultural expectations of masculinity' (Gay, 2018: 10), whereas the codes attributed to women's clothing seem very definitely to emanate from cultural expectations of femininity.

The Power Dressing project discussed in this chapter takes up the impossible paradox and visualizes the constantly shifting and contradictory conditions and subjectifications women have to negotiate in the workplace. The project alerts others to the issues of dressing for work, how it is not easy for women due to the persistence of their objectification as sexual bodies (Tan, 2006: 1), and how this sexualization is so highly conditional, contingent and dependent upon bodies that are the right age, size, colour, orientation, culture, ability, proportion and more. Recent global, feminist, awareness-raising campaigns, such as the #MeToo movement, The Women's March and #TimesUp, mean that many men are beginning to realize how privilege has worked and continues to work in their favour. Awareness does not mean change, however, and research such as Casanova's attests to this when she realized participants 'see gender parity as a goal, or at least pay lip service, but don't seem to have the motivation, the tools, or the standing to push their organizations toward this goal' (Casanova, 2015: 123). Casanova conducted her research in corporate, white-collar workspaces in the United States, in organizations that employed higher numbers of men, so it is easy to see why the men she interviewed adopted an apathetic approach to the working conditions of women in their workplace. But what about workplaces that employ large numbers of women? How is it that in female-dominated spaces (like universities), women still endure disproportionate scrutiny of their appearance and dress choices?

The academy is an interesting context in that it doesn't overtly impose a strict dress code. It does, however, exert influence and pressure through conservatisms that permeate more widely and deeply through the contemporary university. Women are still tasked, even in the liberal-minded university, with the labour of curating their appearance. Like their business and corporate counterparts, women academics often perform additional invisible labour as they find ways to adopt and adapt their appearances to fit a narrow male ideal (Mavin and Grandy, 2016; Peluchette, Karl, and Rust, 2006). The Power Dressing project does not emerge from a stereotypical vision of all academic women being forced to fuss over their workplace dressing choices because many women academics do not worry about how they look. We are aware, however, that many women think and perhaps worry about what messages and significations their appearance might generate. Many women undertake additional labour as they cultivate and curate their appearance, irrespective of their ranking or professional seniority. Generally speaking, this labour is not something men in academia undertake (McClintock, 2018; Stavrakopoulou, 2014; Wolff, 2014).

We curated the Power Dressing project because we see the negative impact that appearance politics has on women in the workplace. Scholars such as

Joanne Entwistle (2015: 4) have called for sociological studies into workplace dress codes to expose the interrelated ways 'in which fashion determines dress and dress interprets fashion', and how the sociology of dress is not a study of fashion design but is a way to understand 'fashion/dress as situated bodily practices [and how] the fashion system impose parameters' (Entwistle, 2015: 40) that are mediated 'by other social factors, such as class, gender, ethnicity, age, occupation, income' (Entwistle, 2015: 49).

The Power Dressing project exists as a transdisciplinary intervention because it breaks through the disciplinary borders of politics, sociology, feminist theory, gender studies, photography, fashion design and performance to hold up the subtle sexisms of workplace dressing experienced by women in the academic workplace. As an artistic project Power Dressing collectively draws upon forms of knowledge production emerging from different intellectual and creative work. Power Dressing is informed by feminist writing, research, and activism, as well as creative practice, which it weaves through the details of the project. For example, the feminist, sociological and political scholarship of the authors cited throughout this chapter helped to shape the specific intention to focus on power dressing, Knight's background in fashion design and sewing informed the design and making of the jacket, the tactic to use photography to create irreverent visual comments is directly informed by feminist artists which include the Guerrilla Girls, Julie Rrap, Cindy Sherman and Tracey Moffatt. In an artistic project like Power Dressing the specific sources and forms of knowledge are taken up and implemented through every stage of the work. This means that the academic scholarship is as present in the end pieces as are the artistic influences.

Power Dressing is an important project because the women who work at universities are incredibly diverse and face discrimination in various ways. For example, Gay (2018: 9) points out that 'women of color, and Black women, in particular, have faced discrimination in the workplace when they choose to wear their hair in natural styles'. Normalizing or homogenizing dress codes also have a negative impact 'by discriminating against faith-based practices' (Gay, 2018: 9) of women academics who might cover their hair and/or parts of their face. We responded to this by making a jacket that is a pastiche of the most diversity-flattening of any item of workplace clothing (i.e. a suit jacket has a ubiquitous status so it does not pay attention to or respect difference, identity, subjectivity, individuality). The jacket, as a single item, is worn by each photographed subject. In putting on the single item of clothing, the jacket speaks to the ways in which diversity gets covered up in the neoliberal, homogenized workplace.

Design and curation of the Power Dressing project

Power Dressing is a project that emerges from a transdisciplinary morphing of photography, performance, textile art, personal narrative and network-based collective activism. It is transdisciplinary because it is simultaneously an idea, an activism, a research experiment, a collective action, an arts intervention, an exhibition and an academic output. The main intention of Power Dressing is to examine how conventional academic dress codes which masculinize, streamline, tailor and unify, create and uphold identity expectations in the academy. The Power Dressing project consists of a textile jacket that participants wear. Wearers are then invited to strike a pose of power, however they interpret that word, and a photograph is taken of them in the pose. The photographs contribute to an exhibition featured on the #FEAS website www.feministeducatorsagainstsexism. com.

The jacket is reversible because women must constantly switch roles in the various contexts they find themselves in as professionals. There is a metallic side. It is marked and tarnished, not a perfect sheen. This side symbolizes the armour women develop to fend off blows to their confidence and legitimacy, and the common feelings women have as imposters in the academy. There is a fur side. The fur is fake snow leopard symbolizing the ways that older women are portrayed as predatory – as 'cougars', preying on the young, driving sports cars, dressing inappropriately, liking loud music and so on. It also refers to the ways senior women are seen as predatory in the academy when they take up senior roles such as Deans, and roles in the executive. And yet, the fur side is also about being prey. Wild cats are rare, prized for their fur and distinct markings. Women can be powerful in the academy, but they are always, also, prey. Their presence in the academy is always at risk, always contingent.

The Power Dressing project sartorializes the original concept of power dressing, a term that began to appear in the United States in the late 1970s/early 1980s 'as an explicitly feminine discourse on how to present yourself at work' (Entwistle, 2015: 187) not only in reference to personal professional appearance but as a technocratic approach to '"manage" one's sexuality so as to acquire "authority," respect and power' (Entwistle, 2015: 187). The best-selling book *Women: Dress for Success* by John Molloy (1980) presented this technocratic approach as 'wardrobe engineering' (Molloy, 1980: 18), a seemingly straightforward approach that women could use to gain status in the workplace:

> By making adjustments of a woman's wardrobe, we can make her look more successful and better educated. We can increase her chances of success.
> (Molloy, 1980: 18)

Molloy advocated for a strict dress code that 'diminishes the potential sexuality of the female body' (Entwistle, 2015: 189) including a jacket that hides the contours of the bust and does not hug the waistline which also accentuates the bust. Molloy paid special attention to the suit jacket because it is 'the primary signifier of "professional"' (Entwistle, 2015: 189) – at least, it was for men. The premise for power dressing was to fit women into the dominant, existing mould of male dress codes but with some alterations (literally) to try and contour the female body of women working 'in occupations where sexuality is deemed inappropriate' (Entwistle, 2015: 188), i.e. the corporate sector, into more appropriate shapes. The emergence of the concept of power dressing and the work clothing that appeared initiated 'a new kind of "technology of the self"' (Entwistle, 2007a: 208): the woman worker as a distinct individual, self-curating their body in response to multiple pressures from fashion design and business commentators to conceal, disguise, and present herself – in distinctly individual ways – in the workplace.

Again, women face an impossible paradox of trying to fit in to corporate workplaces that champion team player mentality while they themselves are individualized, reminded constantly of the individual attributes of their own body. Women remain distinctly individual because they continue to be subjectified and objectified as they balance 'the need to diminish sexuality ... in a man's world' (Entwistle, 2015: 189) within terms that are often strictly normalizing and homogenizing.

Much of the scholarship on workplace dress codes does not critique or problematize the underlying heteronormative semiotics attached to items of clothing people are expected to wear (Brower, 2013). There is a lack of commentary on how workplace clothing, no matter who wears them, how they are adapted or how they are restyled over time signify 'membership of a particular group ... of an "assigned" rather than "chosen" gender' (Geczy and Karaminas, 2013: 20). Critiques into workplace dress must therefore acknowledge queer style and the ways that diverse women including butches and femmes do not 'replicate heterosexual gender roles and styles ... [but are] in fact "rewriting" them in order to signify their own desires and sexualities' (Geczy and Karaminas, 2013: 24). The Power Dressing project theatrically interrogates the semiotics of 'female worker' through a transdisciplinary process of photography, performance, textile art and feminist art to create an open translation or performance of power that may be playful, political and declarative. The theatricality of donning a jacket and power posing is a humorous performance enacted differently by each person. For example, posing disrupted the heteronormative representations of queer women often seen in popular culture that assume queer women 'tend to dress like men' (Geczy and Karaminas, 2013: 23). The purposeful reference of the jacket to cult 1980s shows such as *Dallas* and *Dynasty*, popular with gay and lesbian audiences, prompted playful adoption of poses and stances that affirm different ways of dressing and being in the corporatized academic institution. In the Power Dressing project, the jacket is a symbolic object that activates the wearer to think about identity, appearance, diversity, status, education, and feminism.

The Power Dressing project exaggerates the semiotics of dress and fashion via a jacket that humorously plays with those signs. Inviting the wearer to strike their own pose of power queers the 'power' of the jacket and encourages the wearer to consider the impositions around what clothing is permitted in the workplace and how women work within constraints 'to interpret what is and what is not appropriate wear' (Entwistle, 2015: 51). As a singular object, the jacket prompts the wearer to consider uniformity, restriction, individualism and the impossible paradox of women trying to get their professional appearance right (Woodward, 2007) when they are starkly aware that 'a woman's sexuality ... [is] a major obstacle to her career development' (Entwistle, 2015: 188).

The Power Dressing project purposefully references the fashions and styles of the 1980s as a transdisciplinary citational practice. Paying homage to TV shows such as *Dallas* and *Dynasty* references the cultural shift that these shows captured and dramatized through their high-powered, power dressing women characters who channelled the extreme and exaggerated dimensions of the fashion and workwear that emerged in the 1980s created by designers who were responding to the extremes between class, culture and lifestyle differences at that time, translated by designers into clothing that extended shoulders, celebrated individualism through neckties and flounces which drew attention to faces and heads altered by garish makeup and big hair, used opulent fabrics with strident prints, and dressed up/dressed down the wearer.

The schizophrenic, split style of 1980s fashion (Stanfill, 2013) is something the Power Dressing jacket taps into. It is outrageous, opulent, tasteless, cheap, oversized, exaggerated and two-sided to capture the extremes that took place in that decade. The fur side and the lamé side reference the schizoid social and cultural constructions of women that were starkly obvious in the 1980s and are still present today, especially for academic women who have membership to the powerful and privileged (academic) establishment but who are also vulnerable outliers in that establishment. These tensions create a powerful symbolism to draw upon for a transdisciplinary arts intervention into the precariousness of being a woman in the academy.

Even though the power dressing woman appeared initially in the business sector, technologic ways for constructing the self through dress have since seeped into the tertiary education sector. Women academics now have to contend with the competitive, corporatized workplace conditions that business women endured in the 1980s. Contemporary versions of the 1980s dress manual 'where the rules of "dress for success" were explicated' (Entwistle, 2007a: 210) are now the executive or corporate image consultant, who will, for a consultancy fee, workshop or coach you in managing and curating your professional appearance for maximum impact. Dress and appearance are becoming more noticed in university contexts because more of the work is deeply connected to the industry and private sectors. Now, academic roles, and senior/executive roles, encourage a corporate look to match the increasingly corporatized and bureaucratized university. The arts-based, transdisciplinary nature of the Power Dressing project is particularly valuable for irreverently and playfully critiquing entrenched assumptions around dress, power and success. The project exposes how hard it is 'for any professional or business woman today to escape its notice' (Entwistle, 2007a: 209) by facilitating large-scale and inclusive participation in a performative, transdisciplinary intervention by a diverse group who experience the academy differently.

Having outlined the curatorial rationale for the Power Dressing project and the design of the Power Dressing jacket, we now discuss the transdisciplinary, participatory aspect of the work.

Power dressing with women academics and students

We installed the Power Dressing project at conferences and at events connected to academic work. This involved setting up signage about the work, and photography equipment, in an indoor space that would result in good quality portrait photographs, akin to the professional photographs taken and used for ID cards, and staff profile pages on university websites. Participants were invited to turn the jacket to their preferred side and then put on the jacket. Each person was asked to strike a pose of power, and to interpret this in whatever way they chose. Some interpreted power as strength and so adopted stances that conveyed physical capacity and presence, some considered power as an intellectual capacity, and others presented power as resistance and adopted gestures and poses of retaliation and protest. A reflector screen was used to throw a soft glow on the face to enhance the individual character of each face and to pay attention to the expression (Figures 5.1–5.6). The six examples included in this chapter show how diversely each person reacted to striking a power pose. Some chose to disguise themselves with sunglasses, or to emphasize the messages on their t-shirt. Often the direction the person faced varied, as the examples show here. Some people decided to face the camera full-on, while others turned their back to the camera (and the viewer). Often the person made a resistance gesture, subtly, or more obviously. Each person wore the jacket differently. There were two sides of the jacket to choose from, but the actual wearing of it varied from being worn casually open, to being tightly wrapped around the body.

Common to the photographs, however, is the strength of the subject. Posing while thinking and enacting a gesture of power gave each person a strong and agentic presence that seemed to emerge as the photograph was taken. The power stance and the power jacket initiated a transdisciplinary encounter with the politics of dressing in the academy.

It is a key intention of the Power Dressing project to explore how the photographed subjects react once they put the jacket on. The transdisciplinary nature of the project attends to the relationships between appearance, subjectivity and how dress is 'a situated bodily practice … for understanding the complex dynamic relationship between the body, dress and culture' (Entwistle, 2007b: 277) theoretically through the concept of the intervention, and methodologically through the enactment of the intervention.

Participants take turns to wear a single jacket. Although the jacket is reversible the photographs take on a certain sameness due to the presence of the one jacket. The jacket thereby comments on the impossible paradox of being a good corporate academic citizen and working up through a neoliberal system 'and the discourse on the so-called enterprising self' (Entwistle, 2007a: 209), generating income for the university through grants, publications and postgraduate completions while being a self-managing, self-generating individual that is clever and savvy enough to work the system to self-advantage. The poses of power struck by each wearer can only go so far in declaring that individuality, however, while they all wear the same item of clothing. This is because the design and curation of the Power Dressing project is egalitarian, in that everyone who participates has equal presence in the collection irrespective of rank or experience.

The Power Dressing project also signifies a queering of corporate, 'success' dressing. The overstated jacket playfully ridicules heteronormative office wear and a technocratic approach to smashing the 'glass ceiling' by enabling the wearer to present their power stance through 'a dynamic of slippage' (Geczy and Karaminas, 2013: 3) that renegotiates, undermines, overstates and reinstates. The gaudy overemphasis of the fake snow leopard fur, and the marked silver lamé celebrates diversity and comments on the pressure contemporary academics face to conform. Dress codes are important to queer communities; they allow for recognition, fetish, role play and signify community membership, 'important to queer identity is the role of clothing in constructing material identity and its shaping of personal and social space' (Geczy and Karaminas, 2013: 3). The Power Dressing jacket nods to queerness through the way in which it signifies membership of a group – women academics, and also in its deliberate camp.

The individually-dressing, technologized self has permeated into the academy over the years since power dressing emerged in the 1980s. The #FEAS Power Dressing project critically examines the conservative creep of the academic workplace and how conservatism impacts on women's subjectivity and objectivity by asking diversely identifying feminists to wear the same item of clothing as they strike their power poses. The Power Dressing project is a case study of transdisciplinary research seen in the scholarships, actions, reactions in each wearer, and across the collection.

Figure 5.1 Power Dressing 1. 2017.
Image courtesy of the artist: Linda Knight.

54 *L. Knight* et al.

Figure 5.2 Power Dressing 2. 2017.
Image courtesy of the artist: Linda Knight.

Figure 5.3 Power Dressing 3. 2017.
Image courtesy of the artist: Linda Knight.

Powerful dressing 55

Figure 5.4 Power Dressing 4. 2017.
Image courtesy of the artist: Linda Knight.

Figure 5.5 Power Dressing 5. 2017.
Image courtesy of the artist: Linda Knight.

Figure 5.6 Power Dressing 6. 2017.
Image courtesy of the artist: Linda Knight.

Conclusion

The Power Dressing project exemplifies how #FEAS uses hybrid research practices and embraces experimentation to generate empirical data that intervenes in everyday academic sexisms. The project, through the various ways in which women struck power poses with the power jacket, queers the identity politics that they often find themselves trapped within. The project allows women academics to play with appearance politics that were powerful, meaning, and irreverent. For instance, by playing with the ways appearance and dress perpetuate inequities in the academic workplace.

Power Dressing allows participants to poke fun at the academy, and thus to interrupt the power dynamics that are at play within it. It allows wearers to reflect upon power, on the ways in which they embody, resist or challenge power within their workplaces. Power Dressing also brings women academics together; the photo shoots are convivial spaces, networking opportunities and a place to air and share grievances. As a transdisciplinary project, Power Dressing has activated research into the ways appearance and dress perpetuate inequities in the academic workplace, and how these inequities often disadvantage women.

The Power Dressing project will continue to run as we intend to have future pop-up 'power shoots' at several academic conferences where women academics will be attending. Each time that a photo shoot is done, women's photos will be added to the online gallery (see https://feministeducatorsagainstsexism.com). We are intending to exhibit these photos at a gallery and will invite viewers to respond to the photos adding another layer to understanding the issues that women academics continue to face in the workplace. We are also intending to interview a sample of women who participated in the project to find out how or if they are using the photos in activist ways. We are curious to find out if or how the Power Dressing project has intervened in everyday sexisms that women face in their academic lives and enabled us to laugh at some of the ways in which power operates within the academy.

If readers are interested in joining #FEAS we have a private FaceBook group (search for #FEAS – Feminist Educators Against Sexism), a Twitter account (@FEAS_project) and our website. Joining through one of these media platforms will connect you to the global community of #FEAS.

Figures 5.7, 5.8, 5.9 From left to right: Linda Knight, Mindy Blaise, Emily Gray.
Images courtesy of Mindy Blaise, Emily Gray, Linda Knight.

References

Brower, T. (2013). What's in the closet: Dress and appearance codes and lessons from sexual orientation. *Equality, Diversity and Inclusion: An International Journal*, 32(5), 491–502, doi: 10.1108/edi-02-2013-0006

Casanova, E. M. de (2015). *Buttoned Up: Clothing, Conformity, and White-Collar Masculinity*. New York, NY: Cornell University Press.

Entwistle, J. (2015). *The Fashioned Body: Fashion, Dress and Modern Social Theory* (2nd Edition). Cambridge: Polity.

Entwistle, J. (2007a). 'Power dressing' and the construction of the career woman. In M. Barnard (Ed.), *Fashion Theory: A Reader* (pp. 208–219). London: Routledge.

Entwistle, J. (2007b). Addressing the body. In M. Barnard (Ed.), *Fashion Theory: A Reader* (pp. 273–291). London: Routledge.

Gay, R. (2018). Foreword. In S. Massey, A. Albert and E. Jacobs (Eds.), *Dress Like a Woman: Working Women and What They Wore* (pp. 9–11). New York, NY: Abrams Image.

Geczy, A. and Karaminas, V. (2013). *Queer Style*. London: Bloomsbury.

Gunaratnam, Y. and Hamilton, C. (2017). Introduction: the wherewithal of feminist methods. *Feminist Review*, 155, 1–12.

McClintock, E.A. (2018). The gendered double standard of academic attire. *Psychology Today*. Retrieved from www.psychologytoday.com/intl/blog/it-s-man-s-and-woman-s-world/201805/the-gendered-double-standard-academic-attire. Accessed October 6, 2018.

Mavin, S. and Grandy, G. (2016). Women elite leaders doing respectable business femininity: How privilege is conferred, contested and defended through the body. *Gender, Work and Organisation*, 23(4), 379–396, doi: 10.1111/gwao.12130

Molloy, J. T. (1980). *Women: Dress for Success*. New York, NY: Peter H. Wyden.

Peluchette, J. V., Karl, K., and Rust, K. (2006). Dressing to impress: Beliefs and attitudes regarding workplace attire. *Journal of Business and Psychology*, 21(1), 45–63, doi: 10.1007/s10869-005-9022-1

Pulkkinen, T. (2015). Identity and intervention: Disciplinarity as transdisciplinarity in gender studies. *Theory, Culture and Society, Special Issue: Transdisciplinary Problematics*, 32(5–6), 183–205, doi: 10.1177/0263276415592683

Stanfill, S. (2013). *80s Fashion: From Club to Catwalk*. London: V&A Publishing.

Stavrakopoulou, F. (2014). Female academics: don't power dress, forget heels – and no flowing hair allowed. *Guardian*, Australian Edition. Retrieved from www.theguardian.com/higher-education-network/blog/2014/oct/26/-sp-female-academics-dont-power-dress-forget-heels-and-no-flowing-hair-allowed. Accessed October 6, 2018.

Tan, C. Lu-Lien (2006). Pursuits; business attire: the office cover up. *Wall Street Journal*, Eastern Edition, August 5, 2006.

Wolff, J. (2014). Why do academics dress so badly? (Answer: they are too happy). *Guardian*. Retrieved from www.theguardian.com/education/2014/oct/21/why-do-academics-dress-so-badly. Accessed October 6, 2018.

Woodward, S. (2007). *Why Women Wear What They Wear*. Oxford: Berg.

6 Listening to water

Situated dialogues between Black, Indigenous and Black-Indigenous feminisms

Fikile Nxumalo and Marleen Tepeyolotl Villanueva

Orientations

In this chapter, we put transdisciplinary feminist theory-practice to work by engaging in dialogues between situated Black, Indigenous and Black-Indigenous ways of knowing and relating to place. Our materialized emplaced engagements constellate around the possibilities for orientations to water that are situated within current times of environmental damage and human and more-than-human vulnerability. We are interested in the ways in which Black, Indigenous and Black-Indigenous feminist knowledge-theory-practice might help us to locate early childhood education within current times of ecological precarity while also creating openings towards imagining different kinds of futures – futures marked by resistance, hope and more relational ways of living with human and more-than-human life.

Our bringing together of theory and practice using the term 'theory-practice' is intended to highlight our view of theory and practice as inseparable. Theories are constituted by and constitutive of practices (Lenz Taguchi, 2009). We also want to challenge the idea that 'academics do theory; early childhood educators engage in practice' (Pacini-Ketchabaw et al., 2014: 5). As academics who also work pedagogically with children and educators, we (Marleen and Fikile) also see our work as disrupting the theory/practice divide, and in so doing materializing transdisciplinary feminist research-practices that unsettle hierarchical binaries.

In our work we also want to challenge the hierarchical divide between 'academic theories' and knowledges that emerge from communities, such as those in this chapter, which are Indigenous, Black and Black-Indigenous knowledges. We are not arguing that theories that primarily reside in the academy are the same as community-based knowledges, or that they necessarily always belong in the academy. Nonetheless, we want to trouble the marginalization of these knowledges while also challenging the assumption that these knowledges are not informed by rigorous theory-practice. Our intentional unsettling of multiple normative and inequitable power-laden binaries is also an inherently feminist approach.

Methodologically, we engage with the potentials of multiply situated feminisms alongside mundane everyday early childhood pedagogies. The visual and textual juxtapositions that we bring forward in this chapter are an intentional and an intrinsic part of what Eve Tuck (2009) compels us to name – our theories of change. That is to say we are suggesting that change requires making visible the inadequacies of dominant child-centered water pedagogies *and* animating possibilities for different kinds of pedagogies for young children. We are particularly interested in pedagogical imaginaries that are more explicitly situated within children's unevenly distributed inheritances of current and future watery precarities. Put another way, our feminist material-discursive-embodied engagements with water seek to enact otherwise pedagogical possibilities through emplaced water stories that situate children as always already within specific frictional watery entanglements. At the same time, we are guided by an ethical commitment to unsettle the anthropocentrism of normative, developmental pedagogies. In this regard, we share the perspective that positioning (certain) humans as separate from and superior to nature is implicated in producing the environmental challenges we now face (Grande, 2015; Kimmerer, 2002). This perspective suggests to us that learning to respond to environmental precarity requires a paradigm shift in the ways in which children and their learning are situated in relation to the natural environment. Such a paradigm shift includes creating movements away from dominant universalizing, individualist and child-centered approaches (Nxumalo, 2018; Nxumalo, Delgado and Nelson, 2018). These approaches, which are underpinned by linear developmental understandings of children are a part of shaping children into neoliberal modernist subjects; perpetuating unstable modes of relating to the natural world (Grande, 2015). In this chapter, we make visible how such a shift might be enacted by feminist pedagogies that unsettle disciplinary and colonial divides such as those that privilege: cognitive learning from affective/embodied learning; theory from practice; science from art; Euro-Western onto-epistemologies from Indigenous knowledges; human(culture) from more-than-human(nature); the material from the discursive; and the universalized huMAN from the multiple inequitable instantiations of the human (Barad, 2007; Haraway, 2003; Wynter, 2003).

While acknowledging the significant challenges of enacting the radically different everyday pedagogies that are required by such a paradigm shift, we are interested in what it might look like to situate children's learning in ways that move away from learning *about* the environment as an external observer, and instead create movements towards the kinds of learning that takes place when children's situated and asymmetrical relationality with the environment is foregrounded (Nxumalo and Pacini-Ketchabaw, 2017; Pacini-Ketchabaw and Nxumalo, 2015). In this perspective, nature is not a perfect and separate site that children must be 'returned to' (Taylor, 2013; Nxumalo, 2015). Rather, children's relations within their local environment are seen as always interdependent and relational – including inherited relations to environmental damage and vulnerability.

Our theory-knowledge-practice is situated in geographically dispersed watery lands, including Coast Salish forest in what is now British Columbia; the sacred springs of Texas known as Yana wana; the Missouri river on Lakota and Dakota territories at Standing Rock; oceanfront Zulu territories; and Flint Michigan water pipes. Our intent is not to collapse the particular ways in which water and water injustice come to matter in these particular places. Rather, we see the Indigenous, Black-Indigenous and Black feminist teachings that these places embody as intimately connected with our ongoing attempts to do early childhood environmental education differently. We purposefully think with Black, Indigenous and Black-Indigenous feminist theorists and artists, including Christi Belcourt, Christina Sharpe and our elders. They walk with us in this work and inspire us to envision more hopeful futurities, even as we make visible the unlivability of the present. For the remainder of the chapter, we enact our transdisciplinary feminist methodologies through performative assemblages of visual-sensory-auto ethnographic fragments that place into conversation events, memories, poetics, stories, encounters, teachings and relational knowledges and becomings.

Ocean estrangements

Fikile: My people are predominantly scattered throughout the places known as eSwatini (Swaziland) and South Africa but Nkambeni, in the country now known as eSwatini, is the most recent ancestral home of my clan, surrounded by mountain relatives which are also the resting places for many of my human ancestors. eSwatini is a land-locked country surrounded by South Africa and Moçambique. The absence of ocean mattered to my becoming in a number of ways – here I emphasize just two. The first is that I grew up with the story, inside and outside of formal school curriculum – that the absence of ocean territories to the people of eSwatini was due to colonial dispossession – when the British colonizers allocated land that was previously Swati territories to what is today the Mpumalanga and KwaZulu-Natal provinces of South Africa. Today about double the number of Siswati speakers live in these areas of South Africa than in the nation of eSwatini. The ocean then is an intrinsic part of my Black-Indigenous belongings, yet it is also marked by loss and estrangement due to anti-blackness and settler colonialism.

This sense of estrangement bleeds into my second story; imprinted memories of family road trips to the beach city of Durban on Zulu territories, where our family, like other Black families were limited to rocky and crowded segregated 'Blacks only' beaches; leaving prime beachfront spaces accessible only to white families.

Siwasho remembers

My grandmother instructs us to collect sea water to bring back home to eSwatini; where she will bring it to a healer to make traditional medicine – we call this medicine *siwasho*. Ocean water and my grandmother have not forgotten each other.... Knowledges and relations to the ocean still remain within my ancestors and elders despite the ruptures of colonialism.

Developmental watery pedagogies in early childhood education

I never played with water inside the classroom as a child growing up in an urban setting in eSwatini … I have since immigrated to Canada on unceded Coast Salish (Kwikwetlam Musqueam, Stó:lō, Squamish and Tsleil-Waututh) territories, where I am an early childhood educator and pedagogista (Nxumalo, Delgado and Nelson, 2018) and it seems every classroom I have seen has a water table or 'water play' as part of the curriculum.

On one day, I set out clear containers of water together with the plastic cups, some jugs and bowls in the toddler classroom in which I am working (Figures 6.1 and 6.2). My written documentation of these learning moments reflects the child development theory that is the backbone of early childhood

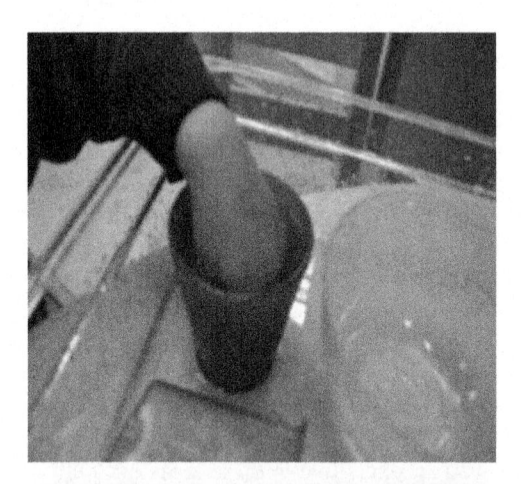

Figures 6.1 and 6.2 Water play in a toddler classroom.

education training (Pacini-Ketchabaw et al., 2014); I describe what the children do to water – *pouring, suctioning, filling, emptying and scooping, and making sounds*. I note down the children's requests for 'more water' as part of their encounters. I struggle to find words to describe these encounters as more than a sensory and science learning activity for children.

In another classroom, where I have been working with preschool children and educators, we engage with readings (Chen, 2010, 2013; Wong, 2011) that inspire us to engage in an inquiry with children on thinking with water in ways that engage with water's liveliness and anthropogenically damaged watery places (Nxumalo, 2016; Nxumalo and Rubin, 2018). We begin to ask different questions about our curriculum-making with the children. For instance, how does water actively participate in the encounters? How might we ethically respond to children's requests for 'more water' amidst our embeddedness in fraught ethics and responsibilities around water use? How might we learn to become affected by and respond to both watery relationalities and watery tensions?

Our pedagogical provocations reflect our struggles in engaging curriculum otherwise to the developmentalism and anthropocentrism in which we are embedded as educators of young children. For example, one day, we (educators) set up a provocation for children to explore the movement of water through pipes. Clear and black pipes are set up at the sink and the water table, and there is a steady stream of water running from the sink to the water table. While children's engagements evoke control of the water, such as diverting and stopping water flows, other unexpected encounters emerge – water after-all is always a lively collaborator in children's engagements whether or not educators pay attention to it in this way. In this particular encounter the entanglements of water and sound come together to shift children's attention. We spend a long time listening to the water: 'the water is saying shhhhh,' one child says.

Water pipes and racial capitalist abandonment

What else might water be telling us then have not yet learned to hear? For example, as I return to the pedagogical encounter with water and pipes several years later, I think about the tensions between this made-innocent science water pipe-play, and the corroded pipes of Flint Michigan, where the combination of crumbling water pipe infrastructure, lead-polluted Flint River water and a myriad of racial capitalist abandonments gathered together to poison thousands of predominantly Black children born and unborn (Pulido, 2016). Lambert (2017: 14) comments:

> In 2014, after the municipality switched the predominantly Black city's water to the lead-polluted Flint River, the amount of fetal deaths and miscarriages, as well as brain, kidney, and liver disorders for residents increased drastically

Thinking with Black feminists brings complexity to our water pedagogies by situating them within vastly unequal and racialized worlds; worlds that continually circulate anti-blackness. These are the kinds of worlds that Christina Sharpe (2016: 104) describes, where 'the weather is the totality of our environments; the weather is the total climate; and that climate is anti-black.' Amidst the pervasiveness of anti-blackness Sharpe also offers hope: '[t]he weather necessitates changeability and improvisation; it is the atmospheric condition of time and place; it produces new ecologies' (106). In looking back at our water-pipe pedagogies and the ways in which they enacted repetitions of unequal ecologies, I stay with the question of what it might look like to enact pedagogies that create movements, however small, towards new justice-oriented ecologies in children's watery relations? What might be needed in early childhood education to engage critically with our complicities in what Moapa scholar Kristen Simmons (2017: n.p.) refers to as 'normalized settler atmospherics.' How might children's water pipe play, lead-leaching water pipes, and the Flint Black community's resistance movements discursively and materially encounter each other in early childhood spaces in ways that do not reproduce otherness (Nxumalo and Cedillo, 2017; Nxumalo, 2018)?

Troubling mastery and control

Feminist scholars have underlined the urgency of finding ways to avoid reproducing Euro-Western colonial practices that privilege mastery and control as primary modes of knowing the more-than-human world (Wynter, 2003). Instead they suggest that a key task of human life is learning to live in more reciprocal ways within our uneven human and more-than-human relationalities (Marin and Bang, 2015; Tallbear, 2016). Drawing inspiration from this work, we wonder what possibilities might emerge for disrupting early childhood education water pedagogies as-usual if, alongside Western scientific modes of knowing water, educators nurtured multiple modalities of curiosity, reciprocity and responsiveness in young children. We are unsettled by our developmental and anthropocentric water pedagogies. We remain troubled by the dominance of Western science in early childhood, even as we are implicated in its persistence. This dominance remains despite clear support for the contention that there are multiple transdisciplinary ways of relating to water that are profoundly pedagogical and that unsettle the bifurcation of humans and nature (Bang et al., 2014).

Black sand–water encounters

In continuing to try out different ways of relating to water with children, the focus of our inquiry shifts to a focus on pedagogical possibilities that encourage relating to water's liveliness. We also want to unsettle engagements with water as an unlimited resource for children's developmental benefit. We are particularly inspired by early childhood pedagogies that encourage children to think collaboratively with water (Pacini-Ketchabaw and Clark, 2016). Our tentative, imperfect provocations to the children, as we try to shift our practices include intentionally providing children with a limited, small amount of water. In one such provocation two small glass jars holding tap water are placed on the ground beside some black sand. In this provocation black sand is included to invite material-discursive messiness into children's water relations. Our intention is also to invite children's attention to what water can do and become with-sand through relations of impermanence, absorption and permeability both within and beyond Western science understandings. What can water do and become in relation to black sand and children's embodied inquiries? (Figures 6.3–6.6) Nearby to the black sand–water provocation, a projector plays a video clip of a water documentary that features brown water crashing through a dam as several people pose for photographs with the crashing water waves in the background. This video clip visualizes the powerful agency of water in juxtaposition with human (in)difference. The murky forceful water on the screen invites children's curiosities as they wonder if the water is full of garbage.

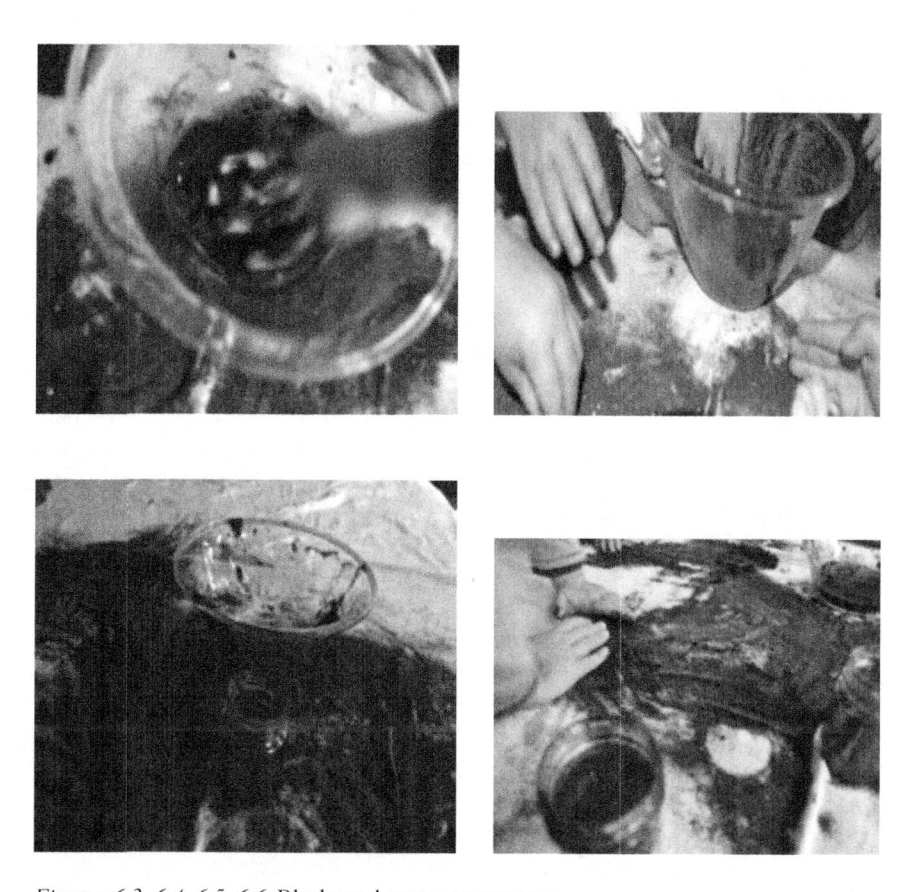

Figures 6.3, 6.4, 6.5, 6.6 Black sand–water encounters.

Children notice the marks the black sand–water leaves on hands. Paying close attention to water's collaborations with black sand perhaps disrupts engagements with water as a simply a subject of children's scientific discoveries. Water, sand and children are all lively entangled collaborators even as children attempt to shape what water and sand can do together. Children's dialogues also often seem to resist objectification of water as static; some children evoke the lively active force of water as they describe what water is doing to the sand. Perhaps, read through the lens of transdisciplinary feminist posthumanist intra-activity, this attention to the liveliness of water, sand and child-bodies might be connected to what Astrida Neimanis (2014: 17) calls 'ethical engagements of responsivity between bodies of water … [where children] … co-emerge with the watery world [they] participate in bringing about.' However, these feminist posthumanist pedagogies still evade difficult questions on water-as-play-material, water-as-resource, water-as-property and questions on the silences on anti-Black and settler colonial inheritances that make possible water-as-play material in this early childhood classroom.

Mni wiconi, water is life

Many Indigenous communities across Turtle Island lack access to clean drinking water. For example, the First Nations Health Authority states that, 'As of July 31, 2018, there were 12 Boil Water Advisories and 4 Do Not Consume Advisories for a total of 16 Drinking Water Advisories in effect in 15 Water Systems across 13 First Nation communities in British Columbia' (First Nations Health Authority, 2018: n.p.).

Standing Rock Oceti Sakowin Camp was set up in April 2016 to resist construction of the Dakota Access Pipeline on Great Sioux Nation territory, including beneath the Missouri River. An important part of this camp was a school, named the Defenders of the Water School (Mní Wičhóni Nakíčižiŋ Owáyawa), which brought children together to engage in the emancipatory curriculum (Grande, 2017). This curriculum included Lakota language and culturally situated science and math. The children also learned from witnessing the water protectors' actions (Grande, 2017). One student at the school describes this learning: 'they make a difference when they pray at the frontlines … many nations as one … we're going to try and kill the black snake, we gotta defeat it' (Cheyenne and Arapaho Television 47, 2016). This story of the water protectors' acts of prayer and ceremony as a source of resistance, counters the dominant media story of 'protest.' This story stands in powerful juxtaposition to the visualities of violence faced by the water protectors including:

> Attack dogs, handcuffs, flex cuffs, stress positions, water cannons, fists, feet, assault rifles, arrest warrants, rural county jails, felonies, misdemeanors, private property, body armor, drones, private security, tear gas, mace, [and] armored Humvees [and] the intentional defilement of gravesites.
>
> (Estes, 2017, as cited in Simmons, 2017: para. 13)

Standing Rock Oceti Sakowin encounters

Marleen: I am from Pame, Chichimeca lands, in what is commonly known as San Luis Potosí, México. I am the first person in my family to not be born in the *cerros* (hills); I have found home in Central Texas, Yana wana lands. While I am not from Central Texas, Yana wana (water of the spirit/spirit of the water) has taken me in as her daughter. Throughout my years living in Central Texas, I have had the fortune of being guided by the Miakan-Garza Band of Coahuiltecan people in Texas, which has led me to my reciprocal relationships with Yana wana.

Our journey to Standing Rock began in the dreamworld: I dreamt that I was at a river that I had not been to. It was so cold that the river had frozen over. I cradled Yana wana in one hand in a jar. I merged her with this soon-to-be known river. Three days after this dream, at a medicine ceremony we received the message that the dream was to become a reality and that the unknown river was at Standing Rock. How were we going to make this happen? We did not know, because as first-generation college students, we did not have the funds to complete the task that Yana wana had asked of us. So we did what we know best. We put our prayers out and asked for guidance. We reached out to Maria Rocha, a Coahuiltecan elder and leader in the community. We relayed the messages we had received through the dream and ceremony and asked for permission to complete the task at hand: merging Yana wana with the Missouri River. She gave us permission to collect Yana wana from four sacred springs in Central Texas: tza wan pupako (Barton Springs in Austin), ajehuan sohuetiau (Spring Lake in San Marcos), saxop wan pupako (Comal Springs in New Braunfels), and Yana wana (the Blue hole headwaters of the San Antonio River). A group of six of us decided to hear Yana wana's call to be merged with the Missouri River.

We are still here; we have that right to pray in these ways. Standing Rock is a beautiful teaching for us. Yana wana continues to guide us on this journey of remembering. Yana wana, water of the spirit/spirit of the water, has taught me about reciprocity with the places I encounter.

Forest–water encounters

On one of our almost daily walks to the nearby second growth forest that surrounds the early learning center on what is now Burnaby mountain, a large water tank and water pipe cover invite children and educators (Figures 6.7 and 6.8). Children are curious about where the water comes from and where it goes – this encounter with forest nature-cultures (Haraway, 2003) reminds us the forest is not outside of human imposition; a reminder that becomes even more present when a few months later the forest becomes a site of protest in relation to a proposed oil pipeline that would pass through the mountain (Nxumalo, 2017). Looking back over these mundane everyday encounters, I wonder what might have emerged from asking children about their ideas on the co-existence of water and oil pipelines in this place – what different kinds of water pedagogies and water relationalities could emerge?

68 *F. Nxumalo and M. T. Villanueva*

Figure 6.7 and 6.8 Forest–water pipe encounters.

Listening to water 69

We have begun to engage with what it means to do forest pedagogies with young children on unceded Coast Salish territories. Our efforts include reading multiply situated Indigenous teachings on water. From one such reading, we are inspired by Violet Poitras, the Nakota/Cree Elder's words. She says:

> I think once we understand each other a bit more clearly, we can tell the rest of the people, this is what's happening to our water and how to take care of it – because it's taken care of us up till now.
>
> (Poitras, 2015: n.p.)

This teaching inspires us to think with an ethic of reciprocal care in our water pedagogies. We are curious about the kinds of reciprocal relations that the waters in this place can invite to children and educators. What possibilities might there be for encounters with water that create movement away from romantic visions of water, water as play material, and water as only knowable through developmental-Western science, and towards an engagement with the 'messiness' in which our relations with water are entangled in this time of the Anthropocene? We struggle with what it might look like to pay attention differently to water. How might we respond pedagogically to the ethics of water use, the taken-for-granted availability of water amidst ongoing water injustice in Canada and beyond? Our provocative questions seem to be in tension with common understandings of the emergent curriculum and we struggle with how to embrace and sustain the messiness of non-anthropocentric watery pedagogies alongside the demands of child-centered curriculum-making (Nxumalo, Delgado, and Nelson, 2018).

Yana wana

The first element that we encounter is water in our mother's belly. We swim around, embraced by life. Water flows, nourishing our heart, our brain, our lungs, our entire body. I loved it so much that I did not want to leave my mama's belly. So when nine months rolled around, I decided to sit criss cross and object to leaving. They ended up having to cut into my mother to pull me out onto this side of the belly. I remember the first time I swam with my grandmother at San Sebastian. I must have been about five years old. I know it was not my first time there, but it is the first time I have visual memories from the spring. I have the memory of holding my Abuela's hand and she has a chair in her left hand. We walk towards the left side of the spring, where the water is calm and clear.

Downstream is a big pool of spring water where people are swimming, laughing and having a good time with their loved ones. I wonder why we are not there with them. She leads me to a spot under a tree where the water is not deep enough to cover my child body. She sets her chair down and sits comfortably. I ask her why we are not down at the pool area with the rest of the family. She says, '*Espérate mija, ahorita hay que sanar, y luego jugar*' (Hold on my child, right now we must heal, then we go play). She sits comfortably in her chair, letting the water flow under her feet carrying them in place. I play in the water, but seeing her sit so still makes me stop and watch. She is caressing the water with her fingertips and her toes are making circles in the water. She has her eyes closed and is sending her face up to the sun. She opens her eyes and says, '*¿Ves ahí? Ahí hay buen lodo. Es bueno para la cara y para las rodillas. Ve y tráeme unos puños nena*' (You see there? That is good mud. It is good for your face and for your knees. Go bring some fist fulls). I go play with the mud and I put some on my face, then I take some in my little fists and apply it to Abuela's knees. I can look back at this memory with my Abuela and smile. I hope she knows how much this memory means to me. How grateful I am to have been able to share mud medicine on her hurting joints. How grateful I am to have been able to witness her healing with the waters of the spring just minutes away from our family's home. It took my familia leaving Mexico in order for me to reconnect with my antepasados (ancestors).

I did not know it then, but the prayers my grandmother was saying for me in that spring as a young child, were carried through my mother's journey to the United States, which allowed me to migrate to Texas. Texas, the land where the Coahuiltecan people have taken me in as their familia. Their niece. The land where Yana wana has accepted my grandmother's prayers to the sacred springs back home in Mexico. Yana wana has let my grandmother know that she will continue to care for her people although they are far away from the motherland. She lets my grandmother know that she will look after her daughter, my mother, and her children. In that way the waters connect in prayer. The grandmother water spirits recognize each other and Yana wana holds me in the same loving embrace that my Abuela held me in the springs in Mexico.

Yana wana is the Indigenous name for water here in central Texas. Yana most closely translates to spirit in the Coahuiltecan language and wana translates to mean water. This spirit of the water, or water of the spirit, has come to hold sacred meaning to Indigenous communities that continue to reside in central Texas. For some, water is seen as a mere element that one pays for as a service and that because one pays for this service, one has a right over it. However, our spiritual practices and ways of allowing for a different understanding of water. We see water as life and as being a sacred spirit. We speak of water as a living being, a spirit that thinks, hears, has life and gives life. For generations, our elders have told us what many are now beginning to see: water listens to what we say and think. She listens and holds memory. She understands.

Yana wana early childhood pedagogies

In this section, our writing comes together as we (Fikile and Marleen) both write in relationship with Central Texas, Yana wana lands where we have been working with young children and early childhood educators in outdoor education (Saint-Orens and Nxumalo, 2018).

We have been spending time at the creek once a week with a small group of kindergarten children at this Austin school. Just as in the setting on Coast Salish territories, here on Coahuiltecan territories, we are also inhabiting the question of what it might look like to engage non-anthropocentric and decolonial water pedagogies. Today Marleen decides to teach the children a water song whose name translates to '*we will always remember the sacred water.*'

After explaining the story behind the song and practicing it a few times, Marleen hands the children rattles to accompany their singing. The children and Marleen approach the creek, ask the creek for permission to share the song and then we began singing to the water. After singing, we invite the children to draw in their water journals (Photo 6.9). Several children's drawings and words connect to how the water felt as we were singing ... echoed as happiness.

- *'The water was happy'* ... *'The water was happy because we sang to it with instruments.'*
- *'This is the water spirit, it is the water's happy ...'*
- *and raining – they heard the song.'*

While these offerings to water by predominantly White settler children are fraught and always risk slippage into appropriation, anthropocentrism and settler emplacement (Tuck, McKenzie and McCoy, 2014), we see them as opening possibilities for an ethics of knowing and relating to water in the everyday

Figure 6.9 Happy water drawing.

places and spaces of early childhood education in ways that move towards respect, gratitude and reciprocity and away from instrumentalism and Euro-Western mastery and control pedagogies.

Atzintli – A water song

> *Atzintli Chalchiuhtlicue Tlaloc Ometeotl*
> *Tu medicina, que limpia, limpia*
> *Que cura, cura mi corazón.*
> *Medicina del agua heyyana heyneyyoway*
> *Son tus rios, tus lagunas,*
> *La lluvia del cielo.*
> *Son los regalos de la vida que purifican mi corazón.*
> *Medicina del agua heyyana heyneyyoway*

Songs are a powerful mode of carrying knowledge intergenerationally, including creating new knowledges across generations. As Māori scholar Linda Tuhiwai Smith (2013: 146) reminds us, 'the story and the storyteller both serve to connect the past with the future, one generation with the other, the land with the people and the people with the story.' *Atzintli* is one of the first songs that I learned to sing for ceremony. Within the song's teachings are the cultural values of deep respect for the water as is exemplified by the first word: Atzintli or raindrop. Atl means water in Nahuatl and -zin refers to reverence that is given to such element. The next three words speak to the importance of masculine and feminine energies within everything and everyone, which break away from the dichotomous and binary ways in which we have been taught about gender. The song incorporates the Spanish language in saying that water cleanses, heals the heart and is medicine. Here we are sharing the knowledge that has been passed down to us in knowing that water has healing properties and the power to cleanse. The song reminds us of various places where water is found (rivers, lagoons, rain) and teaches gratitude for these healing gifts of life through water. *Xanē yohui* pronounced *hey-ney-yo-way* refers to the Coahuiltecan phrase that closely translates to 'with all that I am and with all that there is.' The coming together of three languages (Coahuiltecan, Nahuatl and Spanish) speaks to a collective storying in the origination and carrying of the song across places where 'every Indigenous person has a place' (Smith, 2013: 145). This song has been passed down within and across generations; its genealogy is complex and cannot be described through singular ownership. A member of the Peace and Dignity Journeys community was gifted this song by a relative at the waters in Chalma, Mexico and she in turn shared the song with many community members during the Journeys. This song is sung in many ceremonies throughout Central Texas and around Turtle Island. I have also heard it sung at Standing Rock.

Towards a water revolution in early childhood education

Michif (Métis) visual artist Christi Belcourt powerfully witnesses our current times as part of a water revolution that we are all challenged to participate in when she says:

> We are witnessing, around the world, the rise of what is to be a water revolution led by regular people who want nothing more than to have clean water for their children and a clean world for the next generations.
>
> (Belcourt, 2018: 118–119)

Importantly, Christi Belcourt reminds us that relational and protective actions with and for water, as revolutionary acts, can take a multiplicity of situated forms, wherever we are, guided by positive affects for water. This includes protest and protective offerings such as the water song that we, alongside the children, offer to the creek. Our creek encounters are ongoing and in these encounters we are taking seriously this call to participate in the water revolution through a multitude of ways that enact transdisciplinary research-knowledge-theory-practices (see for example Saint-Orens and Nxumalo, 2018). We see this invitation into water revolution as a provocation to continue to invigorate our water pedagogies with relational and reciprocal acts that disrupt child-as-saviour stewardship discourses (Taylor, 2013) and instead center water and situated child–educator watery relations as a lively effective and affected participant in our curriculum-making. At the same time, the water stories and feminist teachings in this chapter also remind us to pay attention to and respond to anti-Black and settler colonial water injustice. In other words, water revolution cannot separate off certain privileged children from unjust worlds; we need to find ways to consider how transdisciplinary watery childhood pedagogies and curriculum might also inhabit and respond to the ways in which racialized and settler colonial hierarchies have (often deadly) implications for those on those always already deemed as less-than within the interconnected effects of environmental racism and settler colonialism.

References

Barad, K. (2007). *Meeting the Universe Halfway: Quantum Physics and the Entanglement of Matter and Meaning*. Durham, NC: Duke University Press.

Bang, M., Curley, L., Kessel, A., Marin, A., and Suzokovich, E. (2014). Muskrat theories, tobacco in the streets, and living Chicago as Indigenous lands. *Environmental Education Research*, 20(1), 37–55.

Belcourt, C. (2018). The revolution has begun. In E. Tuck and K. W. Yang (Eds.), *Toward What Justice?: Describing Diverse Dreams of Justice in Education* (pp. 118–119). New York, NY: Routledge.

Chen, C. (2010). *Watering Mapping: Thinking with the Lachine Rapids* [blog post]. Retrieved from http://thinkingwithwater.net/category/water-practices/representation

Chen, C. (2013). Mapping waters: Thinking with watery places. In C. Chen, J. McLeod, and A. Neimanis (Eds.), *Thinking with Water* (pp. 274–298). Montreal: McGill-Queen's University Press.

Cheyenne and Arapaho Television 47 (October 26, 2016). *CATV 47 visits Mni Wiconi School at Standing Rock* [Video file]. Retrieved from www.youtube.com/watch?v=AZwhq1z11Nw&feature=youtu.be

First Nations Health Authority (2018). *Drinking Water Advisories*. Retrieved from www.fnha.ca/what-we-do/environmental-health/drinking-water-advisories

Grande, S. (2015). *Red Pedagogy: Native American Social and Political Thought*. Lanham, MD: Rowman and Littlefield.

Grande, S. (2017). *The Future of US Education is Standing Rock*. Truthout|Op-Ed. Retrieved from www.truth-out.org/opinion/item/41146-the-future-of-us-education-is-standing-rock. Accessed July 4, 2017.

Haraway, D. (2003). *The Companion Species Manifesto: Dogs, People and Significant Otherness*. Chicago, IL: Prickly Paradigm Press.

Kimmerer, R. W. (2002). Weaving traditional ecological knowledge into biological education: A call to action. *BioScience*, 52(5), 432–438.

Lambert, L. (2017). Introduction: A 'breathing combat' against the toxicity of the colonial/racist state. *The Funambulist*, 14, 12–15.

Lenz Taguchi, H. (2009). *Going Beyond the Theory/Practice Divide in Early Childhood Education: Introducing an Intra-Active Pedagogy*. New York, NY: Routledge.

Marin, A. and Bang, M. (2015). Repatriating science teaching and learning: Finding our way to storywork. *Journal of American Indian Education*, 54(2), 29–51.

Neimanis, A. (2014). Alongside the right to water, a posthumanist feminist imaginary. *Journal of Human Rights and the Environment*, 5(1), 5–24.

Nxumalo, F. (2015). Forest stories: Restorying encounters with 'natural' places in early childhood education. In V. Pacini-Ketchabaw and A. Taylor (Eds.), *Unsettling the Colonial Places and Spaces of Early Childhood Education* (pp. 21–42). New York, NY: Routledge.

Nxumalo, F. (2016). Storying practices of witnessing: Refiguring quality in everyday pedagogical encounters. *Contemporary Issues in Early Childhood*, 17(1) 39–53.

Nxumalo, F. (2017). Geotheorizing mountain-child relations within anthropogenic inheritances. *Children's Geographies*, 15(5), 558–569.

Nxumalo, F. (2018). Situating Indigenous and Black childhoods in the Anthropocene. In A. Cutter-Mackenzie, K. Malone and E. Barratt Hacking (Eds.), *International Research Handbook on ChildhoodNature: Assemblages of Childhood and Nature Research* (pp. 1–22). New York, NY: Springer, doi: 10.1007/978-3-319-51949-4_37-2

Nxumalo, F. and Cedillo, S. (2017). Decolonizing 'place' in early childhood studies: Thinking with Indigenous onto-epistemologies and Black feminist geographies. *Global Studies of Childhood*, 7(2), 99–112.

Nxumalo F., Vintimilla, C. and Nelson, N. (2018). Pedagogical gatherings in early childhood education: Mapping interferences in emergent curriculum. *Curriculum Inquiry*, 48(4), 433–453.

Nxumalo, F. and Pacini-Ketchabaw, V. (2017). 'Staying with the trouble' in child-insect-educator common worlds. *Environmental Education Research*, 23(10), 1414–1426.

Nxumalo, F. and Rubin, J. C. (2018). Encountering waste landscapes: more-than-human place literacies in early childhood education. In C. R. Kuby, K. Spector and J. Johnson Thiel (Eds.), *Posthumanism and Literacy Education: Knowing/Being/Doing Literacies*. New York, NY: Routledge.

Pacini-Ketchabaw, V. and Nxumalo, F. (2015). Nature/culture divides in a childcare centre. *Environmental Humanities*, 7, 151–168.

Pacini-Ketchabaw, V., Nxumalo, F., Kocher, L., Elliot, E., and Sanchez, A. (2014). *Journeys: Reconceptualizing Early Childhood Practices through Pedagogical Narration*. Toronto: University of Toronto Press.

Pacini-Ketchabaw, V. and Clark, V. (2016). Following watery relations in early childhood pedagogies. *Journal of Early Childhood Research*, 14, 98–111.

Poitras, V. (2015). *Water, the Sacred Relationship* (documentary interview). Retrieved from www.sacredrelationship.ca/why-water/

Pulido, L. (2016). Geographies of race and ethnicity II: Environmental racism, racial capitalism and state-sanctioned violence. *Progress in Human Geography*, 4, 524–533.

Saint-Orens, L. and Nxumalo, F. (2018). Engaging with living waters: An inquiry into children's relations with a local Austin creek. *Journal of Childhood Studies*, 43(1), 68–72.

Sharpe, C. (2016). *In the Wake: On Blackness and Being*. Durham, NC: Duke University Press.

Simmons, K. (2017). Settler atmospherics. *Dispatches: Cultural Anthropology*. Retrieved from https://culanth.org/fieldsights/1221-settler-atmospherics

Smith, L. T. (2013). *Decolonizing Methodologies: Research and Indigenous Peoples* (2nd Edition). London: Zed Books.

TallBear, K. (2016). *Failed Settler Kinship, Truth and Reconciliation, and Science*. Presentation retrieved from www.kimtallbear.com/homeblog/category/democratizing%20science

Taylor, A. (2013). *Reconfiguring the Natures of Childhood*. London: Routledge.

Tuck, E. (2009). Suspending damage: A letter to communities. *Harvard Educational Review*, 79(3), 409–428.

Tuck, E., McKenzie, M., and McCoy, K. (2014). Land education: Indigenous, postcolonial, and decolonizing perspectives on place and environmental education research. *Environmental Education Research*, 20(1), 1–23.

Wong, R. (2011). *Downstream: Reimagining Water* [website]. Retrieved from http://downstream.ecuad.ca/

Wynter, S. (2003). Unsettling the coloniality of being/power/truth/freedom: Towards the human, After Man, its Overrepresentation – An argument. *New Centennial Review*, 3(3), 257–337.

7 The bathroom polemic

Addressing the ethical and political significance of transgender informed epistemologies for feminist transdisciplinary inquiry

Wayne Martino and Jennifer C. Ingrey

Introduction

In this chapter we examine the tensions that continue to afflict feminist accounts of trans informed perspectives on gender embodiment which centre around questions of gender 'authenticity' and gender legitimacy. We address the extent to which such tensions are a result of subscribing to cisgenderist logics that refuse the political terms of trans informed onto-epistemological understandings of female embodiment. For readers unfamiliar with 'cisgenderism', Lennon and Mistler (2014: 63) define it as 'the cultural and systemic ideology that denies, denigrates, or pathologizes self-identified gender identities that do not align with assigned gender at birth as well as resulting behaviour, expression, and community'. We illustrate such tensions by focusing on a particular incident to do with transinclusive bathroom signage at our own university and which gave rise to some debates in our academic community involving an email exchange with feminist, queer and trans scholars and students. We first discuss the specific bathroom policy in question and the nature of the tensions that emerged and set this discussion against a critical trans informed engagement with questions of female embodiment and spatiality. We argue that the terms of such debates illuminate the persistence of a particular trans-exclusionary radical feminist (TERF) account of trans embodiment that cites and relies on problematic discourses about gendered authenticity and legitimacy (Hines, 2019). We then go on to provide further contextualization of the historical legacy of this particular strand of anti-transgender feminism, which focuses on debates about the 'presence of trans women in women's spaces' (Hines, 2019: 146). We use this particular case to reflect on the necessity of trans informed scholarship in transdisciplinary feminist inspired inquiry that calls into question the cisgenderist logics underpinning the question of who can be considered a woman, which sets limits to establishing the legitimacy and authenticity of female embodiment (Namaste and Sitara, 2013).

In addressing the terms of such a polemic we point to the necessity of feminist and gender studies as transdisciplinary fields in highlighting the political and ethical exigency to engage with trans informed epistemological perspectives on gender and embodiment. At the heart of our discussion is an understanding of transdisciplinarity as it pertains to both the practice of feminist theory and epistemological concerns of transgender studies for addressing critical concepts of gender. As Sandford (2015: 160) instructs, while interdisciplinarity entails an individual drawing on more than one discipline and multidisciplinarity involves a team of researchers from different disciplines working together, what is characteristic of transdisciplinary approaches to research is a commitment to

> the idea of specific disciplinary knowledges, concepts, practices and methods maintained in the context of recognition of the virtue of communication between them, according to the presumption that different disciplines can learn from each other and can contribute differently, but complementarily, to the analysis or understanding of a given phenomenon or problem.

At the heart of transdisciplinary approaches in feminist research is a critical concern to transcend disciplinary boundaries and logics and a commitment 'to reflect[ing] on its own modes of knowledge production' (Dolling and Hark, 2000: 1195). It is in this sense that we centre trans epistemological concerns about embodiment as they relate to the problem of the public washroom/ bathroom/restroom space for trans and non-binary people which continues to be motivated by cisnormative concerns that pit trans women and non-trans women against each other (see Bettcher, 2018; Stock, 2018a, 2018b).

Western's policy on washroom inclusivity and debates about who gets to count as a woman

Before proceeding to discuss the specific terms of such polemics and their significance, it is important to provide some contextualization and information about the actual washroom policy at the centre of the debate at our own university, which involved an on-line exchange about washroom inclusivity with feminist, queer and trans academics and students at the university. Equity Services had launched a poster campaign about new bathroom signage, which it stipulated was in line with human rights law in Ontario, Canada. It was conceived to address concerns about the safety of trans, non-binary and gender nonconforming people on campus: 'Western respects everyone's right to choose a washroom appropriate for them: Trust the person using this space belongs here' (University of Western Ontario, 2018). The policy preamble accompanying this initiative was clear in its stipulation that the signage was developed to address the problem of access to public bathrooms on campus for trans/non-binary/gender nonconforming individuals, and was crafted after wide consultation with the university community. There is also specific mention of *gender policing*

> where someone imposes or enforces normative gender expressions – i.e., narrow definitions of what a man or woman should do or look like – on an individual who they perceive as not adequately performing, through appearance or behaviour, the sex that was assigned to them at birth.

(1)

Such statements are important because they contextualize the policy as a response to addressing the cisnormative regulatory regimes that govern access to washroom spaces and their consequences for trans/non-binary and genderqueer persons (Browne, 2004; Ingrey, 2018; Lennon and Mistler, 2014; Radi, 2019). The policy explicitly mentions 'the fear of violence or humiliation' that trans people experience in these spaces (2). Ontario based research on trans health is also cited, which documents the high levels of sexual and physical assault experienced by trans people, the fear of harassment that many trans people expressed, which accounts for their decision to avoid public spaces and which is also related to the potential consequences of being perceived or 'outed' as trans (Bauer and Scheim, 2015).

This contextualization of the bathroom signage initiative is important in understanding the various concerns expressed, and which centred on the question of 'trust'. In an email addressed to Equity Services an MA graduate at the university posted an email expressing her concerns, which she also included on another listserv to which a number of faculty across the university had access. This individual took issue with the wording of the second part of the sign, which she believed 'profoundly undermined' women's experiences. Her concern was that the incitement to trust being invoked by the signage denied due acknowledgement of and in fact detracted from the reality of violence enacted against women, especially given that 'since the beginning of time *women* have been raped or hurt by people they have been told to trust' (our emphasis). This diminishment was further highlighted, she argued, by the fact that *women* are constantly being told to be vigilant in public spaces, given the prevalence of (male) violence, a reality that was belied by the signage which she claimed demanded unequivocal trust.

This graduate student, however, while claiming support for transgender people's access to a washroom space that aligns with their gender identity, goes on to assert that prior to the advent of transgender washrooms *women* have always had to exercise caution and vigilance in such spaces, which are referred to as 'inherently private' and where *women* are vulnerable to 'exposure'. What is noteworthy here is a particular invocation of the category 'woman' which is governed by a fundamental cisnormative logics and a failure to address the specific terms of the contextualization of the signage initiative and inclusive bathroom policy which was instigated in response to human rights concerns for the safety of trans people with respect to gaining access to and being in such spaces. It is an appeal to such a logics and a refusal to consider the terms of address – the fact that the trust that is required is being sought from cisgender individuals in their response to trans embodied subjects in the washroom space – that enables this feminist to read such bathroom signage as a failure to acknowledge 'women's physical and psychological reality'. Excluded are the very trans women who are subjected to high levels of violence and harassment in washroom and other public spaces. As such trans women are set apart from those who are assumed to be inherently female-bodied women as determined by their sex-gender assigned status at birth.

These arguments are also reflected by feminist scholars such as Stock (2018a) in the United Kingdom who express concerns about the *Gender Recognition Act* to legislate trans women's rights to legally identify as women – a move she argues will result in supporting 'unscrupulous men [who] will use this legislation in order to access women-only spaces ... to commit crimes such as voyeurism, flashing, public masturbation, and sexual assault' (n.p.). As trans feminist scholar, Talia Mae Bettcher (2018) explains, this position fails to engage with a necessary 'analysis of the concept attached to the ordinary meaning of "woman" [and] to recognize that dominant meanings of political terms are contested "on the ground" through practices that give them different meanings' (n.p.). Such trans informed engagement in these feminist debates highlight the extent to which gender and embodiment are transdisciplinary concepts that are provisional and as such travel across disciplinary boundaries and fields of inquiry. In fact, Sandford (2015) identifies this application or rather travelling of concepts as a characteristic of transdisciplinary scholarship and one that we argue is at the heart of a transdisciplinary problematics as illustrated above (Osborne, 2015). Trans scholars such as Stryker, Currah and Moore (2008: 13), for example, invite their readers to conceive of *transing* as 'a practice that takes place within as well as across or between gendered space' and one that 'assembles gender into contingent structures of association with other attributes of bodily being, that allows for their reassembly'. Thus *trans*, epistemologically speaking, is understood by such scholars in terms of its temporality 'along a vertical axis, one that moves between concrete biomateriality of individual living bodies and the biopolitical realm of aggregate populations that serve as a resource for sovereign power' (ibid.: 14). It is in this sense that Green (2017: 321) conceives of trans studies in transdisciplinary terms as a field that needs to be 'focused on a method or ethic of openness and movement that will continue to be useful for understanding new categories of people'. These are questions of epistemological awareness (Koro-Ljungberg *et al.*, 2009), which, as informed by transgender and non-binary scholars, are central to building on and elaborating the critical terms of gender democratization that are at the heart of transdisciplinary feminist research (Connell, 2012).

The conundrums which irrupt in response to questions about who gets to count as a *woman* emerged in the ensuing debate at our university with one queer feminist academic expressing concerns about the failure of the MA graduate to address the terms of surveillance enacted against trans and non-binary bodies in washroom spaces. The primary issue raised was that such concerns expressed about trust were motivated by cisgenderist logics that not only dismissed the reality of violence enacted against trans individuals, but also deemed such bodies as 'inherently untrustworthy'. As such, this queer feminist academic believed that such a questioning of trust served to further reinforce the transphobic violence that the very bathroom signage was seeking to undo. This academic also made the point that it was disingenuous to read the bathroom signage as a carte blanche requirement for women to trust unequivocally everyone entering the washroom space. Rather the invocation at play was the requirement to trust those trans and gender nonconforming individuals in their use of these spaces, and to ensure their safety in doing so, without having to be subjected to the humiliation and potential violence that results from gender policing. The point is that critiques of the bathroom signage with its emphasis on trust are made possible only by a refusal to pay heed to the contextualization of the actual policy itself with its emphasis on the need to ensure the safety of trans people on campus and to address violence enacted against them in washroom spaces. However, several female academics from the Faculty of Law posted a joint response that took umbrage at the charges of transphobia, which they considered to be a case of unfair labelling of a dissenting viewpoint. They believed that characterizing a critical response or viewpoint in this way amounted to 'turning disagreement into hate' thereby reducing the terms of the debate to delimiting a productive and open exchange of ideas that are central to serving 'the interests of academic inquiry'.

Such responses are similar to those of Stock (2018b: n.p.) who defends her civic and academic freedom to express her views about 'whether there is any legal right for biologically male, genitally-intact trans women to enter female-only spaces where females undress and sleep ... and how facts about structural male violence affects that issue' without having to contend with charges of transphobia levelled against her by students at her university. However, in asserting such a rights-based position what are eschewed are the very cisnormative terms governing the understanding of gender embodiment and a fundamental lack of understanding and reflexivity about the harm that is enacted against transwomen through employing and asserting such discourses. In addition, as Bettcher (2018: n.p.) highlights 'the dangers faced by trans and genderqueer people (and even non-trans women who pass as men) in using the restroom are bizarrely ignored' by such feminists. This critique once again raises important questions about the need for addressing the epistemological, political and ethical tensions that are central to enabling and extending a transgender informed approach to feminist transdisciplinary inquiry (Elliot, 2010).

We draw attention to this case and to these sorts of tensions because they need to be understood against the historical backdrop of refusing trans women access to 'womyn only' spaces. Such further contextualization highlights the necessity for transdisciplinary dialogue in feminist research and scholarship that is committed to a sustained and productive engagement with trans studies and its epistemological and ontological concerns, which entail addressing the cisnormative terms and limits of embodiment (Stryker, 2006; Rubin, 1998). As such we conceive of this washroom debate as a case in point about the limits of a specific feminist account of violence against women in public spaces, which relies on a cisgenderist and exclusionary framing of the material consequences of gender policing for all women. It is in this sense that a more transdisciplinary feminist engagement with trans informed onto-epistemologies on female embodiment and gendered personhood is necessary. Moreover, to conflate charges of engaging in transphobic rhetoric with a desire to shut down debate about violence against women in public spaces such as washrooms is to fundamentally misunderstand the harm that is being perpetuated by the propagation of a cisgenderist logics for trans individuals and specifically transgender women.

Historical backdrop to trans-exclusionary radical feminism

The term TERF, which Stock (2018a) and others consider a 'slur' (see terfisaslur.com), emerged in a blog in 2008 (Hines, 2019: 147) to mark the long-existing 'discursive struggles around gendered authenticity and the tenure of feminism' (147), or a way to mark the historical and current ontological debates between certain feminists and trans folks over who and what counts as a woman. To trace this history of TERF is to start with the release of Janice Raymond's (1979) book, *The Transsexual Empire*, which defined the divided ground between women (who were women-born-women, or cisgender, a less problematic term) and transsexual women (now transwomen), as well as between TERFs and transinclusive feminists (Elliot, 2010), although at the time Raymond did not use these terms but deployed the singular category of 'women' to denote women-born-women and understood transwomen to be, in her estimation, merely 'deviant males' (Raymond, 1979: 145). Raymond, as a non-trans, cisgender or 'woman-born-woman', conceptualized the transsexual empire as a patriarchal colonization of trans bodies manufactured as agents whose mission would be to infiltrate female spaces and culture in order to remake femininity according to a patriarchal agenda. Raymond's text incited a gender panic over the presence of transwomen, who were reduced to agents of the patriarchy; transmen were completely denied as a threat or a legitimate identity as Raymond's rationalization reduced them to mere women. In his pamphlet from 1980, Riddell (2006: 155) denounced Raymond's logic and called *The Transsexual Empire* a 'dangerous book' not only because of its complete dehumanization of trans people, but because it threatened the productivity of feminism itself, led to a scapegoating of transwomen and employed, ironically, patriarchal methodologies. Ultimately, Riddell accuses Raymond's argument of failing at logic for both advocating for the abolition of gender in order to escape the grips of patriarchy while counter-intuitively celebrating the creativity of womanhood. Interestingly, for our purposes of tracing the political motivations of cisgender feminism in the debate over the washroom signage, Riddell's insights into the tactics of exclusion are helpful. Riddell aligns exclusion as a property of male culture and practice, or, a patriarchal methodology. In contrast, female culture is thus rooted in inclusiveness via care, community-building and alliances. To Riddell (2006: 156) then, feminism *should* be about the 'inclusion of marginals' who are perceived not as a threat 'when it is genuine'.

To highlight further the onto-epistemological tensions between TERF and trans informed accounts, Elliot (2010) analyses the case of the Vancouver Rape Relief Centre in Canada during the 1990s to characterize both the concerns of transwomen to be recognized as legitimate and the concerns of TERF women to preserve women's-only safe spaces. The case centres around the exclusion of

Nixon, a transsexual woman whose application to train as a counsellor in the crisis centre was denied under the reasoning that only women-born-women (again, read, 'cisgender') were entitled to work in the organization whose mandate was to provide services to female victims of violence. In this onto-epistemological frame, the definition of 'woman' is tied to a biological determinism that fixes sex as the stable ground upon which gender emerges and thus, the presence of a transwoman, who TERF would argue had once been a man, would represent a threat to the sanctity of the organization leading to a re-victimization of female clients. For TERF, one can only be born a woman; even living as and identifying as a woman is an insufficient basis to qualify as a woman. TERF denies the existence of transwomen as *real* women because these experiences cannot fit into their cis-onto-epistemological frame for understanding the terms of gender legitimacy and authenticity. There is no room for a recognition of the transphobia inherent in this reasoning. For Elliot (2010), Nixon's case represents an act of violence not on the female clients in the rape centre, but one that is directed towards Nixon herself. It also encapsulates not simply an ignorance or unknowing, but a 'refusal of knowledge' (Elliot, 2010: 25), a refusal for TERFs to recognize the legitimacy of Nixon's claim to womanhood alongside their own. Elliot's position is thus that we must now continue to ask, 'who gets to decide what the terms of inclusion or exclusion in feminist organizations might be while *simultaneously* exposing the political strategies enlisted in refusing to recognize transsexual women as women' (Elliot, 2010: 30, our emphasis).

The case of the washroom signage at our university mirrors this conclusion: to untangle the political motivations of certain cisgendered feminists from their voiced concerns over the notions of 'trust' and trans-inclusion in public washrooms is part of the labour involved in an analysis of the regulation of public washroom spaces that reaffirm cisnormativity and trans-exclusion and as such is central to a transgender informed approach to transdisciplinary feminist inquiry as we understand it. Such critical engagement requires attention to addressing the political and ethical concerns at the heart of onto-epistemological questions pertaining to who and what is to count as a woman. These concerns illustrate what Sandford (2015) refers to as 'the transdisciplinary functioning of the concept of gender' which is reflected in polemics pertaining to washroom inclusivity and *woman only* spaces that we document in this chapter and which cannot be considered to be isolated accounts.

However, while it is important to investigate the tensions historically, it is also easy to see all radical feminism as TERF due to literature rife with flattened accounts of the exclusion of transwomen from women's spaces (see Hines, 2019, for an academic discussion of these tensions). A common citation is the exclusion of transwomen from the Michigan Women's Music Festival in the 1990s that led to the creation of Camp Trans; likewise, the attack on Sandy Stone, a transwoman sound engineer employed at Olivia Records in the 1970s, is oft-cited as an epitome of the war between TERFS and transwomen. Even recently, as of fall 2018, this polemic between TERF and trans-inclusion erupted over a Manchester, UK, billboard that merely contained a pseudo-dictionary definition of woman as 'adult human female' (Chart, 2018: n.p.) but was read by trans activists and scholars as trans-exclusive, thus inciting a twitter war and televised media coverage.

Contesting trans-exclusionary radical feminism

What these accounts miss is the nuance in radical feminism that is distinct from TERF as it is simultaneously trans-inclusive; they also miss the intersectional analyses required of transinclusive feminism that would otherwise elide racial and class difference in the interest of prioritizing gender (Koyama, 2006). In an effort to rethink feminism as trans-inclusive, Williams (2016) re-examines the case of Sandy Stone and Olivia Records to centre not the open letter that certain concerned TERFs issued in protest to the employment of Sandy Stone, but to highlight that radical feminists from the Collective of Olivia protected Sandy Stone through months of verbal and physical attacks and threats from a separate TERF activist group.

Prompted by a more current emergence of racism in white feminist and trans movements, Koyama (2006) re-narrates the exclusion of transwomen from 'the Land' in the Michigan Women's Music Festival through an anti-racist, trans informed lens. The no-penis policy, while initially constructed to keep men out of this women's only space, eventually included only post-op transsexual women which Koyama reads as also classist and racist given that access to gender-confirming surgery depends on class and race privilege, a point acknowledged but unaddressed by festival organizers. Indeed, Sreedhar and Hand (2006) examine the no-penis policy as delimiting the ontological legitimacy of trans women in favour of the comfort of a cisgendered women majority. They propose a self-identification policy that would include the multiple and varied embodied ways of being and identifying as a woman, and in this way, avoid the 'double oppression' transwomen face who would be excluded in the no-penis policy (Sreedhar and Hand, 2006: 168).

Hines (2019) re-narrates feminist histories to also delimit what is meant by trans-inclusion. Her argument explains that the policing of women-only spaces relies upon a coherence between femaleness and anatomy; where 'woman' may be understood to include transwomen (albeit post-op in many cases), the ground of 'female' has been preserved in certain feminist rhetoric to contain the authentic sex-based natural-born woman. Hines thus problematizes the reliance on anatomical/chromosomal sex as basis for claiming authentic femaleness in these feminist debates incited over increased trans visibility and claims to women-only spaces. Williams (2016), Koyama (2006), Sreedhar and Hand (2006) and Hines (2019) excavate the histories of (radical) feminism to situate them as trans-inclusive, while also interrogating the embedded racism, classism, and delimited trans-inclusion.

We consider this critical re-narration of feminist histories as trans-inclusive to be in line with Stryker's (2006) framework of desubjugation. Stryker assigns desubjugation as the methodology deployed in trans studies whose task is to excavate the subjugated knowledges of trans histories, trans embodiment and trans experiences so that the embodied trans subject is a part of their own knowledge-making in political discursive processes that result in material effects. Drawing on Foucault's methodology of genealogy, Stryker recommends that desubjugation can be accomplished in two ways: one, in the re-narration of trans histories, to unearth what has been thought under different terms or paradigms; and two, in the recognition of voices and experiences that have been historically disregarded, silenced or denied. In the first instance, Williams (2016) and Hines (2019) re-narrate the histories of radical feminism as trans-inclusive but are also careful to note that trans-exclusive feminism has not expired but is rather a growing and recent trend that must be contested. In the second instance, which we will outline in the subsequent section, Koyama (2003) and Serano (2007) provide manifestos of transfeminism to envisage a future that refuses the binary of trans-exclusive feminism versus trans studies in place of confirming a transinclusive practice of feminism that continues to remain open to the contingencies embedded in trans theory and practices of embodiment.

The trans body reveals its own contingency in these epistemological and ontological debates around embodiment and entitlement to space, becoming not a slate upon which knowledge is drawn as an after-effect, but the site through which knowledge is constructed in the present. The rhetoric and reasoning from the debate surrounding the washroom signage at our university positions the trans body as a spectre of fear, an object of sympathy, as well as a subject with agency, and in some cases, a conflation of two or all of these subject positions. Our concern in this chapter is not to pin certain actors in said debate to a specific epistemic tradition; rather, we are interested in tracing the tensions between feminist rhetoric that subscribes to cisgenderism and the transinclusive responses to underline the importance of trans-centric knowledge around the legitimate access of transwomen, gender nonconforming and non-binary people to particular washroom spaces. In this respect, we highlight the need for a consideration of and engagement with trans informed epistemological accounts of gender and embodiment in enhancing feminist transdisciplinary scholarship.

The epistemological necessity of trans informed accounts of embodiment in feminist transdisciplinary inquiry

It may be prudent to return to the notion of transphobia as it has become the contested ground upon which feminists, trans and queer scholars engage in their battle over who and what even gets counted as transphobic. In so doing, we highlight the political and ethical requirement to engage with transgender studies informed accounts of gender and embodiment as a transdisciplinary necessity in feminist transdisciplinary inquiry that is committed to gender justice. Bettcher (2014), for example, rejects the literal definition of phobia as 'irrationality' arguing instead that transphobia as a systemic, institutional and historically oppressive practice is based in a rationalization that privileges cisgender over trans, which is perceived as a violation of gender norms, a subsequent problem inherent in the term. Not only is a violation a sort of double oppression (i.e. to be the target of transphobia first, and second, to be named a violation in order to qualify as one who has suffered transphobia), it is also a denial of the multiple and varied ways of trans embodiment including trans who do not violate gender norms but rather exist happily within the gender binary. This violation, as Bettcher argues, depends upon a cisgendered logics that deems trans as inherently violating; transphobia as a violation is thus cis-centric and subscribes to a monolithic account of what it means to be trans. Because of the many cultural, racial, postcolonial and other empirical forms of trans embodiment that are at once complex as well as conflicting, we follow the recommendations of trans scholars such as Bettcher (2014), Hines (2019), Koyama (2003) and Stryker, Currah and Moore (2008) to continue to remain open to 'new, unanticipated meanings to "trans-"' (21) and how it can disrupt trans-exclusive feminist rhetoric. This commitment is at the heart of our understanding of a transgender informed approach to feminist transdisciplinary inquiry.

We thus turn to transfeminist manifestos to desubjugate (Stryker, 2006) trans voices and lived experiences that form a robust and nuanced application of transinclusive feminism. Koyama's (2003) Transfeminist Manifesto outlines several components of coalition-building among trans and cis-people that seeks not to overtake feminism, but to expand and advance feminism through a shared liberation of cis and trans women. Given the patriarchal and colonial binary gender system under which gendered subjectivity is constrained, regulated and punished, Koyama (2003: 251) insists a transfeminism must allow gendered self-definition based on 'what feels genuine, comfortable and sincere to us as we live and relate to others within given social and cultural constraint'. This form of gendered agency rejects the scapegoating, derision and dehumanization that Serano's (2007) *Trans Woman Manifesto* calls to end in a combined effort between feminism and trans activism to rely on trusting self-knowledge and authentic gendered self. This rejection is at the heart of our conceptualization and understanding of critical feminist transdisciplinary approaches to inquiry and intervention with its commitment to embracing intersectionality and 'opposition to old disciplines as rigid structures and hegemonic powers' (Pulkkinen, 2015: 189) (see also Hill Collins, 1986; Haraway, 1988). As Pulkkinen (2015: 199) argues, transdisciplinarity in gender studies is not about providing 'an overarching account of what [gender] is' but rather needs to be understood as a practice of 'intervention against the previous totalizing discourses'.

The notion of trust as a part of the washroom signage at our university incited concern and panic in some feminist responses over fear that such trust would be violated by male predators posing as transwomen. Koyama (2003) answers this fear by articulating the particular danger transwomen face who suffer a double oppression of trans-misogyny (Serano, 2007), and transmen are also at risk if they are perceived to be deceivers (Bettcher, 2007). Instead, the focus of transfeminism must be to incite not panic, but collaborative action against violence against *all* gendered minorities, ciswomen, transwomen, transmen, non-binary, gender nonconforming, genderqueer, etc. Koyama (2003) argues for a seamless integration of transwomen into feminism. While not explicitly interpellated in the debate from our university, the exclusion of trans bodies in women-only spaces had historically and ideologically been based on the belief that transwomen still draw from the patriarchal dividend (Connell and Pearce, 2015), or have been able to do so for much of their lives. Koyama (2003) responds to this myth not by refuting it entirely, but by insisting that any privilege, be it class, race, and/or gender, be acknowledged by each stakeholder in transfeminism, including cis women who are not trans. Only through such critical positionality can transfeminism make room for all sorts of embodiments of trans. And transfeminism must not stop challenging oppositional and traditional sexism in the pursuit of also pursuing transphobia and trans-misogyny. Rather, transfeminism aims to 'forge a new type of feminism' (Serano, 2007: 7), one that extricates TERF from trans-inclusive feminism to reclaim feminism as transinclusive. The costs of forging ahead in a feminism devoid of trans-inclusion, according to Elliot (2010), would be to risk the stability of the women's movement entirely.

Transfeminism that forges an alliance between trans and ciswomen is a contested process especially in questions around who is entitled to specific spaces and how gender and sexed identity is read in those entitlements. Elliot (2010: 28) chooses not to negate the onto-epistemological legitimacy of transwomen, but to consider that debates in transfeminism are necessary 'to deepen our understanding of each other … if we are to be allies in the process of improving the material conditions of all women's lives'. Indeed, Riddell (2006: 153) aligns transwomen with cis women in that 'we are all … products of learning conditioned by our existence in a patriarchy', and in the pursuit of a better understanding of the 'condition of female humanness, all of us have to renounce much powerful cultural learning we have been subjected to, and have internalized.' Riddell's vision of transinclusive feminism settles on the collective; she rejects Raymond's dogmatic approach as patriarchal and divisive, and reminds us that feminism includes difference and debate, but through a mutual respect of multiple experiences and understanding of one's own embodiment. Riddell (2006: 157) underscores that 'we can share and develop collectively' as long as we also refuse to 'define and demean' each other's existence in the process. Transfeminism can inform transinclusive practices that do not override feminist concerns, as long as feminist claims to ontological legitimacy do not override trans embodiment or subscribe to a cisgendering logics. Feminism that can continue to exist while simultaneously 'trans-ing' its spaces, debates, and concerns over patriarchal and colonial control is, as Stryker, Currah and Moore (2008: 13) proclaim, a 'pathway toward liberation'.

Conclusion

In this chapter, we have highlighted the necessity of engaging with trans informed accounts of embodiment that expose the limits of cisnormative understandings of what comes to count as a woman. We see such engagement as central to embracing a transdisciplinary approach to building on feminist theory and research as a basis for enhancing gender democratization in public spaces. As Radi (2019) asserts, what is needed is a centring of the writings of trans scholars which we have argued are central to a sustained transdisciplinary feminist commitment to gender justice. Moreover, he claims that 'trans* studies, feminist theory and/or queer theory' each 'offers an array of contributions and concepts with their own inner debates, tensions and rivalries, as well as diverse engagements with the other two fields' (Radi, 2019: 46; see also Martino and Cumming-Potvin, 2018; Wiegman and Wilson, 2015). Through employing the specific case of the bathroom problem at our own university we have attempted to offer a window onto such tensions as a basis for illustrating the limits and possibilities for enacting a feminist transdisciplinary agenda that is committed to addressing transgender marginalization and gender democratization. In doing so, we embrace Spade's (2015: 9) notion of *a critical trans politics* as central to an intersectional approach to transdisciplinary inquiry at the heart of which is the 'need to shift our focus from the individual framing of discrimination and "hate violence" and [to] think more broadly about how gender categories are enforced on all people in ways that have particularly dangerous outcomes for trans people' as a basis for 'properly understand[ing] power and transphobic harm'. The persistence of cisgender conceptualizations of *woman only* bodies and spaces that continue to afflict debates about gender authenticity that we have outlined in this chapter with respect to the bathroom problem serve to highlight the necessity for a transdisciplinary commitment to feminist inquiry that is inclusive of a sustained engagement with transgender informed epistemological accounts of gender and embodiment.

Note

The writing of this chapter is supported by SSHRC (Social Sciences Humanities and Research Council of Canada) grant entitled: *Supporting transgender and gender minority youth in schools* (435-2015-0077).

References

Bauer, G. R. and Scheim, A. I. (2015). *Transgender People in Ontario, Canada: Statistics from the Trans PULSE Project to Inform Human Rights Policy* (Trans PULSE E-Bulletin) (p. 11). London, ON: Trans PULSE Project.

Bettcher, T. (2014). Transphobia. *TSQ: Transgender Studies Quarterly*, 1(1–2), 249–251.

Bettcher, T. (2018). 'When tables speak': On the existence of Trans Philosophy. Retrieved from http://dailynous.com/2018/05/30/tables-speak-existence-trans-philosophy-guest-talia-mae-bettcher/

Bettcher, T. M. (2007). Evil deceivers and make-believers: On transphobic violence and the politics of illusion. *Hypatia*, 22(3), 43–65.

Browne, K. (2004). Genderism and the bathroom problem: (Re)materializing sexed sites, (re)creating sexed bodies. *Gender, Place and Culture*, 11(3), 331–346.

Chart, N. (2018). What's current: Second billboard defining woman as 'adult human female' goes up in the UK. *Feminist Current*. Retrieved from www.feministcurrent.com/2018/10/02/whats-current-second-billboard-defining-woman-adult-human-female-goes-uk/. Accessed 2 October 2018.

Connell, R. W. and Pearse, R. (2015). *Gender In World Perspective* (3rd Edition). Cambridge: Polity.

Connell, R. (2012). Transsexual women and feminist thought: toward new understanding and new politics. *Signs: Journal of Women in Culture and Society*, 37(4), 857–891.

Dolling, I. and Hark, S. (2000). She who speaks shadow speaks truth: Transdisciplinarity in women's and gender studies. *Signs*, 25(4), 1195–1198.

Elliot, P. (2010). Feminist embattlement on the field of trans. In *Debates in Transgender, Queer, and Feminist Theory: Contested sites* (pp. 17–31). Surrey: Ashgate Publishing.

Green, K. (2017). Trans* movement/trans* moment: an afterword. *International Journal of Qualitative Studies in Education*, 30(3), 320–321.

Haraway, D. (1988). Situated knowledges: The science question in feminism and the privilege of partial perspective. *Feminist Studies* 14(3), 579–599.

Hill Collins, P. (1986). Learning from the outsider within: The sociological significance of Black Feminist thought. *Social Problems*, 33(6), S14–S32.

Hines, S. (2019). The feminist frontier: On trans and feminism. *Journal of Gender Studies*, 28(2), 145–157.

Ingrey, J. (2018). Problematizing the cisgendering of school washroom space: interrogating the politics of recognition of transgender and gender non-conforming youth. *Gender and Education*, 30(6), 774–789.

Koro-Ljungberg, M., Yendol-Hoppey, D., Smith J., and Hayes, S. (2009). (E)pistemological awareness, instantiation of methods, and uninformed methodological ambiguity in qualitative research projects, *Educational Researcher*, 38(9), 687–699.

Koyama, E. (2003). The transfeminist manifesto. In R. C. Dicker and A. Piepmeier (Eds.), *Catching a Wave: Reclaiming Feminism for the 21st Century* (pp. 244–259). Boston, MA: Northeastern University Press.

Koyama, E. (2006). Whose feminism is it anyway? The unspoken racism of the trans-inclusion debate. In S. Stryker and S. Whittle (Eds.), *The Transgender Studies Reader* (pp. 698–705). New York, NY: Routledge.

Lennon, E., and Mistler, B. J. (2014). Cisgenderism. *Transgender Studies Quarterly*, 1(1–2), 63–64.

Martino, W. and Cumming-Potvin, W. (2018). Transgender and gender expansive education research, policy and practice: reflecting on epistemological and ontological possibilities of bodily becoming. *Gender and Education*, 30(6), 687–694.

Namaste, V. and Sitara, G. (2013). Inclusive pedagogy in the Women's Studies classroom: Teaching the Kimberly Nixon case. In S. Stryker and A. Aizura (Eds.), *The Transgender Studies Reader 2* (pp. 213–225). New York, NY: Routledge.

Osborne, P. (2015). Problematizing disciplinarity, transdisciplinarity problematics. *Theory, Culture and Society*, 32(5–6), 3–35.

Pulkkinen, T. (2015). Identity and intervention: Disciplinarity as transdisciplinarity in Gender Studies. *Theory, Culture and Society*, 32(5–6), 183–205.

Radi, B. (2019). On Trans* Epistemology: Critiques, contributions, and challenges, *TSQ: Transgender Studies Quarterly*, 6(1), 43–63.

Raymond, J. (1979). *The Transsexual Empire: The Making of the She-Male*. Boston, MA: Beacon Press.

Riddell, C. (2006). Divided sisterhood: A critical review of Janice Raymond's The Transsexual Empire. In S. Stryker and S. Whittle (Eds.), *The Transgender Studies Reader* (pp. 144–158). New York, NY: Routledge (Original work published in 1980).

Rubin, H. (1998). Phenomenology as method in trans studies. *GLQ: A Journal of Lesbian and Gay Studies*, 4(2), 263–281.

Sandford, S. (2015). Contradiction of terms: Feminist theory, philosophy and transdisciplinarity. *Theory, Culture and Society*, 32(5–6), 159–192.

Serano, J. (2007). Trans woman manifesto. In *Whipping Girl: A Transsexual Woman on Sexism and the Scapegoating of Femininity* (pp. 11–20). Emeryville, CA: Seal Press.

Spade, D. (2015). *Normal Life: Administrative Violence, Critical Trans Politics and the Limits of the Law*. Durham, NC and London: Duke University Press.

Sreedhar, S. and Hand, M. (2006). The ethics of exclusion: Gender and politics at the Michigan Womyn's Music Festival. In K. Scott-Dixon (Ed.), *Trans/forming Feminisms: Trans-feminist Voices Speak Out* (pp. 161–169). Toronto, ON: Sumach Press.

Stock, K. (2018a). *Academic philosophy and the UK Gender Recognition Act*. Retrieved from https://medium.com/@kathleenstock/academic-philosophy-and-the-uk-gender-recognition-act-6179b315b9dd

Stock, K. (2018b). Text of email recently sent to Philosophy students. Retrieved fromhttps://medium.com/@kathleenstock/text-of-email-recently-sent-to-philosophy-students-f38c8f0a1a2a

Stryker, S. (2006). (De)Subjugated knowledges: An introduction to transgender studies. In S. Stryker and S. Whittle (Eds.), *The Transgender Studies Reader* (pp. 1–17). New York, NY: Routledge.

Stryker, S., Currah, P., and Moore, L. J. (2008). Introduction: Trans-, trans, or transgender? *WSQ: Women's Studies Quarterly*, 36(3), 29–65.

University of Western Ontario (2018). *Inclusive Washrooms at Western*. Retrieved from www.uwo.ca/equity/doc/inclusive_washrooms.pdf

Wiegman, R. and Wilson, E. (2015). Introduction: Antinormativity's Queer Conventions. *Differences: A Journal of Feminist Cultural Studies*, 26(1), 1–25.

Williams, C. (2016). Radical inclusion: Recounting the trans inclusive history of radical feminism. *TSQ: Transgender Studies Quarterly*, 3(1–2), 254–258.

8 Performance practice and ecofeminism
A diffractive approach for a transdisciplinary pedagogy

Cara Berger

Introduction

What role does pedagogy play in transdisciplinary feminist research? Although exchanges between disciplines are increasingly encouraged in research activities through funding calls, research clusters and other forms of recognition such as the Research Excellence Framework in the UK, teaching practices, particularly at undergraduate level, remain largely structured around disciplinary formations. The larger fields of the sciences on the one hand, and the arts and humanities on the other, especially remain disconnected. However, as much of the recent rush of scholarship in the 'posthumanities' emphasises, keeping apart culture and nature, science and art, ecological and more obviously 'human' concerns seems increasingly wrong-headed since 'in this new planetary age of the Anthropocene, defined by human-induced climatic, biological and even geological transformations, we humans are fully in nature' (Åsberg and Braidotti, 2018: 1). Pedagogical practice, like research beyond the classroom, needs to take seriously the new challenges of a posthuman age in which 'we can no longer up-hold the division of labour where "nature" is left to science and "culture" to the humanities' (ibid., 2). As feminists strive to de-centre the curriculum from an intersectional perspective by drawing attention to and countering the multiple exclusions that are perpetuated within or even constitutive of disciplinary bodies of knowledge, the intersection between feminism and ecological concerns should not be left out.

The term ecofeminism as a critical perspective has somewhat fallen out of fashion, largely due to a fear of 'contamination-by-association' (Gaard, 2011: 27) based on a tendency in some ecofeminist texts towards troubling gender essentialism and an overly romantic approach to both nature and women (Gaard, 2011; Saeger, 2003). Nonetheless the intersection between ecological thought – in the widest sense encompassing the numerous ways we might engage with a more-than-human world – and feminist critique is thriving in the guise of new transdisciplinary fields such as new materialism, feminist posthumanism, Anthropocene feminism and so on. While I see no use in trying to subsume these under a term they deliberately depart from (hence my use of a hyphen between 'eco' and 'feminism' in the title of this article to signal both an intersection of the two and a difference from ecofeminism), it is nonetheless clear that the ecofeminist aim to counter a culture 'built on the domination of nature, and the domination of woman "as nature"' (Salleh, 1997: 12–13) is vital. If some of the liveliest sites of feminist thought and practices are increasingly transdisciplinary, they pose a conundrum for feminist pedagogues in HE many of whom teach within discipline-specific courses. On top of this, students' increasing self-understanding as consumers of education and the related pressure to attain particular numeric degree outcomes, might drive them away from transdisciplinary areas which are often 'messy, complex, unpredictable and performative rather than representational of any pre-existing structure' (Palmer, 2012).

Despite this, I suggest that transdisciplinary work can and should play a fundamental role for feminist pedagogues supporting students to face life in the Anthropocene. Given the emergent, uncontrollable and situated qualities of transdisciplinary endeavours, they afford an important opportunity for students and teachers to collaborate on knowledge-creation in a way that dismantles illusions of mastery (an important feminist aim), models more cooperative forms of labour and resists the neoliberal commodification of education by taking the classroom seriously as space for mutual exchange and becoming. While it is tempting to fantasise about a fully post-disciplinary curriculum in which students can freely collaborate across specialisms and skill sets, my goal here is slightly more modest and may be more realistic (for the moment). I explore how teaching within a disciplinary context, in my case Theatre and Performance Studies, nonetheless can take on transdisciplinary methods and add to transdisciplinary discourses, which differ from interdisciplinary work in crucial ways as discussed below. Specifically, I look at a course in which I used performance practice as a form of (eco-)feminist pedagogy that tackled a transdisciplinary concept – diffraction – as both *topic* of and *method* for learning. In doing so the labour shared between the students on the course and me led to innovative findings relevant to both Theatre and Performance Studies (where this concept has seen reasonably little application so far) and the wider transdisciplinary discourse.

A transdisciplinary concept: diffraction as metaphor/metaphor as diffraction

Etymologically, the prefix 'trans-' indicates a crossing, a traversal through which the one that does the crossing is changed. It speaks to a mode of travelling that affects the traveller who is altered by her encounters. To trans, to travel in the search for a transformative encounter is as Mieke Bal (2002: 4) writes a 'hazardous, exciting, tiring' undertaking since you do not know what the encounter might produce. I begin from this understanding of the 'trans' in transdisciplinarity to differentiate it from interdisciplinarity which as Stella Sandford (2015: 160) suggests often maintains 'specific disciplinary knowledges, concepts, practices and methods … in the context of a recognition of the virtue of communication between [disciplines]'. If interdisciplinarity is primarily about valuing how disciplines 'contribute differently, but complementarily, to the analysis or understanding of a given phenomenon or problem' (ibid.), transdisciplinarity as I understand it in the following is better likened to a process of translation with the shifts, slippages and deviations this entails. Specifically, I am interested here in what Bal (2002: 24) calls 'transdisciplinary concepts', that is concepts which 'travel between disciplines, between individual scholars, between historical periods, and between geographically dispersed academic communities'. Through her case studies, which include image, *mise-en-scène*, performance and performativity, Bal shows that concepts that travel in this way do not remain the same throughout their journey. She stresses the 'differing' (ibid.) that occurs as they undergo a series of translations through which new capacities for meaning and application are shaped.

Bal's (2002) attention to concepts that lie in the proximity of Theatre and Performance Studies is no coincidence as both theatricality and performance make possible a 'meeting between (aesthetic), art(ifice) and (social) reality' (97). Such potential 'meetings' which are so crucial to the specific mediality of theatre and performance also underpin the research I present here. However, I look to how transdisciplinary concepts may travel *into* theatre and performance. To move from the general to the specific: in the following, I track my research and practice as a pedagogue, performance-maker and dramaturg (who takes on the role of framing or curating the performance material, acting as an 'outside-eye' to the director or company) journeying with a particular kind of transdisciplinary concept, a metaphor. New materialist theorists have called for innovative methods for figuring and producing knowledge in a posthuman world. To do so, thinkers such as Donna Haraway and Karen Barad have suggested replacing reflection as a 'pervasive trope for knowing' (Barad, 2007: 72) with an alternative optical metaphor: diffraction. Whereas reflection remains tied to representationalism and the reproduction of self-same knowledges and identities since it tends to merely 'displace the same elsewhere' (Haraway, 1997: 273), diffractions 'produce patterns that mark difference' (Barad, 2007: 82) and '[attend] to specific material entanglements' (ibid.: 88). Barad takes off from the counter-intuitive insights of quantum physics – namely, that waves exhibit particle-like behaviour and particles wave-like behaviour given the right circumstances and measuring devices – since it directs us away from the 'distance-learning practice of reflection from afar' (ibid.: 90). Instead she champions modes of knowledge-making that take seriously the 'pattern emerging from the entanglement of object (like light) and measuring device' (van der Tuin, 2018: 101). This attention to the emergence of difference beyond static binary opposition – how it is produced and how it can be recognised – is also a feminist endeavour in so far as feminism, as Elizabeth Grosz writes, has moved 'beyond [its] common focus of dealing with women as empirical objects' and instead expands into a mode of research that is able to:

> Raise new questions about materiality, cosmology, the natural order, about how we know and what are the limits, costs, and underside of our knowledge … in order to develop new ideals, new forms of representation, new types of knowledge, and new epistemological criteria.
>
> (Grosz, 2005: 129)

It might seem banal at first sight to hinge a transdisciplinary endeavour on a metaphor, after all it is quite normal for metaphors to cross fields of meaning without necessarily accomplishing the kind of deep shifts outlined by Grosz. However, Barad is quick to stress that diffraction for her is both a metaphor and a method. As such it might be likened to Gilles Deleuze and Félix Guattari's paradoxical stance towards metaphors: despite their philosophy being premised upon figurative language, they seek to, as Helen Palmer explains, 'eliminate the analogical conjunction' (2012: 150) of metaphor which would keep things in their habitual place. When figurative language goes beyond mere analogy towards the production of new differences it might, to return to Barad, be performing diffractively, participating in the production of difference.

As a transdisciplinary concept – or as Nina Lykke (2011: 143) might call it 'a thinking technolog[y] ... not owned by any specific disciplines' – which is assembled from embodied scientific processes, feminist theory, philosophy of knowledge and a keen attention to metaphorology, diffraction has diffractive effects: it interrupts disciplinary silos, highlights that there is always already 'exteriority within' (Barad, 2007: 93) that pushes back against disciplinary cuts, and produces emergent differences across bodies of thought and practice. For Barad (2018: 816) there is an inextricable entanglement of object and apparatus of research. She frames research apparatuses not simply as 'observational devices or mere laboratory instruments' but instead asks us to consider them to be performative in so far as they produce 'dynamic (re)configurings of the world, specific agential practices/intra-actions/performances through which exclusionary boundaries are enacted'. In this case, metaphorology might be considered such an apparatus. It is an instrument through which diffraction is made sensible, and through which transdisciplinary pathways and potentials may be (re)configured. Iris van der Tuin, for example, has translated diffraction into an anti-canonical feminist reading method that tracks the sudden, unexpected crossings of texts in the situated experience of the reader with the effect that 'diffractive readings take off elsewhere and have differing effects' (van der Tuin, 2018: 100). Anna Hickey-Moody, Helen Palmer and Esther Sayers (2015: 218) in turn argue that art-based curricula can produce diffractive effects by giving students the opportunity to experience the 'entanglement of matter and meaning' through embodied activities, pushing against a model of education in which bodies are '[governed]' and disciplined rather than considered vital sites of production (ibid., 223).

The metaphor of diffraction has then seen various translations and has itself been diffracted along various paths. I aim to add to this by exploring what happens when performance is used as an apparatus to produce diffractive 'differencing' in Higher Education (HE) teaching. Specifically, I hope to refract the paths and patterns of difference that were produced in a performance practice module entitled 'Performing (with) Matter' that I led at the University of Glasgow in 2016 with undergraduate Theatre Studies students. Doing so, I want to ask how a creative arts curriculum, in this case one that is engaged with both theoretical and practical study of theatre and performance, might make use of a transdisciplinary metaphor. This means translating the concept of diffraction through a particular disciplinary apparatus, with the aim of further refracting its discourse and producing differencing effects in the experience of student performance-makers and the spectators of the performance alike. Working on extending the reach of diffraction can be considered an ecofeminist practice since, as Donna Haraway (2013: 69) suggests, diffraction is a 'means of making potent connection that exceeds domination'. That is, it can give rise to a form of praxis that seeks new modes of connection between humans and non-humans, beyond the double domination of women and the natural world that ecofeminist thought reveals.

Aspects of diffraction for an ecofeminist performance pedagogy

Since Theatre Studies departments tend to teach across theory and practice (though this varies in degree according to national context), they are often well-positioned as Jill Dolan (2001: 50) writes, to 'experiment with the construction of knowledge and new ways of learning'. In the UK some level of practical learning is the norm for Theatre Studies degrees, and often such courses will variously entangle text-based with experiential and craft-based learning. This was also the case in 'Performing (with) Matter': over the course of one semester the eight third-year students taking the module had classes twice a week in a seminar room and a black box performance space, that is, a room painted black without fixed seating but fitted with theatre lights and a sound desk. Work undertaken in the seminar room involved discussing theoretical texts (both on theatre practices and texts from other disciplines such as essays by Barad and Haraway) and examples of existing professional performance, while practice workshops later in the week investigated the ideas developed in the seminars through creative activities. The assessed outcome of the course was a piece of performance, created in response to a research question set by the students after the initial seminar and practical workshop series.

To work with a transdisciplinary concept in a discipline-specific class room can in the best case mean that tutor and students together embark on forging new capacities for that concept, drawing on their particular tools, training and skills. I suggest that the activity of translation that I endeavour to unpack here might be considered, in Kélina Gotman's (2016: 18) words, as a 'temporary [clustering]' in which a transdisciplinary concept is 'rooted temporarily' to a set of disciplinary practices. Any one rooting does not amount to the final destiny of the concept (which would equate to a discipline fully appropriating and incorporating a concept) but should be considered one translation amongst others, presented in the knowledge that it awaits manifold future translations. In the following, I discuss how this kind of teaching – which is paralleled by practice-based methods in research – affords an important opportunity for integrating transdisciplinary methods and concerns within disciplinary curricula, allowing students to become active researchers rather than consumers of knowledge. To do so, I look at two elements of the course I taught that add a practice and vocabulary drawn from theatre and performance pedagogy to the evolution of the notion of diffraction. First, I suggest that the form of the workshop as a pedagogical tool (within but also beyond arts subjects) is a productive way for translating diffraction into a practical, feminist pedagogy. Second, I move on to discuss how the practice of dramaturgy – the ordering of sensory materials in time and space in theatre practice – is a way in which diffraction can be translated into theatre-making. With this second point, in particular, I am deeply indebted to the work undertaken by the students in this class and my writing here should be seen as reporting on our collective thinking and doing.

Enter the assemblage: the workshop as diffractive pedagogy

One week I bring a bag of apples to the practice workshop. Why apples? Apples have emerged as a kind of rhythm in my reading and class preparation; for reasons that I can only partially retrace they have been traversing my thoughts. Apples connect a number of texts I have been thinking about and suggesting to students: Hélène Cixous's (1988: 16) *Extreme Fidelity* that reads Eve's eating of the apple as a sensual-material epistemology in defiance of the 'Word of the Law', Annemarie Mol's (2008: 29) *I Eat an Apple* in which the process of eating is viewed as a kind of transspecies becoming that '[interferes] with traditional models of the Western subject', and Astrida Neimanis's (2012: 216) suggestion that we turn to collaboration – 'doing-in-common' – to understand ontology in a posthuman world (though Neimanis's writing starts from a bag of peanuts, not apples). Apples – Eve's legendary apple, Mol's hypothetical apple, all the mythical, textual, sensual memories of apples contained within me – have set off a series of diffractive moments, 'interpellations and affectations' in van der Tuin's (2018: 100) words, that I feel compelled to join up and bring to class with me.

In the session, I ask students to spend time sensually engaging with the apples (through vision, touch, smell, taste) while reading bits of these texts to them. We experiment with treating the apples as dance partners, getting frustrated by their refusal to move of their own accord, then delighting in how the doing-in-common of apple, gravity and body can be used to create scores over which we do not have full control. In discussion afterwards the apples stimulate some of the core concerns of the project from there on: How can a performer collaborate with more-than-human materials? What are the particular asymmetries of such collaboration? What modes of attention can do justice to the 'strange agencies of the material world' (Alaimo, 2014: 16) without recapturing them in the anthropomorphic imagination? What are the (productive) contradictions of making more-than-human performance for a human audience?

The workshop for theatre practitioners is typically a place of experimentation and of play. Whereas rehearsals are about defining and honing sequences of a performance, working out what is 'right' for public presentation, workshops are usually much more open in format and less immediately aimed at creating presentable material. They are then concerned, as John Matthews (2012) suggests, with producing a set of circumstances within which *poeisis* can emerge. Based typically around a set of tasks or instructions (for example: 'Try balancing the apple on different parts of your body', 'Create a movement sequence with the apple and gravity') interspersed with discussions of what was done and seen, workshops speculate on the productive power of improvisation and coincidence. Matthews rightly cautions against seeing such workshop coincidences as merely 'chance', rather we might conceive of the workshop 'as creating conditions in which something unexpected can occur, and to which performers can react, shaping and constructing stage phenomena in a duet with an uncontrollable force. This uncontrollable force is ... *poiesis*' (ibid.: 352–353). It is important to note that the workshop within HE has additional aims to those undertaken as part of professional practice: next to producing artistic material they are also supposed to fulfil an academic function, to allow students to discover, articulate and eventually respond to a set of research questions, for example. Still, much more readily recognisable academic activities are not neatly separable from the overall *poeisis* in the workshop setting. This productive crossing of the creative and the academic, of making and (re)searching is essential to how an arts pedagogy can contribute to transdisciplinary journeying and lends itself to a diffractive form of pedagogy in HE.

Whereas Matthews with reference to Aristotle stresses the appearance of something out of nothing, an ecological and feminist practice might rather want to emphasise the relational possibilities of the workshop. In my example, over and above the content of the workshop engaging with ecofeminist challenges to dominant ideas of self, knowledge and being, the workshop format itself was a vital tool for developing a pedagogical method grounded in diffraction rather than reflection. Workshopping methods highlight and depend on the relative and relational nature of knowledge-creation and exchange, rather than the 'replication, reflection, or reproduction' (Haraway, 2004: 70) of existent knowledge. In the performance workshop what is produced is fully dependent on a specific and situated assemblage of actors, forces, processes, materials and texts: a thought or an action materialises from a particular instruction or something someone else did/said earlier or the things in the room or a hazy memory or association stirred by a sound, texture, smell and so on. By taking part in such emergent processes, what Lisa Mazzei (2014: 743) has referred to as 'entering the assemblage', learners are encouraged to reformulate their relationship to knowledge: instead of static acquisition, they are asked to be involved in its active production and discovery.

Importantly, such contingent and coincidental aspects of learning in a workshop mean that no one participant (human or non-human) is fully in control of its outcomes, including the pedagogue. As a result, the principle of mastery as both a method of instruction and a desired learning outcome is called into question, even actively resisted. With regard to the latter point, the performance workshop can function analogous to van der Tuin's (2018: 101) diffractive reading techniques that attend to 'how texts, artefacts and human beings interpellate or affect each other' instead of transmitting canonical knowledge of literary texts. Similarly, in the workshop participants can experience the co-generation of knowledge; how their own actions and ideas are interpellated with the diverse materialities they encounter (such as the apples). This allows learning to be grounded in the appearance of 'phenomena ... specific material configurations of the world's becoming' (Barad, 2007: 206), a central point for diffractive approaches to knowledge. Such an approach also entails, as already briefly touched upon, a divestment of mastery by the pedagogue since they cannot regulate what phenomena begin to appear. Instead, as my description of a session at the start indicates, the pedagogue becomes a part of the assemblage, arranging some of its elements (the materials, the space, the texts for example) but ultimately they have to step back from controlling what that assemblage produces, how it produces a difference in the world. As Brian Massumi writes: 'processually speaking, a making is always bigger than the made. The making includes, in germ, the form of what will come to be, as well as the functions its being, once arisen, will afford' (2013: xi).

Making a difference: dramaturgy as experimental apparatus

Following the workshop phase, students were confronted with a challenge: to translate and develop their workshop experience into sensate material for an audience. Since, as Deleuze and Guattari (2015: 164) stress, an artwork is a 'bloc of sensations, a compound of percepts and affects' that 'must stand up on its own', independently of its creators and even its spectators (since its latent sensate possibilities cannot be individually exhausted), our focus quickly turned to questions of dramaturgy rather than representation. Students found that attempts to mimetically represent their 'doing-in-common' with non-human materials – for example by simply showing their movement scores with apples, as outlined in the previous section, to an audience – were unsatisfactory because such formats tended to reproduce the kind of mastering distance towards a more-than-human world they sought to challenge. Instead, they chose to investigate how dramaturgical arrangements of materials, bodies, texts and actions might encourage a diffractive form of spectatorship.

The practice of dramaturgy in a theatre-making context is concerned with the composition and arrangement of performance materials or, as Theresa Lang (2017: 7) succinctly puts it, the '[curation of] an experience for an audience'; be that in the way plot points are arranged in narrative-driven theatre or how elements such as images, actions and texts are assembled in more image-based theatre such as the piece eventually created by the student group. For Barad 'a diffractive methodology is a critical practice for making a difference in the world. It is a commitment to what differences matter, how they matter and for whom' (2007: 90). Setting out to investigate how they might create a dramaturgy founded in diffraction rather than reflection, they produced a performance entitled 'There is a lot of activity going on here but no control'. The piece was presented in the black box space with no designated seating for the spectators; rather spectators could move freely through simultaneously presented performance scores, soundscapes composed of noises (including those of eating apples) and spoken text fragments as well as projections of live camera feeds trained on to minute details of the room. Many of the performance scores playfully cited scientific experiments with performers dressed in white boiler suits combining mundane materials (washing up liquid, fizzy drinks, water, ice) to produce chemical reactions that were then amplified visually (via the cameras) or aurally (via microphones).

The effect of this arrangement of materials was that representation was radically destabilised since spectators could never be sure whether the potential meaning of materials was deliberate or a product of coincidence and their own interpretive agency. For example, many images produced on a section of plastic sheeting at the centre of the room (see Figure 8.1), where ice blocks were melted on human skin or through contact with salt, and water began to run through or spill over creases in the sheeting, could potentially evoke associative links with the effects of climate change (melting ice caps, increased flooding) but said links remained fragile and contingent.

Through creating the performance, the student group was able to offer a translation of the concept of diffraction into a dramaturgical form. The optical roots of diffraction invoke the terrain of sight, insight and knowledge, in contrast to dramaturgical forms premised on reflection wherein static beings and already-presumed differences are mirrored back to an audience. Because of this, a diffractive dramaturgy continually brings new phenomena into view. In the piece temporary sensory assemblages (of video images, sounds, kinetic action, smell, taste and so on) became visible, affected or interfered with each other to create yet further different constellations. In a scientific context, diffraction is a feminist intervention into ideas of strong objectivity: it insists that knowledge is always situated through a 'particular and specific embodiment … not a false vision

Figure 8.1 The central performance space.
Source: Photograph: Arianne Welsh.

promising transcendence of all limits and responsibilities' (Haraway, 1988: 582). Diffraction – to think with Barad – emerges from an assemblage of viewer, phenomenon and apparatus (amongst others). Similarly, diffractive dramaturgies move against theatrical forms that depict the more-than-human world as static and surveyable, highlighting instead our fundamental enmeshment with and ultimate dependence upon it. Dramaturgy here became an experimental apparatus, a world-making device, through which diffraction was made sensible.

Since a diffractive dramaturgy creates differences and stages the effects of differentiation, it can be considered, in Barad's words, a way of producing 'a specific engagement ... where part of the world becomes differently intelligible to another part of the world in its differential accountability to and for that of which it is a part' (Barad, 2007: 379). In this way it expands upon the long-standing critique of the theatre-as-mirror metaphor undertaken by feminist theatre scholars who have asserted that the stage should be considered an apparatus that can variously be used to reinforce ideological positions or dismantle them. Taking issue with the assumption that the stage functions akin to a mirror that accurately reflects the world, critics such as Dolan (1985: 7) proposed that we should reorient our critical work from the 'mirror's image, to the mirror's surface and frame'. Whereas these classical materialist-feminist positions are committed to the critical potential of self-reflexive dramaturgies, the new materialist ideas of Barad, Haraway, van der Tuin and others, allow for a further step to be taken: towards diffraction. That is, whereas reflexivity no matter how critical runs the risk of 'remain[ing] caught up in sameness because of its mirroring of fixed positions' (Bozalek and Zembylas, 2017: 112), diffractive dramaturgical forms herald the possibility of making a difference by attuning us to the ways in which differences are constantly being produced, negotiated and transformed through cultural as well as scientific practices.

Drawing from their embodied experience in workshops, engagement with theoretical texts and developing expertise in performance-making in their degree programme, the group of students were able to develop a performance that was not only a transdisciplinary learning opportunity but also made this learning accessible to an audience of colleagues and peers. Doing so the module produced a momentary disciplinary rooting of a transdisciplinary concept, circulating new ideas within a local context and opening up new possible journeys for that concept. Most importantly, it empowered students to become producers of new knowledge, rather than asking them to reiterate already existing positions and practices.

Ecofeminist fabulations in the university

What concepts we choose to translate in our classrooms matter. As Haraway writes:

> It matters what matters we use to think other matters with; it matters what stories we tell to tell other stories with; it matters what knots knot knots, what thoughts think thoughts, what ties tie ties.
>
> (Haraway, 2013: n.p.)

Translations are an act of worlding, and therefore a political act; they have material effects in so far as they produce a 'context or background against which particular things show up and take on significance' (Anderson and Harrison, 2010: 8). Curriculum choices, the materials we present to our students and encourage them to engage with, have a performative dimension since they play an important role in determining what kind of differences appear and who or what becomes intelligible (or at least sensible). Transdisciplinary concepts especially have the potential to create differing effects when brought into disciplinary curricula. From this point of view pedagogical work might be considered in Haraway's terms a type of fabulation (2013: n.p.). By this I mean not so much a practice of narration which is often arranged according to a set of aesthetic norms and traditions (and as such might be associated with the replication of canons) but a mode of speculation which remains 'open to the insistence of the possibles' (Debaise and Stengers, 2017: 19) – and as such is not replicating but diffractive.

Pedagogy so understood treats the classroom as place of creative experimentation – be that through artistic practice or theorising – with the potential to forge new connections between concepts and practices. Just as Dolan (1985: 11) envisaged feminist theatre as a 'workplace' and a 'laboratory' in which feminism could be explored and developed, so in my example the performance workshop and its public outcomes acted as an experimental field in which theoretical positions and material practices could be tested out, drawing on developing ecofeminist practices. That is, the workshop approach and performance dramaturgy became spaces for testing out the possibility of an ecofeminist praxis: experimenting with ways 'to relocate, to diffract embodied meanings' in order to '[gestate] a new world' (Haraway, 2004: 98), a world that challenges the binarised, oppressive logic that has been directed against women and the more-than-human world alike.

While feminist research and pedagogical practices have long insisted on the imbrication of the researcher with the research and of the pedagogue with their pedagogy, the terms and methods arising from the current turn to ecofeminist entanglements take this a step further: 'the human no longer assumes priority as the knowing eye/I organizing inquiry' (Hinton and Treusch, 2015: 3). In other words, ecofeminist practices in HE teaching might seek to take responsibility for and critically interrogate the contents and effects of pedagogical decisions with an emphasis on the historical exclusion of the material world and at the same time highlight the material situatedness of all knowledge, pointing out that 'how the world, and the universe, come to be known is a correlate of the (organic and inorganic) bodies involved in perceiving and understanding, and their social, cultural, technical, and other specificities' (Bleeker, 2017: 3). Such delicate negotiations between human and more-than-human agency, between an ethos of accountability and the struggle to not replicate the humanist assumption that 'man is the measure of all things' (Barad, 2007: 136), is important transdisciplinary feminist work in the era of the Anthropocene. Developing teaching formats that allow students to engage with and generate approaches to such negotiations becomes a vital part of feminist pedagogical activism across and beyond disciplinary boundaries. By discussing one particular example from my own practice, I hope to have offered a novel translation of some of these concerns mediated through my particular disciplinary expertise and methods, and would aim to encourage other translations across disciplinary boundaries in the future.

References

Alaimo, S. (2014). Thinking as the stuff of the world. *O-Zone: A Journal of Object-Oriented Studies*, 1, 13–21.

Anderson, B. and Harrsion, P. (2010). The promise of non-representational theories. In B. Anderson and P. Harrsion (Eds.) *Taking-Place: Non-Representational Theories and Geography* (pp. 1–36). London: Routledge.

Åsberg, C. and Braidotti, R. (2018). Feminist posthumanities: An introduction. In Åsberg, C. and Braidotti, R. (Eds.) *A Feminist Companion to the Posthumanities* (pp. 1–23). Cham: Springer.

Bal, M. (2002). *Travelling Concepts in the Humanities: A Rough Guide*. Toronto: The University of Toronto Press.

Barad, K. (2007). *Meeting the Universe Halfway: Quantum Physics and the Entanglement of Matter and Meaning*. Durham, NC: Duke University Press.

Barad, K. (2018). Posthumanist Performativity: Toward an understanding of how matter comes to matter. In Åsberg, C. and Braidotti, R. (Eds.) *A Feminist Companion to the Posthumanities* (pp. 223–240). Cham: Springer.

Bleeker, M. (2017). Knowing as distributed practice: Twenty-first century encounters with the universe. *Studies in Material Thinking*, 16, 1–12.

Bozalek, V. and Zembylas, M. (2017). Diffraction or reflection? Sketching the contours of two methodologies in educational research. *International Journal of Qualitative Studies in Education*, 30(2), 111–127.

Cixous, H. (1988). Extreme fidelity. In Sellers, S. (Ed.) *Writing Differences: Readings from the Seminar of Hélène Cixous* (pp. 9–36). Trans. Sellers, S. and Liddle, A. New York, NY: St. Martin's Press.

Debaise, D. and Stengers, I. (2017). The insistence of possibles: Towards a speculative pragmatism. *Parse*, 7, 12–19.

Deleuze, G. and Guattari, F. (2015). *What is Philosophy?* Trans. Burchell, G. and Tomlinson, H. London: Verso.

Dolan, J. (1985). Gender impersonation onstage: Destroying or maintaining the mirror of gender roles. *Women and Performance*, 2(2), 5–11.

Dolan, J. (2001). *Geographies of Learning: Theory and Practice, Activism and Performance*. Middletown, CO: Wesleyan University Press.

Gaard, G. (2011). Ecofeminism revisited: Rejecting essentialism and re-placing species in a material feminist environmentalism. *Feminist Formations*, 23(2), 26–53.

Gotman, K. (2016). Translation. *Performance Research*, 21(5), 17–20.

Grosz, E. (2005). *Time Travels: Feminism, Nature, Power*. Durham, NC: Duke University Press.

Haraway, D. (1988). Situated knowledges: The science question in feminism and the privilege of partial perspective. *Feminist Studies*, 14 (3), 575–599.

Haraway, D. (1997). Modest_Witness@Second_Millennium.FemaleMan_Meets_Onco-Mouse: *Feminism and Technoscience*. London and New York, NY: Routledge.

Haraway, D. (2004). The promises of monsters: A regenerative politics for an inappropriate/d other. In Haraway, D. (Ed.) *The Haraway Reader* (pp. 63–124). London and New York, NY: Routledge.

Haraway, D. (2013). SF: Science fiction, speculative fabulation, string figures, so far. *Ada: A Journal of Gender, New Media and Technology*, 3, n.p. Retrieved from http://adanewmedia.org/2013/11/issue3-haraway/. Accessed October 30, 2018.

Hickey-Moody, A., Palmer, H. and Sayer, E. (2015). Diffractive pedagogies: dancing across new materialist imaginaries. *Gender and Education*, 28(2), 213–229.

Hinton, P. and Treusch, P. (2015). Introduction: Teaching with feminist materialisms. In Hinton, P. and Treusch, P. (Eds.) *Teaching with Feminist Materialisms* (pp. 1–22). Utrecht: ATGENDER.

Lang, T. (2017). *Essential Dramaturgy: The Mindset and the Skillset*. London and New York, NY: Routledge.

Lykke, N. (2011). This discipline which is not one: Feminist studies as post-discipline. In Buikema, R., Griffin, G. and Lykke, N. (Eds.) *Theories and Methodologies in Postgraduate Feminist Research: Researching Differently* (pp. 137–150). London and New York, NY: Routledge.

Massumi, B. (2013). Prelude. In Manning, E. (Ed.) *Always More Than One: Individuation's Dance* (pp. ix–xxv). Durham, NC: Duke University Press.

Matthews, J. (2012). What is a workshop? *Theatre, Dance and Performance Training*, 3(3): 349–361.

Mazzei, L. (2014). Beyond an easy sense: A diffractive analysis. *Qualitative Inquiry*, 20(6) 742–746.

Mol, A. (2008). I eat an apple: On theorising subjectivity. *Subjectivity*, 22, 28–37.

Neimanis, A. (2012). On collaboration (For Barbara Goddard). *NORA – Nordic Journal of Feminist and Gender Research*, 20(3), 215–221.

Palmer, H. (2012). *Deleuze and Futurism: A Manifesto for Nonsense*. London: Bloomsbury.

Seager, J. (2003). Rachel Carson died of breast cancer: The coming of age of feminist environmentalism. *Signs*, 28(3), 945–972.

Salleh, A. (1997). *Ecofeminism as Politics: Nature, Marx and the Postmodern*. New York, NY: Zed Books.

Sandford, S. (2015). Contradiction of terms: Feminist theory, philosophy and transdisciplinarity. *Theory, Culture and Society*, 32(5–6), 159–182.

van der Tuin, I. (2018). Diffraction. In Braidotti, R. and Hlavajova, M. (Eds.), *Posthuman Glossary* (pp. 99–101). London: Bloomsbury.

9 Living in the hyphens
Between a here, a there *and* an elsewhere

Veena Balsawer

Introduction: I-m-migrant

This chapter offers a braided, transdisciplinary account of existential questions of identity, belonging and *home*. A sense of belonging in Canada 'is elusive for those of us who share part of our lives here' writes Palmer (1997: v) in the anthology *…But Where Are You Really From*? As an immigrant (I-m-migrant), I feel like I live in the hyphens, or the liminal 'third space' (Bhabha, 1987: 22) where I straddle cultures, homelands, identities and languages. People here ask me where I am from or if I am new to Canada, especially when they see me in a sari or a salwar-kameez (chemise). I feel like a foreigner/stranger when I have to apply for a Visitor's visa in order to travel to India – my home-country. It does not help when my friends and cousins think I look *different* now, or that I talk with a *foreign* accent. Thus I feel that no matter where I go, I seem to walk, and exist amongst strangers, a 'mestiza' (Anzaldúa, 1987: 77), negotiating 'between a here, a there, *and* an elsewhere' (Trinh, 2011: 27). After almost three decades in Canada, I have begun to wonder if it is possible for someone like me, a hyphe-nated, culturally dis-located woman to be completely at home anywhere in the world today. This identity crisis has also aroused my post-colonial and feminist subjectivities to quest/ ion how other I-m-migrant women, especially the Indo-Canadian women in Ottawa, navigate their hyphe-nated existences with/in these hybrid liminal spaces.

Researching the lived experience of 'feeling like a foreigner'

Helen Ralston (1996: v), one of the foremost feminist researchers to interview Indo-Canadian women, has argued that 'from the standpoint of any immigrant woman, departure from the homeland and migration to a strange country in order to settle and start a new way of life in a different climate and unfamiliar surroundings is a dramatic step to take'. Yet, people leave their homes and settle down in *strange* countries all the time even though, one of the effects of immi-gration, according to Kelly (2013: 2) is that 'feeling like a "foreigner" does not end', instead, as years go by it lingers, creating mixed emotions about belong-ing, home and identity. As both insider and outsider, and as someone who has 'deviated from the traditionally prescribed role' (Trinh, 1989: 6) of a *good* Indian woman, I was interested in the live(d) experiences of other Indo-Canadian women as they/we (re)created or per/formed this notion of home and community in Canada, through the constant process of 'adjustment, transformation, negotiation and redefinition' (Ahmed, 2000: 1). How might the live(d) experiences of these women from a *visible minority* community become a 'living pedagogy' (Hasebe-Ludt, Chambers and Leggo, 2009) of my/our be/com/ing and be/long/ing?

As part of my research, I engaged in conversations with 11 Indo-Canadian women who had lived in Ottawa for 20–30 years, to understand how they/we have learned to navigate these liminal sp(l)aces which are both home and not-home. In some ways, this navigation represents how we have found *our way* or found *our-selves* by *getting lost* in terms of being confused, or not being in control and trying to figure out a life in a new country where their/our existence and their/our knowledge(s) was/is constantly being de/constructed, challenged or questioned. As the feminist methodologist Patti Lather (2007: 12–13) explains:

> [T]he concept of getting lost, functions as a paradox. It is a metaphor for a new generation of postcritical/postmodern work. It is a way to engage a new (transdisciplinarity)/interdisciplinarity that is able to question not just the nature of knowledge but its grounds of practice.... Here loss [mourning and nostalgia] bears the very possibility that finally, we can begin to think again. My argument is that a stance of 'getting lost' might produce different knowledge and produce knowledge differently.

My goal was to highlight the experiences of women from the Indo-Canadian community, and to catch the often unheard stories – the 'stories that need to come out' (Weis and Fine, 2000: 2) – of their hybrid lives in their own 'marginalized [*ordinary*] voices' (Munro, 1998: 6). I hoped that the live(d) stories of their/our (im)migrations with/in and out/side homes/not-homes might help me / us understand 'how migration influences [our] lives' [and what they/we do about it, and whether] 'women tend to feel a greater need to belong to a culture, and tend to mourn the losses associated with immigration' (Kelley, 2013: 5).

Drawing on a post-colonial feminist lens, I wanted to engage autoethnographically with these women through 'the emotional/personal/affective dimensions along with the academic and intellectual aspects [in order to understand] the struggles without as well as the conflicts within' (Asher, 2002: 86). In this research, therefore, I am not an 'objective' outsider, rather I 'incorporate elements of my own life experience[s]' (Denzin, 1989: 27) when writing about my participants. This enacts feminist inquiry as experimental writing which combines research, action and praxis. It gives us a sense of autoethnography as:

> Writing [*graphy*] about the personal [*auto*] and its relationship to culture [*ethno*]. It is an autobiographical genre of writing and research that displays

multiple layers of consciousness.... Usually written in first-person voice, autoethnographic texts appear in a variety of forms.... They showcase concrete action, dialogue, emotion, embodiment, spirituality, and self-consciousness. These features appear as relational and institutional stories affected by history and social structure, which themselves are dialectically revealed through actions, feelings, thoughts, and language.

(Ellis, 2004: 37–38)

Such writing sets the stage for considering the emerging complexities and shifting boundaries in women's experiences, places and spaces. My transdisciplinary/ interdisciplinary feminist auto/ethnographical journey spans different cities, countries and continents. It is a story of a here, a there and an every-where. It is a 'complicated conversation with self and others' (Pinar, 2000: 30), part memoir, 'a looking back, a reminiscence' (Goldberg, 2008: xx), part 'biotext ... an innately cumulative performance' (Wah, 2006: ix), part auto-bio-graphy and life writing where I write 'about the personal and its relationship to culture' (Ellis, 2004: 37). In this bricolage (Kincheloe, 2005) I address questions about home and identity, cultural dis/placement and hyphe-nations. This writing is also a quilt (tissage/weaving) where I 'borrow from other disciplines/methods' (Denzin and Lincoln, 2008: 4) namely, feminist research methodologies (Anzaldúa, 1987; Lather, 2007; Mohanty, 2003; Olsen, 2005; Tong, 1989; Trinh, 2011), cultural and post-colonial studies (Bhabha, 1987; Hall, 1990; Narayan, 1987), narrative inquiry (Chase, 2005; Clandinin and Connelly, 2000), poetic inquiry (Butler-Kisber, 2010) and performance auto-ethnography (Alexander, 2000). By interrogating the various inter/secting forces that define us and create us, I wanted to understand the process of my/our be/com/ing and be/long/ing in these (sub)liminal spaces which are both home and not-home. The process/performance of weaving/braiding the *messy* conversation bits of my participants' live(d)-through experiences/stories and the artefacts is what I call as my storied-quilt or a 'literary métissage ... a way to generate, represent and critique knowledge/ experience through [life] writing and braiding autobiographical texts' (Hasebe-Ludt, Chambers, and Leggo, 2009: 34–35).

Being conscious of the fact that I might *silence* or *over-shadow* my participants' voices/identities with my 'signature and voice' (Clandinin and Connelly, 2000: 147), I decided to re-create/perform my participants' unique live(d) experiences by drawing on the notion of 'found poetry' or 'generated poetry' which 'use[s] only the words of the participant(s) to create a poetic rendition of a story or phenomenon [to recreate lived experience]' (Butler-Kisber, 2002: 232). What emerges is the hidden, unplanned, unpredictable, dislocated 'curriculum-as-live(d)' (Aoki, 2000: 169) experiences of the Indo-Canadian women – wives, m/others, grand/m/others – in Ottawa who are often silent, silenced or in/visible on the Canadian landscape. My hope is that this transdisciplinary literary métissage might be a transformative 'living pedagogy' (Hasebe-Ludt, Chambers and Leggo, 2009: 205) for both the reader and the writer.

Living in-between: Trishanku's curse

In Canada, the Indian diaspora is comprised of people who identify themselves as Indo-Canadian, East Indian or South Asian. With the influx of immigrants from India, there are cultural centres, societies, temples and gurudwaras that have been established to fulfil the needs of the different regional and religious groups within the diaspora. Immigrants are attracted to join their ethnic social networks or 'enclaves of people from their first culture' says Kelley (2013: 82), because these networks provide information about jobs and residences and help immigrants adjust to their new country, although Parameswaran (2003: xlviii) notes that the tendency of members to bond exclusively with their diasporic family can be dangerous and unhealthy because 'a diaspora could end up ghettoizing itself'.

According to Gnanamony (2008: 61) 'wherever they go, these [diasporan Indian] migrants carry with them a profound sense of attachment to their former place of residence [and] their souls are always found to be divided; in other words, they are neither there nor here fully'. As a member of the Indian diaspora, Parameswaran (2003: xlv) confirms this and states that like some others, she has 'felt a sense of both exile *and* of home within Canada'. She further goes on to say that people who move away from their native countries 'occupy [and transmit to future generations] a liminality, an uneasy pull between two cultures' which she calls 'Trishanku's curse' after the mortal King from Indian mythology, who was suspended in-between heaven and earth (middle-ground) when he could not achieve his ambition to reach heaven in his mortal body.

I have talked to some of my friends about the Trishanku dilemma I/we all face. I seem to experience this 'curse' more acutely after a nostalgic trip back 'home'. When I go to India, I realise that home is not what it used to be and somehow I have become a stranger in my own imagined home. I am not sure how much of this feeling has anything to do with the fact that I have to apply for a Visitor's visa to go there in the first place! Perhaps, it is also because I feel the absence/presence of my parents more intensely when I am there. Thus, within a week or so, I get homesick for Canada and want to come back. But in Canada, too, I am the *other*. This is why I feel like Trishanku existing in the hyphens somewhere between India and Canada – between wor(l)ds. My I-m-migrant friends also tell me that because of their/our dilemmas, they fear their children might have be/come hyphe-nated, or 'mixed-up hybrid kid[s]' (Aoki, 1999: 28).

In my quest to understand this notion of diasporic or 'Trishanku' experience, I turned to some writers who have experienced this phenomenon. In *Imaginary Homelands*, the British Indian writer Salman Rushdie (1991: 17) asks the quintessential question: 'What does it mean to be "Indian" outside India'? Trinh (2011: 12) says,

> [t]oday when I am asked where home is for me, I am struck by how far away it is, and yet, home is nowhere else but right here, at the edge of this body of mine. The source has been travelling and dwelling on hybrid ground.

Behar (1996: 162) tells us that she was drawn to anthropology because she was raised within three cultures – Jewish, Cuban and American – and writes 'I am here because I am a woman of the border: between places, between identities, between languages, between cultures, between longings and illusions'. For Tang (2003: 30), a Chinese-English translator, diaspora implies 'movement and change ... the ambiguity of who one is and is becoming in the midst of displacement and re-location'. Aoki (2000: 323) talks about 'Yû-mu as both "presence" and "absence" [that] marks the space of ambivalence in the midst of which humans dwell ... the ambiguity in yû-mu is understood as a site [space] pregnant with possibilities [hope]'. Hasebe-Ludt (2009: 148) says that through her own experiences of exile and migration, and as a European living in Canada, she has realised that the 'tensioned space of cultural and geographic displacement ... can be/come a generative possibility'.

Asher (2002: 84–85) uses the term 'hybrid consciousness' to describe the awareness that emerges out of the struggle to situate oneself in relation to multiple borders, hybrid identities, cultures and representations; 'it is the process of rethinking "Self" via encounters with the "Other"', she says, that develops our hybrid consciousness of the social forces that shape us, and helps us to engage with difference in productive, meaningful ways. Anzaldúa (1987: 78) calls it a 'mestiza consciousness, or a consciousness of the borderlands' that emerges out of racial, ideological, cultural and biological 'cross-pollinization'. This mestiza consciousness, which can be a source of intense pain, makes us 'conscious of our own borderlands' and allows us to recognise that the 'clashes and contradictions we encounter are located within *and* outside of the Self' (78). Selvadurai (2004: 3) says that it was his arrival in Canada that 'shook his sense of I-dentity' which he had never quest/ioned before. For Hall (1990: 235), the diaspora experience is defined

> not by essence or purity, but by the recognition of a necessary heterogeneity and diversity; by a conception of 'identity' which lives with and through, not despite, difference; by hybridity. Diaspora identities are those which are constantly producing and reproducing themselves anew, through transformation and difference.

Radhakrishnan (1996: xiii–xiv) explains that

> diasporic subjectivity is thus necessarily double: acknowledging an earlier elsewhere in an active and critical relationship with the cultural politics of one's present home ... 'Home' then becomes a mode of interpretive in-betweenness, as a form of accountability to more than one location.

As Kelley (2013: 118) says,

> This is because for some, 'a full commitment to a specific home is not possible ... a dual belonging is preferable to the alternative of losing either home, and this is becoming increasingly common in today's globalized world.

These theorists provide analytical frames for conceptualising Trishanku's curse. But how is that experience lived and felt for the women in my study? What follows are the voices of my participants (*all the names are pseudonyms*). Their words are poetic renditions of our conversations in response to my research question: I sometimes feel like I live in-between. What does it mean for you to be an Indo-Canadian? Have a listen to what they have to say about their Trishanku experiences as they navigate and per/form their hyphenated identities with/in the hybrid liminal spaces which are both home and not-home.

Roopa
I never think of it. I am who I am!
I take the best of both sides and it has become a habit.
Canada is home and India is a foreign country for me.
I think language has a lot to do with it
I grew up in a convent, so, my mother tongue is English.
You cry in your mother tongue, and laugh in your mother tongue,
and for me it was always English.
So you see, language was a big thing that helped me here.

Maya
Maybe it's my age, because I am very comfortable in my skin –
comfortable with who I am.
But yes, when you come to Canada, the first decade you go through
a sort of an identity crisis and you need to sort it out.
I remember a few years after being in Canada,
it was such a shock when it dawned on me that I will die in Canada,
that I will die amongst strangers.
Then my daughter died of a brain haemorrhage
She was only 14 and Canada came into the house
with such kindness and compassion and caring
that I suddenly realized
I am the one keeping Canadians at bay
I am the one who is aware that they are white and I am not.
That experience rooted me in Canada.
Her death rooted me in Canada!
So where I am now it is fine as it is.
If it is Trishanku then it is fine.
I accept.
That is the Buddhist belief.
This is how it is.

It is not a conflict.
So, like Shakespeare said 'we are all on a stage' aren't we?
We are playing a role and now we are in Canada, our role is
Indo-Canadian.

Kanak
Yes, there is sadness, there is struggle inside
Sometimes you feel there is blend.
It is a mixture and I am aware
I can choose now.
I am trying to take the best here
and trying to bring the best from there
at least that is what we are trying to do
and sometimes it is hard to mesh the two.
As immigrants here, we have tried to maintain the good values
that we got there
and we are more Indian than the Indians in India now.
I am grateful that the system allows us to be free to some degree
but we have to make an effort too to understand what is good here.
If you take a rigid position then I think the children will fail
and you have failed your children.
They have to live here.

Devi
A big Thanks to the already existing Canadian community
who really accepted me and us (my family) the way we are.
We didn't have to change anything.
It is all in our outlook.
They are so very accepting.
That is why I keep saying it is all in our outlook.
If you are doubtful, if you are not confident,
then you start thinking of these other possibilities.
But if you are confident, those possibilities may be there
but it won't debilitate us.

Padma
Of course we all live like Trishanku.
All the Indo-Canadians because you have spent your prime time there
and when you came here, at that time you were not accepted
so you missed that what you got from home.

And now when we start accepting here, we lose back there.
It is not easy.
When you hear your parents are not doing well
or you hear someone is getting married,
you just want to drop everything and go but you just cannot!
When I first came, calling home was so expensive.
You had to place a call and then wait and wait.
Now-a-days because the phone is so much better,
I can call home every day.
I can keep in touch with my friends on Gmail, Facebook, WhatsApp
and I am kind of at peace that I am getting the best of both worlds.

Gomati
I don't think of myself as Indo-Canadian.
Like it is said in the Bhagwad Gita,
I consider myself as part of this whole universe.
In my whole family everyone is included
There was one time in my daughter's life
where I felt that this child has to keep her identity.
We need to learn goodness from others
and yet keep our intrinsic nature – our Swa-dharma.
If we let go of our Swa-dharma we will be miserable
and go through an identity crisis.
In order that she does not go through that
we have encouraged her to follow our Sanskaras (ways of living)

Aarya
Like I said before, I feel like I have two homes
but I don't have any.
There is a saying in Hindi which could quantify where we are
Dhobi ka kutta | na ghar ka | na ghat ka! [Hindi transliteration]
[*Like a washer-man's dog, you don't belong there,*
you are not here, you are nobody's
You are just in the middle of nowhere!]
Because whatever you say, this is my life
and this is where I am going to be.
Yes, sometimes you feel like you don't belong in either place
but at the same time you try to get merged into the culture here
by doing different things.

*For our children, there won't be Trishanku feeling
because they have grown up here.
But for people who live away like that, Trishanku feeling will not go away.
It does not matter which country/province you come from.
I talked to somebody at work who is from Europe
and she has exactly the same feeling of being lost,
of not belonging anywhere, and it was kind of uncanny.*

Aparna
*Yes, [I think of this] when I see my children.
They are born here and brought up here.
Whatever we used to do back home in India culture-wise,
they don't do [follow] it.
They do [behave] like Canadian children.
They are completely Canadian-ized even though we don't [can't] accept emotionally.*

Gowri
*Trishanku feeling because of the 2 cultures we have gone through in our lifetime.
It is also because of our accent.
When you go home you realize that your accent has changed
but not to the extent that you can speak like a 'native' Canadian
that is why we feel we are not there nor here.
Our habits have changed.
We have lived here so long,
our way of living, our way of thinking, everything has changed.
These days it doesn't feel as if I am in-between 2 cultures.
I have lived here longer than I have lived in India.
I don't know the India that I left anymore
This is home now.*

Shreesha
*The more you cook Indian food it keeps your connection with the place
The more I was getting used to the food here,
I was losing my attachment from there.
Not having my immediate family in India
has reduced that 'caught-in-between-2-worlds' feeling remarkably.*

> *But when my parents were there, I used to feel*
> *'Oh! When am I going to go back and see them again?'*
> *My children are calling this place as home.*
> *Canada is home for them.*
> *So when they say that, then I want to be where the home is for them.*
> *When we say home, it is there.*
> *But now when I don't have a family there, it is hard for me.*
> *Having an extended family is just not the same.*
>
> **Maanasi**
> *Trishanku!*
> *When somebody asks me 'why don't you go back to India'?*
> *then I say 'Don't even talk about it'.*
> *Basically we have decided that we will stay here.*
> *We are happy here.*
> *The only part that worries me is my parents as they get older*
> *They are there and we feel we are not doing our part*
> *that is why this Trishanku.*
> *When I came here I had to go back to the university, study for 3 years*
> *and then spend time looking for a job.*
> *Now we are settled here, we don't want to go back to India at this stage.*
> *Now we are in Canada, we are well settled*
> *I have friends who always talk about going back.*
> *We are staying what-ever happens.*
> *We came here for a better life and for the children.*

Conclusion: to be and to belong

This chapter offers a glimpse into my autoethnographical existential query to understand the live(d) experiences of Indo-Canadian women – m/others, wives, grand/mothers – 'keepers and transmitters' (Trinh, 1989: 121), of home and bearers of language and stories as they (re)produced and (re)created this notion called ho[me] with/in these diasporic spaces. Their poetically rendered stories offer lived and felt insights into the point Gedalof (2003: 101) makes about how 'the myth of home as a source of stable origins clashes against the reality of being called upon to reproduce that "home" in the context of forced displacement'. These stories indicate that home as a concept can 'integrate many levels of meaning and emotion: home can be a structure, a town, a country and a feeling ... [and that] home, belonging, and identity are interconnected but not interchangeable' (Kelley, 2013: 9–10). These narratives tell of how complicated it is for the 'diasporic person to define or find home'

(Tang, 2003: 29) and yet, how important it is to search for a place where one might find stability and happiness (Trinh, 2011). 'Home' is a place 'we speak from', that it materialises our struggles for identity and the need for a sense of personal coherence and intelligibility centred on this threshold between interior and exterior, between self and other (Rutherford, 1990: 24). Importantly, Thompson and Tyagi (1996: xv) tell us that writing is activism when shaped as 'a way of finding home'. Since Canada is said to be a land of I-m-migrants, and given the current social and political environment here and across the globe, I hope that the stories/narratives in this chapter will resonate with anyone who is an I-m-migrant in Canada, or with anyone who thinks of themselves as a transnational visitor/so-journer/traveller/pilgrim/wanderer/refugee/orphan, and one who might have at some point felt lost or home-less. To borrow Rashmi Luther's (2015: 5) words from her Introduction to the book *Resilience and Triumph*, 'these stories highlight lives lived in liminal spaces, the spaces in-between – spaces of discovery, strength, resistance, and transformation, spaces in which to be and to belong'.

References

Ahmed, S. (2000). *Strange Encounters: Embodied Others in Postcoloniality*. London and New York, NY: Routledge.

Alexander, B. K. (2000). Performance ethnography. In N. K. Denzin and Y. S. Lincoln (Eds.), *The Sage Handbook of Qualitative Research* (3rd Edition) (pp. 411–441). Thousand Oaks, CA: Sage Publications.

Anzaldúa, G. (1987). *Borderlands/La Frontera: New Mestiza*. San Francisco, CA: Spinsters/Aunt Lute.

Aoki, T. (1999). In the midst of doubled imaginaries: The Pacific community as diversity and difference. *Interchange*, 30(1), 27–38.

Aoki, T. (2000). Language, culture, and curriculum. In W. F. Pinar and R. Irwin, (Eds.), *Curriculum in a New Key: The Collected Works of Ted T. Aoki* (pp. 321–333). Mahwah, NJ: Lawrence Erlbaum Associates, Publishers.

Asher, N. (2002). (En)gendering a hybrid consciousness. *JCT: Journal of Curriculum Theorizing*, 18(4), 81–92.

Bhabha, H. (1987). Interrogating identity. In L. Appignanesi (Ed.). *ICA Documents 6*. London: Institute of Contemporary Arts.

Butler-Kisber, L. (2002). Artful portrayals in qualitative inquiry: The road to found poetry and beyond. *Alberta Journal of Educational Research*, 48(3), 229–239.

Butler-Kisber, L. (2010). *Qualitative inquiry: Thematic, Narrative and Arts-Informed Perspectives*. London: Sage.

Behar, R. (1996). *The Vulnerable Observer: Anthropology that Breaks your Heart*. Boston, MA: Beacon.

Chase, S. E. (2005). Narrative inquiry: Multiple lenses, approaches, voices. In N. K. Denzin and Y. S. Lincoln (Eds.), *The Sage Handbook of Qualitative Research* (3rd Edition) (pp. 651–679). Thousand Oaks, CA: Sage Publications.

Clandinin, D. J. and Connelly, F. M. (2000). *Narrative Inquiry: Experience and Story in Qualitative Research*. San Francisco, CA: Jossey-Bass.

Denzin, N. (1989). *Interpretive Biography*. Newbury Park, CA: Sage Publications.

Denzin, N. and Lincoln, Y. (Eds.) (2008). *Strategies of Qualitative Inquiry*, Thousand Oaks, CA: Sage Publications Inc.

Ellis, C. (2004). *The Ethnographic I: A Methodological Novel About Autoethnography*. Walnut Creek, CA: AltaMira Press.

Gnanamony, S. R. (2008). Diasporan divided souls and 'Identity constituting' in Jhumpa Lahiri's *The Namesake*. In T. S. Chandra Mouli and J. Sarangi (Eds.), *Indian Women's Writings in English* (pp. 61–72). New Delhi: GNOSIS.

Gedalof, I. (2003). Taking (a) place: Female embodiment and the re-grounding of a community. In S. Ahmed, C. Casteñada, A.-M. Fortier and M. Sheller (Eds.), *Uprootings/Regroundings: Questions of Home and Migration* (pp. 91–115). Berg: Oxford International Publishers Ltd.

Goldberg, N. (2008). *Old Friend from Far Away: The Practice of Writing Memoir*. New York, NY: Simon and Schuster.

Hall, S. (1990). Cultural identity and diaspora. In Jonathan Rutherford (Ed.), *Identity, Culture, Difference* (pp. 222–237). London: Lawrence and Wishart Limited.

Hasebe-Ludt, E. (2009). Cosmopolitan conversations. In E. Hasebe-Ludt, C. Chambers and C. Leggo (Authors), *Life Writing and Literary Métissage as an Ethos of our Times* (pp. 217–219). New York, NY: Peter Lang.

Hasebe-Ludt, E., Chambers, C. and Leggo, C. (2009). *Life Writing and Literary Métissage as an Ethos of our Times*. New York, NY: Peter Lang.

Kelley, C. E. (2013). *The Accidental Immigrants and the Search for Home: Women, Cultural Identity, and Community*. Philadelphia, PA: Temple University Press.

Kincheloe, J. (2005). Rethinking critical theory and qualitative research. In N. Denzin and Y. Lincoln (Eds.), The Sage *Handbook of Qualitative Research* (3rd Edition) (pp. 303–342). Thousand Oaks, CA: Sage Publications.

Lather, P. A. (2007). *Getting Lost: Feminist Efforts toward a Double(d) Science*. Albany, NY: State University of New York Press.

Luther, R. (2015). Introduction: Celebrating liminal spaces. In The Book Project Collective (Ed.), *Resilience and Triumph: Immigrant Women Tell Their Stories* (pp. 4–15). Toronto: Second Story Press.

Mohanty, C. T. (2003). *Feminism without Borders: Decolonizing Theory, Practicing Solidarity*. Durham, NC: Duke University Press.

Munro, P. (1998). *Subject to Fiction: Women Teachers Life History Narratives and the Cultural Politics of Resistance*. Buckingham, Philadelphia: Open University.

Narayan, U. (1997). *Dislocating Cultures: Identities, Traditions and Third-World Feminism*. New York, NY, and London: Routledge.

Olsen, V. (2005). Early millennial feminist qualitative research challenges and contours. In N. Denzin and Y. Lincoln (Eds.), *The Sage Handbook of Qualitative Research* (3rd Edition) (pp. 235–278). Thousand Oaks, CA: Sage Publications.

Palmer, H. (1997). '... *But Where Are You Really From?' Stories of Identity and Assimilation in Canada*. Toronto: Sister Vision.

Parameswaran, U. (2003). Dispelling the spells of memory: Another approach to reading our yesterdays. In M. Fludernik (Ed.), *Diaspora and Multiculturalism: Common Traditions and New Developments* (pp. xxxix–lxv). New York, NY: Rodopi.

Pinar, W.F. (2000). Strange fruit: Race, sex, and an autobiographics of alterity. In P. Trifonas (Ed.), *Revolutionary Pedagogies: Cultural Politics Instituting Education, and the Discourse of Theory* (p. 30). New York: Routledge.

Radhakrishnan, R. (1996). *Diasporic Meditations: Between Home and Location*. Minneapolis, MN: University of Minnesota Press.

Ralston, H. (1996). *The Lived Experiences of South Asian Immigrant Women in Atlantic Canada: The Interconnections of Race, Class, and Gender*. Queenston: The Edwin Mellen Press.

Rushdie, S. (1991). *Imaginary Homelands: Essays and Criticism 1981–1991*. London: Granta Books.

Rutherford, J. (1990). A place called home: Identity and the cultural politics of difference. In J. Rutherford (Ed.), *Identity: Community, Culture, Difference* (pp. 9-27). London: Laurence & Wishart.

Selvadurai, S. (2004). Introducing myself in the diaspora. In S. Selvadurai (Ed.), *Storywallah: Short Fiction from South Asian Writers* (pp. 1–14). Canada: Thomas Allen Publishers.

Tang, S. (2003). Generative interplay of/in language(s) and culture(s) midst curriculum spaces. In E. Hasebe-Ludt and W. Hurren (Eds.), *Curriculum Intertext: Place/Language/Pedagogy*. NewYork, NY: Peter Lang.

Thompson, B. and Tyagi, S. (Eds). (1996). *Names We Call Home: Autobiography on Racial Identity*. (pp. ix–xix). New York, NY: Routledge.

Tong, R. (1989). *Feminist Thought: A Comprehensive Introduction*. Boulder, CO: Westview Press.

Trinh, M. (1989). *Woman, Native, Other: Writing Postcoloniality and Feminism*. Bloomington, IN: Indiana University Press.

Trinh, M. (2011). *Elsewhere, Within Here: Immigration, Refugeeism and the Boundary Event*. New York, NY: Routledge.

Wah, F. (2006). *Diamond Grill*. Alberta: Newest Press.

Weis, L. and Fine, M. (2000). *Speed Bumps: A Student-friendly Guide to Qualitative Research*. New York, NY: Teachers College Press.

10 Caster Semenya

The surveillance of sportswomen's bodies, feminism and transdisciplinary research

Belinda Wheaton, Louise Mansfield, Jayne Caudwell and Rebecca Watson

Introduction

Across international competitive sport events, women and girl's bodies are scrutinized, surveyed and regulated to enforce a lean and toned, strong but sexy and heterosexually feminine version of female athleticism, positioning others as outsiders in the field of play. To police these female body boundaries, governing bodies of sport including The International Olympics Committee (IOC) and International Association Federation of Athletics Federation (IAAF), have endorsed a range of regulatory practices. These have included femininity certificates, 'naked parades', chromosome screening, 'sex tests', gender examinations, gender suspicion policy, gender verification policy, hyperandrogenism regulations and Differences of Sexual Development (DSD) regulations (Caudwell, 2012; Schultz, 2011). This often-officious regulation started in the 1930s and, while the testing methods have changed, these practices continue today. They are applied to women and girl athletes, but not men and boys. As Pieper (2016: 2) discusses, 'sex testing' functions 'to uphold a notion that women's sexed bodies must align with an absolute binary: woman–man. Furthermore, this policing of gender in sport has operated to 'privilege white gender norms and hamper female athleticism'. Pieper is one of a line of critical feminist writers to offer well-informed and insightful accounts on the topic. Sport feminists, sport sociologists, philosophers, historians and cultural studies scholars have presented convincing critiques that demonstrate the abuse, discrimination, prejudice and violence that accompanies global sport gender policy aimed at determining who can and cannot participate (Cole, 2000; Dworkin and Cooky, 2012; Teetzel, 2006, 2014; Wackwitz, 2003). In this short chapter we continue this line of feminist inquiry through a focus on the recent public science, legal, sport and media response to one sportswoman, the African middle-distance runner Caster Semenya.

Caster Semenya and her battle for legitimacy

Semenya's outstanding career is well documented including Commonwealth Games, World Championship and Olympic gold medals. Yet while her incredible athletic record has made headlines, these have often been overshadowed by the sustained set of assertions from International Sport's governing authorities, athletes and the mass media, that she is not a 'real' woman, and that her athletic achievements are somehow 'unfair' (Schultz, 2011). While these allegations have ranged from scrutiny of her physical appearance (she is said to be too muscly, too flat-chested, too manlike) to her sexuality, recent cases have focused on her bodies' physiology and so-called Differences of Sex Development. In contrast, exceptional male athletes whose bodies do not comply with biological norms are celebrated rather than scrutinised. For instance, swimmer Michael Phelps's Olympic record has been attributed to a range of extraordinary physiological characteristics, including unusually long arms, flipper-like feet, double-jointed limbs and his body's ability to produce less than half the lactic acid of many of his competitors. Sport governing authorities have 'praised how lucky he is to have such an insane genetic advantage' (marthafitat55, 2019).

The most recent episode in the scrutiny of Semenya's 'unnatural' body, centred around her 1 May 2019 challenge to the International Association of Athletics Federation's ruling to enforce new regulations for athletes who naturally produce higher levels of testosterone than those considered to be 'normal'. The IAAF's case went to Sport's Court of Arbitration (CAS), which ruled that women with so-called DSD cannot compete against other women in distances ranging from 400m to the mile, unless they take synthetic drugs (medication and hormonal contraceptives) to reduce and suppress their natural production of testosterone to IAAF defined levels adapted from medical standards (below 5nmol/l for a continuous period of at least six months) (Kelly, 2019). Semenya's lawyers argued this ruling is discriminatory to her and other female athletes with DSDs.

The case featured in media headlines worldwide; newspapers and social media feeds were deluged with 'expert' commentaries from scientists, lawyers and bioethicists to activists. Those in favour of the IAAF ruling, including some high-profile sportswomen, argued that its purpose was to ensure a fair and level playing field for all women (O'Sullivan, 2019). Others were critical of the IAAF, condemning the ruling as 'discriminatory', 'violating women's bodies and integrity' in ways that neither 'protect' nor 'benefit' women's sport (Zirin, 2019). The World Medical Association (WMA) (April 2019) questioned the ethical validity of a decision that requires women who want to compete to undergo a drug intervention that is not medically necessary, and furthermore, as CAS have recognised, could be potentially harmful. The WMA have urged physicians not to break codes of medical ethics by giving hormones to DSD athletes based on the IAAF rule. Semenya's testimony told the judges that testosterone-suppressing medication she was forced to take in the past affected her mental and physical health, including nausea, abdominal pain and regular fevers (Ingle, 2019). Following Semenya's subsequent appeal to the Swiss supreme federal court (7 August 2019), the IAAF was ordered to suspend its testosterone regulations, but only for Semenya (who mounted the legal challenge), not, at this point, other athletes with DSD. This issue clearly has wide-ranging implications for the world of sport and its long-held belief in the biological 'purity' of two distinct sexes and genders. This, in our view, is an issue which would be well served by a feminist analytical lens in developing an understanding of the complex sport, medical, scientific, ethical and social justice issues that frame the debate. In the following discussion we draw attention to some of the so-called justifications that have been made for the regulation of Caster Semenya's body. We demonstrate that arguments claiming women with naturally high testosterone levels have an unfair advantage reflect the authority of particular medical science perspectives that are repeatedly used to justify the regulation. We conclude that the ways in which Sport Governing bodies operate within these discourses constitutes powerful and privileged knowledge that needs to be challenged through critical, transdisciplinary feminist approaches.

Testosterone: the discourse of science and sport

Testosterone is a hormone; an androgen, often called the 'male' hormone that has a range of effects on the body, including muscle building. While testosterone is produced by both men and women, individual levels vary and fluctuate; on average, men have higher levels than women. Yet, as many researchers point out, beyond these facts, the science is complex and there have always been plentiful misconceptions about testosterone. The question about whether naturally-produced testosterone builds stronger and faster athletes is a complex and contested issue (Singer, 2006). Scientists interviewed by Gina Kolata (2019: 1) claim to have clear evidence that androgenised bodies 'have a performance advantage'. However, other scientific experts contest these claims, arguing that while synthetic steroids do stimulate muscle building, the impact on athletic performance is much less clear (Kelly, 2019). Bradly Anwalt, hormone specialist and Chief of medicine at University of Washington Medical Centre, admits that trying to quantify 'competitive advantage in naturally occurring levels of the hormone' are 'fraught with difficulty in interpretation' (cited in Gollom, 2019: 3).

Bad sport science: a public health issue?

The key scientific basis of the IAAF policy on hyperandrogenism, compelling female athletes to receive medical intervention to lower testosterone levels in some events, is based on a paper on serum androgen levels and their relation to performance in track and field published in the *British Journal of Sport Medicine* (*BJSM*) in 2017 (Bermon and Garnier, 2017). This mass spectrometry study of 2127 observations of male and female high-performance track and field athletes (1332 female; 785 male) concluded that female athletes with high levels of free testosterone have a significantly higher competitive advantage over those with lower levels in the 400 m, 400 m hurdles, 800 m, hammer throw and pole vault (see Harper *et al.*, 2018). However, researchers were unable to independently replicate the results in their entirety, thus missing a key principle of validity and reliability in scientific research. Significantly, in a letter to the *BJSM*, these scientists have called for the retraction of the IAAF commissioned research study on testosterone in women because the data is unreliable and provides a weak and inaccurate evidence base on which to make policy decisions (Pielke, Tucker and Boye, 2018).

Furthermore, this key study in the IAAF evidence was funded and supported by the IAAF itself, along with the World Anti-Doping Association (WADA). Meanwhile, the report's authors declare that they had no competing interests in conducting the study. Competing interests in research occur when professional judgement concerning the primary interest of research validity and ethics may be influenced by a secondary interest such as financial gain from funding and professional gain from publication. There is nothing inherently unethical about competing interests and we are not suggesting this to be the case in this study. The lead author of the paper does identify, as a disclaimer, IAAF consultancy and working group, and expert witness roles for high-profile organisations. Yet such involvement with key decision makers and a failure to recognise and declare such interests as *competing*, reveals an inability to recognise the impact of the relationship between the researchers and the commissioners of that research, a relationship which in this case controls the scientific basis to the IAAF policy agenda. Madeline Pape, an Australian athlete who competed against Semenya in the 800 m at the 2009 world athletics championships in Berlin explains how this type of bias can influence the way people think about the issues. Pape (2019: 1) recounts how at the time she was quick to join the 'chorus of voices condemning Semenya's performance as unfair'; on reflection, she recognises how she was influenced by the IAAF's constant questioning of Semenya's biological sex and her right to compete. She said that she is astounded by the continued lack of information, weak leadership and 'refusal to reflect critically' on what 'biases might be underpinning their absolute views informing notions of women's bodies, sex and gender' (Pape, 2019: 1). In July 2015 Pape testified for India's top female sprinter Dutee Chand, in her landmark victory at CAS against an IAAF ban for hyperandrogenism, and subsequently has been vocal in asserting that the decision by CAS about Semenya is an outdated and indefensible position.

The inability of a powerful international governing body of sport like the IAAF, and their scientific consultants to take an independent, rigorous and systematic approach to the scientific evaluation of the issues in Caster Semenya's case is akin to the type of bad science identified by Ben Goldacre (2010). Goldacre is a British physician, academic and science writer specialising in unpicking the misuse of science by journalists, politicians and drugs companies. Like much of the science translation and dissemination Goldacre explores, the IAAF use of testosterone evidence is selective, concealing facts that enable full evaluation of the issues of female athletes and testosterone levels. It is an exemplar of cherry-picking scientific data that favours the IAAF's own views, politics and agenda while at the same time ignoring wider critical analysis that suggests something different is going on.

Policing women's bodies: critical intersectional analysis

Mobilising scientific authority in this way to discipline those bodies, like Semenya's, that do not fit the normative subject position has a long history in sport. Feminists charting the past and present control of sportswomen's sexed bodies have illustrated the ways governance of femininity and femaleness has been embedded within West versus East geopolitical conflicts, for example, during the Cold War, and Global South and North colonial relations. Heggie (2010) and Pieper (2016) indicate that these histories tell of the pernicious treatment of women athletes from non-dominant nations, ethnicities, classes and femininities – such as Ukrainian-born Irina and Tamara Press; Polish-born Ewa Janina Kłobukowska; Indian-born Dutee Chand and Soundarajan Doha; and South African Caster Semenya – by the IOC, IAAF, sport media and sport publics. Racial difference has long been invoked to explain the perceived dominance of Black male as well as female athletes: as Spracklen (2008: 221) argues, sport normalises scientific racism, reproducing a discourse that reflects and reproduces what he labels the 'folk genetics' of Black athletic physicality. Dissenting voices, particularly in South Africa, claim that 'blatant racism' (Bull, 2018: 1) underpins this apparent witch-hunt (New Frame, 2019). The South African Sports Confederation, Olympic Committee and African National Congress have joined the growing international voice to publicly condemn the ruling. Supporting their case is the question about why this ruling has *only* been applied to the specific running events that Semenya competes in? If the IAAF's scientific case is to be believed, then events including the shot put, and pole vault are also ones where elevated testosterone levels would be seen to have an advantage. As other commentators have also highlighted, this selectivity suggests, 'a racially motivated stance, as athletes who do well in those codes tend to be white, while athletes of colour dominate the 400m, 800m and 1500m events' (New Frame, 2019).

Critical feminist work in sport highlights complexities in the way sexism, misogyny and biological racism are inscribed on sporting bodies (Jamieson, 2003; McDonald and Birrell, 1999; Scraton, 2001). We need to apply this critical lens to challenge how gender is constructed in and through sport (Ratna and Samie, 2018). Calls for intersectional analysis point to the necessity to link individual biographies of sportswomen to the structural and ideological contexts of sport. However, prioritising difference should not be at the expense of working towards gender justice in sport (Watson and Scraton, 2017). Thus, individual cases, such as Semenya's, need to be examined in ways where complex power relations, across gender, race, nation, class are exposed rather than diminished or deemed less significant in efforts to account for the specific experiences of certain athletes.

Conclusions: addressing the wrong decision in the right way and feminist transdisciplinary movements for change

The case of Caster Semenya illustrates how women's sexed, gendered and racialised bodies continue to be surveyed in and through elite sport. We, along with many other feminist researchers internationally, have called out the antiquated views of gender that many national and international sport leaders continue to perpetuate. This feminist challenge focuses on the paradoxes, inconsistencies and inequalities that have long underpinned the institution of 'modern' sport (Mansfield et al., 2017a, 2017b). Feminist work has helped to open up the sporting world for females by transforming gender-related rights and athlete welfare. This work must continue to highlight the ways in which sporting institutions, including governing bodies, sport educators, the sport workforce and the media can be called to account. Too many sports institutions continue to operate under a veil of secrecy allowing practices including prejudice, discrimination, sexual abuse and child protection to continue without adequate scrutiny (Caudwell, Mansfield, and Watson, 2017). As Karkazis (2019), the author of *Fixing Sex: Intersex, Medical Authority, and Lived Experience* persuasively argues, although international sports governing bodies like the IOC have for decades 'sought a single biological criterion by which to exclude some women from the female category … the idea of a true sex is mistaken, and tries to make something incredibly complex seem simple and binary'. It is time for these organisations to recognise this fallacy, and instead of using their powerful position to perpetuate the myth, take the lead in addressing the injustices it engenders.

Feminist work within the social science of sport has for a long time evidenced the unequal and unjust treatment of people with different bodies based on their sex, gender, ethnicity and class. Sport feminists have done so by drawing on different disciplinary perspectives including history, philosophy, sociology and cultural studies. Legal experts have utilised gender-related law and human rights instruments to challenge, case-by-case, individual exclusions arbitrated by powerful governing bodies. In turn, sport social science scholars have drawn from this judicial work as well as the emerging work within sport and exercise science to strengthen their analyses (Caplan, 2010; Henne, 2015). While feminist approaches are multiple and have sought to be multi- and inter-disciplinary, this chapter puts forward a case for a *trans*disciplinary approach to sportswomen's and girls' sexed bodies. The cross-disciplinary conceptualising that is a hallmark of a transdisciplinary approach has the potential to create new ways of thinking and theorising.

We have shown above that the treatment of Caster Semenya – and numerous female athletes throughout the course of modern sport – requires a transdisciplinary framing within which evidence from different epistemological perspectives is acknowledged, shared and incorporated. An approach that recognises the importance of knowledge from the social and biological sciences, legal, policy and practice perspectives as well as from athletes themselves, can, we suggest, provide a robust knowledge base to challenge decisions made on bad science. This transdisciplinary approach would bring together scholars, medics, lawyers, national and international organisations and athletes to develop a deeper knowledge of the powerful socio-cultural and political effects of concepts such as gender, sex, the sexed body, binary sex and embodiment. This transdisciplinary knowledge can then be applied through global gender sport policy to achieve a version of 'fairness' that is not imbued with sexism, misogyny and racism.

References

Bermon, S. and Garnier, P.-Y. (2017). Serum androgen levels and their relation to performance in track and field: mass spectrometry results from 2127 observations in male and female elite athletes. *British Journal of Sports Medicine*, 51(17). Retrieved from https://bjsm.bmj.com/content/51/17/1309.info

Bull, A. (27 April 2018). IAAF accused of 'blatant racism' over new testosterone level regulations. *Guardian*. Retrieved from www.theguardian.com/sport/2018/apr/27/iaaf-accused-blatant-racism-over-new-testosterone-regulations-caster-semenya

Caplan, A. L. (2010). Fairer sex: The ethics of determining gender for athletic eligibility: commentary on 'Beyond the caster Semenya controversy: The case of the use of genetics for gender testing in sport'. *Journal of Genetic Counseling*, 19(6): 549–550.

Caudwell, J. (2012). Sex watch: Surveying women's sexed and gendered bodies at the Olympics, in J. Sugden and A. Tomlinson (Eds.), *Watching the Games: Politics, Power and Representation in the London Olympiad* (pp. 151–164). London: Routledge.

Caudwell, J., Wheaton, B., Mansfield, L. and Watson, R. (8 August 2017). New Premier League season begins … but child abuse scandal hangs heavy over football. *The Conversation*.

Cole, C. L. (2000). Testing for sex or drugs. *Journal of Sport and Social Issues*, 24(4), 331–333.

Dworkin, S. L. and Cooky, C. (2012) Sport, sex segregation, and sex testing: Critical reflections on this unjust marriage. *The American Journal of Bioethics*, 12(7), 21–23.

Goldacre, B., (2010). *Bad Science: Quacks, Hacks, and Big Pharma Flacks*. Toronto: McClelland and Stewart.

Gollom, M. (2019). *Caster Semenya Case Reignites Debate Over Testosterone's Impact on Athletic Ability*. Retrieved from www.cbc.ca/news/technology/caster-semenya-testosterone-athletic-ability-iaaf-1.5119865

Harper, J., Lima, G., Kolliari-Turner, A., Malinsky, F., Wang, G., Martinez-Patino, M., Angadi, S., Papadopoulou, T., Pigozzi, F., Seal, L., Barrett, J. and Pitsiladis, Y. (2018). The fluidity of gender and implications for the biology of inclusion for transgender and intersex athletes. *Current Sports Medicine Reports*, 17(12), 467–472, doi: 10.1249/JSR.0000000000000543

Heggie, V. (2010). Testing sex and gender in sports; reinventing, reimagining and reconstructing histories. *Endeavour* 34(4), 157–163.

Henne, K. E. (2015). *Testing for Athlete Citizenship: Regulating Doping and Sex in Sport*. New Jersey: Rutgers University Press.

Ingle, S. (18 June 2019). Caster Semenya accuses IAAF of using her as a 'guinea pig experiment'. *Guardian*. Retrieved from www.theguardian.com/sport/2019/jun/18/caster-semenya-iaaf-athletics-guinea-pig.

Jamieson, K. (2003). Occupying a middle space: Toward a Mestiza sport studies. *Sociology of Sport Journal*, 20, 1–16.

Karkazis, K. (2019). *Fixing Sex: Intersex, Medical Authority, and Lived Experience*. Durham, NC: Duke University Press.

Kelly, D. (2 May 2019). Caster Semenya: How much testosterone is too much for a female athlete. *The Conversation*. Retrieved from https://theconversation.com/caster-semenya-how-much-testosterone-is-too-much-for-a-female-athlete-116391

Kolata, G. (1 May 2019). Does testosterone really give Caster Semenya an edge on the track? *NY Times*. Retrieved from www.nytimes.com/2019/05/01/health/caster-semenya-testosterone.html

Mansfield, L., Wheaton, B., Caudwell, J. and Watson, R. (27 July 2017a). Sportswomen still face sexism, but feminism can help achieve a level playing field. *The Conversation*.

Mansfield, L., Caudwell, J., Wheaton, B. and Watson, R. (Eds.) (2017b). *The Palgrave Handbook of Feminism and Sport, Leisure and Physical Education*. London: Palgrave

marthafitat55. (2019). Women, sport and sex tests: Why Caster Semenya matters a great deal. Retrieved from https://fitisafeministissue.com/2019/05/03/women-sport-and-sex-tests-why-caster-semenya-matters-a-great-deal

McDonald, M. and Birrell, S. (1999). Reading sport critically: A methodology for interrogating power. *Sociology of Sport Journal*, 16(4), 283–300.

New Frame (2019). Caster Semenya and the IAAF witch-hunt. *New Frame*. Retrieved from www.newframe.com/caster-semenya-and-iaaf-witch-hunt/

O'Sullivan, S. (2019). Sonia O'Sullivan: Why CAS upholding IAAF ruling on Caster Semenya is correct. *Irish Times*. Retrieved from www.irishtimes.com/sport/other-sports/sonia-o-sullivan-why-cas-upholding-iaaf-ruling-on-caster-semenya-is-correct-1.3877615

Pape, M. (1 May 2019). I was sore about losing to Caster Semenya. But this decision against her is wrong. *Guardian*. Retrieved from www.theguardian.com/commentisfree/2019/may/01/losing-caster-semenya-decision-wrong-women-testosterone-iaa

Pielke, L., Tucker, R. and Boye, E. (2018). Letter to BJSM reinforcing call for retraction of IAAF research on testosterone in women. Retrieved from https://sportsscientists.com/2018/08/letter-to-bjsm-reinforcing-call-for-retraction-of-iaaf-research-on-testosterone-in-women/?doing_wp_cron=1567553563.4275629520416259765625

Pieper, L. (2016). *Sex Testing: Gender Policing in Women's Sports*. Illinois: University of Illinois Press.

Ratna, A. and Samie, S. F. (2018). Mapping the field: ethnic "Other" females, in A. Ratna and S. F. Samie (Eds.) *Race, Gender and Sport: The Politics of Ethnic 'Other' Girls and Women* (pp. 10–32). London: Routledge.

Schultz, J. (2011). Caster Semenya and the 'Question of Too': Sex testing in elite women's sport and the issue of advantage, *Quest*, 63(2), 228–243.

Scraton, S. (2001). Reconceptualising race, gender and sport: The contribution of Black feminism, in B. Carrington and I. McDonald (Eds.) *Race, Sport and British Society* (pp. 170–187). London: Routledge.

Singer, N. (10 August 2006). Does testosterone build a better athlete? *The New York Times*. Retrieved from www.nytimes.com/2006/08/10/fashion/10Fitness.html

Spracklen, K. (2008). The Holy Blood and the Holy Grail: myths of scientific racism and the pursuit of excellence in sport, *Leisure Studies*, 27(2), 221–227, doi: 10.1080/02614360801902257

Teetzel, S. (2006). On transgendered athletes, fairness and doping: An international challenge, *Sport in Society*, 9(2), 227–251.

Teetzel, S. (2014). The onus of inclusivity: Sport policies and the enforcement of the women's category in sport. *Journal of Philosophy of Sport*, 41(1), 113–127.

Wackwitz, L. A. (2003). Verifying the myth: Olympic sex testing and the category 'woman'. *Women's Studies International Forum*, 26(6), 553–560.

Watson, B. and Scraton, S. (2017). Gender justice and leisure and sport feminisms, in J. Long, T. Fletcher and B. Watson (2017) (Eds.) *Sport, Leisure and Social Justice* (pp. 43–57). London: Routledge

Zirin, D. (2 May 2019). The Caster Semenya ruling is nonsense. *The Nation*. Retrieved from www.thenation.com/article/iaaf-cas-ruling-caster-semenya-nonsense/

11 Womanist and Chicana/Latina feminist methodologies

Contemplations on the spiritual dimensions of research

Michelle Salazar Pérez and
Cinthya M. Saavedra
(alphabetical listing; equal authorship)

Introduction

With growing recognition in the Global North of the urgency to disrupt oppressions experienced and lived for centuries by Indigenous peoples and people of color around the world, research practices that move beyond siloed academic disciplines are needed. Although feminist research has always traversed disciplines such as philosophy, sociology and educational, ethnic and gender studies (Sandford, 2015), we posit that theorizing from the flesh (Moraga and Anzaldúa, 1983), particularly with/in spiritual realms, is a necessary and often underrepresented transdisciplinary feminist research practice. Through Womanism and Chicana/Latina feminism, methodologies can cross not only academic disciplines but also intertwine with otherworldly ways of knowing and being. This can push transdisciplinary feminist research in new directions that can at least begin to heal colonial wounds.

We position transdisciplinary feminist research within the description that Dölling and Hark (2000, as cited by Sanford, 2015: 162) provide, in which one reflexively transgresses artificially imposed boundaries:

> Dölling and Hark see transdisciplinarity as a way for gender studies to avoid the perils of institutionalization – that is, its disciplinarization. For them, transdisciplinarity, 'characterized by a continual examination of artificially drawn and contingent boundaries and that which they exclude' (2000: 1197), is essential for the future of gender studies, allowing it to 'reflect on its own modes of knowledge production' (2000: 1195), on 'the contingency of its own premises and constructions.'
>
> (2000: 1197)

As part of transdisciplinary feminist praxis, we wish for Womanist and Chicana/Latina feminist spirituality to not merely co-exist alongside other research practices, rather for it to be understood as enmeshed throughout any mode of inquiry. Moreover, we suggest that spiritual realms are always present with/in and among us as methodological instruments, whether one is aware of or acknowledges their presence.

Enfleshed praxis across disciplines and dimensions

We have chosen to theorize from Womanism and Chicana/Latina feminism, as both purposefully center spirituality. We are drawn to these perspectives as they have emerged from the everyday lived and spiritual experiences of women of color, uniquely situating the socio-geo-political and material realities of power and oppression, while recognizing the complexity, intersectionality, and interconnectivity of our socially constructed worlds and identities.

Womanists have taken on a multiplicity of fluid/transdisciplinary approaches. Existing in and outside of academia, Womanists have mainly drawn upon the her/his/tories and philosophies of women of color (such as those that have theorized Black feminist thought and Chicana feminism) and Indigenous peoples, with aims to act as spiritual change instruments. Practicing spiritual activities like meditation and dialogues with a range of beings (including human, land and supernatural), Womanists infuse not only what one might consider academic traditions but also metaphysical traditions such as astrology and cosmology. As such, Maparyan (2012: 16) explains that womanism is more than just theory; she describes it as a 'spirit,' 'mindset' or 'worldview:'

> Womanism is not argument based, it does not privilege rationality, and it does not rest its case on academic intelligibility. Rather, it privileges the experience of inspiration, a heightened, nonrational spiritual state that makes the seemingly impossible possible – materially, socially, politically, economically, ecologically, psychologically, and relationally – and contributes to an ongoing sense of inner well-being and power that defies, and in turn, transmutes external conditions. Womanists know this state personally and they draw from it to do their social change work.
> (Maparyan, 2012: 33)

Similarly, Chicana/Latina Feminism was born out of theories in the flesh (Moraga and Anzaldúa, 1983) because of the necessity to express, document and examine the lived and embodied experiences of mujeres (women) who were marginalized by white middle class feminist and Chicano studies (Roth, 2003). Drawing from an array of fields (anthropology, sociology, education, women's studies, literary studies, history and psychology) as well as epistemologies and theories such as Black feminism, postcolonialism, poststructuralism and critical feminism, Chicana feminism intersects with Indigenous, transnational and decolonial lenses to challenge postconquest colonialities and offer new possibilities for rethinking theories, methodologies and pedagogies (Delgado Bernal et al., 2006; Saavedra and Pérez, 2017).

Both Womanism and Chicana feminism have multiple intersections and extend across numerous disciplines and areas of study. This includes the generation of theory from the lived experiences of women of color and attention to social justice for minoritized peoples. In this chapter, we focus not only on their fluidity across disciplines and epistemologies, but also on how they intertwine with spiritual realms. We first discuss how Womanists and Chicana/Latina feminists have theorized notions of spirituality and then apply these ideas to how one approaches research methodologies. We specifically focus on how Womanism and Chicana/Latina feminism changes the purposes for inquiry, how one engages in research, and what spiritually-centered methodologies can offer in terms of healing (both humans and more than humans) in an increasingly racist, sexist, colonialist, and violent world. We then discuss how spiritually-centered methodologies further transdisciplinary feminist research by opening dimensions and ways of engaging with/among the world that are often closed off and thought of as nonexistent, intangible or separate from our research.

Womanism and Chicana feminism as spiritual facilitators

Womanism and Chicana feminism unearth ways to re-examine and re-read our world. Though mainly situated within the Global North and, in some ways, entangled in a western epistemology, Chicana feminist and Womanist scholarship continues to provide tools that help to navigate entanglements and construct new visions to understand and experience the world. For us, and in these times, Womanist and Chicana feminist spirituality facilitates a recapturing of wisdom lost and provides a means to re-incorporate these wisdoms back into our lives, both personal and professional. Maparyan (2012: 56) explains that 'to live without spiritual practices, individually or collectively, is to live in a perpetual state of drought.' As such, Womanism and Chicana feminism can revitalize us in times of conflict, ethnocentrism, and neoliberal colonialism.

Chicana feminists, such as Anzaldúa (2002, 2015), and Womanists like Alice Walker (1983), believe/d in the power of spirit to guide and heal us. They and others (Dillard, 2006; Elenes, 2011, 2014; Espin, 1996; Facio and Lara, 2014; Hudson-Weems, 1993; Lara, 2005; Maparyan, 2012; Ogunyemi, 1996; Rendon, 2009/2014; Saavedra and Pérez, 2017) have championed the spirit as a way to challenge the rationalist epistemology that grounds much of our world and the postmodern skepticism that engulfs academia (Levine, 2005). The separation of the sacred from the mundane, our bodies, nature and dreams have been secularization tactics of colonization that have and continue to be a technology of power to suppress Indigenous, ancient and Other cosmologies. For many Chicana feminists and Womanists, it is in these Indigenous, ancient and Other cosmologies that tools for navigating entangled colonialist structures (sexism, racism and classism, to name a few) can be found and revived (Alexander, 2005; Anzaldúa, 2015; Christian, 2005; Delgadillo, 1998; Dillard, 2006; Facio and Lara, 2014; Espin, 1996; Holmes, 2002; Maparyan, 2012). These tools are pertinent to all facets of life, including academic spheres. Noticeably, however, many across disciplines have shied away from mentioning spirit or spirituality in their work (Keating, 2007) for fear of not sounding 'scientific,' credible and rigorous. Anzaldúa (2012: 18) points to how '[t]raditional science has such a grip on us, it's become the *only* way to describe reality.' We agree and acknowledge that spirit is not something we can tangibly connect to but permeates all facets of life. For many women of color, it has been a guiding force, and one that compels us to examine the purposes of why and how we engage in research. It's worth quoting Fernandes at length:

> All expansive feminist scholarship which has pointed to the partiality of the knowledge we produce within the constraints of our institutions ... questioned the notion of objectivity ... enabled forms of writing where it is legitimate to insert ourselves ... visions ... emotions ... conscience and heart; all of this has in many ways has been a kind of collective struggle and plea for a space where we are allowed to write with spirit.
> (Fernandes, 2003: 21)

Spiritual activism

Spirituality for Womanists and Chicana feminists is centered on the relationship between the self and world. One is interconnected to a larger web of people, places, the land, inanimate objects and Otherbeings. As an example, drawing from Indigenous concepts such as the Mayan law of In Lak'ech (I am you and you are me), interdependence becomes a central component in Chicana feminist spirituality (Rendon, 2009/2014). Most importantly, as Lara and Facio (2014: 4) point out, 'the claiming [of] spirituality goes hand in hand with a deep sense of respect for and accountability to their community including ... land base or specific traditions.' This sense and understanding of an interconnected world compels many Womanists and Chicana feminists to examine their role in acting upon the injustices in their communities, be it economic, gendered, or racist practices, in order to enact transformative research, in addition to revolutionizing pedagogies and policies (Dillard, Abdur-Rashid and Tyson, 2000; Elenes, 2014). A symbiotic relationship, then, exists between spirituality and social justice. Spirituality not only allows one to find 'meaning, purpose, and wholeness in life' (Rendon, 2009/2014: 9), but it also facilitates engagement in social justice work. As Maparyan (2012: 124) explains, 'the implication for spiritual activism is that human beings, as spiritually infused energy transformers, both respond to and create morphogenetic fields [and] we become able to use this ability toward social change ends.'

Anzaldúa (2002, 2015) inspires such spiritual activism as a stage in the path to conocimiento, which includes the healing that takes place as we work on ourselves and our communities. Anzaldúa's (2015: 120) spiritual activism begins with conocimiento, or the 'breaking out of your mental and emotional prison and deepening the range of perception ... [that] enables you to link inner reflection ... with the social political action and lived experiences to generate subversive knowledge.' With conocimiento, one can link the self/inner and outer worlds of action as a nepantlera. Nepantlera is a term that Anzaldúa (2015) uses to theorize those that work in the in-between spaces of ideas, epistemologies and beliefs and become bridges of understanding to many. According to Anzaldúa (2015: 83), nepantleras 'know that each of us is linked with everyone and everything in the universe and fight actively in both the material world and spiritual realm. Thus nepantleras are 'spiritual activists engaged in the struggle for social, economic, and political justice, while working on the spiritual transformations of selfhoods' (Anzaldúa, 2015: 83).

Womanist scholar Maparyan has been heavily influenced by the spiritual activism of Anzaldúa and AnaLouise Keating, a friend and collaborator of Anzaldúa who has carried on her work posthumously. Maparyan (2012: 115) explains how these authors 'have bravely and boldly – if not systematically – explored how deep spirituality, including metaphysics, mysticism, and the supernatural, as well as orthodox and indigenous forms of religion, interrelate with social/ecological transformation.' Maparyan's womanism has also been inspired by M. Jacqui Alexander (2005) and Akasha Gloria Hull (2001), among others (Ryan, 2005; Holmes, 2002), as feminists who have written extensively about the intersections of African and Black women's spirituality, quantum physics and New Age traditions. As Maparyan (2012: 115) explains, Ryan and Holmes 'inspired me to proceed intrepidly with my refiguration of how Black women's spirituality relates to the whole of humanity and possess/embodies transformative, redemptive and liberatory dimensions that have been underexplored, academically or otherwise.' Spiritual activism, then, can be enacted in all aspects of life, including with/in research. Through spiritualized methodologies, transdisciplinary feminist research opens often untapped realms that incite healing and social change.

Spiritualized methodologies as transdisciplinary feminist research praxis

Spiritualized methodologies have been enacted in ways that rethink approaches within disciplines, and in turn, create new possibilities grounded in multiple vantage points, ideas and research. For example, in education, Rendon (2009/2014) has developed a pedagogy called sentipensante (sensing/thinking) that draws from Indigenous epistemologies, holistic education, learning theories, feminist teaching and critical pedagogy. Her purpose is to create a spiritualized social justice pedagogy that is 'less fragmented and more relational; less autocratic and more democratic; less passive and more active; and less focused on information and facts and more focused on the shared construction of meaning' (Rendon, 2009/2014: 17). Implementing a sentipensante pedagogy asks us to center a curriculum that is

> *multihuman* ... multicultural and humanistic in nature. This is an integrative, transdisciplinary pedagogy that affirms the dignity of and worth of all people and respects and honors diverse ways of accessing truth [including] the traditional scientific paradigm as well as qualitative methods.
> (Rendon, 2009/2014: 139)

In women's studies, Fernandes (2003) has encouraged a feminist practice that promotes not only social transformation but also a spiritual revolution. She writes:

> [T]here is an historic moment now where an individual, regardless of their own personal backgrounds, are beginning to see the interconnections of a fully globalized world; writers and activists have increasingly moved away from older models of social change that focus on single issues to coalition work and to a deeper understanding of the interconnections between what appears to be separate structures of oppression ... [i]n this endeavor, it is critical that we understand that a transformation of such vast structures of inequality must also simultaneously engage in a transformation of spirituality within this world.
>
> (Fernandes, 2003: 15)

Fernandes' arguments stem from an array of women of color theorizing, spiritual leaders and activists to invoke spiritualized transdisciplinary models of engaging in social justice. Though not to create a model for which to follow, there are aspects one can consider to begin to enact a spiritualized engagement with social justice pursuits. Fernandes (2003) offers ideas to contemplate, such as seeing spiritual lessons in the contemporary world and in our lives by radicalizing and liberating the divine in various forms and ways that lead to transformations. Reclaiming the spirit in our work necessitates that projects are conceptualized from multiple vantage points in order to engage as researchers with an interconnected spiritualized world. Thus, transdisciplinary methodologies become central and necessary in these endeavors.

Healing colonial wounds through spiritualized methodologies

Womanists and Chicana/Latina feminists have theorized about suturing our mind/body/spirit splits through energy work, meditation, accessing our spiritual guides and ancestral knowledges, curanderismo (Mexican healing traditions) and mysticism. Gloria Anzaldúa (1990) has urged us to look for and create new teorías and metodologías in order to find solutions to problems and the consequences of oppression and colonization. Anzaldúa has engaged deeply with how to unlearn societal and our own oppressive restraints, offering many tools for healing. Her approaches and life's work have earned her, as Hartley (2010: 135) proclaims, the title of the 'curandera of conquest ... a healer of la herida abierta, the open wound created by the borders that neocolonialism has imposed – borders policing class, national, gender, sexual, racial, and religious divisions.' Research that moves inter-dimensionally, not just across academic disciplines but also among spiritual realms, becomes a transformative and redemptive praxis.

Spiritual praxis: energy work

A central aspect of spiritual praxis is energy work, which entails shifting vibrational frequencies that exist within everything: ourselves as human beings, objects, light and the earth. In this energy expanse, with even thoughts, one can influence her experiences in/with the world and the world itself. Maparyan (2012: 122) explains:

> Scientists have documented that thoughts impact matter [McTaggart, 2007]. The natural implication of this finding is that thoughts, when applied with intentionality, can change things in predictable and desired ways, for the better or the worse. This is the basic foundation upon which spiritual activism rests. In a nutshell, spiritual activism is the conscious transformation of vibration.

Similarly, Anzaldúa's spiritual activism rests upon changes from within to transform the outer world as a cyclical, iterative practice. Inner work not only involves learning the colonial herstories of our-selves, the land and ancestors, but it also involves detoxification of the body and thoughts through spiritual exercises such as meditation. Without this inner work, colonial wounds can diminish our health and wellbeing, and perpetuate forms of oppression that have, at times, been taken on as colonized peoples (Pérez, 1999).

How does energy work change methodology?

When framing our work in academia with the notion of humans as energy transformers (Maparyan, 2012), the purposes for inquiry shift. As mid-career scholars, we have both engaged in research that has social justice aims. Michelle, for instance, has used Black feminist situational analysis to challenge the privatization of public education, and Cinthya has used Chicana feminist testimonios to provide counter-narratives of colonialism in education. While much of this work has resulted in recommendations for outer transformations (such as rethinking pedagogy and how educational reform is conceptualized), we contemplate what inner transformations spiritualized energy work incites. We posit that as women of color that have been profoundly impacted by colonial educational systems (among other systems of oppression), that when we engage in doing the outer work of academic research, we cross spiritual boundaries to coalesce inner work with the outer in order to heal the wounds inflicted by self, culture, patriarchy, racism, heteronormativity and linguicide. This healing can be imagined as putting ourselves back together, or what Anzaldúa (2015) calls the Coyolxauhqui imperative. According to Mexica mythology, Coyolxauhqui was planning to kill her mother, Coatlicue, the goddess of creation and destruction because she became magically pregnant one day by a ball of feathers that fell on her. But upon the birth of Huitzilopochtli, the god of war, to save his mother he dismembered and banished Coyolxauhqui to the sky as the moon.

Anzaldúa (2015: 20) uses the Coyolxauhqui imperative as the 'symbol of for reconstruction and reframing ... an ongoing process of making and unmaking. There is never a resolution, just the process of healing.'

Spiritualized social justice methodologies can be seen as a recursive journey of rebuilding ourselves and communities that leads to an ongoing healing process. As such, the purpose and goals of social justice methodologies must be rethought to include healing of wounds, fragmentation and rationalism that have been imposed on the Self, Others and communities of color. For researchers, this can be seen as a response to Denzin and Lincoln's (2005) call for methodologies that are disruptive, decolonial and that lead to social transformation. We believe that the transdisciplinary nature of Womanist and Chicana feminist spiritualities, when centered in research methodologies, have the potential to create such transformative inner and outer work (Anzaldúa, 1987, 2002, 2015).

One example of spiritualized healing is through the work of curanderismo, or healing that examines an illness of a patient through psychology (mind), the physical (body) and religion (soul, spirit). The roots of curanderismo are from different belief systems such as Judeo-Christian, Arabic, Greek, Indigenous and Western science (Hartley, 2010; Trotter and Chavira, 1981). The approach is to examine all dimensions of illness, dis-ease or imbalance. The curandera/o deals with mind, body and spirit. Reflections upon this inner work, in which we ourselves and our family members have engaged, guide us to think about how our outer work should focus not only on symptoms (e.g., privatization of education or colonial curriculums) but also root causes of such phenomena, including the fragmentation of humanity's bodymindspirit.

From these spiritual considerations, Cinthya has begun to rethink the purposes and roles of research based on her current study with mujeres with low-income status in the borderlands of the U.S. and Mexico. What was designed to be a project about gathering stories to change deficit perspectives of literacy among public housing residents has transformed into research that heals the soul. Cinthya has paid careful attention to how the actual telling of stories, rather than only the stories themselves, has influenced the women's emotional and spiritual wellbeing. Even for Cinthya, the researcher, through sharing her own story and memory of the civil war in Nicaragua, emotions of fear were released that have been buried deep within her body. Healing this fear-based emotion has opened her to develop her inner warrior goddess in order to face other aspects of life with courage and strength. In this way, research has facilitated the transformation of material and emotional/spiritual conditions. This could be a potential encounter for both researchers and participants, to experience healing through a form of curanderismo. What began as the initial purpose of inquiry – changing deficit perspectives of mujeres' literacy – is equally important and needed. However, through spiritualized methodologies, one can also engage with her spiritual selves to work across other dimensions that heal colonial wounds.

Spiritual praxis: interconnectivity

Womanists and Chicana feminists have centralized the interconnections that exist among each other as spiritual beings, including across more than human realms. Examples are encounters with the air, land and wind. Anzaldúa (2012: 58) recalls, 'I remember listening to the voices of the wind as a child and understanding its messages.' In our own life, Cinthya has connected deeply with energies from crystals and has experienced emotional and physical healing that has resulted in positive spiritual changes in her life. Michelle recalls being one with the water and the sand through meditative practices as she negotiated a childhood of abuse, not only to resist and survive gendered and racialized violence, but to also find peace, joy, vitality and serenity (Pérez, 2014).

To cross such dimensions, some have practiced spirit embodiment. When accessing sacred energies through divine figures such as Yemayá, Goddess of the living Ocean, one's corporeality, as Alexander (2005: 322) explains, is:

> Pushed past modernity's mode of reason and [the Spirit has] taken up temporary sojourn on the insides of this artificial enclosure, come to accept, cleanse, to bless, to remind us that in the same way the breaking of the waves does not compromise that cosmic flow to wholeness. The body cannot but surrender in order to make way for this tidal flow.

Engaging in otherworldly encounters can teach us about acknowledging connections between each other, animals and the earth, and provide new ways to reimagine opposition. Oppositions can manifest in an issue one views as problematic, such as an educational policy, or with someone, such as Trump, who has perpetrated (and perpetuated) racist, sexist, nationalist and homophobic (to only name a few) hegemonies. Western thought has imposed a dualistic way of knowing and viewing such people and phenomena. As Maparyan (2012: 153) explains 'even our conceptions of "fighting for the oppressed" often involve taking sides [making] it impossible to realize the oneness of humanity so long as such a dualistic perspective about warring or oppositional factions is maintained.' Theorizing opposition, Alexander (2005: 325–326) suggests:

> One of the effects of constructing a life based principally in opposition is that the ego learns ... simultaneously how to hate.... My point here is not to reduce radical political movements to mass psychologies of hatred. Rather it is to suggest that the field of oscillation between the two might be quite small.... We learn how to hate in our hatred of injustice, and it is these psychic residuals that travel, sometimes silently, sometimes vociferously, into social movements that run aground on the invisible premises of scarcity – alterity driven by separation, empowerment driven by external loss – and of having to prove perpetual injury as the *quid pro quo* to secure ephemeral rights.

As a form of spiritual praxis, attempts to find ways to unpack and rethink opposition can give light to new approaches to negotiating conflict – negotiations that are sought to provoke peace and justice within and outwardly. To actualize this, Maparyan (2012: 197) suggests a radical forgiveness that can cultivate 'a shift in perception that allows one to see the larger spiritual meaning of events,' which can provoke one to reconsider 'the victim/perpetrator duality.' She cautions, however, that radical forgiveness does not imply an '"anything goes" morality' (197), rather it allows for a shift in energies to enact strength and healing, as well as a means to incite 'peacebuilding more broadly' (197).

How does working with/in opposition change methodology?

At the 2018 Reconceptualizing Early Childhood Education Conference (RECE) in Denmark, Norma Rudolph, captured what we view as an example of how one might rethink opposition to an issue or a problem. Rudolph suggests a methodology that shifts from problem solving to appreciation. Based on her work during South African apartheid, Rudolph witnessed how communities became accustomed to people coming in and asking about problems to be solved which, when they were expressed, often felt insurmountable. In the end, the problems discussed wouldn't be resolved, leaving the community feeling just as, or even more, frustrated. As a different approach, Rudolph (2018) has engaged in collective conversation and participatory research focusing on what communities in South Africa felt they were doing well in terms of supporting their livelihoods and activism. From there, communities conceptualized dreams. These included smaller dreams in which action could be taken immediately (based on what the community felt they did well), in addition to 'middle sized' dreams and larger dreams that could be broken into more manageable efforts. This allowed for action to not only be immediate and iterative, but also for an approach that celebrated what the community felt was working for them and to experience small successes with their imagined dreams, ultimately providing energy to take on bigger issues. In considering action-based research, looking to Rudolph's (2018) work encourages a shift in methodology from engaging in opposition with a problem, to starting at what communities believe have been working. From this vantage point, grappling with issues that may feel insurmountable, such as those that stem from colonialism, are viewed and approached differently.

In thinking through oppositions that can occur with others, spiritualized methodologies may help us to reconceptualize where we lay our energies. For instance, what if inquiry sought to engage with (rather than against) oppositional vantage points? Drawing from a larger social example, there has been media coverage over the years about how social justice activists have engaged with members of movements seeped in hatred, such as white nationalism. Daryl Davis is a Black blues musician in the United States who, since the 1980s, has been having conversations with members of the Ku Klux Klan, many of whom have changed their racist viewpoints, and in turn, their participation in the KKK (Burke, 2018). Using Daryl Davis' approach, perhaps the purposes of a spiritualized research praxis would shift to seeking opposition with which to engage, instead of working against it.

To conceptualize the 'how' of this provocation, careful and intentional spiritual practices would need to be sought to provide spiritual guidance and protection. This arises out of the need to acknowledge the dangers that such encounters could pose, especially for women and women of color, and other minoritized people who would consider entering oppositional spaces. Importantly, this is not only the work of minoritized peoples, but also those with social privilege with whom we are interconnected. Working with, rather than against, opposition as a form of spiritualized praxis would not exist without controversy. Daryl's relational approach has been criticized by some in the Black Lives Matter movement, to which he has responded that he believes we need to take a multipronged approach to dismantling oppressions, one that entails movements like Black Lives Matter in addition to changing people's perspectives in order to change the system (Burke, 2018).

We recognize that our example is part of a much larger issue that Rudolph (2018) in her work in South Africa would consider a 'bigger dream,' and is perhaps an advanced effort that initiates multiple, smaller, spiritualized efforts. However, we believe discussing the prospect of such larger possibilities, and looking towards those who have engaged in these forms of spiritual activism, could reimagine why and how we do research.

Expanding transdisciplinary feminist research: Womanist and Chicana feminist spiritual possibilities

This chapter has suggested that transdisciplinarity means more than crossing disciplines, and has argued strongly for the need to include spiritual realms. Feminist methodologies have centered corporality through approaches like performance autoethnography (Spry, 2011), and there has been a growing movement in educational studies, psychology and other fields to recognize the benefits of practices like meditation (Janesick, 2015; Windle et al., 2014). Each of these are openings to a more radicalized methodology that incorporates the Spirit and which seeks to enact a transdisciplinary feminist praxis in which transformative methodologies are possible. Maparyan (2012: 171), in her reflections on Sister Chan Khong's Buddhist activism during times of war, speaks of inspired tenets that can guide transformational praxis. These include cultivating vibrational power, a spiritual community, and a refuge 'whether that refuge is a practice, like mindfulness ... or a spiritual collaboration with one or more other human beings [as] part of self-care, and thus a pillar of social and ecological transformation.' In a similar vein, the provocations discussed in this chapter concern enacting spiritualizing methodologies through energy work and interconnectivity. As we have contemplated these forms of spiritual praxis, we have been compelled to consider the reciprocity of inner and outer work and to question oppositional worldviews. We, therefore, close this chapter with what we consider to be two urgent proposals for incorporating spiritualized praxis as part of transdisciplinary feminist research.

First, we propose that the Western hold on speaking of the Spirit in academic realms be lifted. As we have shown, women of color are engaging in Chicana feminist, Womanist and Black feminist methodologies (among other Global South theories) and have been accessing and utilizing spiritual energies through crystal healing, meditations with ancestors and metaphysical encounters. However, these practices are often not spoken of in mainstream/dominant academic or professional spaces, nor are they explicitly addressed in much women of color scholarship. This rings true for much of our own work. Even though spiritual practices have often guided feminist research, in our experience it has typically only been acknowledged during intimate conversations. As such, spiritualized methodologies remain hidden, even though they are very much alive and active. Writing and talking more about our spiritual practices through research collaborations, during lectures and conferences, and by welcoming dialogue about such approaches with grassroots activist networks are some ways we have used to inspire others to consider their relations in research/with other worlds, and to consider how this re-purposes inquiry toward social justice orientations.

Second, we return to Maparyan's (2012: 171) reflections on Sister Chan Khong's Buddhist activism during times of war: she encourages all to 'do it yourself. Don't wait for authority; do what's needed, exercise leadership where you are, question laws and policies that don't work. Answer only to peace, love, respect, and healing.' This inspires our second proposal – to work within oppositional tensions. We, ourselves, struggle with this point of contention; however, we see much promise and value in making attempts to utilize spiritualized research practices to move us towards collective healing. This is imperative during times of war, conflict, and violence. Feminist transdisciplinary approaches, which may have led to (fragmented) justice and equity for some, have a long way to go to fully actualize emancipation from oppression. One reason may be that we have used the same oppositional, and at times violent tactics, that create and maintain oppression. Spiritualizing methodologies can, we suggest, incite different encounters with social injustice that then incites peacebuilding (as Maparyan has suggested), not just for humanity, but also for the healing needed for Otherbeings and land with which we share the earth. Spiritual methodologies, we suggest, might then offer powerful possibilities by expanding transdisciplinary feminist research to other worldly realms.

References

Alexander, M. J. (2005). *Pedagogies of Crossing Mediations on Feminism, Sexual Politics, Memory, and the Sacred*. Durham, NC: Duke University Press.

Anzaldúa, G. E. (1987). *Borderlands/La Frontera*. San Francisco, CA: Aunt Lute Books.

Anzaldúa, G. E. (1990). Introduction. In G. E. Anzaldúa (Ed.), *Making Face, Making Soul/Haciendo Caras: Creative and Critical Perspectives by Women of Color* (pp. xv–xxviii). San Francisco, CA: Aunt Lute Books.

Anzaldúa, G. E. (2002). Now let us shift ... the path of conocimiento ... inner work, public acts. In G. Anzaldúa and A. Keating (Eds.), *This Bridge We Call Home: Radical Visions for Transformation* (pp. 540–578). New York, NY: Routledge.

Anzaldúa, G. E. (2012). *Borderlands/La Frontera* (4th Edition). San Francisco, CA: Aunt Lute Books.

Anzaldúa, G. E. (2015). Light in the Dark/Luz en lo Oscuro. In A. Keating (Ed.), *Light in the Dark/Luz en los Oscuro: Rewriting Identity, Spirituality, Reality* (pp. 1–257). Durham, NC: Duke University Press.

Burke, C. (January 15, 2018). *How One Black Blues Musician Convinced Dozens of KKK Members to Quit.* CBN NEWS. Retrieved from www1.cbn.com/cbnnews/us/2016/july/how-one-black-blues-musician-changed-25-members-of-the-kkk. Accessed October 31, 2018.

Christian, B. M. (2005). *Belief in Dialogue: U.S. Latina Writers Confront their Religious Heritage.* New York, NY: Other Press.

Delgado Bernal, D., Elenes, C. A., Godinez, F. E. and Villenas, S. (Eds.) (2006). *Chicana/Latina Education in Everyday Life: Feminist Perspectives on Pedagogy and Epistemology.* Albany, NY: State University of New York Press.

Delgadillo, T. (1998). Forms of Chicana feminist resistance: Hybrid spirituality in Ana Castillo's So far from God. *Modern Fiction Studies*, 44(4), 888–916.

Denzin, N. K. and Lincoln, Y. S. (2005). Introduction: The discipline and practice of qualitative research. In N. K. Denzin and Y. S. Lincoln (Eds.), *The Sage Handbook of Qualitative Research* (pp. 1–32). Thousand Oaks, CA: Sage.

Dillard, C. B. (2006). *On Spiritual Strivings: Transforming an African American Woman's Academic Life.* Albany, NY: State University of New York Press.

Dillard, C. B., Abdur-Rashid, D., and Tyson, C. A. (2000). My soul is a witness: Affirming pedagogies of the spirit. *International Journal of Qualitative Studies in Education*, 13(5), 447–462.

Dölling, I. and Hark, S. (2000). She who speaks shadow speaks truth: Transdisciplinarity in women and gender studies. *Signs*, 25(4), 1195–1198.

Elenes, A. C. (2011). *Transforming Borders: Chicana/o Popular Culture and Pedagogy.* Lanham, MD: Lexington Books.

Elenes, A. C. (2014). Spiritual roots of Chicana feminist borderland pedagogies: A spiritual journey with Tonantzin/Guadalupe. In E. Facio and I. Lara (Eds.), *Fleshing the Spirit: Spirituality and Activism in Chicana, Latina, and Indigenous Women's Lives* (pp. 43–58). Tucson, AZ: University of Arizona Press.

Espin, O. M. (1996). *Latina Healers: Lives of Power and Tradition.* Encino, CA: Floricanto Press.

Facio, E. and Lara, I. (Eds.) (2014). *Fleshing the Spirit: Spirituality and Activism in Chicana, Latina, and Indigenous Women's Lives.* Tucson, AZ: University of Arizona Press.

Fernandes, L. (2003). *Transforming Feminist Practice: Non-violence, Social Justice and the Possibilities of a Spiritualized Feminism.* San Francisco, CA: Aunt Lute Books.

Hartley, G. (2010). The curandera of conquest: Gloria Anzaldúa's decolonial remedy. *Aztlan: A Journal of Chicano Studies*, 35(1), 135–162.

Holmes, B. A. (2002). *Race and the Cosmos: An Invitation to View the World Differently.* New York, NY: Bloomsbury.

Hudson-Weems, C. (1993). *Africana Womanism: Reclaiming Ourselves.* Troy, MI: Bedford Publishers.

Hull, A. G. (2001). *Soul Talk: The New Spirituality of African American Women.* Rochester, VT: Inner Traditions.

Janesick, V. J. (2015). *Contemplative Qualitative Inquiry: Practicing the Zen of Research.* Walnut Creek, CA: Left Coast Press.

Keating, A. (2007). *Teaching Transformation: Transcultural Classroom Dialogue.* New York, NY: Palgrave.

Lara, I. (2005). Daughter of Coatlique: An interview with Gloria Anzaldúa. In A. Keating (Ed.), *Entre Mundos/Among Worlds: New Perspectives on Gloria Anzaldúa* (pp. 41–55). New York, NY: Palgrave.

Lara, I. and Facio, E. (2014). Introduction: Fleshing the spirit, spiriting the flesh. In E. Facio and I. Lara (Eds.), *Fleshing the Spirit: Spirituality and Activism in Chicana, Latina, and Indigenous Women's Lives* (pp. 3–17). Tucson, AZ: The University of Arizona Press.

Levine, A. (2005). Champion of the spirit: Anzaldua's critique of the rationalist epistemology. In A. Keating (Ed.), *Entre Mundos/Among Worlds* (pp. 171–184). New York, NY: Palgrave Macmillan.

Maparyan, L. (2012). *The Womanist Idea*. New York, NY: Routledge.

McTaggart, L. M. (2007). *The Intention Experiment: Using your Thoughts to Change your Life and world*. New York, NY: Free Press.

Moraga, C. and Anzaldúa, G. (1983). *This Bridge Called My Back: Writings by Radical Women of Color*. Watertown, MA: Persephone Press.

Ogunyemi, C. O. (1996). *Africa Wo/man Palava: The Nigerian Novel by Women*. Chicago, IL: University of Chicago Press.

Pérez, E. (1999). *The Decolonial Imaginary: Writing Chicanas Into History*. Bloomington, IN: Indiana University Press.

Pérez, M. S. (2014). Complicating 'victim' narratives: Childhood agency within violent circumstances. *Global Studies of Childhood*, 4(2), 126–134.

Rendon, L. I. (2009/2014). *Sentipensante (Sensing/Thinking) Pedagogy: Education for Wholeness, Social Justice and Liberation*. Starling, VA: Stylus Publishing, LLC.

Roth, B. (2003). *Separate Roads to Feminism: Black, Chicana, and White Feminist Movements in America's Second Wave*. Cambridge: Cambridge University Press.

Rudolph, N. (2018). *Resisting Dominant Discourses in Early Childhood Policy: Reinvigorating Collective Activism that Ended Apartheid in South Africa*. Paper presented at the 26th Reconceptualizing Early Childhood Education Conference, Copenhagen, Denmark.

Ryan, J. S. (2005). *Spirituality as Ideology in Black Women's Film and Literature*. Charlottesville, VA: University of Virginia Press.

Saavedra, C. M. and Pérez, M. S. (2017). Chicana/Latina feminist critical qualitative inquiry: Meditations on global solidarity, spirituality, and the land. *International Review of Qualitative Research*, 10(4), 450–467.

Sandford, S. (2015). Contradiction of terms: Feminist theory, philosophy, and transdisciplinarity. *Theory, Culture, and Society*, 32(5–6), 159–182.

Spry, T. (2011). *Body, Paper, Stage: Writing and Performing Autoethnography*. Walnut Creek, CA: Left Coast Press.

Trotter, R. T. and Chavira, J. A. (1981). *Curanderismo: Mexican American Folk Healing*. Athens, GA: The University of Georgia Press.

Walker, A. (1983). *In Search of Our Mother's Gardens*. New York, NY: Harcourt Brace Jovanovich.

Windle, C., Newsome, S., Waldo, M. and Adams, E. M. (2014). Mindfulness and group therapy: Mindfulness-based stress reduction and dialectical behavior therapy groups. In J. DeLucia-Waack, C. Kalodner, and M. Riva (Eds.), *The Handbook of Group Counseling and Psychotherapy* (2nd Edition) (pp. 474–483). Thousand Oaks, CA: Sage.

12 Hear me roar

Sound feminisms and qualitative methodologies

Walter S. Gershon

Introduction: Resounding feminisms, or what would feminism sound like?

The past two decades have seen a good deal of attention to the many ways that women and girls have been silenced and, conversely, the significance of their voices (Oliveros, 2005; Rogers, 2010). Further, there is a long tradition of attending to questions of sound from a feminist perspective (Cooper, 1892; Chow and Steintrager, 2011; Love, 2012; Salvaggio, 1998). While feminist perspectives on voice and silence strongly inform the backbone of contemporary qualitative research methods (Behar, 1996; Bhattacharya, 2017; Lather, 1991), how transfeminist qualitative research might be applied to, activated by, or otherwise engage sound methods, is generally overlooked.

As Samantha Pinto (2016) makes clear, there is a Black and feminist sound study. However, although there are overtures to sound and soundscape, the focus is most often musical rather than sonic. This is a false distinction in many regards, for music is comprised of sounds and a central form of sonic expression is music. Nevertheless, a distinction between scholarship primarily focused on the sonic rather than on a particular kind of sound or music is a helpful heuristic. Further complicating matters, Pinto (2016) argues that sound studies cannot be feminist because of its masculinist histories, understandings and practices. In linking sonic studies to masculinist approaches, Pinto incidentally presses back at avowedly feminist methodological approaches to the sonic (Oliveros, 2005), not that Pinto is incorrect about the masculinist constraints of those structures.

The central point here is nonetheless significant: there has long been attention to music and talk in qualitative research from a variety of perspectives, along with longstanding concerns about the gendered nature of talk and music, and their patriarchal normative false assumptions (Cooper, 1892; De Graaf, 2008; Diamond, 2010; Hale, 1994; Oliveros and Maus, 1994). This continuing absence of women and girls in awareness and citation forms a feedback loop of intentionally dampened resonances and reverberations, a null curriculum (Flinders, Noddings and Thornton, 1986).

What, then, might a critical qualitative transfeminist sonic methodology sound like and how might it function in practice? This chapter articulates possible answers to this still open question. It does so in the spirit of Aunt Hester's (Moten, 2003) and Abbey Lincoln's scream in Max Roach's 'Freedom Suite/Triptych (Prayer/Protest/Peace)' (Holiday, 2016), Pauline Oliveros' (2005) calls to deep listening, Cathy Lane's (2016) articulation of often missing voices of women and girls in sound arts, my own calls for sonic arts-based research (Gershon and Guy, in press), and ongoing conversations in feminist qualitative research practices noted above. Methodologically centering the voices of women of color and girls, these understandings are filtered through braided transdisciplinary feminist theories where resonances necessarily grate yet are given the space to ring out without being resolved either in the sense of being 'solved' or subsumed under another form, including other feminisms. Together, these methodological reverberations form an impossibly entangled polyphonic cacophony of interrelated understandings, an inseparability of theoretical possibilities and material practices I have come to call ways of beingknowingdoing (Gershon, 2017: 2).

Consider, for example, a few of the many fields and disciplines that attend to sound feminisms: affect theory, anthropology, critical Black and Brown feminisms, ethnomusicology, (critical) improvisation studies, musicology, qualitative methodologies, queer studies, sociology, sensory studies, sound studies, women's studies. In addition, there is this singular braid in the tapestry: from an arts-based research perspective, every woman who has composed, played, orchestrated, edited or otherwise worked on musical practices at any time, in any way, in any place can be conceptualized as a feminist qualitative researcher.

Really.

In light of such complications, this chapter traces critical feminist tendencies in conceptualizing and enacting qualitative research in, with and through sound. It does so by addressing three potential pathways, three understandings that echo ongoing interventions and developments in critical feminist sound making: attunement, embodiment, alterity, silence and noise, the impossibility of hearing, and affect. Each section is grounded in a different set of parameters and scholarship that indicates how such feminisms might be conceptualized through the sonic. As with the chapter as a whole, these are offered as resonances and reverberations of feminist sonorities among ongoing waves of potential expressions.

Feminisms can be understood as that which in some fashion addresses the power and potential of the feminine without the need for comparison to maleness; as efforts oriented to working towards liberation and equality for all who identify as female. As this volume indicates, there are myriad positions, theoretical, material and otherwise, that can be categorized as feminisms (see Humm, 1992; Nash, 2019). Of the many gifts critical feminisms has given qualitative research, perhaps most central is the construct of reflexivity (Anzaldúa, 2015; Lorde, 1986; St. Pierre and Pillow, 2000), and reflexivity resonates deeply in feminist approaches to the sonic – as can be heard, for example, in Pauline Oliveros' understandings of deep listening (Oliveros, 2010; Oliveros and Maus, 1994), and others whose work examines the intersection of feminisms and sound (Bresler, 2005; Koskoff, 2014).

What could feminist methods sound like?

1. Attunement

Andra McCartney (2006) provides one possible answer in her chapter in *How am I to Listen to You?: Soundwalking, Intimacy and Improvised Listening*. McCartney's argument about love, relation and the intentionality of listening for her soundwalking is grounded in Luce Irigaray's (1996) *I Love to You: Sketch of a Possible Felicity in History*. Here is the passage from Irigaray that McCartney's chapter takes up:

> I am listening to you, as to another who transcends me, requires a transition to a new dimension. I am listening to you: I perceive what you are saying, I am attentive to it, I am attempting to understand and hear your intention. Which does not mean: I comprehend you, I know you, so I do not need to listen to you and I can even plan a future for you. No, I am listening to you as someone and something I do not know yet, on the basis of a freedom and an openness put aside for this moment. I am listening to you: I encourage something unexpected to emerge, some becoming, some growth, some new dawn, perhaps. I am listening to you prepare the way for the not-yet-coded, for silence, for a space for existence, initiative, free intentionality, and support for your becoming.
>
> (Irigaray, cited in McCartney, 2006: 53–54)

McCartney (2006: 57) states that, 'when I am introducing soundwalks, I encourage participants to engage in intimate listening; that is, listening to the sound environment as if it were a dear friend or lover.' This intimacy, the depth of attention necessary to really hear another, is what McCartney seeks to engender in her process:

> I want to listen openly, creatively, alert to the moment and to the chance, improvising ... When I am out doing individual listening and recording work for a sound project, it is the moments of discovery that teach me the most, that engage me most strongly.
>
> (Ibid.: 58)

What is perhaps most significant here is a vulnerability of receptivity. For, what McCartney is after are moments in her decades-long practices of soundwalking that surprise her in ways that she can hear something she had not previously considered. She is asking of the world: how can I listen to you? While McCartney's focus is on attention to the fluid, liminal ecologies that are part of her and of which she is part as she moves, each nested in scales of yet another nested set of environments, her practice is reflexive in its entirety. How to consider encounters of all kinds in ways that operate in an intimate ethics of interruption? How can I listen to you so that I might hear beyond myself? How can I work to transcend the impossibility of my self so that I might be simultaneously a) more aware of the infinite resonances and their reverberations to which I am not attuned, and b) become more than I already am through such attunement?

Becoming attuned is, then, a relational reflexivity that acknowledges significance outside the self for the purpose of becoming aware of one's own biases and assumptions in order to gain knowledges. Reflexivity is not only critically seeking to notice and attend to one's proclivities but also to be in dialogue with others in positions to aid in those processes. As McCartney (2006: 60) writes, thinking with Ellen Waterman (2006) and Waterman's construction of 'creative improvising:'

> I want to find a way of making soundwalks that encourage the kind of listening Waterman describes [as] 'intersubjective and dialogic,' where the focus is less on sensitizing numbed listeners to the sound environment and more on exploring the multiple ways that people listen, and how those ways of listening are conjoined, during the silence of the walk and the flow of the conversation after it, in reciprocal exchange.

Attunement requires a degree of generosity, of vulnerability, the possibility that one may well need to alter one's own understandings, a letting go of certitude and a giving in to the sonority of moments. It is an encouragement to truly pause and listen to a polyphonic, especially when it is silences that speak volumes (Jardine, 2004; Miller, 2005; Vogelin, 2010). Such attunement is deeply complex, in its everyday and extra-ordinary resonances, in that it works via a form of sonic reflexivity and an embodied entanglement with nested and layered ecologies. It is that beingknowingdoing I referred to earlier which brings one's own predilections into a deeply reflexive awareness of things outside of one's self. Attunement is – bringing together McCartney, Oliveros, Irigaray and Édouard Glissant – deep listening to the entangled rhizomes that are poetics in relation.

2. Vibrational affects: resonances, reverberations and reverb

Sounds impact things and ecologies in a never-ending stream of vibrational affects, resonances that reverberate, continually moving, amplified and dampened, waves in crests and troughs, decaying only to be replaced by others. A constant cacophony that impacts things – flora and fauna, water and land, alike – as much as those things themselves are vibrating, sending waves of their own while refracting and reflecting waves from outside, vibrational affects that travel as much through as around things (Gershon, 2013, 2017, 2018).

As with other fields of study, such as area studies and political theorizing, affect has also become central in fields associated with sound (Thompson and Biddle, 2013). However, as Ana Hofman (2015) argues about ethnomusicology, affect and being sonically affected has long been part of theorizing relations between environments, people and the organized sounds they create and express (music and talk). While it must be recognized that recent turns in affect and relational ontology are unnecessary for those whose conceptualizations already partake of complexities and interconnectedness, for example, those who live in/with Indigenous ontologies or Aboriginal Dreamtime, for those seeking to move beyond Enlightenment dualisms and paternalisms, new materialisms have been a boon in two significant interrelated areas (Berlant, 2011; Bennett, 2010; Massumi, 2015): conceptualizing relations and movement and the language utilized to describe such processes. These understandings are outgrowths of Gilles Deleuze's (1995) and Deleuze and Guattari's (1987) theorizing.

At the core of affects are an understanding of the inescapable inseparability of all things, the significance of their relationalities, and the centrality of ontologies. From this vantage, humans are no longer central to ecologies but parts of them and all things become agential, flattening relations, the stapler and the paper and the person and the tree, each acting upon the other. Following Deleuze, and often Guattari, affect theorists refer to relations as intertwined and entangled and understandings of those relationalities as an assemblage, a mesh of entangled associations. In a similar vein, Barad (2007) and others (Kohn, 2013; Tsing, 2015) make a theoretical move to deploy physical science to conceptualize human and interspecies relationalities in flatter ontologies, which means that new materialisms might also have the possibility if not the inclination to overlook aspects of oppression, violence and aggression (Gershon, 2016). It is for this and associated reasons that I find myself much more aligned with affect when placed through Weheliye (2014), Katherine McKittrick's (2006, 2015), and Sylvia Wynter-inspired takes on affect and being affected. Theirs is an attention to the significance of affect that firmly retains the human, not as a means to ignore the ecologies in which humans exist but, rather, as a means to examine contexts and impacts of affect on bodies towards justice and liberation or oppression (Gumbs, 2016; Sharpe, 2016; Stewart, 2007). In terms of sound studies, these social justice conceptualizations of affect as entangled in questions of race and of noise are closely aligned to Brandon LaBelle's (2018) most recent work on sonic agencies, Weheliye's (2000, 2005, 2014) understandings of Black sonorities, Jennifer Stoever's (2016) discussions of affects of race that echo Mark M. Smith's (2008) historical discussions and Fred Moten's (2017) responses to Glissant and Spiller.

These works share a theoretical understanding of two other areas of attention in sonic studies: resonances and reverberations (Erlmann, 2010; Price, 2011). Operating from an understanding that vibrational affects are ubiquitous, in the same way playing a certain pitch on a saxophone will cause a glass to ring, their relations are forms of resonance, sympathetic sonic attunements. While the ongoing, always already present nature of vibrational affects is an ontological inescapability, resonances and reverberations are not apolitical but are instead intentionally amplified and dampened depending on who has the power to do so (Gershon, 2013, 2017, 2018). Thus, sounds are agential in that they move in ways that impact things as much as things impact sounds (Gershon, 2013; LaBelle, 2018; Thompson, 2017). Sounds can also be used by those who have agency and, as Ortner (2006) reminds us, just as there is no outside of power (Foucault, 1991) so too is there no outside of agency. This is precisely how minority perspectives survive: by people using their available agency in the face of ongoing dominant groups and individuals' oppression and suppression. This is why sonic practices as decolonizing research (as for example McKittrick, 2016; Pedri-Spade, 2016; Wynter, 2003, 1984, 1989) are so important.

Attention to vibrational affects as resonances and reverberations provide important methodological possibilities for qualitative researchers in two central ways. First, anything can resonate with any other thing and those reverberations can trigger further resonances and reverberations. They provide a language and a theoretical means for considering relationships between or within ecologies, between or within any and all things, also as their own lines of flight and entanglements. Second, resonances and reverberations are political. Their examination can reveal seemingly hidden patterns that work rhizomatically, tracing trajectories over time, amplified and dampened by event, context, thing (including people) and their combinations. From this perspective, ideas, ideals and processes are always connected to other understandings and experiences, and human relations are audibly reflexive and responsive: one always emits, reflects, refracts and otherwise engages resonances and reverberations, as much as one is pressed by them. We are constantly bombarded and emit sounds regardless of their audibility for humans. Conceptualizing ecologies, things and the patterns they produce underscores the necessarily polyphonic nature of human experiences. Similar to Bakhtin's (1983) argument for heteroglossia, resonance and reverberation insist on the multiplicity of all things. Just as one cannot close an earlid the way one can blink an eye (Kim-Cohen, 2009), a sonic awareness reminds us that any such singularities are in fact questions of framing that are quite literally impossible with sounds. As Gloria Anzaldúa (2015) and Eve Kosofsky Sedgwick (2003) argue, one cannot split or foreground an aspect of self without creating loss, false splits and errors of equivalency. In sum, vibrational affects, resonances and reverberations entail attunement as attention to the world around one's self.

3. Voice, silence and noise

Questions of voice, silence and noise are deeply interconnected with one another, in embodied material and theoretically methodological ways, and are central to many trajectories of feminisms (Lane, 2016; Miller, 2005; Spivak, 1988). They are similarly central to questions of organized sounds, music and talk, as well as having relations to feminisms (Cash, 1991; Viswaseran, 1994; Walker-Hill, 1992). Given ongoing discussions about the significance of voice, silence and noise across fields and disciplines (Bonnenfant, 2018; Erickson, 2004), this section first speaks to the ocular nature of correctness, then places two arguments about voice, silence, noise and the feminine in conversation to contribute another set of methodological potentialities and cautionary parameters.

Reflecting her life's work in qualitative methodologies and musicalities, Liora Bresler (1995, 2004, 2005, 2015) attends to musical aspects of musicianship such as form, timbre and polyphony, and addresses what she calls 'Doing and Becoming as a Nested Participation' via five interrelated themes: improvisation, empathy, embodiment, three-pronged connection and collaborative research. Where empathy, embodiment and collaboration are now well-traveled paths in qualitative methodologies, improvisation and three-pronged connection are not. Bresler explains (2005: 178) that three-pronged connection – one that is central to processes of making music and understandings from which qualitative researchers might gain important insights – is the combination of 'reaching towards the phenomenon under study,' 'reaching into oneself, to unravel subjectivities and values as shaping perception and interpretation' and 'reaching to the audience.' Likewise, improvising, in all its forms, is an underutilized and undervalued resource for qualitative researchers in education.

Fredrick Erickson's (1984, 2002) life's work at the intersection of talk, social theory and education documents the significance of improvising. While Erikson is one of a very few qualitative researchers to document the deep skills and negotiations of everyday talk, its improvisational nature, and the significance of that improvising, what sets Erickson's work apart is his ability to interpose musical notation with transcriptions of talk to note their deep similarities, how that talk is contextualized by sociocultural pathways through which talk constrains, enables and engenders particular trajectories and theoretical implications for talk in understanding our worlds and one another.

The remaining points in this section continue conversations about the challenges and potential for talk about voice, silence and noise in qualitative research methods, for, just because something is complex doesn't mean that it is necessarily not either normed or need of un-straightening. As Brent Davis and Dennis Sumara (2006) elucidate, constructs for right, straight and correct, all have to do with mathematical linearity that were then given ethical heft over time. What once was linear is good and what was not, was not. The same with

> the notion of normal [that] originally referred to a carpenter's square. As the adjective version for the noun *norma*, normal was used to describe angles that were reasonably close to 90 in much the same way the word "circular" is used for shapes that are reasonably close to being round.
>
> (Davis and Sumara, 2006: 41)

This understanding makes even more apparent concerns about utilizing constructs such as 'normal' in sound methodologies, given its ocular derivation and which has tipped the balance away from the sonic. The other difficulty with understandings of hearing something 'correctly' or perceiving a sound as 'normal' is that not only are such constructs unhelpful for understanding an always messy, never linear sound (wave forms) but they are also physically impossible. Due to the ways that physical hearing and the ear (otology) combine with liminally haptic resonances and reverberations of media involved in hearing (sounds move from one space to another through solids, liquids, gasses and fluctuate), hearing 'correctly' is impossible. Just as you do not hear yourself as others hear you, you do not hear what someone says, or a sound from any source, precisely the way others do. What is normal in hearing is actually already queered. Or, people always already mishear (Gershon, 2017, 2018).

A central theme in Marie Thompson's (2016, 2017) scholarship has been attention to relations between the feminine and noise. Thompson (2016: 86) 'outline[s] various intersections of noise and femininity through which noise has been feminized and the feminine has been produced as noise.' Significantly, Thompson argues that, although 'feminine silence has been construed as "virtuous" … the feminine shares with noise connotations of disorder, chaos, complexity, and excess' (87). Further, 'vocalisations and speech deemed feminine have often been construed as negatively noisy' (87).

Thompson's position echoes Jane Roland Martin's (1981) argument about how an ideal of the educated person places girls and women in a double bind, making its attainment a gender-bound impossibility. Education, Martin (1981: 101) argues, at once excludes women from curriculum and knowledge and then constructs women according to men's images, biases and deficit perspective; thus patriarchy ensures that the feminine is always a deficit position to the masculine, while they 'deny the truly feminine qualities she does possess.' According to this logic, if women behave like men, they are negatively judged for not being women and alienate themselves from their selves and experiences; if women behave like women, they do not express the male-gendered traits of the ideal for an educated person. Although such framing hurts women in ways it does not hurt men and is undeniably oppressive, this framing hurts both women and men in the narrowness of definitions for gender and knowledge.

Echoing significant resonances with the scholarship of Mark M. Smith (2008) and Jennifer Stoever (2016), Thompson (2016) notes that the sexist sociocultural norms and values that render the feminine noisy deepen further when heard through social class and what Stoever (2016) calls 'the sonic color line.' If women are noisy, working class women are more so than middle class women; if white women are noisy, Black women are necessarily more so. As they intersect, a poor white woman will be heard as less noisy than a poor woman of African descent. Such knowledges are rooted in historical constructions: in the American South, for example, poor white sharecroppers marked themselves as Black sharecroppers' betters by making sonic differences into socio-cultural differences (M. M. Smith, 2008).

It is this hidden curriculum – the often-implied norms and values students are taught through educational processes – that Signithia Fordham's (1993) now-foundational work, *'Those Loud Black Girls:' (Black) Women, Silence, and Gender 'Passing' in the Academy* address. In another version of a double bind, African American young women cannot be feminine because they are not men but also because their very selves cannot possibly embody the necessary whiteness that serves as a baseline for feminine norms and values. Their resistance is often sonic: pressing into the 'nothingness' of the double bind with their loudness, part of a system of interrelated oppressions that tend to negatively impact Black girls' and women's academic achievement in school. Such knowledges reverberate with Carter G. Woodson's (1933) argument about the impossibility of lynching without Black students' educational lynching in school, and with Boni Wozolek, Lindsey Wootton and Aaron Demlow's (2017) talk about queer teens and suicide that they call the school-to-coffin pipeline. Such studies underscore the ongoing nature and damage of such sonic misogynoir.

Finally, Thompson (2016: 87) adds another key distinction in her discussion of sound, warning 'against the conflation of the two terms' feminine/feminized and, 'by extension, the hurried labeling of [such] projects and artworks in inherently "feminist" – or indeed "not feminist."' For Thompson, the difference between feminized and feminist noise is that feminist noise works towards justice and liberation. Stepping back a layer of scale, Thompson provides doubled means for disrupting or playing outside the kinds of double binds presented above. Her arguments indicate the construction of noise as a sociocultural construction rather than fact and provide ammunition to support claims that women and girls can utilize noise to their advantage. Such work complexifies notions that if noise exists, it can work for rather than against women; if it doesn't, they are sonic differences rather than sonic deficits.

This reclaiming of sound feminisms and their intersections with race, class and queerness also resonates with Fred Moten's (2017) opening arguments in *Black and Blur*. Explicitly grounded in the work of Black feminists, Moten makes a case for the analytic and liberatory possibilities for sonic Blackness. From the theoretical, talk of amplification and harmonics, to the material, expressed as the trilogy 'consent not to be a single being' (Moten, 2017, 2018a, 2018b). Arguing for sound aesthetics as central to both Black study and blackness, Moten (2017: xii) states that: 'jazz does not disappear the problem; it is the problem.' Following a discussion that winds through questions about jazz as an unsolvable problem, including whether an aporia is a problem or its avoidance, Moten (2017: xiii) arrives at the following: 'Then, this absent problem ... is the problem of the alternative whose emergence is not in redress's impossibility but rather in its exhaustion. Aunt Hester's scream is that exhaust.' Moten (2017: xiii) continues:

> This is why, as Wadada Leo Smith has said, it hurts to play this music. The music is a riotous solemnity, a terrible beauty. It hurts so much that we have to celebrate. That we have to celebrate is what hurts so much.

This exhaustion of the push–pull of suffering is how Moten defines Black study; Black feminism is 'the anti*mater*ial ecology of black and thoughtful stolen life as it steals away' (ibid.).

Moten's mode adds to the above understandings of voice, silence and noise. If that which is noise speaks against categorization, at once diffuse, exhausting and present, then the very sounds to which one often pays least attention might hold the most significant understandings. In a similar fashion, following in the footfalls of Black, Brown, Indigenous, and queer feminisms, how women's voices and silences move from being feminine to doing tools for the work of feminism, sound feminisms are that exhaust, the irreducibly complex, liminally powerful presence that obliterates commonplace constructions and, yet again, gives birth to new possibilities (Anzaldúa, 2015; Sedgwick, 2003; Sharpe, 2016; Taylor, 2017).

Combined, these theoretical understandings have practical implications for qualitative researchers, particularly those working with the sonic in transdisciplinary ways. In attuning oneself to the impossibility of singularities, sound feminisms insist on hearing sounds within and outside of dominant, patriarchal socio-cultural constructions. It is in pressing in this fashion that we can better interrupt our understandings and more deeply learn how others use their available agency to shape their ecologies as well as how those ecologies continue to shape all the things that reside within, including peoples and their relations to all things and ecologies. For, how else will we perceive not only how resonances and reverberations are amplified and dampened but also that, when doing sound feminist qualitative research, we too become the problem, the irreducible presence for giving birth to new paths for justice and liberation?

Conclusion

Praise and thanks to our foremothers
Who knew as much and told us to
Listen
Child, listen!
Who pressed so we could
Be
Knew we could be then made us
Literally
Felt the breath in the silence
Were loud
Grinned in the face of fools
Put themselves between us and harm
Pushed us to be ourselves
Got their feet as they were pushed
Screamed
Our existence
From their exhaust
So that we too might
Hear

Positing one possible combination of reverberating resonances, this chapter provides three central arguments that take seriously Samantha Pinto's (2016) critiques about the masculinist nature of sound studies and the potential for sound feminisms in transdisciplinary qualitative research. First, yes. Yes, sounds of all kinds are deeply masculinist expressions of ongoing patriarchies, misogynoir, and anti-feminine(presenting)-queerness. It is always high time for their interruption at all times across all fields and disciplines, including sound studies.

Second, the notion that sound studies, and associated sound methodologies including all forms of composition regardless of its mode of expression (as graphic score, traditional Western Art Music notation, transmitted through thousands of years by example, poems, novels, etc.), is both by men and masculinist is simultaneously a deeply false and dangerous narrative to continue to evoke. Sounds are central to our worlds and their presence and use offer ways to do serious counter-patriarchal, counter-whiteness work; continuing to privilege masculinist constructions limits our worlds, harms over half of the world's population and contributes to injustice rather than liberation.

Third, this chapter documents multiple ways that sound feminisms can positively shape qualitative research methodologies and its potential for feminist transdisciplinary research possibilities. It has sought to introduce readers to the scale of the problem and some of the key ways in which feminist sonic methodologies function in practice; it has noted how sound feminisms retain central understandings in feminist theorizings, speak to key tonal centers of feminisms in qualitative research methodologies such as reflexivity and power, and can be utilized in concert to powerful affects and effects. My aim has not been to document any kind of definitive expression of linearity, rather to offer one of many possible trajectories for sound feminisms in qualitative methodologies.

Finally, in addition to noting that my own musical life has been deeply and irrevocably impacted by women, not least of whom is my sister from another mother Maura Bank who was my first percussion teacher, this chapter would not have happened without listening to a long list of feminists whose sounds and spirits helped me along this path. Given the already generous space I have been provided, this reference list can be found by selecting the following QR code.

These are usually the citations that fall by the wayside when we write, reading twice or three times the works cited. In this case, sound feminisms insist that I make transparent the silences so that their powerful impact on my thinking can be acknowledged. This too is but a partial list of all the pieces I've read over time and is offered as another set of starting places for those interested in sound or sonic feminisms. A playlist with examples of their work can be found using the QR code below. The soul stirring is theirs, the errors here are mine.

References

Anzaldúa, G. (2015). *Light in the Dark: Rewriting Identity, Spirituality, Reality*, A. Keating (Ed.). Durham, NC: Duke University Press.

Bakhtin, M. M. (1983). *The Dialogic Imagination: Four Essays*. Trans. M. Holquist. Austin, TX: University of Texas Press.

Barad, K. (2007). *Meeting the Universe Halfway. Quantum Physics and the Entanglement of Matter and Meaning*. Durham, NC: Duke University Press.

Behar, R. (1996). *The Vulnerable Observer: Anthropology that Breaks your Heart*. Boston, MA: Beacon Press.

Bennett, J. (2010). *Vibrant Matter: A Political Ecology of Things*. Durham, NC: Duke University Press.

Berlant, L. (2011). *Cruel Optimism*. Durham, NC: Duke University Press.

Bonnenfant, Y. (2018). Voice, identity contact [Special Issue]. *Journal of Interdisciplinary Voice Studies*, 3(2).

Bresler, L. (1995). The subservient, co-equal, affective, and social integration styles and their implications for the arts. *Arts Education Policy Review*, 96(5), 31–37.

Bresler, L. (Ed.) (2004). *Knowing Bodies, Moving Minds: Towards Embodied Teaching and Learning*. New York, NY: Springer.

Bresler, L. (2005). What musicianship can teach educational research. *Music Education Research*, 7(2), 169–183.

Bresler, L. (2015). Toward connectedness: Aesthetically based research. *Studies in Art Education*, 48(1), 52–69.

Bhattacharya, K. (2017). *Fundamentals of Qualitative Research*. New York, NY: Routledge.

Cash, A. H. (1991). Feminist theory and music: Toward a common language [Conference Report]. *The Journal of Musicology*, 9(4), 521–532.

Chow, R. and Steintrager, J. A. (2011). The sense of sound [Special Issue]. *Differences: A Journal of Feminist Cultural Studies*, 22 (1–2).

Cooper, A. C. (1892). *A Voice for the South by a Black Woman from the South*. Xenia, OH: Aldine Printing House.

Davis, B. and Sumara, D. (2006). *Complexity and Education: Inquiries into Learning, Teaching, and Research*. New York, NY: Routledge.

De Graaf, M. J. (2008). 'Never call us lady composers': Gendered receptions in the New York Composer's Forum, 1935–1940. *American Music*, 26(3), 277–308.

Deleuze, G. (1995). *Difference and Repetition*. Trans. P. Patton. New York, NY: Columbia University Press.

Deleuze, G. and Guattari, F. (1987). *A Thousand Plateaus: Capitalism and Schizophrenia*. Trans. B. Massumi. Minneapolis, MN: University of Minnesota Press.

Diamond, B. (2010). Native American contemporary music: The women. *The World of Music*, 52(1), 387–414.

Erickson, F. (1984). Classroom discourse as improvisation: Relationships between academic task structure and social participation structure in lessons. In L. C. Wilkinson (Ed.), *Communicating in the Classroom* (pp. 153–181). New York, NY: Academic Press.

Erickson, F. (2002). *Talk and Social Theory: Ecologies of Speaking and Learning in Everyday Life*. Malden, MA: Polity Press.

Erlmann, V. (2010). *Reason and Resonance: A History of Modern Aurality*. Cambridge, MA: Zone Books.

Flinders, D. J., Noddings, N. and Thornton, S. J. (1986). The null curriculum: It's theoretical basis and practical implications. *Curriculum Inquiry*, 16(1), 33–42.

Fordham, S. (1993). 'Those loud Black girls': (Black) women, silence, and gender 'passing' in the academy. *Anthropology and Education Quarterly*, 24(1), 3–32.

Foucault, M. (1991). *Discipline and Punish: The Birth of the Prison*, A. Sheridan, (Trans.) (2nd Ed.). New York, NY: Vintage.

Gershon, W. S. (2013). Vibrational affect: Sound theory and practice in qualitative research. *Cultural Studies ↔ Critical Methodologies*, 13(4), 257–262.

Gershon, W. S. (2016). The sound of silence: The material consequences of scholarship. In N. Snaza, S. E. Truman, D. Sonu and Z. Zowiska (Eds.), *Pedagogical Matters: New Materialisms and Curriculum Studies*. New York, NY: Peter Lang.

Gershon, W. S. (2017). *Sound Curriculum: Sonic Studies in Educational Theory, Method, and Practice*. New York, NY: Routledge.

Gershon, W. S. (2018). Reverberations and reverb: Sound possibilities for narrative, creativity, and critique. *Qualitative Inquiry*. [Online First], doi: 10.1177/1077800418807254

Gershon, W. S. and Guy, C. (2020). Policing normalcy: Men of Color speak back at a Ridiculously White Institution. *Cultural Studies ↔ Critical Methodologies*, 20(1), 52–62.

Gumbs, A. P. (2016). *Spill: Scenes of Black Feminist Fugitivity*. Durham, NC: Duke University Press.

Hale, T. A. (1994). Griottes: Female voices from West Africa. *Research in African Literatures*, 25(3), 71–91.

Holiday, H. (2016). Abby Lincoln's scream: Poetic improvisation as a way of life. *Poetry Foundation*. Retrieved from www.poetryfoundation.org/harriet/2016/10/abbey-lincolns-scream-poetic-improvisation-as-a-way-of-life

Hofman, A. (2015). The affective turn in ethnomusicology. *Музикологија /Musicology*, 18, 35–55, doi: 10.2298/MUZ1518035H

Humm, M. (1992). *Feminisms: A Reader*. London: Routledge.

Irigaray, L. (1996). *I Love To You: Sketch for a Felicity within History*. New York, NY: Routledge.

Jardine, D. (2004). A bell ringing in the empty sky. In W. F. Pinar (Ed.), *Contemporary curriculum discourses: Twenty years of JCT* (pp. 262–277). New York, NY: Peter Lang.

Kim-Cohen, S. (2009). *In the Blink of an Ear: Toward a Non-cochlear Sound Art*. New York, NY: Continuum.

Kohn, E. (2013). *How Forests Think: Toward an Anthropology Beyond the Human*. Berkeley, CA: University of California Press.

Koskoff, E. (2014). *A Feminist Ethnomusicology: Writings on Music and Gender*. Urbana, IL: University of Illinois Press.

LaBelle, B. (2018). *Sonic Agency: Sound and Emergent Forms of Resistance*. London: Goldsmiths Press.

Lane, C. (2016). Why not our voices? *Women and Music: Journal of Gender and Culture*, 20, 26–110.

Lather, P. (1991). *Getting Smart: Feminist Research and Pedagogy Within/in the Postmodern*. New York, NY: Routledge.

Lorde, A. (1986). *Sister Outsider: Essays and Speeches by Audre Lorde*. Berkeley, CA: Ten Speed Press.

Love, B. (2012). *Hip Hop's Li'l Sistas Speak: Negotiating Hip Hop Identities and Politics in the New South*. New York, NY: Peter Lang.

Massumi, B. (2015). *Politics of Affect*. New York, NY: Polity.

Martin, J. R. (1981). The ideal of the educated person. *Educational Theory*, 31(2), 97–109.

McCartney, A. (2006). Gender, genre and electroacoustic soundmaking practices. *Intersections*, 26(2), 20–48, doi: 10.7202/1013224ar

McKittrick, K. (2006). *Demonic Grounds: Black Women and the Cartography of Struggle*. Minneapolis, MN: University of Minnesota Press.

McKittrick, K. (Ed.). (2015). *Sylvia Wynter: On Being Human as Praxis*. Durham, NC: Duke University Press.

McKittrick, K. (2016). Rebellion/invention/groove. *Small Axe*, 49, 79–91.

Miller, J. (2005). *Sounds of Silence Breaking: Women, Autobiography, Curriculum*. New York, NY: Peter Lang.

Moten, F. (2003). *In the break: The Aesthetics of the Black Radication Tradition*. Minneapolis, MN: University of Minnesota Press.

Moten, F. (2017). *Black and Blur* (consent not to be a single being). Durham, NC: Duke University Press.

Moten, F. (2018a). *Stolen Life*. (consent not to be a single being). Durham, NC: Duke University Press.

Moten, F. (2018b). *The Universal Machine* (consent not to be a single being). Durham, NC: Duke University Press.

Nash, J. C. (2019). *Black Feminism Reimiagined: After intersectionality*. Durham, NC: Duke University Press.

Oliveros, P. and Maus, F. (1994). A conversation about feminism and music. *Perspectives of New Music*, 32(2), 174–193.

Oliveros, P. (2005). *Deep Listening: A Composer's Sound Practice*. Lincoln, NE: Deep Listening Publications.

Oliveros, P. (2010). *Sounding the Margins: Collected Writings 1992–2009*. Lincoln, NE: Deep Listening Publications.

Ortner, S. (2006). *Anthropology and Social Theory*. Durham, NC: Duke University Press.

Pedri-Spade, C. (2016). 'The drum is your document': Decolonizing research through Anishinabe song and story. *International Review of Qualitative Research*, 9(4), 385–406.

Pinto, S. (2016). Una esquela rara: feminist methodologies, innovation and the sound of what is to come in diaspora studies. *small axe*, 49, 175–184, doi: 10.1215/07990537–3481462.

Price, P. (2011). *Resonance: Philosophy for Sonic Arts*. New York, NY: Atropos Press.

Rogers, T. (2010). *Pink Noises: Women on Electronic Music and Sound*. Durham, NC: Duke University Press.

St. Pierre, E. A. and Pillow, W. S. (2000). *Working the Ruins: Feminist Poststructural Theory and Methods in Education*. New York, NY: Routledge.

Salvaggio, R. (1998). *The Sounds of Feminist Theory*. Albany, NY: SUNY Press.

Sedgwick, E. K. (2003). *Touching Feeling: Affect, Pedagogy, Performativity*. Durham, NC: Duke University Press.

Sharpe, C. (2016). *In the Wake: On Blackness and Being*. Durham, NC: Duke University Press.

Smith, M. M. (2008). *How Race is Made: Slavery, Segregation, and the Senses*. Chapel Hill, NC: University of North Carolina Press.

Spivak, G. (1988). Can the subaltern speak? In C. Nelson and L. Grossberg (Eds.), *Marxism and the Interpretation of Culture*. London: Macmillan,

Stewart, K. (2007). *Ordinary Affects*. Durham, NC: Duke University Press.

Stoever, J. (2016). *The Sonic Color Line: Race and the Cultural Politics of Listening*. New York, NY: NYU Press.

Taylor, K.-Y. (2017). *How We Get Free: Black Feminism and the Combahee River Collective*. Chicago, IL: Haymarket.

Thompson, M. (2016). Feminised noise and the 'dotted line' of sonic experimentation. *Contemporary Music Review*, 35(1), 85–101.

Thompson, M. (2017). *Beyond Unwanted Sound: Noise, Affect, and Aesthetic Moralism*. London: Bloomsbury.

Thompson, M. and Biddle, I. (2013). *Sound, Music, Affect: Theorizing Sonic Experiences*. London: Bloomsbury.

Tsing, A. L. (2015). *The Mushroom at the End of the World: On the Possibility of Life in Capitalist Ruins*. Princeton, NJ: Princeton University Press.

Visweswaran, K. (1994). *Fictions of Feminist Ethnography*. Minneapolis, MN: University of Minnesota Press.

Vogelin, S. (2010). *Listening to Noise and Silence: Towards a Philosophy of Sound Art*. London: Bloomsbury Academic.

Walker-Hill, H. (1992). Music by Black women composers at the American Music Research Center. *American Music Research Center Journal*, 2, 23–52.

Waterman, E. (2006). Radio bodies: Discourse, performance, resonance. In B. Labelle and E. G. Jensen (Eds.), *Radio Territories*. Los Angeles, CA: Errant Bodies Press.

Weheliye, A. G. (2005). *Phonographies: Grooves in Sonic Afro-modernity*. Durham, NC: Duke University Press.

Weheliye, A. (2014). *Habeas Viscus: Racializing Assemblages, Biopolitics, and Black Feminist Theories of the Human*. New York, NY: Duke University Press.

Woodson, C. G. (1933). *Mis-education of the Negro*. Washington, DC: Associated Publishers.

Wozolek, B., Wootton, L. and Demlow, A. (2017). The school-to-coffin pipeline: Queer youth, suicide, and living the in-between. *Cultural Studies ↔ Critical Methodologies*, 17(5), 392–398.

Wynter, S. (2003). Unsettling the coloniality of being/power/truth/freedom: Towards the human, after man, its overrepresentation – an argument. *The New Centennial Review*, 3(3), 257–337.

Wynter, S. (1984). The ceremony must be found: After humanism. *Boundary*, 2, 12(3), 19–70.

Wynter, S. (1989). Beyond the world of man: Glissant and the new discourse of the Antilles. *World Literature Today*, 63(4), 637–648

13 Inter(r)uptions

Reimagining dialogue, justice and healing

Anjana Raghavan

Introduction

In her introduction to *Muddying the Waters* Richa Nagar (2014: n.p.) advocates for 'muddying theories and genres so that we can continue to embrace risks of solidarities that might fail and of translations that might refuse to speak adequately'. This piece, more than anything else, is about failure, risk and inadequacy. It is written, in part, as a critical-contemplative reflection on my own theory-praxis of decolonial, queer feminism and in part, a vigilant reimagination of dialogue as both feminist method and engagement. It is, in so many ways, also about unravelling the solipsistic and political intertwinings of 'research' as an academic endeavour, and being fully cognizant of both. Transdisciplinary feminism, as it applies both to this chapter, and in my own practice, is about the disruption of the fortress-model of disciplinarity. I therefore write in resistance of an intransigent disciplinarity, and in favour of a trans[ient]disciplinarity, which is simultaneously expansive, as it is specifically located. This chapter is also offered as an act of 'theorying' (Raghavan, 2019), that is, a full acceptance of theory as embodied practice; theory as an active manifestation of the deeply intermeshed life-worlds of the structural, personal, affective and political.

The impetus to write about dialogue comes from the uneasy, yet necessary relationship that I have with it, in personal, scholarly and political spaces. We inhabit worlds where dialogue is dangerous and despotic to oppressed peoples everywhere. The demand for dialogue, most often expressed as a desire for exchange and understanding, masks the dynamic of domination, and yet, inevitably, dialogue remains a powerful form of engagement across multiple realms of inhabitation. As a university lecturer, it also remains key to my own privileged and risky modes of embodied living and working.

This chapter is not intended as a systematic review of dialogic processes as theory and research, or even as an examination of its limits and possibilities, though I do a little bit of both. I want, instead, and in keeping with the framing of this collection, to provide an intervention into, or more appropriately, an *interruption of* my own practice, using it as an opening into the larger modalities of dialogue as it operates in transdisciplinary feminist, queer and decolonial theory-praxis. It is worth noting that I consider decoloniality, and queerness, to be prerequisites for transdisciplinary feminist practice and knowledge production. Thus, the calls for building decolonial, queer practices in this chapter should be seen as integral to transdisciplinary feminist work. I maintain no fixity between theory, positionality, politics and method, understanding them all to be part of an 'intermeshed' (Lugones, 2003: 223) process. I also centre justice, radical vulnerability, and embodied love with Black-decolonial-queer feminist practices. Contextually, much of this piece is set within the fortresses of higher education and academia. The implications and critiques that emerge – and which are the heart of radical, justice-based praxis – will demand that we act to resist and erode that elite specificity of location.

Conventional 'sections' do not really work well for interruptions, and so I imagine this chapter, partly inspired by Lama Rod Owens' teachings, as three interrupting mo(ve)ments (indicative of their emergence-transience) (Williams, Owens and Syedullah, 2016). The first interruption is an ongoing conversation with my work on cosmopolitanism as it is the dialogic space that I identified and worked with, for all kinds of reasons, both problematic, and hopeful. Cosmopolitanism, as both philosophy and identity, is entwined with dialogic imaginaries that range from colonial-racist, to radically anticolonial-liberatory. It was in the possibility of such multiplicity that I framed 'corporeal cosmopolitanism' (Raghavan, 2017) as one imagination of radical dialogic futurity. I therefore begin with a deep reflection (through my own work) on the complex relationship between the *desire* for dialogue and the denial of domination that it so often conceals. This reflection moves, as feminist work so often does, between my own positionalities, blank spots, and denials on the one hand, and the larger matrices of privilege-oppression and marginalization that we (and our work) inhabit, on the other.

The second interruption discusses and investigates some of the modalities of dialogue as trope, method, theory, intervention and 'solution'. I consider critical-contemporary work on dialogue which combines a keen critique of oppressor-violence in dialogic processes with a compassionate desire for radical connectedness. I bring these critical discussions of dialogue-in-practice into conversation with Édouard Glissant's *Poetics of Relation* (1997) as a deeply self-aware and vigilant way of framing the genuine yearning for relationality that might live within the desire for dialogue. This yearning for relationality lived (and lives) at the heart of my own work, but it did so with far less criticality, and self-reflection when I began, and so this second interruption is also about *embodying* personal accountability, and the necessity of transformative justice in our selves-worlds.

The third, and final interruption is perhaps the one that I am most apprehensive of, because it is the one where I presently locate myself. This interruption is about how to *responsibly* feed our desire for connection and 'large' solidarities, and I draw on the teachings of spiritual-feminists and activist-teachers like Lata Mani, Gloria Anzaldúa, Zen Guru Thich Nhat Hanh, Rev. angel Kyodo williams and Lama Rod Owens in this endeavour. Truly inhabiting interconnectedness and deep dialogicity requires enormous energy, heart and honest accountability. Those of us who have inhabited oppressor privileges and modalities will have to hold space for rage, silence and trauma, and also heal from our internalised violence. Those of us who continue to be oppressed and violated will need to create our own spaces, and languages to speak, love and heal. We will have to reject every guise in which oppressor-modes of being approach us, whether they be capitalism, colourism, individualism or amnesia. This final interruption tries to imagine radical futurities which honour the real yearning for relationality through radical love and spiritual-justice work, both of which are made possible only through an abiding commitment to justice by dismantling coloniality, anti-blackness, casteism, heterosexism, imperialism, patriarchy and misogyny.

First interruption: privilege and accountability

My doctoral work and book on corporeal cosmopolitanism, *Towards Corporeal Cosmopolitanism: Performing Decolonial Solidarities*, was invested in 'naming and reclaiming emotional and bodily practices ... into the realm of the political ... through a critical dialogic engagement with ... contemporary visions of cosmo-politanism, liberal Euromerican and Kant-inspired strains, as well as radical, decolonial strains' (Raghavan, 2017: 4) of cosmopolitan thought and visons. The book was an early attempt to bring a vastly (sometimes unwieldy), diverse set of voices and imaginaries into dialogue with one another, underpinned by a genuine, if sometimes naïve, commitment to interdependence. However, if, as David Harvey (2009: 50) argues, 'there is actually not much difference between cosmopolitanism and liberalism, and even neoliberalism', because all Universalist prescriptions are problematic, then, *why cosmopolitanism?* For me, the inspiration came mostly from decolonial, feminist, queer and spiritual understandings and imaginings of cosmopolitanism (historical, contemporary and futuristic), which resisted liberal and neoliberal appropriations of cosmopolitan imaginings. Indeed, an important part of my work was to 'break the unspoken ownership of liberal narratives over cosmopolitan imaginaries' (Raghavan, 2017: 194). I wanted a dialogic cosmopolitanism that was committed to embodiment, queer feminism and decoloniality. I based my theoretical articulations on decolonial, Black, Brown and queer feminist scholarship, and drew on radical practices of Global South queer solidarities in Southern India, and Indo-Caribbean feminist literature, to articulate the existing practices and imagined possibilities of corporeal cosmopolitanism (see Gayatri Reddy, Brinda Mehta, A. Revathi, Kalpana Ram, Gautam Bhan, Arvind Narrain, Shalini Puri).

But there is a further problem of what Harvey terms the over-flourishing of 'adjectival cosmopolitanisms' (of which my work is a part), which can very easily descend into a kind of meaningless abstraction. I respond to this critique with Harvey's own formulation of 'cosmopolitics'. That is to say, I consider corporeal cosmopolitanism to be a deeply political-material practice. We also do not have *enough* queer-feminist-decolonial adjectives in academic spaces, so a little flourishing is no bad thing.

Recognising as critical scholars like Harvey (2009), Paul Gilroy (2013), Pnina Werbner (2008), Gyan Prakash (1990), Walter Mignolo (2000) and others do, that we cannot relinquish vast, planetary imaginaries of resistance and transformation, I chose to work with decolonial, feminist criticality and resistance within the discourses and practices of critical cosmopolitanism (Mignolo, 2000). As I reflect on my work in the present moment, I am struck by the keenness, this strong *desire* for dialogue, I nurtured and, indeed, heard echoed, in most cosmopolitanisms I read about (never more fervently than in Euromerican liberal narratives). Some of the interlocutors in my dialogues were: Kantian cosmopolitanism (Kant, 1917), Heldian cosmopolitanism (Held, 2005), 'enforced cosmopolitanism' (Beck, 2006), 'critical cosmopolitanism' (Delanty, 2009), among other Euromerican liberal cosmopolitanisms. I investigate my desire for dialogue here, embodying the composite lens of what Chela Sandoval (2000: n.p.) terms 'differential consciousness', that is, a complex, contradictory and multiplicitous subjectivity that is vigilant, resistant and loving. Although I began my foray into cosmopolitanism with justifiable postcolonial-feminist anger and frustration, I also felt a genuine willingness to be 'altered by the words spoken' (Keating, 2013: n.p.) as I deepened my engagement with the literature. I hold that compassion is an important element of critique, and so I found it difficult but ultimately generative when a majority of my largely Indian, male supervisory committee told me to read better, and not shoot my mouth off about liberal cosmopolitan scholarship.

So far, so good. This is the appropriate trajectory of rigorous, reflexive scholarship in which we are all careful about 'identity politics', and generous, even though we have every reason to hold Euromerican political philosophy suspect. It is also the precise modality which perpetuates my-our inability to be fully conversant with my-our occupation of what Lugones terms the 'oppressor/ being oppressed↔resisting' complex. Lugones (2003: 7) uses the expression I-we in her writing, to signify the relationality and fluidity between self and collective. I use my-our as a combination of Lugones' usage and Gloria Anzaldúa's use of 'autohistoria' and her insistence that writing only works if it accesses the world through self, troubling the self-world boundary. I use the terms oppressor–oppressed in structural senses, while noting that these can also be literal and visceral. In all cases, I hold these dynamics to be corporeal, epistemological and cultural-political. While my-our capacity to engage with certain forms of dominant scholarship is not devoid of a sincere generosity, it can often be the deliberate obfuscation and denial of crucial accountabilities and acknowledgements of our own oppressor modalities.

I offer three instances, in my own practice, of how these oppressor-modes functioned. In the first instance, my capacity to engage critically-yet-generously with liberal, Euromerican political philosophy was complicated by a deeply internalized epistemic colonialism. This internalisation would *not* permit me to do otherwise, and simply let me begin my doctoral thesis from Chapter 3 (thanks to Dr Rahul Rao, for drawing my attention to this), which is where the decolonial-corporeal cosmopolitanism actually begins to manifest. The second instance was the ways in which I responded to the desperate, gendered fear of being unable to be 'intelligible' and to prove expertise with 'the' literature – so much so that I was advised not to engage with Habermas because I would get in trouble for not treating his work with enough nuance. In other words, if I could not execute *perfect* jumps through the hoops of white, Euromerican, male scholarship, nobody would care about Chapters 3, 4 and 5. Rather than resist this demand to evidence fluency in Master-tropes I felt compelled, instead, to excel at them, executing a complex form of compliance, where the price of legitimacy was the performance of a colonial-epistemic ventriloquism.

These two instances illustrate the (my) internalisation of dominator tropes. A third instance illuminates the obfuscation or denial of the direct forms of privilege I wielded: those of both caste and class. S*avarna* (dominant/dominator castes) identity-narratives exercise enormous power within South-Asian socio-cultural-political contexts in a complex combination of ritual, cultural, corporeal and material discourses of pollution/purity and superiority/inferiority. They also collude with internalised colonialism *and* the resultant desire for colonial-white approval. In this context, my admittance into postcoloniality permitted a relatively uncomplicated commitment to resisting whiteness and Euromerican-centrism, while my relationship of dominance to oppressed-victimised caste and class communities remained largely unexamined. Ironically, it is only in the years that I have taught in predominantly white settings in the Global North, often forced into situations ranging from uncomfortable, to hostile, to racist, that I have fully encountered the implications of both internalised casteism and anti-blackness (which are not the same, but also not unrelated) as systemically built into *savarna*, South-Asian bodies and imaginaries (Patel, 2016). Alison Jones writes of white-identified peoples seeking knowledge from people of colours where 'the very act of "being taught" becomes, most significantly, not an act of logic or an accumulation of information or even a call to action, but an experience of redemption' (Jones, 1999: 313). This desire for a kind of performative absolution, where the act of 'empathetic knowing' and 'confessing ignorance' (313) become proxies both for justice and for a full recognition of oppressor privilege and all the work that dismantling it entails.

This is a sleight of hand and denial of what whiteness does/performs: it shifts the focus onto oppressed peoples when the real work lies within itself. As I continued to throw myself into frightening and heartbreaking 'dialogues' with whiteness, it became apparent to me that I was, in part, performing my own proxy. I was displacing my *own* redemptive desires in particular relation to caste on to my harmful engagements with white supremacy and racism. I was engaging with whiteness for absolution from my caste privilege. Lugones (2003: 14) writes that

> perceiving oneself as an oppressor is harder to sustain morally than deception. There is often a lapse, a forgetting, a not recognising oneself in a description, that reveals to those who perceive multiply that the oppressor is in self-deception, split, fragmented.

As a postcolonial, caste and class elite subject, interpellated with psychic and bodily wounds of misogynistic, sizeist and queerphobic violences, I was not unfamiliar with the co-habitations of privilege and marginality. But intersectionality only means that oppressions are connected; knowing some does not entail knowing others. I recognise my own *savarna* self-deceptions *in and through* my recognition of the self-deception that whiteness performs vis-à-vis me as a Brown, queer, 'third world' woman. I understand this to be the kind of poly-self subjectivity that seeing multiply produces. This vulnerable accountability between ourselves, our worlds and our 'others', is also at the heart of decolonising white and/or elite and *savarna* feminist practice.

The other facet of this complex self-knowledge as oppressor–oppressed is that, once recognised, and fully acknowledged, it opens up the capacity for the responsible and compassionate act of what Leela Fernandes (2003: 92) calls 'active witnessing', that is, to be a witness who will be present, fully involved and articulate in the struggle for justice. 'Differential consciousness' has enabled me to engage in dialogues with white-identified peoples and groups with love. It has taught me to be silent and *actively* witness the rage, anger and grief of Black peoples, Indigenous peoples, disabled peoples, whose oppressions are different (and sometimes untranslatable) to mine, while simultaneously identifying and dismantling my own privileges and blank spots. I have learnt the value and necessity of my own anger, and pain; that engagement and non-engagement are equally difficult, equally valid choices. It is work that is always ongoing. It is why I am still writing about dialogue, working across disciplines and feminism. The next interruption will speak to the larger context and politics of dialogicity, and why it might be necessary to reject dominant forms of dialogue, if we are truly invested in relationality.

Second interruption: vigilance and refusal

Deriving from the Greek *dialogos*, meaning thinking together, dialogue as intrinsically *good*, and virtuous, is an assumption that flows from long histories rooted in the Greco Platonic and Socratic traditions. However, as Burbules (Burbules and Bertram, 2001: n.p.) points out, dialogue's 'different forms express deeper assumptions about the nature of knowledge ... inquiry ... communication, the roles of teacher and learner, and mutual ethical obligations thereof'. Thus, even before we make the critical move to consider contemporary implications, power-dynamics and structures of dialogic interaction, we must already account for the epistemic specificity, and Eurocentricity, of how we *imagine* dialogue as sharing, equal, empowering, etc. Burbules (2001: n.p.) points out how philosophical traditions like Zen Buddhism prefer 'relying ... upon the indirect effect of riddles, paradoxical statements, and questions (koans) that precisely cannot be answered'. The complex, and rich philosophical traditions hailing from different cultures in East Asia, South Asia, Africa, Latin America and the 'Middle-East' (which I understand to be a problematic term) have a plethora of approaches to dialogue, exchange, sharing and learning (Nasr and Leaman, 2005; Eze, 2008). However, none of these understandings really find a place in dominant Enlightenment-based understandings of dialogue which, right up to contemporary liberal-political understandings of dialogue, are bound by forms of didactic dualism and the desperate need for conclusive certainty. Many knowledges and wisdom that come to us from different cultures and traditions (even within 'Europe') are not committed to these strictures of certainty. Indeed, many of them invite us to eschew binaristic certainty, in favour of a more expansive mode of being. While it is true that some *European* (in terms of geographical location) philosophical traditions drew considerably on several other philosophical systems, though often with no acknowledgement, it is equally true that the mainstream ways we learn about 'Europe' (as a political and ideological centre of power) is anything but dialogic.

I want to bring into conversation some critical-contemporary discussions of dialogue in the field of education where we are witnessing a colonisation of the vocabulary of free speech, critique, safety and rigorous scholarship. Sanctioning fundamentalist revisionist history in school curricula, explicit transphobia, explicit racism, the systematic shutting down of scholarly critique of anti-immigration policies, anti-blackness and Islamophobia have all become part of acceptable educational practice, in the guise of 'diverse' viewpoints, one of the cornerstones of dialogic exchange. This wholly disembodied deployment of 'diverse' viewpoints masks how elite, white, enabled, *savarna*, cis-hetero-male (I use all of these tropes as dominator logics, which can be internalised by individuals and communities) bodies sanction the annihilation of poor, Black, disabled, Dalit, queer, female bodies. It also animates a dangerous form of hypercapitalist, adversarial dialogicity that requires no consideration of ethics or justice. In the interests of space, I discuss two relatively contemporary pieces on dialogue in education, from a critical whiteness perspective, and a radical Black perspective. I chose these two pieces for their nuanced understandings of the damage that dialogue can, and does wreak, while at the same time refusing to abandon it. It is this tension between both a deep *suspicion/fear of*, and a *yearning for* certain forms of dialogic engagement that I want to unpack as an important part of decolonial-queer-feminist praxis.

Alison Jones in *The Limits of Cross-Cultural Dialogue* (1999) explores the violence that whiteness perpetrates on Indigenous peoples and people of colours in its demand for dialogue, knowledge and exchange. Identifying her own positionality as *pakeha* (white), she powerfully illuminates white dominator-discourses as they operate in an experimental teaching process. Maori and Pacific Islander students and white students studied the same course (taught by Jones and her Maori colleague Kuni Jenkins) in separate groups. The separation was met with great enthusiasm by the Maori and Pacific Islander students, and considerable hostility by white students. Jones examines white resistance to the rejection of dialogue by people of colours and what it means for liberation visions to exclude dialogues. As Kelsey Blackwell (2018: n.p.) points out in her insightful piece on why people of colours need their own spaces, the values of whiteness are the water in which we all swim. No one is immune. Those values dictate who speaks, how loud, when, the words we use, what we don't say, what is ignored, who is validated and who is not.

The ways in which spaces, modes of speech and voices are regulated and legitimised are fundamentally governed by systems of domination and, as

Jones (1999: 307) points out 'most important in educational dialogue is not the *speaking voice* but the *voice heard*'. This critique runs through the work of much postcolonial, Black and decolonial feminist work. It places emphasis both on the act of listening and on the '*voice heard*' indicating that the question of whether the subaltern can speak is itself already mired in an imperial-colonial episteme. People of colours are labelled perennially 'hysterical' in all of our articulations and are thus rendered mute, either through illegibility, erasure or sheer exhaustion. Jones' piece draws out the important dynamic of domination that is inherent in the demand for dialogue by dominant groups and the important ways in which *that* kind of dialogue differs very differently from the kinds of speaking and listening that took place in the Maori and Pacific Islander group (Jones is also careful about not conflating/romanticising the two identities). The dominant group's aggressive desire for knowledge and understanding is, she shows, a fundamentally exploitative and narcissistic one. It bypasses the difficult, critical work of unpacking and actively giving-up privilege, and instead uses the labour of people of colours to provide 'authentic' knowledge which is then used as a proxy for the work that whiteness must do.

Jones' (1999) work is an important reminder that dominant groups must perform their own labour, and learn to embrace the inevitability of failure, loss and unease. In a radical reformulation of dialogic engagement with specific reference to race, Zeus Leonardo and Ronald Porter (2010) offer a 'Fanonian Theory of "safety" in race dialogue'. For Leonardo and Porter, when it comes to talking about race, *there is no safety* for people of colours. The safe space of race dialogue is reserved exclusively for white people to 'avoid publicly "looking racist"' (Leonardo and Porter, 2010: 139). They build on Frantz Fanon's theory of transformative violence that becomes *necessary* for decolonisation, because of the overwhelming cruelty of colonial violence. In this, Leonardo and Porter offer a nuanced and powerful account of Fanon's (often misunderstood) writings on violence as resistance. Their call is for a 'humanizing form of violence' (2010: 140) which includes non-violent civil-disobedience action as a form of active resistance: 'King's tactic of non-violence was, in content but not in form, an act of violence aimed at liberating both the oppressed and the oppressor' (2010: 144).

Fanon's insistence on revolutionary violence was premised upon the totalising quality of colonial dehumanisation. Not only did it invest colonisers with total, annihilating power, it also internalised an intense sense of fear and self-loathing amongst colonised, enslaved Black peoples. It is to break the vicious grip of this singular and hegemonic understanding of violence that Fanon speaks of a transformative, humanising violence. As Lewis Gordon (2010: 208) points out with specific reference to Black peoples, racism 'locks a group of beings below the self-other dialectic, which means in relation to them there is neither self nor other; there is no-self, no-other'. This is where we begin to discern the true magnitude of how dominant groups perpetrate violence through dialogue. In a situation where 'ontological equality' (Mignolo, 2000) does not exist, the notion of liberal or constitutional equality is a travesty. The demand that people of colours participate in 'dialogues' about race where the biggest threat to whiteness is its own exposure (a fact well known to people of colours) but the threat to people of colours is bodily, psychic, emotional and spiritual violence, is an act of malevolence. Leonardo and Porter (2010: 150) point out that the repeated desire of people of colours to get through to white people might be terribly naïve on the one hand, but it also demonstrates a 'humanizing desire and commitment to the other' despite its risks. Such a humanising violence is an insurgent, resistant act of dialogue where whiteness learns to hold the anger, grief and silence of people of colours. An act of justice where the classroom is a space that *risks* chance, and transformation, to work *through* pain and hostility through a process of full accountability in what I earlier referred to as 'active witnessing' (Fernandes, 2003: 92).

Both Jones' and Leonardo and Porter's pieces are striking in their commitment to transformative justice which I see as integral to the practice of transdisciplinary feminism. As I discussed in the first interruption above, I have had to begin the journey of looking deeply into, and dismantling, my occupation of caste and class privileges, as well as recognising the deep connections between internalised whiteness and anti-blackness, while also holding space for and speaking the anger and grief I hold in the face of racism, misogyny and queerphobia *and* honouring my deep yearning for connection, love and relationality. This second interruption is a call for honest accountability which highlights that the neat time-space continuums of elite, liberal dialogues are simply not adequate to the task. It requires, instead, the kind of journeying that Glissant (Glissant and Wing, 1997: 20) terms errantry:

> one who is errant (who is no longer traveller, discoverer or conqueror) strives to know the totality of the world yet already knows he will never accomplish this – and knows that is precisely where the threatened beauty of the wold resides.

Errant thinking is relational thinking; it is unstable, and uncertain, it recognises the violence of categories like knowledge and understanding (remembering that they are tools of imperial and colonial conquest). Relationality is 'latent, open, multilingual in intention, directly in contact with everything possible' (1997: 32), and lives in the dawn of connected histories and the 'accumulation of sediment' rather than in 'lightning flashes' (1997: 33). For Glissant, relationality *is* an experience, not a knowledge, one which is deeply connected to the inheritance of the abyss, that is the memory of the Middle Passage. If we begin to deeply listen to these 'impossible memories' (Glissant and Wing, 1997: 72) embedded in 'catastrophic time' (Drabinski, 2010: 303), we recognise that the absence of bodies *fundamentally* alters the experience of loss, language, and mourning. How can dialogue function in such a space? How can dialogue demand the articulation of what is held in ancestral, body-and-spirit memory? It cannot.

It is for this reason that Glissant (1997: 190) invokes the 'right to opacity', distance and inarticulability. Opacity weaves and enables relation, it allows us to hold things without having to possess them, to not reduce, or generalise. Opacity is crucial to multiple seeing, and differential consciousness and, as such, opens the way to a much more liberatory, spacious, and loving way to experience relationality. It frees us from the trap of an annihilating sameness, a diktat to *comprehend*, and consume one another into a frightening integration, or an amputating tolerance. Invoking this right is also an important resistance to whiteness and eurocentric ways of knowing that are often locked in a deadly certainty. We must be subsequently vigilant of how this filters into, and shapes Euromerican iterations of feminist knowledge and practice, and the ways in which white feminism continues to silence women of colours everywhere. This second interruption has dwelt on some of the dangers of dialogue while trying to unearth its longing for connection. Nurturing this longing responsibly means that we *must* be vigilant and do the hard work of self-world transformation. The third, and final interruption will try to open up some paths towards such transformation and healing for our selves, worlds, our practices of politics, and decolonial-queer feminism.

Third interruption: radical healing

This third interruption is the newest one in my journey. It is a tentative map, but one without a 'mandate for conquest' (Alexander, 2005: 246). The mapping work of this interruption might be imagined as a relationality of ocean and shore: both always shifting, moving, fluid and changing, the ocean being capable of both great gentleness, and uncontrollable inevitability, in the way that she transforms her shores. This mapping is not governed by a linear sense of direction, space, or time. It requires a crustacean-like sensibility; sideways movements of incredible speed, leaving tiny imprints and trails on the sand that will not always be visible, but also long stretches of incredible, immovable stillness and an amphibious capacity to dwell between terrains. To depart from dominator logics requires a fundamental shift from, and transformation of, the very categories that we operate in and through. Because, as bell hooks (2012: 32) says, 'indoctrination into dominator thinking in a culture governed by the dictate of imperialist white supremacist patriarchy is a process that affects all of us to greater and lesser degrees', we must constantly find paths that are Deleuzian lines of fligh*t* zigzagging in non-linear ways from dominator logics. This is also directly applicable for those bearing structural-cultural-emotional privileges, as Rev. Angel Kyodo Williams explains, referring to the 'mind of whiteness' (Williams, Owens, and Syedullah, 2016: n.p.) that awareness of this mind cannot come from *inside* it. A larger form of witnessing must be practised. As Audre Lorde (1984) rightly insisted: the master's house cannot be dismantled using the master's tools. Thus, what are currently considered as 'valid' forms of knowing, method, theory and justice must all be dismantled from their separated epistemes. This is what Lugones (2003: 134) identifies as 'split separation' as distinct from 'curdle separation' where 'split separation' is a kind of disconnecting separation which annihilates multiplicity but curdling is a process of separation that fundamentally cannot occur without connectedness. Curdling is a state where differences can and do exist within the framework of interconnectedness. It is worth recalling Anzaldúa's (Anzaldúa and Keating, 2009: 106) words here: 'nothing is separate. It all filters through from one world to another, from one mode of consciousness to another'. It is to enable this 'curdling', that I draw on a transdisciplinary combination of both activist-scholarship of feminists of colours writing in-out of the academy as well as the spiritual wisdom of activist-teachers-of-colours who are increasingly bringing healing to wounded peoples.

I return briefly to Glissant's (1997) formulation of the inheritance of 'abyss memory'. Without erasing the specificity of the trauma of enslavement and the Middle Passage, I want to explore the context of trauma in what Zen teacher Thich Nhat Hanh (2010: n.p.) refers to as the 'inheritance of suffering'. Rev. Angel Kyodo Williams, and Lama Rod Owens are both radical, Black, queer, Buddhist teachers and practitioners who centre justice, activism and love in their paths. Thich Nhat Hanh's teachings of the practice of Buddhism are embedded in the desire for transformative justice and the Buddhist teaching of *metta* or loving-kindness. One of his central focuses is the body, and Thich Nhat Hanh (2010: n.p.) stresses the importance of 'returning to the body', identifying it as the site where trauma inheres. One of the abiding problems with the dominant tropes of dialogue is that while it is happy to acknowledge non-verbal or body-based *elements* of dialogue, it does not recognise the body as a primary *site* of suffering, resistance, and transformation. However, as Anzaldúa (2015: 105) writes, 'the unconscious and the physical body do not distinguish between what is really happening and what is imagined or envisioned'. It is this *embodied* wisdom and capacity to connect to different planes of selfhood and consciousness that makes our bodies both sites of enormous vulnerability, as well as liberation. Thich Nhat Hanh (2010) thus advocates deep contemplation of the body as a microcosm of interconnectedness, what he refers to as 'interbeing'. The body, he suggests, is connected to, and animated by, the entire cosmos. The connection of our bodies to ancestral memory is an especially important part of realising connectedness, identity and our sense of being-in-the-world. Colonial, genocidal violence is a systematic amputation of these connections and, in the context of catastrophic loss, where there is neither memory, record nor recoverable names, the body becomes the most crucial medium of ancestral connection. Lama Rod Owens (2016: n.p.), in his teachings, envisions 'intersectionality as lineage', where lineage refers not to a narrow understanding of blood lineage alone but to acknowledging all of our multiplicitous ancestors, teachers, guides, and kin. Inhabiting our lineages in an internally dialogical, conversant way, is critical to being able to connect across differences without being flattened into a violent sameness. In this context, anger emerges as an important emotion-resistance for oppressed peoples across denominations.

Audre Lorde's (1993) extraordinary reflections on anger have offered Black women first and foremost, but also people of colours and other oppressed communities, great strength and power. She identifies the role of anger as a call to attention, as the recognition of and revolution against injustice and as the animating voice of peoples crushed into silence by oppressor logics. Indeed, as Leonardo and Porter (2010: 151) write, the anger of people of colour is not 'a distancing move [but] an attempt to engage, to be vulnerable to and recognized by the other'. Lugones (2003: 116) speaks of a 'generous anger' that occurs between peers or different groups of oppressed peoples who need to be heard and understood in response to the centuries of distortion they have borne. This is a transformative and generative anger, necessary between loved ones, and those working together towards justice, as so many feminists of colours have written about so eloquently. In this context, I want to briefly dwell on the call for vigilance around the connections of anger to hate (which is dominator-logic), and the resultant 'manipulative effects' (Lugones, 2003: 105) of anger. Lorde's (1993: 152) warning is that

> in the long run, strength that is bred by anger alone ... focus(ses) not on what lies ahead ... but what lies behind ... what created it, hatred. And hatred is a deathwish for the hatred, not a lifewish for anything else.

Attentiveness to connections between anger and hatred are important because 'we learn *how to hate* in our hatred of injustice' (Alexander, 2005: 323). The important point, then, is that deployment of anger as a mode of relationality in the desire for justice is different, in crucial ways, from the anger that is produced by hate. But it is not always easy to know or enact the distinction which is why the work of healing becomes even more crucial for oppressed peoples.

Related to this question of healing, Black feminist Barbara Holmes (2002: 40) asks this complex question: 'Can we institute a pedagogy for ... oppressors?', a question that she herself answers in the affirmative. Rev. Angel Kyodo Williams (Williams, Owens, and Syedullah, 2016: n.p.), in her discussion of love in capitalist-individualist Global North framings, notes that whiteness has no access to love other than as a private, personal and secret commodity, observing that 'people don't know how to apply love in the great spheres of society'. If we extend the ways in which Fanon, hooks and other scholars-of-colours describe the totalising effects of colonial-imperial complexes, it might help us begin to navigate the idea that oppression is tied to dominator *logics* rather than identities. Furthermore, that dismantling these logics though primarily in the service of oppressed peoples will also serve to liberate those who have historically enacted dominance-violence (Willams, Owens and Syedullah, 2016), particularly if we understand the perpetration of violence to be a part of the complex of oppressor–oppressed suffering and the cycles of hate. This will need intensive contemplation and bodily inhabitation by all of us who embody and perpetrate dominator logics; it is work that must be done by us, and us alone, in spaces that we create for such work.

For those of us who are enabled by some privileges, and/or lovingly seek, and/or are required to undertake dialogic engagement, it is still necessary to be conscious of certain dangers. *Sometimes* extraordinary love, courage, and compassion may move oppressed peoples to engage with their oppressors. This is a precious gift, not a duty, nor something to be expected (Blackwell, 2018). This gift must be learnt from with the respect and loving humility it so richly deserves. If the internalisation and perpetration of dominance within ourselves is not realised as amputation, deep wounding and imprisonment, but we appear to be invested in the 'other's' liberation, then *we are still perpetrating violence*. The work of deep relationality is the work of justice is the work of love is the work of spirit. It requires, above all else, 'being at the frontlines of your own liberation' (Williams, Owens, and Syedullah, 2016: n.p.). Decolonial-Black-queer-feminisms and spiritual activism are both practised and realised in the belief that there is no world-transformation without self-transformation and, more pertinently, that there *is no boundary that separates the two*. This third interruption has tried to draw on some of this wisdom, to give us pathways into transforming our potentially superficial desire for (dominator) dialogue into a committed desire for relationality, justice and love.

Conclusion

I bring this piece to its pause (because the work has no end), with some reflections on reclaiming slowness and silence as an oblique but necessary addendum to the recuperation of dialogue as radical relationality. Although invested in unravelling binaristic modes of inhabitation, my primary ethical commitments are to justice and to prioritise care for those most wounded. Transdisciplinary, decolonial feminist theory and praxis, in my understanding, inheres most meaningfully and powerfully in its capacity to resist the subtle, sophisticated modalities of dominator logics, as well as in its centring of processes of healing. These words that follow, are in honour of those deepest wounds in need of healing. Maria Lugones (2003: 67) who, in *Pilgrimages/Peregrinajes*, quotes a poem by Inez Hernandez Tovar which emphasises the necessity of decolonising our understanding of time. Tovar, in her poem, categorically resists the linear disciplining of clock-time, suggesting instead that wounded communities must walk their own paths, in their own *time*, to make bonds, to resist, to find solidarity and to heal.

This resonates deeply with some of the practices that I have learnt about and practice to heal from my own traumas of abuse, oppression and loathing (both internalised and externally inflicted), in spiritual-professional-political realms. Buddhist and Hindu conceptions of emptiness, or *shunyata* is described by Thich Nhat Hanh (2010: n.p.) as 'emptiness of a separate existence, but at the same time, totally full of the cosmos'. Just as we must reclaim the right to honour anger, and resist its conflation with hate, there is also, I believe, similar work to be done in relation to stillness, and silence. The words that have been cut out of the tongues of oppressed peoples, and enforced silence, is a dominator-silence. The permanent demand made upon people of colours, women, Dalit, queer, poor, disabled people to speak, defend, explain and justify is also an infliction of violence. Although resistant speech is essential to justice, sound that emerges from *healing* silence takes 'exquisite shape as it travels across the threshold into that which we recognise as a note, a word, a sound' (Mani, 2011: 79). The right to stillness, and pause, to inhabit mystery, our bodies and that which is extra-lingual, is as important to spiritual and material wellbeing as the right to agitation and speech. Systematically refuse to plant your seeds in violent, toxic soil. Leave when you must. Remember to not always be alone; your *sanghas* (community-kin) nourish you – make space to commune with them.

May all beings be nourished in relations of love, justice and accountability to each other and the cosmos.

Acknowledgements

This work owes a great deal to Dr Lata Mani, and Lama Rod Owens, teachers, and healers extraordinaire. This chapter is dedicated to the ceaseless efforts of Black, Queer, People of Colours, and all beings engaged in the work of justice, and healing.

References

Alexander, M. J. (2005). *Pedagogies of Crossing: Meditations on Feminism, Sexual Politics, Memory, and the Sacred.* Durham, NC: Duke University Press.
Anzaldúa, G. and Keating, A. (2009). *The Gloria Anzaldúa reader.* Durham: Duke University Press.
Anzaldúa, G. (2015). *Light in the Dark/Luz en lo Oscuro: Rewriting Identity, Spirituality, Reality.* Durham, NC: Duke University Press.
Beck, U. (2006). *The Cosmopolitan Vision.* Cambridge: Polity.
Blackwell, K. (2018). *Why People of Color Need Spaces Without White People.* Retrieved from https://arrow-journal.org/why-people-of-color-need-spaces-without-white-people/
Burbules, N. C. and Bertram C. B. (2001). Theory and Research on Teaching as Dialogue. In V. Richardson (Ed.), *Handbook of Research on Teaching* (4th Edition). Washington, DC: American Educational Research Association. Ebook.
Delanty, G. (2009). *The Cosmopolitan Imagination: The Renewal of Critical Social Theory.* Cambridge: Cambridge University Press.
Drabinski, J. (2010). What is trauma to the future? On Glissant's poetics. *Qui Parle,* 18(2), 291–307.
Eze, E. (2008). Language and time in postcolonial experience, *Research in African Literatures,* 39(10), 24–47.
Fernandes, L. (2003). *Transforming Feminist Practice: Non-Violence, Social Justice, and the Possibilities of a Spiritualized Feminism.* San Francisco, CA: Aunt Lute Books.
Gilroy, P. (2013). *Between Camps: Nations, Cultures and the Allure of Race.* London: Allen Lane.
Glissant, E. and Wing, B. (1997). *Poetics of Relation.* Ann Arbor, MI: University of Michigan Press.
Gordon, L. (2010). Theory in black: Teleological suspensions in philosophy of culture. *Qui Parle,* 18(2), 193–214.
Harvey, D. (2009). *Cosmopolitanism and the Geographies of Freedom.* New York, NY: Columbia University Press.

Held, D. (2005). Principles of Cosmopolitan Order. In G. Brock and H. Brighouse (Eds.), *The Political Philosophy of Cosmopolitanism* (pp. 10–27). Cambridge: Cambridge University Press.
hooks, b. (2012). *Writing Beyond Race: Living Theory and Practice*. London: Routledge.
Jones, A. (1999). The limits of cross-cultural dialogue: Pedagogy, desire, and absolution in the classroom. *Educational Theory*. 49(3), 299–316.
Kant, I. (1917). *Towards Perpetual Peace*. Translated by M. Campbell Smith. London: George Allen and Unwin.
Keating, A. (2013). *Transformation Now!: Toward a Post-Oppositional Politics of Change*. Urbana, IL: University of Illinois Press. Kindle.
Leonardo, Z and R. K. Porter. (2010). Pedagogy of fear: toward a Fanonian theory of 'safety' in race dialogue. *Race Ethnicity and Education*, 13(2), 139–157
Lorde, A. (1984). *Sister Outsider*. USA: Crossing Press.
Lorde, A. (1993). *Zami, Sister Outsider, Undersong*. New York, NY: Quality Paperback Book Club.
Lugones, M. (2003). *Pilgrimages = Peregrinajes: Theorizing coalition against multiple oppressions*. Lanham, MD: Rowman & Littlefield.
Mani, L. (2011). *Interleaves*. New Delhi: Yoda Press.
Nagar, R. (2014). *Muddying the Waters: Coauthoring Feminisms across Scholarship and Activism*. Champaign, IL: University of Illinois Press, Kindle.
Nasr, S. H. and Leaman, O. (Eds.) (2005). *History of Islamic Philosophy*. London: Routledge.
Nhat Hanh, T. (2010). *Together We are One: Honouring our diversity, celebrating our connection*. Berkeley, CA: Parallax Press.
Mignolo, W. (2000). The many faces of cosmo-polis: Border thinking and critical cosmopolitanism. *Public Culture* 12(3), 721–748.
Patel, S. (2016). Complicating the tale of 'two Indians': Mapping 'South Asian' complicity in white settler colonialism along the axis of caste and anti-blackness. *Theory and Event*, 19(4). Retrieved from muse.jhu.edu/article/633278
Prakash, G. (1990). *Bonded Histories: Genealogies of Labor Servitude in Colonial India*. New York, NY: Cambridge University Press.
Raghavan, A. (2017). *Towards Corporeal Cosmopolitanism: Performing Decolonial Solidarities*. London: Rowman and Littlefield International.
Raghavan, A. (2019). Prayers to Kāli: practicing radical numinosity. *Third World Thematics: A TWQ Journal*, doi: 10.1080/23802014.2019.1622442
Sandoval, C. (2000). *Methodology of the Oppressed*. Minneapolis, MN: University of Minnesota Press. Kindle.
Werbner, P. (Ed.) (2008). *Anthropology and the New Cosmopolitanism: Rooted, Feminist and Vernacular Perspectives*. Oxford: Berg.
Williams, A. K., Owens, R. and Syedullah, J. (2016). *Radical Dharma: Talking Race, Love and Liberation*. Berkeley, CA: North Atlantic Books.

14 Moving with the folds of time and place

Exploring gut reactions in speculative transdisciplinary research with teen girls' in a post-industrial community

Gabrielle Ivinson and Emma Renold

Introduction

The chapter focuses on a gut holding mannerism, observed in an improvised movement workshop with teen girls living in an ex-industrial town in south Wales (UK), as a vantage point from which to explore what more the gesture might be telling us. A transdisciplinary approach enables a more expansive grasp on the complexity of being, doing and having and how these arise in intra-connections with the place, material world and through intergenerational transmissions. The gut is a series of folds of biological matter. Drawing on Gilles Deleuze's (1993) readings of Gottfried Wilhelm Leibniz's concept of 'Fold' as a differential, we speculatively explore scalar orders of time, space and matter. By taking the gut holding mannerism as a fulcrum we imagine folds that become larger and larger expanding into space, place and the universe, or become smaller and smaller by focusing on corporeal-movement, psycho-dynamic experiences and the 'thinking gut' (Wilson, 2015). We question what more the gut mannerism can illuminate, what more girls can be and what more ex-mining communities might become.

Staring with movement folds

The school hall worlds bodies in specific ways (Manning, 2016). On the morning of our first dance workshop, girls huddled or stood in tight knots in a secondary (high) school hall, located in an ex-coal mining town in south Wales, UK. None of them were trained dancers and many had never participated in a movement workshop that did not focus on recognisable moves and routines (e.g. 'street dance'). Hair was tugged; 'T' shirts were repeatedly pulled over bottoms and shoulders tensed. These awkward poses gave pathic knowledge communicated affectively (Guattari, 2006, 25). We read them as possible feelings of being exposed, self-conscious, wary, bored, relieved, tired and maybe excited. Yet the pose that arrested our attention and remained with us was a gut-cradling gesture. Arms were folded tightly across stomachs in a self-hug. The gut-cradling mannerism instantaneously betrayed protecting, hiding, hugging and comforting.

This mannerism seemed to fold the body into the body. The feel of skin on skin seemed to act as a physical-corporeal holding as well as psychological 'second skin' (Bick, 1987, cited in Manning, 2013: 1). Choreographer, Jên Angharad guided us into new socio-corporeal-embodied patternings as part of a series of dance workshops. Girls reverted to the self-holding mannerism in the intervals between the movement exercises. We joined the girls in exercises that encouraged us to stretch, run, crouch and move in unfamiliar ways. As they moved they started to open up physically and psychically.

This tiny corporeal fold inspired this chapter where we unfold speculations on the entanglements of place, gender and bodies. We ask: Can a mannerism provide insight into how girls become in the present while entangled with the distinctive history of a mining community's highs and lows, its closely guarded values and hidden violence? Opening out the enquiry further we ask: What are the new geo-psychical formations of late capitalism in post-industrial societies?

The gut holding mannerism provides a vantage point from which to explore what more might come into view. And to capture that 'more', we necessarily take a transdisciplinary approach. This is because transdisciplinary thinking and analysis enables us to go beyond a uni-dimensional view of the body and the subject. It enables a more expansive grasp on the complexity of being, doing and having and how these arise through our intra-connections with the material worlds in which they are lived. Thus, following an introduction to the concept of mannerism, the paper follows three speculative journeys. The first starts with the pleats of the earth that created the geology of the coal beds in south Wales across vast scales of space and time. The second unfolds issues around the em/bodying of gender. The third speculates about folds of the gut as a thinking organ; folds of anatomy, phylogenesis, species and survival. We use these transdisciplinary speculative forays to break hegemonic discourses that pathologise teen girls living in post-industrial places (Renold and Ivinson, 2015) and to re-imagine their lives and communities differently as part of an on-going exploration of the proto-politics of becoming (Renold and Ivinson, 2019).

Extensive and intensive pleats in/of movement

The gut holding mannerism seemed to hold fragile bodies together by providing a corporeal fold of support. We approach the concept 'mannerism' as it derives from Leibniz, born in Leipzig, Germany in 1646 and interpreted by Deleuze (1993). The mannerism might have been experienced as a reassuring feedback loop of self on self confirming a presence, a beingness, an existence. What was the fold reassuring a girl of? Was it to reassure her that she still existed or belonged? Belonged, yet belonged where and to what?

Inspired by Deleuze's book, *The Fold; Leibniz and the Baroque* (1993), we imagine pleats as transdisciplinary forms that can either unfold by extending their spatial reach into the world or by compressing inward as more and more tightly concealed intricate tucks. Series of pleatings as asymmetric principles (Deleuze, 1994, 106) might move ever more outward from the gut-cradling mannerism into space, hall, school, town, community extending into evermore, far-reaching worlds and the cosmos. The human species can then be imagined as a phylogenetic fold. Phylogenesis comes from the Greek phylon (tribe) and genesis (origin) and refers to the biological process by which a taxon (of any rank) appears (https://en.wikipedia.org/wiki/Phylogenesis). Another series follows increasingly concertina-ed pleats such as those found in semi-porous cell membranes, organs and skin. Holding these series of folds in place is Elizabeth Wilson's (2015) concept of the 'thinking gut', which acts as a fulcrum where series of folds and creases come together and apart.

The broader frame is Deleuze's sense that subjectivity is caught in a crisis of representation and his question of whether or not philosophy can find a way out of the crisis and 'back to the sphere of action' (Hughes, 2011: 86). In our work we strive to break free of discourses that pathologise poor children and young people and which place the blame/responsibility for their lives within a Cartesian, bounded subject. It is here also that we see the power of a transdisciplinary approach as it allows us to escape dualisms such as subject–object, individual–society and allows a fundamental collective concept of the socius (Guattari, 2006) where coming into being is enunciated through assemblages of layers and orders as 'partial levels of existential territorialisation' (Guattari, 2006: 27). This kind of ontology enables us to imagine teen girls fused with, and becoming through the histories of the place where they were growing up.

In searching for a way out of dualistic impasses, Deleuze (1993) explored folds as ways to complicate, disrupt and crumple surfaces. Series of folds hint at asymmetrical differentials (the dx, in calculus). As folds become larger and larger or smaller and smaller, scales of time and space alter. We can think of repetition as a series of pleats that set in play non-linear time and space. The aim is not to draw on a range of place-based, psycho-dynamic and corporeal-movement folds to explain *why* girls seemed to be stuck in place, but to expand terrains and think about more wild entanglements. It is about asking what more the gut mannerism can illuminate, what more girls can be, and what more communities might become. In her critique of the disciplinary focus of scientific knowledge, Wilson (2015: 171) suggests that 'the social sciences are too monochromatic in their ambitions'. We don't want to settle matter; we want to unsettle matters. Imagining transdisciplinary complicating folds seems like one potential way to rumple, untuck and unpick settled hegemonic monochromatic scales of time, place and corporeality.

Like so many experimentations with transdisciplinarity, new materialism(s), new realities and new ontologies (for example, MacLure, 2013; Ringrose, Warfield and Zarabadi, 2018; Coleman, Page and Palmer, 2019; St. Pierre, 2019) we are striving to replace faith in a transcendence anchored in an extraterrestrial mythology (God) and rational progress with a multiplicity of forces belonging to lively world(s) and cosmologies. We imagine an ever-moving and expanding Nietzschean universe where repetition is the eternal return of being, not a return of the identical, but a return that is dissimilar, that agitates, that will not be still. In the speculative forays that follow we hint of pressures above and

Moving with the folds of time and place 171

below surfaces that will not be stilled, of the troubles in the past that have not been reconciled in the life of valleys communities in the present and how girls 'catch these' corporeally, psychically and in their guts. We also hint of social, political and psychic grounds that shift, subside, compress, rupture and will not settle.

We turn to the choreographer and philosopher, Erin Manning (2013, 2016), to elaborate how a gesture such as a gut-hugging mannerism is multiply folded with compressions and extensions of time, space and matter. These can be imagined as partial existential territorialisations (Guattari, 2006). Not being fed, the gut contraction of hunger or not having enough (money, care, attention) eventually become traumatic. It is in the interstices of corporeal folds, just before a movement, that we can glimpse hesitations, quivers before stuckness and where corporeal seizures of trauma take hold. These are moments of immanence.

Focusing on just one mannerism, the gut holding gesture becomes an external, vantage point from which to view the conditions of young people's lives, and girls in particular, growing up in post-industrial places. This mannerism is the spring-board that enables us to think with Deleuze, Guattari, Manning and Wilson among others. The gut-cradling gesture is a non-arbitrary point, or chance to imagine how the world might be restored to us/them. Jên Angharad's pedagogic practices, in effect, helped to get the girls moving again (Ivinson and Renold, forthcoming). This chapter sits within our wider mission to draw on transdisciplinary thinking to imagine young people as part of a restless, forward political momentum of life. For further details on working with the micropolitics of young people's actions see Renold (2018, 2019, 2020).

The more-than of methodology

During the early phases of what became a longitudinal ethnographic study of young people and place we conducted over 60 one-to-one interviews and 12 group interviews with young people aged 12–14 years. As the project progressed we generated multi-sensory ethnographic data that could better get at the qualitative multiplicity of the embodied and affective phenomena of lived experience (Ellingson, 2017). This phase of the research involved inviting young people on walking tours (Ivinson and Renold, 2013b) and film-making activities, one of which focused on the running body, 'Still Running', and another, the captured body 'Shades of Place' (Ivinson and Renold, 2016). In the phase of the research discussed here, we decided to focus directly on the body.

The secondary (high) school was in a valleys town in south Wales where we had been working on the Young People and Place project.[1] The workshops took place in the last week of the summer term, over four days, when the usual school timetable was suspended. The invitation read, 'If you feel like moving, if you feel like jumping, swaying, running and creating stories with your body, this activity is for you'. Eighteen girls between the ages of 12–16 years signed up.

Choreographer and dancer, Jên Angharad, who specialises in dance theatre and improvisation, led the workshops. She encouraged people to develop their styles and become empowered by the movement exercised. Over the four days, Jên used a range of exercises to work with the energies and corporeal movements presented by girls and helped them to move into/with the beat of music she chose for each exercise. Although some girls took dance lessons (mostly 'street dance'), the majority were untrained. We participated in some of the exercises to feel with our bodies what the girls were experiencing. In the intervals between sessions, girls often asked us questions and some spoke spontaneously about what they were feeling and we encouraged them to talk using simple probes such as 'how was that?'

By inviting bodies to move, we found that girls opened up physically and psychically. We captured this through video recordings using three small cameras placed in the corners of the hall. After the workshops, we watched video footage many times and sometimes at slow or fast speeds. This revealed patterns of behaviour and micro-dynamics of specific gestures such as the gut holding gesture (for a more extensive exploration see Ivinson and Renold, forthcoming).

The movement workshops provided the opportunity to create an explicitly embodied, qualitative methodology. We employed a diffractive analysis (Barad, 2007; Haraway, 2008) with a transdisciplinary compass to entangle and read observations, fieldnotes and philosophical concepts of dance and movement through each other speculatively. Next we present three speculative journeys that fold outwards from the gut holding mannerism: folds of time and place; gender unfolds; and gut reactions.

Folds of time and place

The girls' gut holding gesture cannot be separated from the milieu where they are growing up. There is something intense about working in a place where the collapse of the industrial base has been so catastrophic and where attempts at economic regeneration have been largely unsuccessful.

Valleys communities became global coal mining centres during the Industrial Revolution (between the 1870s–1920s). Since the mid-1980s the failure of successive waves of regeneration policies, the increasing neglect of mining communities, and the politics of austerity is the backdrop to the girls' lives. Yet the values of solidarity and close-knit bonds that ensured survival during the harsh and dangerous conditions of industrial mining remain in the psychic landscape (Walkerdine and Jimenez, 2011; Ivinson and Renold, 2013a, 2013b). Holding themselves in place has a specific vibratory resonance given that coal mining is uniquely tied to the geology of place.

In south Wales, coal seams were laid down during the Carboniferous period 298 and 323 million years ago as the earth's surface buckled under tectonic pressure. Coal was created in the syncline folds of the earth as vegetable matter from ancient waterlogged peat bogs was compressed (Figure 14.1).

Coal is found in seven valleys that lie on a north to south axis in parallel formation to the south of what is called the Wales-London-Brabant High.

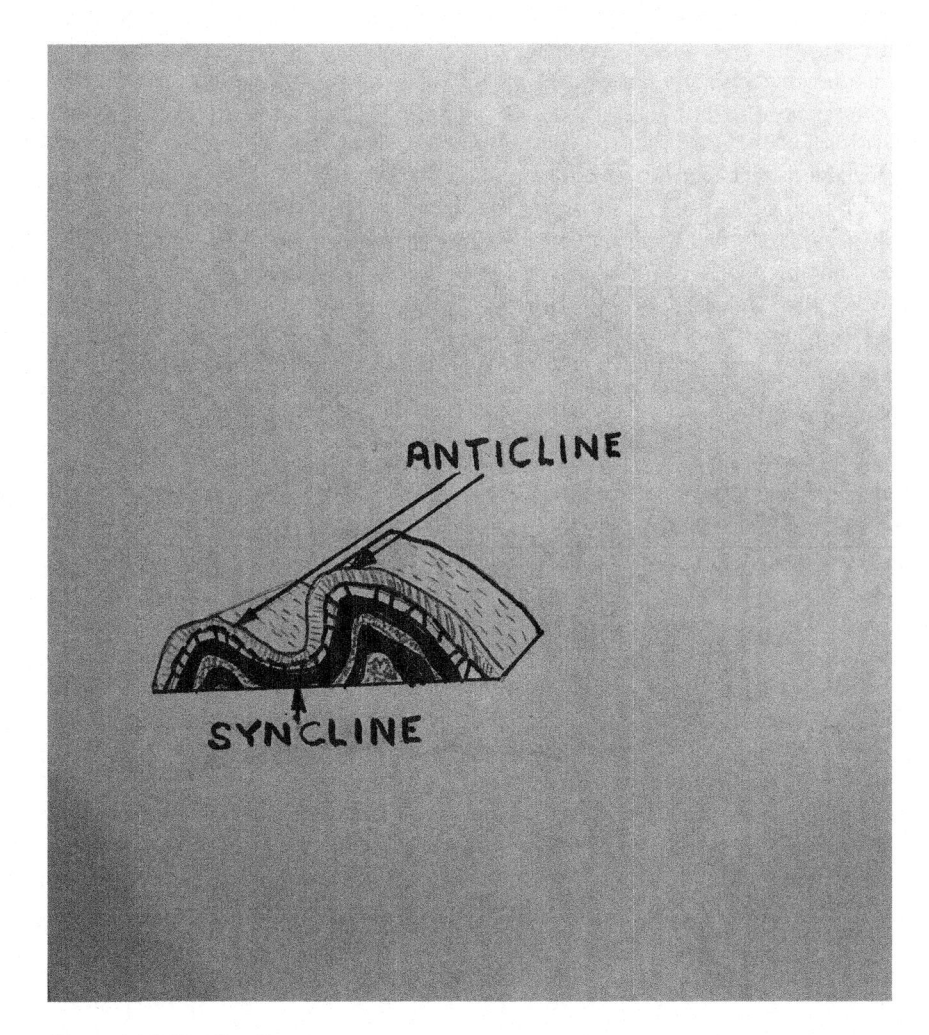

Figure 14.1 The syncline.

Of all the heavy industries mining is, by necessity, placed-based. Gilbert Simondon (2017) suggested that miners develop a specific kind of co-relation with underground nature as intuition, what Beverley Sauer (1998) refers to as 'pit sense':

> He [*sic*] lives in a kind of co-natural relation with underground nature, and this co-naturalness is so profound that it excludes all other feelings or attachment; the true miner is a subterranean man [sic]; the one who descends into the mine without loving it won't discover this essential co-naturalness.
>
> (Simondon, 2017: 107)

Accordingly, ways of being, community practices, and forms of survival are deeply entangled with the earth's geology. Intuitive ways of knowing enabled families to brave the dangers of underground mining and to form a protective community matrix (Walkerdine and Jimenez, 2011) of sociality above ground. This sociality underpins Trade Unions and labour movements and was part of the social glue that keeps valleys communities functioning in times of austerity. Sociality can be traced into the visceral stuff of girls' friendships groups (Renold and Ivinson, 2019) that came stuck and unstuck throughout our work with them. The gut holding mannerism is thus perhaps infused with molar rhythms and fears of being stuck in place, a place which resonates still with patriarchal inequalities exacerbated by the history of harsh labour practices followed by years of austerity.

Gender unfolds

The value of coal and labour, and whose labour was used to extract coal have gendered histories (Penlington, 2010). In the pre-industrial era whole families undertook mining labour together. In this era children and women hauled coal to the surface and men hewed the rock face. We have written elsewhere of how the women's working bodies were both reviled and eroticised during the Victorian era (Renold and Ivinson, 2014, 2019). In the period of industrialisation, labour became subordinated to the temporal rhythms of industry. Through a series of Parliamentary Acts, women and children were banned from working in mines and women's labour was confined to life above ground and by necessity became reciprocal to men's labour within patriarchal family structures. Not only did women have to heat water for baths, at times they had to hand-feed men when their hands were injured or suffered muscular cramps through toiling in hazardous and exhausting conditions (Penlington, 2010). A long tradition of unequal gender labour became more complicated in times of austerity, for it was often women who were able to find jobs outside the mining economy while men were unemployed.

To this day we find legacies of reciprocal and oppositional gender relations among many young people in ex-miming communities (Ivinson and Renold, 2013a). From the first interview phase of the project we learnt much about the highly gendered fears and desires young people associated with urban and rural landscapes. Many girls, for example, talked about the gendered legacies of motherhood and domesticity as a form of 'stuckness' that had been essential for the survival of community life during the industrial era, no longer meaningful to them, yet which continued to haunt them (Ivinson and Renold, 2013b):

> I want to get out of here, I don't like it … it's always the same, like, you see people going to work, coming back, cooking dinner and stuff … I don't wanna be just stuck here with like loads of kids and stuff.
>
> (Rowan, age 12)

In times of austerity, legacies that retain asymmetric gender relations can often become stronger. Some girls spoke of hiding or running from men

(Ivinson and Renold, 2013b). They rehearsed stories of rape and sexual assault (Renold and Ivinson, 2015). Even if they had not experienced such acts first hand, a visceral sense of the fear of violence has been woven into the psychic fabric of girls' and women's beingness in many ex-mining valleys communities. Many girls also anxiously talked about a feeling of always being watched:

> You've got to worry all the time. You have to watch yourself. You just can't go out, not worrying.
>
> (Tanya, age 12)

The girls' fears seem to vibrate with resonances of sedimented, polarised and violent gender/sexual relations and structures. We have witnessed first hand, teen girls' anger with such legacies (Renold and Ivinson, 2019). The fall out of the mine closures is a vibratory geo-psychic landscape, exacerbated by a politics of austerity that creates new folds in gender relations.

It is only recently that women in mining communities are beginning to speak out about the hard time of industrial mining and how hard the men were on them (Bright and Ivinson, forthcoming). Men's superior positioning in the family structure created cultures where fathers felt entitled to 'touch' their daughters, exercising a seigneurial male right to possess. Such abuses were kept hidden, unacknowledged, and silence was often violently enforced (Bright, 2018). It was a 'knowing' that everyone knew, yet which could not be spoken of or surfaced (Bright and Ivinson, forthcoming).

Perhaps, then, the gut-cradling mannerism is a protecting hold; one that shields the body from the perpetrator of violence and the gaze of the other.

Gut reactions

Above we suggest how the gut-cradling mannerism can be traced outward into the syncline folds of the ancient earth and into differential gender relations produced by the heavy industry of coal mining. We see how the very nature of the environment infolds with what was once above ground and what became coal beds below. In this section we speculate about time folds of biological matter, and the blurred boundaries between the inside and outside of organs and bodies.

While the coal beds in south Wales were laid in the Carboniferous period 298 and 323 million years ago, the species *Hominina* probably has origins between four to seven million years ago. We can imagine the human species as a phylogenetic fold, composed of carbons, proteins and oxygen. Minerals are taken in by organs and incorporated, exhaled, expelled and modified over time. The human body is a microcosm of life where the automatic processes of chemical and biologic growth and change are shaped within a multiplicity of milieux, making humans bio-cultural creatures. According to Leibniz, 'the subject lives and re-enacts its own embryonic development as a play of folds – endo-, meso-, and ectoderm' (Deleuze, 1993: xvii). Humans are subjected to a 'very great number of affections' over which they have no control (Hughes, 2011: 81, citing

Deleuze, 1992: 219). These are the non-conscious, anatomical processes of the body. These biological activities complicate notions of will, intentionality and thinking.

Wilson (2015) described the gut as a thinking organ. The gut is a super-folded membrane that ingests and digests, which has an inside that is semi-porous, more a pleat than a boundary. The gut is a series of organs that lie below the skin which itself is a clever semi-porous membrane. Digestion and ingestion are not pre-coded processes, they are environmentally constituted and involve the trafficking of molecules, in which proteins, bustle, barge, roll and communicate (Wilson, 2015). The physiology of the cell membranes that make up the gut involves a pleated accumulation of phylogenetic developments (Figure 14.2).

The gastric folds inside the stomach are called rugae. Rugae are large folds in the mucous membrane of internal surface of the organ.

> In the empty state, the stomach is contracted and its mucosa and submucosa are thrown up into distinct folds called rugae; when distended with food, the rugae are 'ironed out' and flat.
>
> (Bailey, 2019)

Throughout our work in the south Wales valleys, food and hunger were tied to the history of precarious employment patterns and social relations (Bruley, 2007).

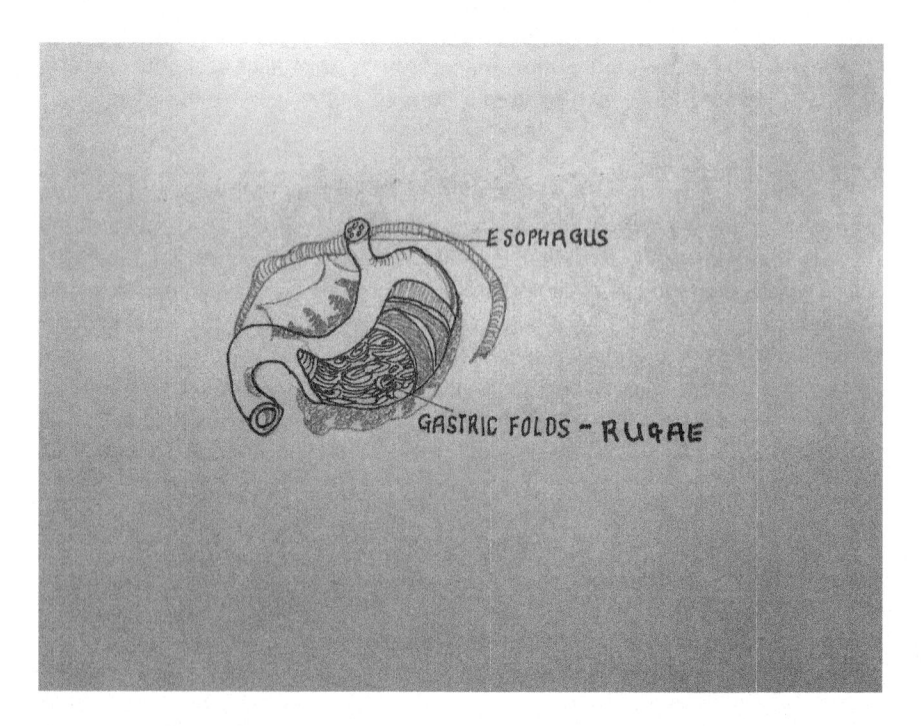

Figure 14.2 Gastric folds.

Hunger involves contractions of the stomach wall and changes in blood sugar levels. Parental/carer relationships sometimes ended abruptly and children experienced dramatic changes in their circumstances, suddenly they had to move house, live off less money or look after grieving relatives. The shift from having a steady income to claiming benefits was further complicated by the introduction of a new benefits system called Universal Credit, which left families with no money for the first six weeks. When food is precarious young people often crave carbohydrates and sugar as their diet becomes about survival. The unpredictable nature of not having enough to eat is folded into place.

Wilson reminds us that the affective intensity of hunger entails that the belly is psychically alive. Calling on Susan Isaacs, she describes this as the gut being 'phantastically alive – from birth, before birth, and in prehistory. Infant minds emerge from an engagement with this unconscious biological mentation' (Wilson, 2015: 41). Multiple folds of organic substrate relate back to prior histories through which human organs evolved, for example, from primates and even earthworms. The pre-given in biology becomes what she calls a 'phantasy'. She suggests that 'regression folds psychic events (from the present, the individual's past, and prehistory) into the heart of organic substrate' (Wilson, 2015: 56, citing Ferenczi, 1919). Accordingly:

> The action of musculature of the intestines is not that of passive substrate awaiting the animating influence of the unconscious but, rather, that of an interested broker of psychosomatic events.
>
> (Wilson, 2015: 53)

Wilson proposes that the gut is the centre of a biological unconscious. She argues, 'one of the gut's archaic feats is minding, apprehending, caring' (Wilson, 2015: 44). Her argument rests on bringing to our attention the unconscious communication that takes place between organs and between organs and the world.

> The belly takes shape from what has been ingested (from the world), from its internal neighbors (liver, diaphragm, intestines, kidney), and from bodily posture. This is an organ uniquely positioned, anatomically, to contain what is worldly, what is idiosyncratic, and what is visceral, and to show how such divisions are always being broken down, remade, metabolized, circulated, intensified, and excreted.
>
> (Wilson, 2015: 43)

Wilson explores the relation between biology and feminist theory, arguing that feminist theory has distanced itself from the biological in a bid to raise awareness about the role of culture in the construction of norms such as masculinity and femininity, and in so doing lost its transdisciplinary potential to not only know 'more' but to know otherwise.

And what might be the gut thinking here in the south Wales valleys? The Welsh artist Nicolas Evans captures the relation between hard labour undertaken underground and the psychic pain of hardship and oppression. One haunting depiction shows colliers crouching in the cramped crevasses of underground mines. Pain and hunger are folded into the anatomy of the men's faces and bodies crumpled into foetal positions within the earth womb. We see regression folds of the prehistory of ancient troglodyte people (Simondon, 2017) affectively connected to the earth.

Evans, who left the mines in his early teens after his father died in a mining accident, conjures the underground hauntings, as the trouble (Haraway, 2016) borne of the injustices in the way the mines were brutally closed and the economic and psychic devastation this caused. The girls inherit these historical injustices as an intergenerational legacy manifest, we speculate, in the folds of the gut holding gesture. Sometimes this mannerism is a protective hold, sometimes a reassuring embrace, and sometimes a way to soothe stomach cramps and hunger pangs.

Movement (un)folds: becoming unstuck

The gut holding mannerism emerged when the girls were standing still. We have speculated that the mannerism could manifest a symbolic projective stuckness, a physiological stuckness and a psychic stuckness. We sensed a wider affective resistance to opening up with us. Many girls literally could not speak in seated interviews. For some, the interview context seemed to close them down, they seemed to become drained of their sense of autonomy and some girls showed a great reluctance to talk. One girl, Rhian, simply slumped across the desk and became unable to respond to our verbal and visual prompts.

> I dunno. [huge yawn. slumps body over desk]
>
> (Rhian, aged 13)

Our speculation intensified when we compared the interview context with Rhian's vivacious account of gardening with her granddad. As she showed us around the school grounds we came across the school allotments. She came alive as she talked of digging, planting and weeding with her granddad. Clearly she became stuck and unable to speak only in some contexts.

Girls who dared to continue moving and practices childhood habits such as running, biking and climbing mountains became entangled with the historical legacies associated with normative masculinity and so for them, engaging in these activities became increasingly risky or subversive (Renold and Ivinson, 2014). Some told us that they gave up practices such as swimming, rugby, football, biking, skating, dancing and horse riding around the ages of 11 to 12 years because the activities seemed to clash with the normative expectations of teen femininity in the local community.

> I had my own bike but I don't use it. It's just, I dunno, I'm too quiet. It's like, you've gotta get dirty and break bones and everything.
>
> (Lucy, aged 13)

Moving with the folds of time and place 179

Being stuck in place such as giving up physical hobbies and standing still is not an absence of movement, it is itself a complex assemblage of beingness, possibly criss-crossed with psychic pain and unconscious legacies of past trauma. As Manning (2013: 43) points out 'standing still' is a difficult posture; it hides a multiplicity of complex muscular efforts required to retain balance. Standing still is an event that is immanent with forces anchored in contrasting fields and existential territories.

Within the school hall Jên created a much-needed place of ontological security and slowly she encouraged the girls to move. As the girls followed the gentle movement exercises we sensed their bodies discovering the power of movement again. Gradually the exercises expanded their/our movement repertoires. Manning writes about how 'rhythm comes to the fore through techniques of invention', drawing on Simondon to suggest:

> Techniques are imbued with rhythm, they move with the machine's own forces of recombination.
>
> (Manning, 2013: 10)

To create intentional movement requires that we commit ourselves to a motion so that mind, body and intention move as one, which Jên referred to as 'e-motion'. Through the workshops girls came into a newfound sense of purposefulness engendered by joyful affections (Ivinson and Renold, forthcoming).

Futures folds

Above we have speculated about a series of transdisciplinary pleats as asymmetric principles (Deleuze, 1994: 106). We moved from the geological formations across vast temporal scales of waves of coal extraction and the appearance of *Hominina*, millions of years ago. In ancient times people mined the earth for minerals possibly using specific kinds of intuitive knowing in co-relation with underground nature (Simondon, 2017). We speculate that this kind of transdisciplinary knowing remains as non-spoken feelings and forms of sensing held in communities and that this develops into specific patterns of sociality, bodily movement and self-relation linked to the geological folds of place. We imagine this as a deep underground vibratory beat.

The forces of culture in terms of capitalism, patriarchy and gender relations swerved the development of mining and disciplined activities into a new beat. Industrialisation created a rupture that separated miners from the activities of mining. We speculate that as factory owners mediated the relation between coal extraction and coal use, a new consciousness, perhaps a more reflective consciousness, was born which can be linked to the rise of Trade Unions movements. Communities' minoritarian (Manning, 2016) tendencies of, for example, solidarities of health care protection, women's domestic labour and socialist political knowledge contributed to the community matrix (Walkerdine and Jimenez, 2011). We speculate that these became minor forces that both unmoored the structural integrity of major forms of industrial practices and contributed to a kind of second skin (Bick, 1968) or Leibniz' ecto-derm of protection and survival in the oppressive working/living/killing/polluting conditions of coal extraction. The reverberations of the harsh brutality of work, the present–absence of male labour, and the hidden violence men enacted on women, together is the haunting trouble of the past that will not be stilled. We speculate that these engender the rhythmic rockings, tummy-cradlings, self-affirming, gentle embrace of the girls' gut holding mannerism standing still yet not still on the ground where too many unacknowledged, gendered and sexual histories vibrate below the surface.

As the girls stood, rocking in a semi-foetal fold of protection, arms wrapped around a thinking gut, mannerism had multiple folds and existential forces coursing through it. The virtual potential of the place could be glimpsed, we suggest, through the movement exercises orchestrated by Jên as she transformed the ground beneath the girls' feet. The music she chose delivered its energy, movement took on a different beat and the space expanded outward, filling the atmosphere and lifting their thoughts into talk. Thus, girls spoke of the need to go fast, to travel far and to be different (Renold and Ivinson, 2014, 2015).

The micro-politics of becoming calls us to ask what more the girls could become if we think of space, the hall, the school, the town, the community extending evermore outward into far-reaching worlds and the cosmos, if we could think beyond the temporal arrow that points to an inevitable, closed down, end point. For Deleuze, 'immanence is a task with a future dimension' (Colebrook, 2002: 78). If the human species is a phylogenetic fold, so another series of increasingly concertina-ed pleats might unfold and vibrate across the surface of the earth and across gut's manifold to create different milieu for appetites and desires to incubate. In our work, we see hope in desires that open up through movement and art. We have been touched by the never-ending labour of care that women show towards others (Bright and Ivinson, forthcoming) and which girls feel, ingest, fear and crave for their own unfolding existences (Renold and Ivinson, 2019).

Wilson argues that, for too long, feminists have been battling against the Freudian thesis that 'anatomy is destiny' (Wilson, 2015: 45). She suggests that, rather than turning away from anatomy, feminists should embrace the potential of transdisciplinary thinking by embracing the anatomical and 'turn towards it more attentively to see what improbable capacities it holds' (ibid.). In our work we have been exploring what improbable capacities are locked in the past waiting to unfolded: what virtually, energetico potentialities might emerge from girls' moving bodies? Activities such as breathing, getting hungry, eliminating, falling asleep, and feeling the coming and going of emotions are within us in the micro beats of living, so as Manning (2013) reminds us, we are never without the presence of vital affects.

Just as women hauled coal out of pits as a means of survival and later as a way to find economic independence, so more purposeful corporeal movements can free girls from the social constraints and surveillance they intuitively sense on/in their bodies. For it is in the ceaseless movement of matter (Nietzsche) that we find the proto-possibility of different beats, of futures that do not move with the sedimented rhythms of the past. Boundaries are dissolving and reforming continuously in the minor and molar bio-geological and cultural folds of time. With Leibniz we speculate of a gut holding mannerism that lives and re-enacts its own embryonic development as a play of endo-, meso- and ecto-dermic transdisciplinary folds of caring and becoming.

Note

1 This project was located within the Wales Institute of Social and Economic Research, Data and Methods (WISERD) and funded by the UK Economic and Social Research Council and the Higher Education Funding Council for Wales (Grant number: RES-576-25-0021).

References

Bailey, R. (2019). ThoughtCo. Retrieved from www.thoughtco.com/anatomy-of-the-stomach-373482. Accessed 10 October 2019.
Barad, K. (2007). *Meeting the Universe Halfway*. Durham, NC: Duke University Press.
Bick, E. (1968). The experience of the skin in early object-relations. *International Journal of Psychoanalysis*, 49, 484–486.
Bright, N. G. (2018). 'A chance to talk like this': Gender, education, and social haunting in a UK Coalfield. In J. Smyth, and R. Simmons (Eds.), *Education and Social Class*. London: Palgrave.
Bright, G. and Ivinson, G. (forthcoming). 'Washing lines, whinberries and (reworking) waste ground: Women's affective practices in the socially haunted UK coalfields' Special Issue 'Social Haunting, Classed Affect, and the Afterlives of Deindustrialization' *Journal of Working Class Studies*.
Bruley, S. (2007). The politics of food: Gender, family, community and collective feeding in South Wales in the general strike and miners' lockout of 1926. *Twentieth Century British History*, 18(1), 54–77.
Colebrook, C. (2002). *Gilles Deleuze. Routledge Critical Thinkers*. London and New York, NY: Routledge Taylor-Francis Group.
Coleman, R., Page, T. and Palmer, H. (2019). Feminist New Materialist Practice: The Mattering of Methods. In *MAI Feminism and Visual Culture*, Spring Issue. Retrieved from https://maifeminism.com/category/focus-issue-intro/
Deleuze, G. (1992). *Expressionism in Philosophy: Spinoza*. Trans. M. Joughin. New York, NY: Zone.
Deleuze, G. (1993). *The Fold: Leibniz and the Baroque*. Foreword and Trans. T. Conley. London: Athlone Press.
Deleuze, G. (1994). *Difference and Repetition*. Trans. P. Paton. London and New York, NY: Bloomsbury.
Ellingson, L. (2017). *Embodiment in Qualitative Research*. London: Routledge.
Ferenczi, S. (1919/1926). '"Materialization" in Globus Hystericus'. *Further Contributions to the Theory and Techniques of Psychoanalysis*. Trans. Jane Isabel Suttie. New York, NY: Brunner/Mazel.
Guattari, F. (2006). *Chaosmosis: An ethico-aesthetic paradigm*. Trans. P. Baines. Sydney: Power Publications.

Haraway, D. (2008). *When Species Meet*. Minneapolis, MN: University of Minnesota Press.

Haraway, D. (2016). *Staying With the Trouble: Making Kin With Chthulecene*. Durham, NC: Duke University.

Hughes, J. (2011). Believing in the world: Toward an ethics of form. In L. Guillaume and J. Hughes (Eds.), *Deleuze and the Body*. Edinburgh: Edinburgh University Press.

Ivinson, G. and Renold, E. (2013a). Valleys' girls: Re-theorising bodies and agency in a semirural, post-industrial locale. *Gender and Education*, 25, Special Issue: Feminist Materialisms and Education, 704–721.

Ivinson, G. and Renold, E. (2013b). Subjectivity, affect and place: Thinking with Deleuze and Guattari's body without organs to explore a young teen girl's becomings in a post-industrial locale. *Subjectivity*, 6, 369–390.

Ivinson, G. and Renold, E. (2016). Girls, camera, (intra)action: Mapping posthuman possibilities in a diffractive analysis of camera-girl assemblages in research on gender, corporeality and place. In C. Taylor and C. Hughes (Eds.), *Posthuman Research Practices in Education*. Buckingham: Palgrave.

Ivinson, G. and Renold, E. (forthcoming). Entanglements of place, corporeality and gender: Exploring teen girls' moving bodies in an ex-industrial place. *Body and Society*.

MacLure, M. (2013). Researching without representation: language and materiality in post qualitative methodology. *International Journal of Qualitative Studies in Education*, 26(6), 658–667.

Manning, E. (2013). *Always More Than One: Individuation's Dance*. Durham, NC, and London: Duke University Press.

Manning, E. (2016). *The Minor Gesture*. Durham, NC and London: Duke University Press.

Penlington, N. (2010). Masculinity and Domesticity in 1930s South Wales: Did Unemployment Change the Domestic Division of Labour? *Twentieth Century British History*, 21(3), 281–299.

Renold, E. (2018). 'Feel what I feel': Making Da(r)ta with Teen girls for creative activisms on how sexual violence matters. *Journal of Gender Studies*, 27(1)1, 37–55.

Renold, E. (2019). Ruler-skirt risings: becoming crafty with how gender and sexuality education research comes to matter. In T. Jones, L. Coll, L. van Lewent and Y. Taylor (Eds.), *Up-lifting Gender & Sexuality Study in Education & Research*. London: Palgrave Macmillan.

Renold, E. (2020). Becoming AGENDA: co-creating of a youth-activist resource to address gendered and sexual violence with a run-a-way pARTicipatory praxis. *Reconceptualising Educational Research Methodology*. 10(2–3), doi: https://doi.org/10.7577/rerm.3677

Renold, E. and Ivinson, G. (2014). Horse-girl assemblages: Towards a post-human cartography of girls' desire in an ex-mining valleys community. *Discourse: Studies in the Cultural Politics of Education*, 35, 361–376.

Renold, E. and Ivinson, G. (2015). Mud, mermaids and burnt wedding dresses: Mapping queer assemblages in teen girls' talk on gender and sexual violence. In E. Renold, D. Egan and J. Ringrose (Eds.), *Children, sexuality and sexualization* (pp. 239–255). Buckingham: Palgrave.

Renold, E. and Ivinson, G. (2019). Anticipating the more-than: Working with prehension in artful interventions with young people in a post-industrial community. *Futures*, 112, doi: 10.1016/j.futures.2019.05.006.

Ringrose, J., Warfield, K. and Zarabadi, S. (Eds.) (2018). *Feminist Posthumanisms, New Materialisms and Education*. London and New York, NY: Routledge.

Simondon, G. (2017). *On the Existence of Technical Objects*. Trans. C. Malaspina and J. Rogove. Minneapolis, MN and London: A Univocal Book, Minnesota Press.

St. Pierre, E. A. (2019). Post qualitative inquiry in an ontology of immanence. *Qualitative Inquiry*, 25(1), 3–16.

Sauer, B. (1998). Embodied knowledge: The textual representation of embodied sensory information in a dynamic and uncertain material environment. *Written Communication*, 15(2), 131–169.

Walkerdine, V. and Jimenez, J. (2011). *Gender, Work and Community After De-Industrialisation: A Psychosocial Approach to Affect*. Basingstoke: Palgrave Macmillan.

Wilson, E. (2015). *Gut Feminism*. Durham, NC: Duke University Press.

15 Transition states

Chemistry educators engaging with and being challenged by matter, materiality and what may come to be

Kathryn Scantlebury, Anita Hussénius and Catherine Milne

Introduction: use of material feminist theory in chemistry education – teaching, learning and research

For several decades, feminist scholars have critiqued science and challenged its premises especially those that separate the researcher from the researched in a search for objectivity or that seek to write out women from the historical development of science (Stengers, 2018). Yet most of these critiques have focused on the disciplines of biology and physics with few offering a feminist critique of chemistry's underlying principles and assumptions. Rather, studies in the construction of chemistry are often atheoretical with regards to gender and race, rarely offering any examination of power structures or any critical examination of the socio-cultural aspects of learning chemistry and the gendered construction of the discipline.

In the late 1980s and 1990s feminist scholars critiqued the gendered nature of science (Schiebinger, 1999; Tuana, 1989). Haraway (1988) challenged feminists to engage with the material because the discourse that built science and technology produced a matrix of domination. More recently, Barad (2007) building upon Haraway's theories, and using Bohr's epistemological framework, published a ground-breaking, field-defining text, challenging us and the rest of humanity to 'meet the universe halfway' by becoming entangled with matter and materiality. Taken together, these authors present us with the question of whether there are transdisciplinary ways to explore the nature of chemistry and chemistry education that undermine the gendered nature of the discipline, while also remaining true to the tenets of feminist materiality. Lykke (2010) noted that transdisciplinary research poses and explores research questions that do not belong within existing disciplines and as such have the potential to generate new knowledge and areas of inquiry not accessible to a traditional discipline such as chemistry.

This chapter responds to these provocations in ways that speak into feminism's critique of the power structures that facilitate/cause inequities, especially as they pertain towards women and girls. In it, we explore the use of research|practices, such as cogenerative dialogues (cogens), snaplogs and shadowing as feminist strategies to illustrate transdisciplinary material feminist research, and how these research strategies entangle humans with images, instruments, matter and material in the construction of chemical phenomena, knowledge, ontology and epistemology. We discuss how cogens, snaplogs and shadowing are research|practices that challenge the current power structures and problematize the hierarchy in teaching chemistry, while generating research questions not yet asked within the discipline.

Our scholarly 'location' within science education/science as feminist researchers places us in a transdisciplinary 'transition state' that produces unsettled feelings. A transition state, in a chemical sense, is explained further below but it represents an unstable 'condition' where it is impossible to halt/remain – you either return back from where you came or move to a new position. Our research identities as chemists/chemistry educators may invoke certain 'scientific' practices in conducting, reporting and teaching in our discipline yet those 'scientific practices' can be in conflict with material feminism practices – and vice versa. These different practices are grounded in different perceptions of knowledge, where 'pure' chemistry and traditional chemistry teaching has not embraced, or is even aware of, Barad's agential realism. Thus, located in a chemistry department surrounded by chemists who are ignorant of material feminism causes tensions that put us in an unstable 'condition'. And gender studies scholars often are uninformed about natural sciences practices and perceptions of knowledge. Regardless, when we are in an unstable transition state connected with unsettled feelings, forced by pressure from the surrounding or our own 'inner' experience of being uncomfortable, we may adjust back within the borders of the local setting/discourse. But transition states have the potential to generate opportunities for something new that would be impossible within a traditional discipline, and thus may constitute a mountain pass (see below) for feminist transdisciplinary change.

Our discipline, our research

Chemistry is the study of matter and energy with the purposes of understanding the chemical processes of nature while also seeking power over nature by developing tools to synthesize both chemicals found in nature and chemicals new to nature. Chemistry is often celebrated for its contributions to humans' quality of life, including such developments as the Haber–Bosch process for making fertilizer from nitrogen gas to improve crop production, pharmaceuticals to prevent or cure disease and chlorofluorocarbons which allowed safer and more effective refrigeration. However, making chemicals new to nature, which are synthesized because of their very stability and usefulness to humans, such as these examples were, has created multiple environmental and social challenges to humans and the organic and material world.

Chemistry education research focuses on studies of the teaching and learning of the discipline, often with a focus on chemical concepts, such as chemical periodicity, chemical equilibrium or thermodynamics, necessary topics for understanding the discipline. Thus, chemistry education research focuses on students' understanding – or lack thereof – of conceptual chemical knowledge. Another major area is pedagogical content knowledge, that is, how teachers of chemistry understand the discipline and what practices they use to 'effectively' teach students.

Sometimes chemistry education research will use socio-cultural theories to frame questions, analyze data and interpret outcomes but in general it ignores the socio-cultural impact of chemistry and rarely (if ever) uses material feminism or posthumanist theories.

In the educational contexts that we have examined, matter and materiality remain passive entities that are moulded into objects for understanding and utility by the efforts of human agency. Chemists and chemistry educators largely ignore the very matter for which they profess a passion for understanding. By acknowledging matters' agentic qualities and applying feminist theories that are more often used in the humanities and social sciences, we challenge the traditional chemistry discipline and thereby engage in and with transdisciplinary practices. In a virtual seminar on 'rethinking interdisciplinarity' Helga Novotny illustrated the concept transdisciplinarity by the analogy that 'knowledge seeps through institutions and structures like water through the pores of a membrane' and therefore is about transgressing boundaries (Novotny, 2006, quoted in Trojer 2017: 56). In this chapter, we connect transdisciplinary practices and our transgressing of boundaries with the chemical concept of transition states because transition states, while key to the formation of new substances also produces a state of 'in-betweenness' as atoms reorganize themselves. We explain this in more detail in the next section.

Transition states: a 'chemical sense' explanation

Transition state theory explains the processes and progress of chemical reactions. Chemical reactions occur when bonds between atomic entities are broken, atoms re-configure into different arrangements and new bonds are established. It takes an input of energy to 'break' bonds for chemical reactions to occur and energy is released when new bonds are formed. Climbing over a mountain is an analogy to illustrate a chemical reaction. There may be several paths over the mountain which can lead a climber to different final destinations. Correspondingly, a chemical reaction can lead to different products depending on which path the reaction takes; that is, how the atoms and the bonds between them can morph from one arrangement to another. For the climber the path across the rock can mean a number of smaller climbs up and down before reaching the final destination. Similarly, a chemical reaction may consist of several sub-steps, where the 'highest points' on each such step are transition states. In each such step the transition state is the highest point on the 'easiest' path, that is, the transformation of atoms and bonds that require the lowest energy to occur. At this point, the chemical bonds undergoing transformation are neither fully broken nor fully developed; instead they are more or less partially broken and formed.

We use the analogy of a transition state to examine chemistry, material feminism and pedagogy to forefront matters' agentic qualities and destabilize the 'status quo' of the discipline. Reactions take time and the rate depends on a variety of factors. A catalyst can lower the energy needed to start the reaction (known as the activation energy) and thus increase the reaction rate. In the analogy of the mountain, a catalyst could be something making it easier to climb a steep rock (like a rope, a ladder or a chair-lift). Material feminism can thus be seen as the catalyst providing a possibility for transformations of chemistry education and beyond, where the agency of matter is taken into account.

In material feminism, matter has agency, humans are de-centred as knowledge-producers and bodies, objects and matter are entangled in meaning-making. Through material feminism researchers are engaged at the micro-level in the social and chemical (sub-micro) 'sense'. A material feminism transition state in chemistry education could be an examination of the power structures that re-configure in different arrangements as students and teachers come together in a learning environment. Also, the humans are moving towards a re-thinking of what it means to know as the agentic nature of matter is acknowledged and an awareness, an awakening of the central role of matter in knowledge production, is realized. Moreover, the transition state can engage researchers, teachers and students in a flattened hierarchy, that provides ways and means to change pedagogical practices to challenge power structures. With respect to our research|practices discussed here, snaplogs and cogens support learning while offering learners opportunities to articulate what they value in the teaching context, while, in a slightly different way, shadowing provides a pathway to increase teachers' awareness of 'what matters', and thus supports students' learning. In the transition state, chemistry educators could make the 'familiar' strange by questioning unconscious practices and critiquing what is taken for granted as 'standard' practice. In the next section we discuss the practices of cogenerative dialogues (Kathryn), snaplogs (Catherine) and shadowing (Anita), and show how these can be regarded as transdisciplinary practices.

Transdisciplinary practices of cogenerative dialogues, snaplogs and shadowing

(1) *Cogenerative dialogues (cogens): Kathryn*

I started using cogenerative dialogues (cogens) with undergraduate science teacher education students to model the practice so they could use cogens when student teaching. Cogens is a form of praxis used by students, teachers and researchers to engage in critical discussions on science classroom practices with the intent of establishing equitable teaching and learning practices through the generation of local knowledge, proposing and enacting changes that promote equity (Stith and Roth, 2006). When focused on structures that impact on women, cogens can act as research|pedagogy and may be considered feminist praxis (Scantlebury and LaVan, 2006). Cogens provide students with a forum to critically examine their engagement with learning science and how that engagement contributes to their scientific identities (Bayne and Scantlebury, 2012). They take place outside of regular instruction time. Important facets of cogens are that all participants have an equal role and responsibility in organizing and managing the cogen. Participants listen to others' perspectives and share their own with the group cogenerating solutions to problems or challenges to science learning and teaching.

Cogen research has yet to utilize material feminist theories and, with cogens focused primarily on the teaching and learning of science, a re-thinking of them to recognize the entanglement of matter, bodies, space, time and discourses is clearly the next stage in this field's research trajectory. In Baradian theory, subjects do not have individual agency but generate agency through intra-action. The uniqueness of entanglements (i.e. material-culture, time, space, human, matter) is that the entities involved are not just intra-acting with each other; instead the entanglement produces something that is greater than the sum of its parts (Barad, 2007). Entanglements produced through cogens can result in girls engaging in science and re-ascribing their identities to include science. The structure of cogens is intended to flatten power hierarchies between teachers and students, as well as provide a forum where students articulate their needs and concerns.

I met Jen, a white, middle class, female science teacher at a low socio-economic urban high school on the east coast of the United States that enrolled predominantly African American students, when we were participating in a science education research group. Teachers were using cogens to improve their understanding of students' science learning needs and for the students to understand the teachers' instructional goals, school and district structures that framed their teaching practices, and the challenges of and their aspirations for the students' science learning.

Jen initiated cogens because her female students did not enact the material-discursive practices she associated with 'appropriate ways of participating in science, and that meant that it looked and sounded a certain way'. Because her female students' material-discursive practices did not demonstrate their engagement with science as defined by Jen, she assumed they were disinterested in science. Six girls volunteered to participate in the cogens which occurred at lunch in Jen's classroom. We provided the girls with lunch and the 'rules' for cogens that included everyone having an equal voice and responsibility in running a cogen (Tobin, 2014). Participants are given and shown respect, ideas and opinions are shared and valued; listening was as important as talking, and solutions would be co-generated to address questions and concerns raised in the cogen. For Jen and the students, the cogen was an example of a transition state where their material-discursive practices focused on enacting changes in the science classroom that would improve the girls' engagement in, and understanding of, the subject.

During the year, the group engaged in cogens focused on how they (students and teacher) would assume co-responsibility for science learning and teaching. Jen stated to the girls that while they did not disrupt the class, they did not engage either. She asked what were the issues that prevented the girls from learning science and what could be done to change that situation. The girls told Jen they found it difficult to follow the lesson as she taught and wrote notes at the same time, asked questions and gave them little time to think about the concepts before moving on. Accordingly, Jen changed her teaching approach and the girls had time to ask questions and respond to Jen's questions. Moreover, through the cogens, the girls' assumed responsibility for their leaning and restructured their environment by changing their lab seats away from students who distracted them during laboratory sessions. This minor change enabled the girls to talk with each other about the science concepts that were illustrated through the labs. Through cogens, Jen and her students critiqued assumptions about science's material-discursive practices and identified ways that would support girls' science learning.

Cogens provided the structure for us to pose new questions about girls' science learning and teachers' practices that challenged science's hegemonic masculinity and moved into transdisciplinary feminist research|practices by sharing the responsibility of ensuring learning science among the girls and Jen. The discussions led to changes in the students and teacher practices such that the girls transitioned from disengaged learners to students who asked and answered questions during formal instruction, completed laboratory work and assumed responsibility for their science learning. These transdisciplinary feminist research|practices (Lykke, 2010) placed the participants in a transition state which raised new questions and required an activation energy from the participants: engaging in cogens produced changes in their practices as learners and teachers. Moreover, these practices offered the girls a pathway through which to restructure their identities to include science learner.

(2) *Using snaplogs to explore learning: Catherine*

As a high school teacher and a university educator, I have grappled with how to support students' awareness of connecting their learning to the world. As a form of self-assessment, I have asked students to identify what they found most interesting in their class experience and explain why. This strategy became more structured when I became involved in implementing a self-assessment model of reflection into university courses (McVarish and Milne, 2014). With this model, I asked graduate or undergraduate students to reflect and write a note of something they learned and, if possible, connect this learning/experience to other life experiences or ask questions connecting their classroom experiences with everyday experiences. Every week I responded to the students' notes. Over the years that I implemented this approach, students responded that they were rarely asked to practice self-evaluation and were unsure of how to reflect. However, I valued the highly variable nature of each student's reflection on the same lesson.

This experience reinforced for me how we use assessments in education to limit what counts as knowing. I know Haraway (1988) rails against the idea of reflecting as reflecting back but I never had that expectation. I explicitly deterred such practices telling students that since I had also been present in class they did not need to describe their reflection on what happened in class. However, I was troubled by the fact that reflection cards tended to privilege text. Barad (2003) argued, and I agreed, that text had too much power and as a consequence material-discursive practices got lost or subjugated in the way Latour (1987) labels 'inscription devices' producing external representations that are for communication through language.

Reading Barad's (2007) and Haraway's (1992: 300) ideas of diffraction as 'a mapping of interference, not of replication, reflection, or reproduction' provided me with a different way of thinking about how students might engage with their learning. From my material-discursive approach, asking participants to think back over their experiences did not place me in a position of having to expect that all participants would reproduce an experience. Diffraction justified difference and offered a strategy for opening up and expanding opportunities for students to highlight their learning and the connections they were making in idiosyncratic ways that were all acceptable. A material-discursive approach meant that I also wanted participants working with a variety of media, so I needed a tool that would complicate the media in which students constructed their diffraction. Bramming *et al.* (2012: 55) introduced me to the 'performativity' of snaplogs as a 'visual method within qualitative research'. Snaplogs are a contraction of 'snapshot' and 'log' and offer a strategy for foregrounding the aspects of practice in a 'process of framing' (ibid., 58). Snaplogs offered students the freedom to document important evidence of learning and, most importantly, their diffractive potential enabled the material world that was a largely ignored agent in their construction of knowledge to be brought more to the fore.

Snaplogs enable each student to produce phenomena of learning through their intra-action with the material world via their smartphones. I negotiated with students in a Liberal Arts course on water and sustainability to use snaplogs at least eight weeks of a 15-week semester. I then responded on their snaplog, which provided me with a way of acknowledging and possibly challenging the connections and claims they made (see Figures 15.1–15.3 below for the first weeks of snaplogging and my responses).

Olivia re-presents her entanglement with water and a paperclip using a snaplog. Her statement: *The surface tension of the water allowed the paper clip to float*, led me to respond (in red): *Olivia, I am wondering how you understand 'surface tension'?* I do not assume that Olivia understands the phenomenon that is captured by her intra-action. I ask another question with the goal of further activating her thinking: *What does 'floating' of the paperclip tell you or suggest to you about how the water molecules that make up the water are organized? Have you seen this phenomenon in your everyday life? If so, where?*

Transition states 191

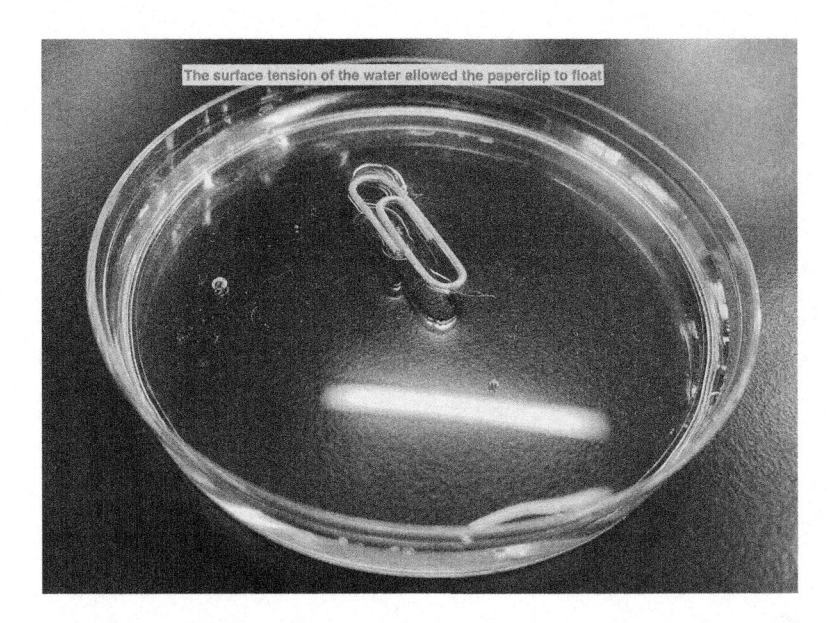

Figure 15.1 Snaplog: water and paperclip.

Figure 15.2 Snaplog: planting peas.

192   K. Scantlebury et al.

In this snaplog, the participant notes the connection between the peas they were planting and a rap music band called The Black Eyed Peas. I reply (in red): *Yes ☺ and can you say 'Frijol carita'? I hope your seeds are still alive. I realized I checked them on Friday but I had a day long course on Saturday and did not get back there.*

> I was able to make the clay float by forming it into a boat-like shape with the edges curved upwards. I never thought about why heavy boats can float and I think it is really interesting to find out that it has to do with density and surface area. I'm intereasted to learn more about water related things like this!

Figure 15.3 Snaplog: clay.

Ashley's snaplog of modelling clay's intra-action with water and in another intra-action the sense she is making of that experience with other experiences she has had.

Each student's snap and log showed the phenomenon constructed as they intra-acted with the material world. Note the snaplog in which a student observed that 'black eyed peas' are not just a band but also seeds that can be planted. For others, it was the intra-actions between water and different matter that produced different phenomena: surface tension and buoyancy, which became the focus of their snap and log as evocative of their experiences in class.

As I reviewed a semester of students' snaplogs, I was struck by the diversity of the images constructed as they variably intra-acted with matter over time. Some of the material was highly evocative. For example, the process of building DIY water monitors, which introduced students to making electric circuits to identify when plants needed watering, evoked emotion, cognition and memory (Turkle, 2007). It became clear that the snaplogs made concrete the phenomena we create.

If we think of snaplogs in terms of transition states, it takes time for students to make connections between what happens in the classroom and their everyday lives – the activation energy can be high at the beginning and that connection may not always be there, so the reaction may not really start. However, with time and experience, students begin to make more connections and their snaplogs become more complex involving time series presentations and multiple images. I came to see snaplogs as a valid feminist (and later transdisciplinary) way to help course participants negotiate a pathway into well-defined disciplines like chemistry.

(3) *Shadowing, agency of matter and its intra-action with students to create new material-discursive practices: Anita*

My contribution comes from acting as a 'shadow' (Czarniawska, 2007) to four male chemistry professors at three different Swedish universities. As a shadow, I examine the material conditions in laboratories, in line with my interest in how social arrangements, specifically those relating to gender hierarchies, develop in connection to these conditions. Although a material feminist perspective might consider how all sorts of material conditions matter in the social construction of gender (Wicke, 1994), my focus is particularly on the equipment used in chemistry laboratory activities.

I have spent most of my academic life in chemistry departments, teaching chemistry and conducting chemistry research. However, for the last decade my academic 'home' has been an interdisciplinary Centre for Gender Research with researchers from humanities, social sciences, medicine and natural sciences. These years have given me a space and temporal distance to have an outsider's perspective, such that former taken-for-granted enculturated aspects of the academic chemistry environment appear in a new light. Interdisciplinary research is commonly associated with a group of scholars with different disciplinary belongings and onto-epistemological positions, carrying out research that requires knowledge from more than one discipline to be accomplished. However, according to Trojer (2017) a single researcher moving from one discipline initially into other disciplines while struggling with a problem, can also be regarded as doing interdisciplinary research, with a likelihood of creating new intertwined theoretical and methodological practices. If this likelihood becomes a reality, then it fits into Lykke's (2010) description of transdisciplinary research. My own journey is a result of struggles connected to power structures and the gendered construction of the chemistry discipline. As a 'shadow' my various perspectives – as chemist/insider and gender researcher/outsider – are intertwined and act as a variant of what Barad (2007) describes as a non-dualistic whole rather than distinguishable positions.

As a chemist embracing material feminist theories, I scrutinize what goes on 'in place' where chemistry takes place. During fieldwork, I was the chemists' shadow from the beginning of the day to the end, I followed them everywhere. These scientists work in their laboratories investigating chemical reactions, material properties, molecules, doing controlled experiments, using vocabulary with stipulated definitions, and they get joy from adding insights to our understanding of matter and materiality. But chemistry's subject culture, language and practical work form gendered knowledge and identities which can both reproduce, amplify and break stereotypical views and power relationships. Key to this is matter as a co-actor constantly intra-acting with the humans. In the excerpt below, from an observation in a course lab during my shadowing of a chemistry professor where the student group consisted of seven women and one man, we can see how students' use of protective gloves illustrates this agency of matter and the evolution of a material-discursive practice (Hussénius, 2018).

> Students wear protective gloves all the time. Sometimes they take them off, but almost immediately put on new ones. I ask if this is something students learn during the introductory chemistry courses, that they are told to always wear gloves as a safety precaution. The professor denies that is the case. I ask how it can be that all students have protective gloves. He says they wear gloves when they look in a microscope and when they are handling deionized water. I wonder if this might be a practice learned in high school and the teacher says 'yes, maybe it is'. However, my feeling is that this is not something raised and discussed with the students – that is, when it is relevant to wear gloves and when it is not.... When I ask the students they respond that they have been told to wear gloves. I ask who told them to do so and they respond 'the teachers'. When I ask whether it is the teachers at the university or at high school, they say 'it's here during this education'.
>
> (Field notes, April 2016)

Disposable plastic gloves are a protective device whose purpose varies depending on context – sometimes they protect the wearer, other times they protect the sample. In addition, the gloves can pose a risk factor for the wearer or the sample. The students had earlier analyzed DNA and worn gloves to protect the sample from their own DNA. In other contexts, particles that adhere to the outside of gloves can contaminate an experiment, thus giving unreliable results. When handling chemicals that can penetrate the skin, wearing gloves can generate a false sense of safety, because you lose sensitivity and may fail to realize that an organic compound has penetrated the gloves. Without gloves, you feel the chemical contact on your skin and then immediately can wash your hands.

In the context I observed, the wearing of protective gloves was not justified. Instead, it was a routine developed within the student group. But the teacher did not question the students' glove-wearing routine, thus giving it the legitimacy of being 'correct' behaviour. When and why gloves are used seemed to be a taken-for-granted knowledge, something students are expected to understand, without it being explicitly communicated. Regardless, the students' wearing of protective gloves imparts a kind of protective-glove-wearing discourse that implies a specific act.

According to Butler (1990) the sense of belonging rests on the re-experiencing and reiteration of socially established meanings. In this context, group belonging and inclusion was demonstrated by wearing gloves, because not to wear gloves meant that you would stand out. Artefacts like lab coats, gloves and goggles are also likely to contribute to students' identification of themselves and each other as prospective chemists. In this way, students mimic the 'right way' to be, embrace the 'correct' behaviour and incorporate these into their self-image as important components of what it means to 'be' and 'do' 'natural scientist' (Bergwik, 2014). Putting on protective gloves works in the same way – as an example of what Barad (2003) calls posthumanist performativity, in which material have agency as co-creators of identities, action and action space. Thus, protective equipment does more than simply protect. It becomes an attribute through which the wearer embraces the feeling of a future professional identity – a chemist to come, an expert. The gloves have an agency that extends beyond their intended purpose and use. Students and gloves intra-act with each other in the creation of a material-discursive practice (Barad, 2007).

The teacher becomes a co-agent in this creation. Due to his inattention regarding the use of protective gloves, or incapability to correct something taken for granted, he is part of the entanglement that contributes to the space and effect of the intra-action between students and gloves. In fact, his inattention or incapability is a prerequisite in subtly enforcing a gendered norm: we could say that he does not recognize this group of students, the majority of which are female, as potential chemists and therefore does not bother to address their improper glove use. And there is more to say about the gloves' agency: the gloves could be perceived as bearers of economic power. They occupy the lab in such a way that the number of gloves consumed is significantly greater than justified by the number of students in the room and their possible need for protection. For the manufacturing companies there is an economic gain in gloves having a positive legitimacy and identity effect. For the chemistry environment, the effect instead becomes an unnecessary cost, where the teacher becomes an unintentional co-creator of the power of this glove-using economy.

To return to the transition state analogy, the glove-students intra-actions and the resulting material-discursive practices of glove-wearing create a path which contributes to the bodily formation and entangled cognitive internalization of a chemist identity in becoming. For the teacher, to become the catalyst that facilitates the students' path to a chemist identity – which can be recognized as such by experienced chemists – both a material awareness is required and self-reflection on the underlying assumptions which affects her/his actions or absence thereof. In other words, not only do chemists and chemistry educators need to acknowledge matters' agentic qualities, but also to recognize the gendered construction of the chemistry discipline and contribute to its change.

As a shadow, I transgressed the disciplinary boundaries of chemistry and gender studies by becoming entangled with and across these disciplines and with and through the material equipment in the setting. These entanglements of discipline-setting-materialities produced interpretations and insights that otherwise would not have been available to me. When a professor in anthropology read the part of my field notes where I wrote about students wearing of gloves, she stated that she would never have pay any attention to this practice if she had been the shadow, she would simply have taken it for granted as something you should wear when working in lab. Similarly, when I was a 'pure' chemist and had not yet engaged with knowledge from gender studies and material feminist theories, I probably would have corrected the students' glove-wearing routine by explaining when and why this equipment should be used, but I am quite sure that I had not reflected about the cause behind this routine. The important point, then, is that becoming aware of our entanglements in different subject areas, different disciplines, and with living and non-living material entities is effective in opening out the significance of transdisciplinary practices in producing new knowledge that is otherwise unlikely to emerge.

Conclusion: kick back at chemistry education

Usually, material feminism focuses on the agency of matter and humans but cogens, snaplogs and shadowing show that for the successful development of these practices both matter *and energy* are important. Often in accounts of intra-actions, the energy is ignored but our exploration of these research|practices suggest that energy is important in facilitating the post human entanglements involved with teaching and learning chemistry. We need to identify and pay attention to how material conditions entangle with humans, influence hierarchies and affect students' transition state for learning.

In this chapter, we have indicated that material feminist transdisciplinary practices can both open up other opportunities for students to engage in chemistry, and also challenge the power structures within the discipline. We suggest that these practices expand and extend how chemistry participants engage with phenomena and then re-present their perceptions and understandings of chemical concepts. Snaplogs expand the pathways for learners to share their knowledge, rather than being confined to text answers. Both snaplogs and cogens seek to flatten power structures and lower the activation energy students need to engage with learning chemistry thereby establishing a more collaborative space in which knowledge is constructed. Shadowing provides new perspectives on scientific practices and culture. By considering posthuman theories, the three research|practices work towards a transdisciplinary approach that offers new knowledge for chemistry education. At the same time, these practices fit within a material feminist approach to research and teaching as they are comfortable with difference and do not seek uniformity.

References

Barad, K. (2003). Posthumanist performativity: toward an understanding of how matter comes to matter. *Signs*, 28(3), 801–831, doi: 10.1086/345321

Barad, K. (2007). *Meeting the Universe Halfway: Quantum Physics and the Entanglement of Matter and Meaning*. London: Duke University Press.

Bayne, G. and Scantlebury, K. (2012). Cogenerative dialogues as pedagogy|research in science education. In K. Irby, G. Brown and R. Lara-Aleci (Eds.) *The Handbook of Educational Theories* (pp. 239–250). Charlotte, NC: Information Age Publishing Inc.

Bergwik, S. (2014). The historicity of the physics class: Enactments, mimes and imitation. *Cultural Studies of Science Education*, 9(2), 495–501.

Bramming, P., Gorm Hansen, B., Bojesen, A. and Gylling Olesen, K. (2012). (Im)perfect pictures: Snaplogs in performativity research. *Qualitative Research in Organizations and Management: An International Journal*, 7(1), 54–71. doi: 10.1108/17465641211223465

Butler, J. (1990). *Gender Trouble. Feminism and the Subversion of Identity*. New York, NY: Routledge.

Czarniawska, B. (2007). *Shadowing and Other Techniques for Doing Fieldwork in Modern Societies*. Malmö: Liber.

Haraway, D. (1988). Situated knowledges: The science question in feminism and the privilege of partial perspective. *Feminist Studies*, 14(3), 575–599.

Haraway, D. (1992). The promises of monsters. In L. Grossberg, C. Nelson, and P. A. Treichler (Eds.), *Cultural Studies* (pp. 295–337). New York, NY: Routledge.

Hussénius, A. (2018). Bland provrör och spektrometrar. Materiens agens och materiell dysfunktionalitet. [Among test tubes and spectrometers – agency of matter and material dysfunctionality] *Tidskrift för Genusvetenskap*, 39(4), 31–50.

Latour, B. (1987). *Science in Action: How to Follow Scientists and Engineers Through Society*. London: Open University Press.

Lykke, N. (2010). *Feminist Studies: A Guide to Intersectional Theory, Methodology and Writing*. London: Routledge.

McVarish, J. and Milne, C. (Eds.) (2014). *Teacher Educators Rethink Self-assessment in Higher Education: A Guide for the Perplexed*. New York, NY: Peter Lang.

Scantlebury, K. and LaVan, S.-K. (2006). Re-visioning cogenerative dialogues as feminist pedagogy|research [33 paragraphs]. *Forum Qualitative Sozialforschung/Forum: Qualitative Social Research* [On-line Journal], 7(2), Art. 41. Retrieved from www.qualitative-research.net/fqs-texte/2-06/06-2-41-e.htm

Schienbenger, L. (1999). *Has Feminism Changed Science?* Cambridge, MA: Harvard University Press.

Stengers, I. (2018). *Another Science is Possible: A Manifesto for Slow Science*. Cambridge: Polity Press.

Stith, I. and Roth, W.-M. (2006). Who gets to ask the questions: The ethics in/of cogenerative dialogue praxis [46 paragraphs]. *Forum Qualitative Sozialforschung/Forum: Qualitative Social Research* [On-line Journal], 7(2), Art. 38. Retrieved from www.qualitative-research.net/fqs-texte/2-06/06-2-38-e.htm

Tobin, K. (2014). Twenty questions about cogenerative dialogues. In K. Tobin and A. Shady (Eds.), *Transforming Urban Education* (pp. 181–190). Rotterdam: Sense Publishers.

Trojer, L. (2017). *Sharing Fragile Future. Feminist Technoscience in Contexts of Implication*. Kampala, South Africa: Makerere University Press.

Tuana, N. (Ed.) (1989). *Feminism and Science*. Bloomington, IN: Indiana University Press.

Turkle, S. (2007). *Evocative Objects: Things We Think With*. Cambridge, MA: MIT Press.

Wicke, J. (1994). Celebrity material: Materialist feminism and the culture of celebrity. *The South Atlantic Quarterly*, 51–78.

16 Embodying critical arts-based research
Complicating thought/thot leaders through transdisciplinary discourse

Gloria J. Wilson

Introduction

This chapter advances my arts-based autoethnographic work (Wilson, 2018), and how I, through acts of arts-based inquiry and representation, make sense of how I experience the intersections of racialized and gendered identity as an art and visual culture educator/thought leader. I draw from Michlin and Rocchi's (2013) work on transdisciplinarity and Crenshaw's work (1989, 2013) on intersectionality, in order to represent and preserve the nuances and complexities of my specific raced/gendered experience (Michlin and Rocci, 2013).

Figure 16.1 (Re)Mixed. Gloria J. Wilson, 2013, Screen print on linen. 36 × 84 in.

Constructing a transdisciplinary narrative

> **mixed.**
> /mɪkst/.
> *adj.*consisting of different qualities or elements

Over the years, my artwork and research have served as a guide for understanding the complex nature of racialised social identity locations (Wilson, 2018; Wilson and Shields, 2019). In creating visual images, I create a representation of my understanding of the world. This understanding is often derived from my embodied lived experience.

In '(Re)Mixed' (Figure 16.1), I trouble the notions of identity by creating a printed image of a geisha figure and inserting her into a culture where she performs in a serendipitous context. For me, *mixing* utilizes the tone of hybridity, border crossings and complexity of identity – my own and that of the geisha's (Daniel et al., 2014). *Mixed* also acknowledges a compilation of music performed by a DJ, combining complementary qualities and elements of varied beats and tones in order to create a seamless new track, which is often intended to 'move' a crowd of dancers. I intended for this artwork to fluidly utilize the unique disciplinary aspects of the visual and the performance arts while also aiming to capture aspects of the social world through visual, aural and embodied aesthetic. The combination of these disciplines – one complimenting the other – creates new meanings and understandings of lived experience in order to advance theoretical understanding.

> **transdisciplinary**
> /ˌtranzˈdisəpləˌnerē/
> *adj.* relating to more than one branch of knowledge

My arts-based response (Figure 16.1) serves to represent transdisciplinarity (Michlin and Rocchi, 2013) and a development of new ways of synthesizing various approaches to understanding the world and those who inhabit it. To this end, *(Re)Mixed* also serves as a window into the intersectional aspects (Crenshaw, 1989) of my lived experience as a woman of color (WoC) art educator and perceived thought leader, who also seeks to complicate an 'academic hegemony' of feminist discourse. Specifically, I am interested in unpacking what it means to be a WoC thought leader/artist within these dominant discourses.

In order to do this I begin by describing my inspiration for art making. I situate myself within a hip-hop feminist paradigm and complicate the word/acronym T.H.O.T., while also considering the role critical feminisms play in my work. I round out my discussion with future considerations for critical arts-based work.

Textile and fiber arts: the surface treatment

I trace my earliest love for textiles to faint memories of my Filipino uncles preparing and making garments for me. It was not until I grew older that I would understand how sewing came to be associated as a gendered act. However, knowing that my uncles and mother were connected to this craft would eventually lead me down a path to explore the possibilities of fabric. Introduced to printmaking for textiles in graduate school, I was challenged to create a 'novelty print' on a length of fabric (Figure 16.1). Novelty prints are often conversational in nature in that they push the boundaries beyond a simple pattern of shape and color. Usually novelty prints contain a theme and are often associated with places and activities. Knowing that I would be able to design an original pattern on a stretch of textile was beyond exciting to me. I would use the method of screen printing to create a 'repeat' (repeating pattern) of images associated with the complexities of human identity.

By this time in my life, I had grappled quite a bit with notions of identity (both raced and gendered) and had recently returned from a month-long stay in Japan. Still feeling connected to my recent understanding of women's status in Japan, I decided to merge the less-discussed social status of these women with my deep desire to problematize the idea of women's bodies as patriarchal sites for entertainment. I drew inspiration from my adjacency to hip-hop culture and music and re-imagined the woman/geisha as a different type of entertainer (see Figure 16.1). In this work, I envisioned the geisha as liberated from her role as entertainer *for* men while simultaneously giving a nod to powerful women thought leaders/emcees/DJ's of a male-dominated hip-hop culture.

Women of color as thought/t.h.o.t leaders

As a child who grew up in the early stages of the hip-hop era in North America (1970s and 1980s), I could be found writing down and 'spittin' lyrics, fashioning myself to emulate the women lyricists of the day. I was proud to wear my 'bamboo' earrings, asymmetrical hairstyle and embody the empowering messages of women MC's. Thought provokers and icons, MC Lyte, Queen Latifah, Salt n Pepa, Monie Love and Roxanne Shante to name a few, could be seen as occupying the first wave of Black/Brown feminism within hip-hop culture. Often considered the women who shaped hip-hop, these MC's would project their voices in direct response to the misogyny of male counterparts.

As the movement traveled into the 1990s, women's voices expanded to include a range of styles, blending rhyme with melody, sexual empowerment and spirituality. Women such as Lauryn Hill, Foxy Brown, Erykah Badu and Missy Elliot pushed the boundaries of Black female identity and sexuality, minimizing a desire to directly respond to the male voices in the industry. In the 2000s, a new generation of Black/Brown women lyricists have taken the stage, and a potential new wave of feminism inspired a re-framing of what constitutes liberation from patriarchal structures. Like Foxy Brown and Lil' Kim, newer lyricists like

Cardi B (Williams, 2017) have continued to bump against a binary (e.g., good girl versus bad girl trope) and a new label, 'Thot' (an acronym for 'That Ho Over There'), has surfaced. Pronounced just as it is spelled, it is intended to serve as the equivalent of calling someone a 'bitch' or 'whore.' These labels have storied histories and have often carried a derogatory connotation and dismissal of women's agency for liberation. A theory of intersectionality (Crenshaw, 1989) helps to reveal the complexity of interlocking oppressions (race/gender) and systemic marginalization of the voices of WoC, across professional lines.

I return to *(Re)Mixed* and to the image I designed, which expresses a re-imagined possibility of liberation for the geisha figure. At one level, I am responding to identity-boundaries and power differentials. At a deeper level, my own image-making serves as a critical arts-based autoethnographic reflection of my own racialized/gendered status within academic feminist discourse and power differentials (Guyotte et al., 2018). As such, I trouble the notion of the thot/thought leader and claim 'thot' as a position of power to argue that women lyricists (and writers, art-makers, scholars, etc.) have much to say (e.g., knowledge-production) about the lived realities of women of color (Acuff, López and Wilson, 2019). The history of the sociopolitical and creative acts of women has proven hopeful, yet is still fraught with a politics of respectability (Higginbotham, 1993) – which brings me to think about how this is relevant for me and others like me.

Hip-hop feminism

Hip-hop feminist theory (Lindsey, 2015: 54) is 'generationally specific,' which allows me to draw from my own personal experiences growing up in the middle of a burgeoning hip-hop culture, where beats, lyrics and rhymes were central forms of expression of the day within working class Black and Brown communities. Locating myself within this culture, I shift between these questions as I expand on my prior autoethnographic musings: First, how might the voices of WoC thought/t.h.o.t. leaders inform my movements as a WoC researcher/artist/educator? And second, how might this be materially represented through arts-based modes of expression?

My own material (arts-based) responses to these questions merge my articulations through textile-based printed image. These responses are my way to illuminate the intersections of various social and political locations: Black/Brown, woman, scholar and artist. I lean on the backs of the WoC scholars and artists who have expressed their frustrations and aspirations of hope through their material expressions (Moraga and Anzaldúa, 2015). Crenshaw (1989) and Collins (1998, 2009, 2015) have offered intersectionality as just the way to do this. In the next section, I complicate feminist discourse via these transdisciplinary mixings and expand on a *theory in the flesh* (Moraga and Anzaldúa, 2015: 19), in order to locate myself as a woman of color within and beyond traditional feminist discourse. Throughout, my writing draws reference to the words and lyrics of WoC activists, writers and performers, which helps further contextualize their voices within critical feminist frameworks.

Complicating feminist discourse

In a recent lament Rebecca Traister (2018) noted, 'we need to think differently about how we are hearing, receiving and responding to women's voices raised in passion and dissent.' Traister brings into clear view how the power of women's voices have been the catalyst for many of the social movements that have occurred in U.S. history. For instance, in the 2018 U.S. midterm elections, women participated in full force, and made U.S. political history with the record election of women of color in the U.S. Congress.

This brings into sharper focus the historic systemic challenges for WoC whose ontologies/epistemologies are marginalized within the larger narrative of U.S. culture and ultimately within feminist discourse. With the first publishing of *This Bridge Called My Back: Writings by Radical Women of Color* (1981), the sentiment that WoC somehow *needed* to 'radically' galvanize their voices within a collective space, was telling of the larger systemic inequities. It is now in its 4th edition. Moraga (2015: xxi) argues that 'women of color have traditionally served as the gateways – the knowledge-holders – to those profoundly silent areas of expression and oppression.' A recent argument made by art educator Joni Acuff (2018) is closely representative of my story, as a WoC artist and researcher in the field of art education. Acuff (2018) notes that we should ask critical questions regarding minoritized women's access to knowledge-making opportunities. Further, that when given the opportunity, these women are forced to participate using the dominant discourses, theories and methods. Bumping against a normative space of traditional feminist theoretical approaches, which centralizes gender inequality without considering (or acknowledging) simultaneous racial oppression (Combahee River Collective, 1983), WoC have experienced what Smart and Smart (2017: 518) refer to as a gentrification of space or 'academic hegemony.' In other words, it becomes difficult for WoC to introduce theoretical approaches that make their voices central, without being challenged as less rigorous (Acuff, 2018). If we add to this a 'whitening use of citations' within poststructuralist and new material feminist theories (Edenheim, 2016: 285), then we see that WoC continue to fight an uphill battle.

These insights resonate in the lyrics of American lyricist, Lauryn Hill's song 'Everything is Everything' (Hill, 1999: 1–23), 'It seems we lose the game before we even start to play. Who made these rules?' Her lyrics draw attention to systemic inequities that begin in youth, particularly for working class and minoritized peoples. These inequities continue throughout the lives of those who have been historically marginalized. When viewed through the lens of race and gender, these felt-realities are ever-present.

In reviewing Cherrí Moraga's (2015) description of a *theory in the flesh*, I am reminded of the double bind WoC experience: that in feminist scholarship, we are 'too similar to be different [yet] too different to be the same' (Ngai, 2004: 813). The physical realities of our lives 'fuse together to create a politic born out of necessity' (Moraga and Anzaldúa, 2015: 19). The notion of *being too different to be the same* aligns with the particular embodied ways of knowing of WoC and the simultaneous 'othering' by the very feminists who purport to fight for the equality of all women. WoC live this reality daily (Moraga, 2015). The very structures that contemporary feminisms critique (Thiel and Jones, 2017) are unhelpful when words are not put into action to think differently about the frustrations of WoC.

Racialized identities and social locations have been pinned down by historical U.S. legislation (Harris, 1993) and constructed (Wilson, 2018) as an intentional marker of difference (Miller, 2010). The double bind also includes that WoC also experience a gendered marginalization. To these ends, Crenshaw's (1989) theory of intersectionality has been omitted from new(er) feminist theories (Edenheim, 2016).

While this chapter is not a direct critique of this omission, I utilize this realization to advance theories of intersectionality and womanism (Crenshaw, 1989, 2010; Walker, 2012) within the body of contemporary feminisms (Lindsey, 2015). In order to acknowledge and make central my own racialized/gendered ways of being and knowing, I must also utilize critical race and hip-hop feminisms (Peoples, 2008). As a pointed solution toward transfeminist inclusiveness of my voice as a WoC within feminist scholarship, I present how my critical arts-based focus (Finley, Vonk and Finley, 2014) has not only informed but also nourished my racialized embodied movements within these dominant discourses.

Theory in the flesh

A theory in the flesh (Moraga and Anzaldúa, 2015: 19) means one where the bodily and material realities of the lives of WoC create a politic of necessity, one which has been advanced at least since the arrival of 'white feminist movements' in the U.S. Echoing my earlier sentiments that in order to become part of the larger narrative of women, WoC need to write/cite themselves/one another into the literature.

The lyrics in American songwriter and performance artist Solange Knowles' 'Don't Touch My Hair' (Knowles, 2016) activates a space that speaks ontologically and epistemologically to the *hair experiences* of Black women and, in my case, women of mixed African lineage. Specifically, the lines 'Where we choose to go. Where we've been to know,' connects to an axiology and acknowledgment of unregulated blackness. Depending on what era in U.S. history, women of African lineage have stories to tell about their hair. Particularly, women who have chosen to wear their hair 'natural' have had to manage any number of attempts codified by policy to tame their hair in order to maintain a sense of 'professionalism.' Additionally, many WoC have fielded any number of requests made by white people who desire to touch their locks. An invasion of space at worst, these 'innocent' requests become emotionally, mentally and, over time, physically taxing. Solange's words 'where we choose to go … where we've been to know' read as a liberatory manifesto. To remove oneself from regulatory standards is to also liberate one's self.

Much like the sentiments of womanism, a theory in the flesh places my own lament as a WoC front and center and highlights how I have managed to artfully tell my story through modes of arts-based and material representations. This theoretical framing embraces both a critical race feminism and intersectionality.

Critical race feminism and intersectionality

The hit single 'Ladies First' from the album *All Hail the Queen*, asserts a message that promotes powerful Afrocentric womanhood (Roberts, 1994). Performed by Queen Latifah and Monie Love, I see these Black women creatives as thought/thot leaders, who respond from the intersections of race and gender and also respond to the patriarchal power structures of hip-hop. Specifically, the line 'desperately stressing I'm the daughter of a sister who's the mother of a brother' (Latifah and Love, 1999: 2–45) references matrilineal lineage. This verse also serves as a lyrical materialization 'of mothering' to include its role in the development of world civilisation (Roberts, 1994: 255).

As a WoC thought leader interested in materializing my own sensibilities and interests in art making and popular culture, I find particular resonance in hooks' decades of work examining the intersections of race, feminism, and cultural studies (hooks, 1990, 1995, 2001; hooks, Yancy and Brod, 2017). As a maker of things, I have found that this allows me to give critical voice to the interlocking systems of privilege and marginalization in a way that simply writing about them cannot. Most recently, for example, I documented my embodied experiences as a WoC in academia by making a doctoral gown as a response to the criterion of university expectations: teaching/service/research. I sought to address critical issues through sewing, using familiar garment construction concepts of *marking*, *pinning*, *tracing* and *stitching* as a means to engage an audience in a broader discussion of multiple feminist legacies of stitching and sewing, racial identity formation and systemic racial inequities of academia (Wilson, 2018).

As a salient lens for my work, critical race feminism (hooks, 1990) not only champions a liberatory stance with great aims to end systemic oppression and domination, it also foregrounds systemic, social justice-oriented change efforts. With similar yet distinct aims, Crenshaw (1989) and Collins (1998, 2008, 2015) remind us that by emphasizing the intersectionality of raced and gendered locations within feminist thought and principles, we are able to throw into greater relief the experiences of WoC.

A critical feminist critique of the traditional feminist canon, challenges the primacy given only to gendered locations of women. Without examining the intersections of race along with gender and class, the narrative is short of holistic (Collins, 1998). Yet, as it relates to a being a racialized and gendered body, Ngai (2004: 816) notes, 'there are discursive limitations to our ability to capture the complex and reiterative processes of social categorization.' In this case, Ngai is referring to the impossibility for WoC, and specifically Black women, to name themselves within a traditional feminist theory, as their issues are both similar (as women) and different (raced) in relation to white women. As such, Few-Demo

(2014: 169) notes, 'intersectionality as a concept is fundamental in the articulation of racialized and gendered analyses and serves as an extension of racial/ethnic feminisms and critical race theories.' Yet Carbado (2013) cautions that intersectionality should not be misunderstood as a theory only suited for the examination of race and gender as much as it is a way to examine the multiplicity of social and political locations of *all* human beings. I would add caution, in that a theory of intersectionality should not be misused to refer to a 'theory of difference.' It should be understood as a theory of oppression.

Material feminist narratives

Yara Shahidi (2018) comments that 'A fight to help one person belong, belongs to all of us.' The transdisciplinary nature of the visual and performing arts practices I enact is well-suited for expanding a discussion of a 'politics of materiality' (Irni, 2013: 347). Strands of critical/materialist feminist work (Irni, 2013) serve as salient and powerful tools for critiquing dominant political structures for close engagement with social concerns. My engagement with these material forms of expression/ communication allow for a multi-sensorial experience for viewers as well as a coping strategy for myself. Like the writings of Moraga and Anzaldúa (2015), these material engagements are deeply personal and rooted in my own ways of being and knowing. Artful and feminist modes of expression by women of color have proven to spark debate when applied to a canonical expressive and theoretical forms (hooks, 1995). This is made apparent, particularly when modes of expression are taken up in popular culture forms, such as hip-hop (Lindsey, 2015).

If we are to inquire from a new materialist perspective, critical ways of questioning non-human forms come into view. For instance, when considering distributive agency what type of thing-power (Bennett, 2010) does a record player hold, when placed at the hands of a DJ who happens to be a Black/Brown/middle class woman versus when used in a mid-century modern home occupied by a White/middle class woman? What about when you add the agency of statistical information that reveals that hip-hop consumerism is largely taken up (and sometimes 'put down') by the White middle class (Kopano and Brown, 2014), yet still largely undervalued as a serious and rigorous body of knowledge?

As I think of my arts-based work with and through fibers/textiles, I ask: what are the optics of distributive agency when women have historically, in large numbers, occupied a 'domestic sphere' of textile arts and fabric manipulation, but the yet gatekeepers of the canonic art world are men? What role does race play in this equation? An intersectional approach (Collins, 2015; Crenshaw, 1989) provides the lens for examining such questions. In this context, then, I am prompted to ask: what thing-power do my own art works have? What new matterings does my geisha textile prompt? What onto-epistemological and axiological shifts might my doctoral gown produce?

Activist and screen artist Amandla Stenberg would once recite, 'what would America be like if we loved Black [Brown] people, as much as we loved Black [Brown] culture?' (Stenberg, 2015). This begs us to consider the ways in which

Black/Brown voices within feminist scholarship have dealt with the double bind (too similar, yet too different) thereby, unable to be fully recognized within this work. Within contemporary feminist scholarship, critiques of systems of power and domination are easily 'called out' (Thiel and Jones, 2017), yet there is a less-obvious empowerment of those who have been historically written out of the narrative.

Coping and forward movement

The visual and performing arts, as expressive forms of communication, are useful to step between social issues and forms of work. This is their beauty. This chapter explores my use of arts-based approaches to critical forms of inquiry as a way to explore my embodied experiences as a WoC artist/academic. In using these approaches, I aimed to re/consider and complicate feminist discourse by utilising intersectionality and critical race and material feminist lenses. My use of creative practice, alongside a hip-hop feminist theory, served as a provocation and my response led me to inquire into my entangled movements both within and outside of normative feminist spaces. I sought to represent my experiences and understandings of embodying these spaces.

As a WoC, I acknowledge an intrinsic value of 'theory of the flesh' as a primer for exploring issues extending beyond those of gender and into racialized women's issues often submerged in traditional feminist scholarship. I also highlight the utility of the academic disciplines of the visual and performing arts as an opening for critical theoretical positioning and means of producing a new aesthetic of knowledge to expand transdisciplinary feminist approaches for authoethnographic inquiry. My aim in advancing the conversation between arts-based autoethnography and critical feminist theories is to complicate the possibilities that an intersectional theory and approach offers to qualitative research. In my own work, this critical arts-based process works as a way-finding mechanism toward a hip-hop feminist inquiry and as a way to further a transformative critical aesthetic practice.

For me, hip-hop culture is an extension of who I am. I am as much a part of this culture as I am the cultures of education and research and the visual arts. It is at these intersections that I am able to aspire toward feminist futures. My engagement with the 'energetic contributions' (Hood and Kraehe, 2017: 33) of this material world propels me to *think with* and *through* these diverse intellectual resources in a variety of ways. One example of this was when I joyfully performed (slam poetry) an academic paper about race at a Qualitative Inquiry conference about experiences as a WoC art teacher while utilising the technique as a form of arts-based research (Wilson and Shields, 2019). Traces of my connection to hip-hop can also be seen in my curricular decisions as I have students analyse pop culture texts and transform them into action-oriented projects (Wilson, 2019). But larger than this, it serves as a survival strategy and coping mechanism to work through the contradictions (Durham, Cooper and Morris, 2013) and contested spaces I find myself in as a researcher, educator and artist.

Passion and dissent: addressing the weight of race via art, critical feminism and intersectionality

I return to my (art)making. *(Re)Mixed* contains a complex narrative, meant to provoke questioning of hybridity of identity and boundary crossing. As the art maker, working within and influenced by a variety of systems and cultures (academia, art world, U.S. census/legislative bodies), I now ask: what creative practices might be embraced within Womanist-oriented education (Crenshaw, 1989) and research spaces? Within traditional feminist scholarship, which voices are being heard, received and/or elevated? Ignored, tokenized, submerged?

It was my work with a collective of white women researchers that would bring into sharp focus the inability of postmodern feminist frameworks to operationalize intersectional axes of difference (Collins, 1998; hooks, 2001) and provide tools for empowerment, rather than simply offer a critique of power (Wilson et al., 2016). For such projects, there is a need for additional critical lenses to expose the relational intersections of domination and oppression that people of color (PoC) experience. What came of the project was a deeper engagement with seemingly oppositional theories (post versus critical, for instance) and deeper engagement with one another. This is not to say that my colleagues have shifted to become critical theorists or that I have taken a deep dive into the post-, yet as educators, each of us is able to work alongside fellow researchers who reside at the intersections, who might see and exist differently than us (Traister, 2018).

What I am now wondering is, like the story I shared in the beginning, what prevents deeper material engagements from happening among women who do feminist work *differently*, yet are unable to see the similarities across difference? Is it simply a limitation of time? Perhaps. Then, what of the 'material' world continues to widen the gaps of engagement between human-things/academics? A mere citation (or omission of one)? We might also ask questions like the ones Hood and Kraehe (2017: 35) offer: *What might it be like to be this* [racialized] *thing? What might* [race] *be doing that you have never considered?*

As a relational construct, race holds palpable weight unlike any other bodily identifier in the U.S. In recent U.S. events, we are able to notice the gravity of conversations about race due to the violence against Black men and women and youth. It is a relational construct that has been institutionalized judicially (Harris, 1993) and visually (Harris, 2003). Early time-based media productions like *Birth of a Nation* reveal how ideologies of race were constructed and further supported by other structures (educational policy, etc.) in order to maintain inequitable hierarchies based on skin color (Wilson, 2019).

Addressing the topic of race within feminist discourse is laden with contradictions (Lindsey, 2015). Critiques of traditional feminist scholarship address the failure to institutionalize and operationalize the voices of women whose racialized locations are often ignored and yet, when included in the discourse, are often ghettoized (Lorde, 2015). In her 1979 letter to feminist Mary Daly, Audrey Lorde (2015: 91) noted, 'the history of white women who are unable to hear Black women's words, or to maintain dialogue with us, is long and discouraging.' Lorde's lament was an attempt to point toward the stronghold of a Western-European patriarchal frame of reference. In 2017, bell hooks joined a panel discussion at St. Norbert College to discuss feminist futures and noted that 'patriarchal masculinity' (hooks, Yancy and Brod, 2017) harms all of us – including men.

Like hooks (2017), my own transdisciplinary feminist arts-based intersectional work aims to support a critical feminist/Womanist (Crenshaw, 1989) future by suggesting that we can educate ourselves to learn from the past to end domination in order to free us to be who we are – liberated from exploitation and oppression. This must undergird everything that we do. In these critical times, what then is our role as educators/artists/women/researchers? How might the visual and performing arts provoke us to think differently about how we are hearing, receiving and responding to women's voices raised in passion and dissent? What can we *do*? What *are we doing?*

References

Acuff, J. B. (2018). Black feminist theory in 21st-century art education research. *Studies in Art Education*, 59(3), 201–214.

Acuff, J. B., López, V. and Wilson, G. J. (2019). Lunch on the grass: Three women art educators of color. *Souls: A Critical Journal of Black Politics, Culture, and Society*, doi: 10.1080/10999949.2019.1647084

Bennett, J. (2010). *Vibrant matter*. Durham, NC: Duke University Press.

Carbado, D. (2013). Colorblind intersectionality. *Signs: Journal of Women in Culture and Society*, 38(4), 811–845.

Collins, P. H. (1998). *Fighting Words: Black Women and the Search for Justice*. Minneapolis, MN: University of Minnesota Press.

Collins, P. H. (2008). *Black Feminist Thought: Knowledge, Consciousness, and the Politics of Empowerment*. 2nd Edition. New York, NY: Routledge.

Collins, P. H. (2015). Intersectionality's definitional dilemmas. *Annual Review of Sociology*, 41(1), 1–20.

Combahee River Collective (1983). The Combahee River Collective Statement. In B. Smith (Ed.), *Home Girls, A Black Feminist Anthology* (pp. 264–274). New York, NY: Kitchen Table: Women of Color Press, Inc.

Crenshaw, K. (1989). Demarginalizing the intersection of race and sex: A Black feminist critique of antidiscrimination doctrine, feminist theory and antiracist politics. *The University of Chicago Legal Forum*, 140: 139–167.

Daniel, G. R, Kina, L., Dariotis, W. and Fojas, C. (2014). Emerging paradigms in critical mixed race studies. *Journal of Critical Mixed Race Studies*, 1(1). Retrieved from https://escholarship.org/uc/item/2db5652b

Durham, A., Cooper, B. C. and Morris, S. M. (2013). The stage hip hop feminism built: A new directions essay. *Signs: Journal of Women in Culture and Society*, 38(3), 722–737.

Edenheim, S. (2016). Foreclosed matter – On the material melancholy of feminist new materialism. *Australian Feminist Studies*, 31(89), 283–304.

Few-Demo, A. (2014). Intersectionality as the 'new' critical approach in feminist family studies: Evolving racial/ethnic feminisms and critical race theories. *Journal of Family Theory and Review*, 6(2), 169–183.

Finley, S., Vonk, C. and Finley, M. L. (2014). At home at school: Critical arts-based research as public pedagogy. *Cultural Studies/Critical Methodologies*, 14(6), 619–625.

Guyotte, K. W., Hofsess, B. A., Wilson, G. J. and Shields, S. S. (2018). Tumbling from embodiment to enfleshment: Art as intervention in collective autoethnography. *Art Research International: A Transdisciplinary Journal*, 3(2), 101–132.

Harris, C. I. (1993). Whiteness as property. *Harvard Law Review*, 106(8), 1707–1791.

Harris, M. D. (2003), *Colored pictures: Race and visual representation*. Chapel Hill, NC: University of North Carolina Press.

Higginbotham, E. B. (1993). *Righteous Discontent: The Women's Movement in the Black Baptist Church, 1880–1920*. Cambridge, MA: Harvard University Press.

Hill, L. (1999). Everything is everything [L. Hill]. On *The Miseducation of Lauryn Hill* [Album]. New York, NY: Sony Music Studios.

Hood, E. J. and Kraehe, A. M. (2017). Creative matter: New materialism in art education research teaching, and learning. *Art Education*, 70(2), 32–38.

hooks, b. (1990). *Yearning: Race, Gender, and Cultural Politics*. Cambridge: South End Press.

hooks, b. (1995). *Art on My Mind*. New York, NY: The New Press.

hooks, b. (2001). *Reel to Reel: Race, Class and Sex at the Movies*. New York, NY: Routledge.

hooks, b., Yancy, G. and Brod, H. [St. Norbert College]. (April 11, 2017). *Feminist Future: Mutual Dialogue Featuring Bell Hooks, George Yancy and Harry Brod*. [video file]. Retrieved from www.youtube.com/watch?v=PErPxdEBdn8andt=1302s

Irni, S. (2013). The politics of materiality: Affective encounters in a transdisciplinary debate. *European Journal of Women's Studies*, 20(4), 347–360.

Knowles, S. (2016). Don't Touch My Hair [Recorded by S. Knowles]. On *A Seat at the Table* [Medium of recording]. New York, NY: Columbia Records.

Kopano, B. and Brown, T. (Eds.) (2014). *Soul Thieves: The Appropriation and Misrepresentation of African American Popular Culture*. New York, NY: Palgrave MacMillian.

Latifah Q. and Love, M. (1999). Ladies First [Q. Latifah and M. Love]. On *All Hail the Queen* [Album]. New York, NY: Tommy Boy.

Lindsey, T. B. (2015). Let me blow your mind: Hip hop feminist futures in theory and praxis. *Urban Education*, 50(1), 52–77.

Lorde, A. (2015). An open letter to Mary Daly. In C. Moraga. and G. Anzaldúa (Eds.), *The Bridge Called My Back* (pp. 90–93). Albany, NY: State University of New York Press.

Michlin, M. and Rocchi, J.-P. (2013). Introduction: Theorizing for change: Intersections, transdisciplinarity, and Black lived experience. In M. Michilin and J.-P. Rocchi (Eds.), *Black Intersectionalities* (pp. 1–20). Liverpool: Liverpool University Press.

Miller, J. W. (2010). Beyond Skin Deep: An analysis of the influence of the one-drop rule on the racial identity of African American adolescents. *Race, Gender, and Class*, 17(3), 38–50.

Moraga, C. and Anzaldúa, G. (2015). *The Bridge Called My Back*. Albany, NY: State University of New York Press.

Ngai, M. (2004). *Impossible Subjects: Illegal Aliens and the Making of Modern America*. Princeton, NJ: Princeton University Press.

Peoples, W. A. (2008). 'Under construction': Identifying the foundations of hip hop feminism and exploring bridges between Black second-wave and hip hop feminisms. *Meridians* 8(1), 19–52.

Roberts, R. (1994). 'Ladies first': Queen Latifah's Afrocentric feminist music video. *African American Review*, 28(2), 245–257.

Shahidi, Y. (20 October 2018). *Star Tribune*. Retrieved from www.startribune.com/yara-shahidi-urges-fight-against-identity-blind-narrative/498113521/

Smart, A. and Smart, J. (2017). Ain't talkin' 'bout gentrification. The erasure of alternative Idioms of displacement resulting from Anglo-American academic hegemony. *International Journal of Urban and Regional Research*, 41(3), 518–525.

Stenberg, A. (2015). What would America be like if we loved Black [Brown] people, as much as we loved Black [Brown] culture? Retrieved from http://clandesteen.tumblr.com/post/107484511963/dont-cash-crop-my-cornrows-a-crash-discourse-on

Traister, R. (9 November 2018). [The Daily Show with Trevor Noah]. *How 'good and mad' women continually reshape America*. [video file]. Retrieved from www.youtube.com/watch?v=kAQG-8XY6N4

Thiel, J. J. and Jones, S. (2017). The literacies of things: Reconfiguring the material-discursive production of race and class in an informal learning centre. *Journal of Early Childhood Literacy*, 17(3), 315–335.

Walker, A. (2012). Womanist. *Buddhist-Christian Studies*, 32(1), 45. Retrieved 31 August 2019, from Project MUSE database.

Williams, S. (2017). Cardi B: Love and Hip Hop's unlikely feminist hero. *Feminist Media Studies*, 17(6), 1114–1117.

Wilson, G. J. (2018). Construction of the Blackademic: An arts-based tale of identity in and through academia, *Visual Inquiry*, 7(3), 213–226.

Wilson, G. J. (2019). Pre-service art education: Examining constructions of Whiteness in/through visual culture. *Journal of Cultural Research in Art Education*, 36(1), 73–89.

Wilson, G. J. and Shields, S. S. (2019). Troubling the 'WE' in art education: Slam poetry as subversive duoethnography. *Journal of Social Theory in Art Education*, 39(1), 5–18.

Wilson, G. J., Shields, S. S., Guyotte, K. and Hofsess, B. (2016). Desirable difficulties: Toward a critical postmodern arts-based practice, *Journal of Social Theory in Art Education*, 36(1), 115–125.

17 (Un)disciplined
What is the terrain of my thinking?

Susan Naomi Nordstrom

Introduction

In many ways this chapter materializes the following quote from Ahmed (2017: 16): 'Sometimes we need distance to follow a thought. Sometimes we need to give up distance to follow a thought.' My original proposal for this collection centered on thinking with three objects that materialized key ideas of my feminist transdisciplinary work in the core areas of United States faculty evaluation: research, teaching and service. When I wrote the proposal, I was one-year away from submitting tenure and promotion materials. The original proposal became a space for me to write a version of the research, teaching and service statements (part of the materials submitted for tenure and promotion) I wish I could have produced at that time. I thought that this would be generative work. But, each time I set out to write from that proposal, I became mired in cynicism and despair.

In the editors' review of that proposal, they asked me to consider the disciplines I draw from in my feminist and transdisciplinary research and how my work is feminist transdisciplinary. When confronted with this review, I realized that transdisciplinary thought and research is so normal to me that it has become natural. How did feminist transdisciplinary work become normal and natural for me?

To explore this question as well as the cynicism and despair I encountered while attempting to fully develop the original proposal, I turned to Stengers and Despret (2014: 78) who invited numerous established European women scholars to consider the following question 'What does thinking demand today?' Such a question, the authors claimed, asked the scholars to consider not only the terrains in which they think but also how those terrains generate thought (Stengers and Despret, 2014). What is the terrain of my thinking? How does that terrain create enabling conditions for certain thoughts? What does thinking demand of me now?

To respond to these questions, to 'offer a version of the problem [they] propose' (Stengers and Despret, 2014: 79), I turn my attention to the nonhuman objects that populate my terrain that have allowed me to explore 'what thinking could mean for [me].' These objects create an ensemble of a transdisciplinary scholarly life and thought. This version consists of an ecology of practices that is at once hopeful, instructive, obstructive, creative and responsive. In this chapter, I respond to the thought(s) generated by an inability to write what I proposed and the aforementioned question by examining my ensemble of a scholarly life. In so doing, I open a space to examine the thoughts that need(ed.) both distance and closeness.

A method

To answer the questions I pose to myself in the introduction, I draw on my previous work about the ensemble of life, a concept I created to describe the work of family history genealogists and the nonhuman objects (e.g., documents, photographs, and other artifacts) that they use to construct their ancestors (Nordstrom, 2019). The ensemble of life is a loose grouping of objects that temporarily assemble a person's life and is open and connectable to other ensembles. In my tenure and promotion dossier research statement, I explained this concept by referring to the dossier itself as an ensemble of my scholarly life. The dossier consists of publications, syllabi, student evaluations, and other contributions I have made to the scholarly community in the realms of research, teaching, and service during my time at the University of Memphis. The dossier, then, constructs an ensemble of my scholarly life. In this section, I expand on this explanation and develop it as a method to examine the questions listed in the introduction of this chapter.

In this chapter, I expanded the dossier to include more artifacts of my scholarly life. I assembled documents (e.g., transcripts, past syllabi from my coursework and letters), artifacts of thought (e.g., class papers, conference presentations, journal articles, art work and so on), and nonhuman ephemera (e.g., gifts from students and colleagues). This work allowed me to see how I have moved between, against, and with different disciplines in my scholarly life. Moreover, it allowed me to see how feminism has been a constant in this scholarly life, sometimes in more prominent ways than others. A life that has become so normal and natural to me that transdisciplinary thinking is just something I do, not something I aim to do. This transdisciplinary life is lived the middle where things pick up speed (Deleuze and Guattari, 1987) – a life that many times passes through me too quickly to examine.

The process of assembling these objects for this chapter has offered a momentary slowing down (Ulmer, 2017a). These objects disrupt the 'I' of autoethnography (Jackson and Mazzei, 2008). In this slowing down, I became aware of how each object becomes a coordinate in a terrain and materializes an event in the *agencement*, or assemblage, in which I live and work. The *agencement* is a non-fixed space of coordinates that enable conditions for events and how that event comes into being (Manning, 2016). Each event becomes a moment in which the 'I' (myself) materializes in space and time. Each iteration of an 'I' expresses these events, a vector in the ever-shifting and arranging field of experience (Manning, 2016).

Using the ensemble of life as a method has allowed me to map these I's as they materialize through nonhuman objects to explore the questions that guide this chapter. The ensemble of life helped me to consider the terrain of my thinking. How does the terrain come into being? How does the terrain enable transdisciplinary thought? What does transdisciplinary thinking demand of me now (Stengers and Despret, 2014). More importantly, the ensemble of life helped me to examine my iteration of feminist transdisciplinary thinking and research that has become so normal and natural to me that it is difficult for me to think otherwise.

(Un)disciplined: What is the terrain of my thinking?

Some colleagues have assumed that because I am in the field of educational research that I logically progressed through an undergraduate teacher education program, followed by a masters in education, and a doctorate in education. Their assumption is proved sorely wrong by my transcripts, curriculum vita, class papers and published papers, and other objects within my ensemble of scholarly life. These objects materialize how forces generate a shifting 'I' in an (un)disciplined and transdisciplinary terrain of thought.

I first began my undergraduate studies in vocal performance. To better understand the languages in which I frequently sang, I took classes in German and independently studied Italian. Slowly, I began to enjoy my language studies more than singing itself. There was something magical in learning a different way to think and be in the world through language. During this time, I returned to Spanish, my first foreign language, and took a course. In that course, we read Carlos Fuentes (1973) *Chac Mool* in which an art collector purchases a Chac Mool, a Mesoamerican sculpture associated with rain. The Chac Mool shifts from nonhuman to human form. It smells of lotion. It floods the art collector's home. It talks back. The story ends with the art collector drowning from rain produced by the Chac Mool. This short story animated something, a something I could not name, but knew I had to follow.

Consequently, I changed my major to Spanish and later added Latin American Studies, itself an interdisciplinary major. For the Latin American Studies major, I took courses in political science, history, women's and gender studies, literature and sociology. Through that work, the stories of women who participated in politics and war compelled me to study them ... From the soldaderas who fought in the Mexican Revolution of 1910 to the arpilleristas, women family members (primarily mothers) of victims of political violence under Pinochet in Chile, who made intricate tapestries that depicted political violence and working-class conditions, I became fascinated by Latin American women doing extraordinary things in times political turmoil.

To further explore that area of study, I completed a senior honor's thesis that examined the roles of women in Pre-Columbian Wars to the Revolution of 1910 in Mexico. In particular, I studied how actions attributed to Aztec goddesses later materialized in women's practices and roles during wartime. I relished the time spent digging through archives, writing with feminist thinkers such as June Nash (1997) and her work with the Zapatista uprising in response to the

North American Free Trade Agreement in Chiapas Mexico, and crafting a historical argument. During my senior year, I presented that research at both university-level and regional conferences. Following graduation, I was unsure as to whether I would pursue Spanish or History in graduate school. As I considered my options, I took graduate-level coursework in Spanish and worked odd jobs to make a little extra money.

One such odd job became more than an odd job. I accepted a job teaching Spanish to second and third grade students in an after-school program. Both my parents taught elementary school, and I swore I would never teach school. I fell prey to the adage 'never say never.' Planning lesson plans for the program began to draw me in and I began spending more time doing that work than reading literature and writing papers for my graduate-level courses. Another option materialized, a degree in education. At that time (early 2000s), U.S. state governments required that all teachers must earn a teaching license to teach in public schools through an accredited program found in colleges of education. The curriculum of these programs usually entail courses on pedagogy and other areas. Consequently, I applied and was accepted to a Master of Education program that offered licensure and a master's level degree.

While I had balanced scholarly and teaching activities in my odd job, I desired such a balance in my teacher preparation and brief career as a K-12 teacher. I enjoyed teaching, but something was missing. I found the coursework to be method-centric, with one exception. I adored my educational philosophy course, because I finally felt at home because it was most familiar to my undergraduate training. It was in that course that I read about the history of education and how that history made possible present realities. In my methods courses, I learned what to do as a teacher. I did not learn how and why those methods came into being and what purposes they served. Instead, I made portfolios of lessons full of best practice methods rather than write papers about the historical and philosophical background of those methods. I then put those methods into practice as an elementary technology teacher, third grade teacher, and eighth grade teacher.

While I enjoyed teaching in the K-12 setting, I still longed for the rich discussions of philosophy, deconstructing texts and the archival work of my undergraduate thesis. I needed these elements in my intellectual life. These absences created desirous forces that drove me back into the academy. At the time, I was unable to articulate why I sought a Ph.D., I just knew the forces were drawing me back to the academy. I had to listen. I began doctoral work in my third year of teaching, which would be my last year of teaching K-12.

Forces exploded in that first doctoral course, a required introductory course that traversed the *a priori* theoretical landscape of educational research. Each week's readings and conversations animated new forces that, in turn, generated becomings. It seemed that I was finally able to merge my past scholarly interests with future endeavors. The final paper I wrote for that course materialized those becomings as I explored literature, philosophy, history and educational research. I enrolled in every class that professor taught, and soon she became my dissertation advisor. U.S.

doctoral students work closely with a faculty advisor throughout their doctoral program. The advisor helps shape the program of study and is instrumental in facilitating the dissertation proposal and the dissertation itself. She advised me to 'read, read, read.' And, I read, read, read. I enrolled in courses across the university, qualitative research courses and independent studies. That final paper written for my first course marked a beginning that begins again.

My course papers merged disciplines as I read literature, listened to music, made art and watched films to generate the knowledge presented in the papers. For example, a qualitative research course paper used arts-based research to describe philosophical musings about the self/other binary in qualitative research. A course paper for a course in comparative literature drew on art (Goggin's 'Defenestration' (1997–present) to Goya's (1823) 'Saturn Devouring his Son') and music (tracks ranging from The Beastie Boys to Pink Floyd) to argue for different writing practices. Another course paper used a music video, The Faint's (2001) 'Agenda Suicide,' as a way to consider poststructural subjects. These course papers and my Ph.D. transcript (or list of courses taken during the Ph.D.) materialize an eclectic iteration of a Ph.D. in Language and Literacy Education. Language and literacy education became broadly defined as a practice invested in the dynamic practices of reading and writing across disciplines.

This narrative drawn from the ensemble of a scholarly life, an ensemble of nonhuman objects (e.g., transcripts, syllabi, course papers and a senior thesis) aims to illustrate the generation of an (un)disciplined terrain, a transdisciplinary terrain, upon which I live and work. These objects are the litter on the terrain from the movements that generate iterations of 'I's.' Manning (2016: 37) wrote, '"I" is the movement of thought destabilized by the act, the coming-into-itself of a capacity to regulate experience, but only until it is destabilized again.' In other words, the 'I' is in the middle of the *agencement*. The 'I' that materializes through this narrative is lured by events to become something otherwise, become unknowable.

With the objects, I am able to see how forces drew me in, asked me to think differently, and, in so doing, helped me to stretch the bounds of disciplined terrains. The pattern was already happening (Haraway, 2018) and a contingent terrain of thought materialized from that pattern. This terrain of thought resists the disciplinary boxes set forth by the historical forces of academic disciplines. This terrain draws from literary studies, history, art, philosophy, feminism, qualitative research and education to generate thought and knowledge. These disciplines move and shift on the terrain such that they become (un)disciplined and, in so doing, the terrain becomes transdisciplinary. In this flat space of movement, forces from these disciplines move together to generate thought.

How does an (un)disciplined), transdisciplinary, terrain create enabling conditions for certain thoughts?

Similar to Virginia Woolf's (1986: 109) claim that 'As a woman, I have no country. As a woman I want no country. As a woman my country is the whole world,' a feminist transdisciplinary terrain does not pledge allegiance to any particular discipline as it moves across academic disciplines. This terrain generates a series of I's that move too quickly across the spaces of academic disciplines. These 'I's' have no discipline. They want no discipline. The world is their discipline as they move across it, hungry for affirmative becomings that generate different enabling conditions for thought.

Before addressing conditions for thought and what it does, it is necessary to conceptualize thought. Deleuze's (1994) work on thought is instructive in this instance. He wrote:

> Something in the world forces us to think. This something is an object not of recognition but of a fundamental *encounter*. What is encountered may be Socrates, a temple or a demon. It may be grasped in a range of affective tones: wonder, love, hatred, suffering. In whichever tone, its primary characteristic is that it can only be sensed.
>
> (Deleuze, 1994: 139)

According to Deleuze, thought passes through a person as an encounter, an event. This encounter or event may be materialized in an idea read in a book, a person, an object, for example. As the encounter passes through, it leaves affective residues that are imperceptible (Deleuze, 1994). Thought, then, is working at the limit of recognition, something that stretches possibility. In this way, thought perplexes sense-making as it moves between and stretches the possible and impossible. Deleuze (1994) goes on to suggest that people use faculties, or dogmas, of thought that seek to make sense of the thought-encounter. Deleuze (1994) argues that the faculty of thought should not be given as the only way to think a thought-encounter. Rather, the thought should initiate a 'disturbing unfamiliarity [something that] has been seen, but in another life, in a mythical presence' (142).

The narrative in the preceding section seeks to illustrate a Deleuzian (1994) notion of thought and Foucault's (1994) archaeological work that studied how knowledge practices come into being. Something always forced me to think (Deleuze, 1994), and I eagerly followed those forces as they carried me from academic discipline to academic discipline. Academic disciplines can function as a faculty of thought because they and their discursive practices articulate possible and impossible thoughts in grids of intelligibility (Foucault, 1994). Within each discipline, I was taught through discursive practices how to think and be within that discipline and what was both possible and impossible to think within that discipline. This was done via syllabi, lectures in courses, responses to course papers and so on. For instance, a class paper in a qualitative research methodology course (my current discipline and a discipline in which I have had extensive PhD coursework) usually carries with it expectations of disciplinary knowledge and practices. Students are expected to demonstrate disciplinary knowledge by selecting appropriate citations of key methodological texts and be able to put those texts into practice by completing research that both aligns with and extends those texts. Simply put, a course paper asks students to enter into a discursive practice, develop knowledge about it, put that practice to work, and, in turn, further knowledge and practices about the discursive practice. Instructor feedback aims to help students successfully learn both the knowledge and practices. Discursive practices, such as these, helped me understand what was both possible and impossible to think within a discipline.

What is deemed both possible and impossible through discursive practices is systematically repeated through a discipline's curriculum. For example, I studied syllabi from my teacher education program. In syllabus after syllabus, certain ways of thinking and being were practiced over and over so as to make them normal. In this instance, the development of certain ways of lesson planning, teaching methods, and so on was standardized. That standardization set assessment criteria for how well teacher candidates performed the disciplinary practices throughout the coursework. In this way, my teacher education program systematically repeated discursive practices so as to normalize them and make them natural to thinking. So much so that it becomes dogmatic.

In this way, the discursive practices become sense-making apparatuses. When a thought-encounter happens, a particular sense-making apparatus is put to work. The goal of such an apparatus is to limit thought and being within those structures. Is the thought-encounter possible, impossible or some kind of in-between? How might someone think that thought? What discursive practices are needed to make sense of that thought? As this process happens, the sense-making apparatus churns out possibilities and impossibilities within a discipline.

However, my movements between disciplines, created a unique sense-making apparatus. As I moved from grid to grid, I picked up discursive practices that became normal for me while in a particular discipline. These practices did not somehow disappear once I moved to another discipline. The practices stayed with me and influenced how I made sense of thought-encounters. For example, in my undergraduate majors, I learned of the importance of theory in developing arguments. In fact, I remember a Spanish professor during that time telling me one cannot think without a theoretical framework. That practice bristled with the seemingly atheoretical approaches to teaching methods (which, as many realize, are far from atheoretical) and generated friction, which I described in the previous section. It was not until my first class as a doctoral student that the normalized discursive practice of theory in literary and historical studies is also used in educational research. What was normal and natural (theory work in an academic discipline) for me was finally normal and natural in another discipline. Still, there are others (and it is beyond the scope of this chapter to illustrate all of them) that I carry with me as I travel the grids of academic disciplines and discursive practices.

As I picked up discursive practices, I also began to consider how my thought might be thought of in another discipline. For instance, during my research with family history genealogy, I considered the following questions. How might a historian think the objects of family history genealogist? How might an archivist think this thought? How might a qualitative researcher think this thought? How might a literacy scholar think this thought? And so on. This work allowed me to see the realms of possibility for thinking such a thought in different disciplines. This is transdisciplinary thought, a way for multiple disciplines to converge on a topic in order to think the possibility of a thought in multiple ways.

The previous section, then, consists of parts of an assemblage that are constantly moving together to make sense of thought-encounters. The assemblage generates the thought-encounter and asks sense-making questions within the disciplines that comprise the assemblage. These questions aim to articulate the topic's possibility and impossibility within the terrain-assemblage. This assemblage, however, is not static (Deleuze and Guattari, 1987). Rather, the assemblage is always assembling itself, becoming otherwise, becoming imperceptible (Deleuze and Guattari, 1987). The possibility to think otherwise is always possible. As I think a thought, the thought moves through the contingent assemblage. The thought moves across grids of intelligibility (Foucault, 1994) as the imperceptible becomes perceptible within realms of possible thought within a discipline. In this way, this work is about becoming, about creating knowledge that is 'at once never-seen and yet already-recognized, a disturbing unfamiliarity' (Deleuze, 1994: 142).

In an (un)disciplined transdisciplinary terrain of thought in which thought is encountered and becoming, research is different. It does different things. Deleuze (1994: 143–144) wrote:

> For nothing can be said in advance, one cannot prejudge the outcome of research: it may be that some well-known faculties – too well known – turn out to have no proper limit, no verbal adjective, because they are imposed and have an exercise only under the form of common sense. It may turn out, on the other hand, that new faculties arise, faculties which were repressed by that form of sense.

I rarely know in advance what research might do. When a thought-encounter happens, I usually cannot anticipate which faculties are warranted to make sense of the thought and explore that thought's possibilities. Consequently, I cannot delimit myself to only thinking with one framework. I must let the terrain keep moving rather than stratify it with disciplinary forces. For example, when I commence any project, I have to trust where that thought-encounter leads me. For my dissertation, it was my parents' home that is filled with objects of my family's history. Those objects became thought-encounters, encounters that developed into a more formal research project. I read deeply in family history genealogy, novels, scholarly research about family history genealogists, philosophical work about objects, material culture and multi-modal literacies, just to name a few. This work did not happen in some orderly fashion. Rather, it is one thought-encounter that led to another, and so on and so forth. Simply put, I have to trust procedural ontology and resist the temptation to put it into dogmatic ways of thinking about family history genealogy that are many times set forth by academic disciplines. In many ways, this work led to the conceptualization of the data assemblage (Nordstrom, 2015), an assemblage of data that generates knowledge about phenomena. The data assemblage does not follow a linear path. Instead, lines connect, disconnect and reconnect. In so doing, they generate thought-encounters that grow and morph the possibilities of a data assemblage.

A motley crew of feminists, poststructuralists (most notably Deleuze), novelists, poets, musicians and so on populate my assemblage. In describing her reading practices as an assemblage, St. Pierre (2001: 150) wrote: 'The work of reading and interpretation is such that we always create assemblages, multiplicities, within which writers across space/time speak with each other and ourselves.' As my motley crew speaks to each other and to me, they generate 'I's' across the terrain. Each 'I' is a delicate arrangement of this crew. In each doing of philosophy (Deleuze, 1991) in whatever form (e.g., research, teaching and mentoring) in which it materializes, each member of the motley crew is there. In this (un)disciplined terrain, no one member stands out and above the assemblage. For example, the 'I' that writes this chapter is one such doing, an assemblage materializing a motley crew of characters (please see reference list and attend to how the citations move through the text). As this motley crew continues to assemble itself, different iterations of this 'I' are sure to follow as they have in the past.

Returning to Virginia Woolf's (1986) quote that opened this section, I have no country, no discipline. I am assemblage. Each thought that I encounter pledges allegiance to the assemblage. These pledges are the sense-making processes as the thought-encounter moves across to disciplines to consider possibilities. Each pledge considers how disciplinary frameworks shift the thought-encounter into different possibilities and impossibilities. Each pledge becomes something other than itself.

What does thinking demand of me now?

As soon as I wrote the sentence comparing the tenure and promotion dossier to the ensemble of life (which I describe in the section 'A method'), something changed. The previous versions of the statements about research, teaching and service expressed cynicism and despair. The force of that one sentence about the dossier as an ensemble of a scholarly life shifted everything. I revised the statements with the joy that sentence gave me. The statements became celebrations of an ever-arranging self. The statements shifted to an expression of a self that is unabashedly feminist and transdisciplinary not a subject trying to shapeshift herself into a neoliberal box (Collective, 2017). I wrote the statements I wanted to write by strategically enacting a neoliberal subject that joyfully assembles herself in feminist and transdisciplinary ways (Nordstrom, 2018). More importantly, I realized how I fell prey to the dogma of the singular and what that dogma and assemblage can do. Dogma = despair. Assemblage = joyful creation.

All this happened months after I wrote the proposal for this chapter. To be in touch with my present, to be 'open to the world's aliveness, allowing oneself to be lured by curiosity, surprise, and wonder' (Barad, 2012: 207), I had to write the present – the inability to write what I proposed and respond to a curious question. I could not respond to the proposal I wrote because it was no longer my present. The assemblage, the terrain of thought, shifted and I had to respond. Much like Alexandra Bergson did when she looked upon the empty Nebraska prairie and imagined possibilities, I, too, 'felt the future stirring' (Cather, 1989: 45).

I returned to my goddesses – Barad, Stengers, Despret, Haraway and Ahmed – to help me consider the present. I turned toward their wise words and extended my hand to them. Stengers (2011: 147) wrote:

> But knowing that what you take has been held out entails a particular thinking 'between.' It does not demand fidelity, still less fealty, rather a particular kind of loyalty, the answer to the trust of the held out hand. Even if this trust is not in 'you' but in 'creative uncertainty,' even if the consequences and meaning of what has been done, thought or written, do not belong to you anymore than they belonged to the one you take the relay from, one way or another the relay is now in your hands, together with the demand that you do not proceed with 'mechanical confidence.'

I had missed something. Or rather the cynicism and despair had masked key parts of my iteration of transdisciplinary thinking. It is in-between thinking, thinking between resistance and creation. This work is about resisting the norms that unjustly bind us but also create possible futures. It is work dominated by a responsible practice that threads humans and nonhumans together in affirmative becomings toward a justice-to-come (Barad, 2012). This work mobilizes creative experimentations that announce possibilities of living differently. This work is loyal to the creativity generated by the thought-encounter. This work is about making a fuss.

Making a fuss is an ecology of practices. Haraway's (2018) conclusion to her essay about Stengers' work is instructive. Haraway included the texts of protest signs she saw during a protest following the United States 2016 election. She (2018: 63) wrote:

> Instruct. Obstruct. Construct.
> Run Fast, Bite Hard.
> Listen. Think. Respond.
> Teach. Organize. Resist. Change. Hope.

Studying my ensemble of a scholarly life has helped me to see how these verbs materialize movements, relays, and a sense of being in touch with the world. Palmer (2014: 87) wrote, 'the infinitive is the undetermined problem and the conjugation is the solution.' The objects that constitute my ensemble of a scholarly life materialize problems in which I found myself caught. Subsequent objects demonstrate how I used conjugations – and, and, and … – to generate solutions. In other words, I did not just wake up and become transdisciplinary. Object by object I engaged with the verbs listed by Haraway. Object by object I became and continue to become with transdisciplinary thinking and research. Object by object transdisciplinary thinking and research has become my normal and natural sense-making apparatus. The pattern was already in my hands (Haraway, 2018).

By sharing the ensemble of my scholarly life, and the terrain of thought that it generated, and what that terrain generates, I have attempted to do the work that Barad, Haraway, Stengers and Despret have called upon me to do. As transdisciplinary feminist scholars relay these words to each other, we engage in feminist world making (Ahmed, 2017). We become with the world, rather than apart from it. We focus on the lively curiosities that demand in-between thinking and research. We move across disciplines in search of conjugative solutions. We engage in hope. In love (Ulmer, 2017b). In Resistance. In Creation. If the pattern is in our hands as Haraway (2018) suggested, then it is up to us to harness the power of transdisciplinary thought and research to think and do research otherwise.

References

Ahmed, S. (2017). *Living a Feminist Life*. Durham, NC: Duke University Press.
Barad, K. (2012). On touching – The inhuman that therefore I am. *Differences: A Journal of Feminist Cultural Studies*, *23*(3), 206–223, doi: 10.1215/10407391-1892943
Cather, W. (1989). *O Pioneers!* New York, NY: Bantam Books.
Collective. (2017). I am Nel: Becoming (in)coherent scholars in neoliberal times. *Cultural Studies ↔ Critical Methodologies*, *17*(3), 251–261, doi: 10.1177/1532708617706120
Deleuze, G. (1991). *Empiricism and Subjectivity: An Essay on Hume's Theory of Human Nature*. New York, NY: Columbia University Press.
Deleuze, G. (1994). *Difference and Repetition*. Trans. P. Patton. New York, NY: Columbia University Press.
Deleuze, G., and Guattari, F. (1987). *A Thousand Plateaus: Capitalism and Schizophrenia* (B. Massumi, Trans.). Minneapolis, MN: University of Minnesota Press.
Foucault, M. (1994). *The Order of Things: An Archaeology of the Human Sciences*. New York, NY: Random House.
Fuentes, C. (1973). *Chac mool y otros cuentos*. Mexico City: Salvat Editores.
Goggin, B. (1997–present). *Defenestration*. Retrieved from www.metaphorm.org/portfolio/defenestration. Accessed June 4, 2019.
Goya, F. (1823). *Saturn Devouring His Son*. Retrieved December 9, 2006 from www.ibiblio.org/wm/paint/auth/goya/goya.saturn-son.jpg
Haraway, D. (2018). SF with Stengers: Asked for or not, the pattern is now in your hands. *SubStance*, *47*(1), 60–63.
Jackson, A. and Mazzei, L. (2008). Experience and 'I' in autoethnography: A deconstruction. *International Review of Qualitative Research*, *1*(3), 299–318.
Manning, E. (2016). *The Minor Gesture*. Durham, NC: Duke University Press.
Nash, J. (1997). The fiesta of the word: The Zapatista uprising and radical democracy in Mexico. *American Anthropology*, *99*(2), 261–271.

Nordstrom, S. (2015). A data assemblage. *International Review of Qualitative Research*, 8(2), 166–193, doi: 10.1525/irqr.2015.8.2.166

Nordstrom, S. (2018). Antimethodoogy: Postqualitative generative conventions. *Qualitative Inquiry*, 24(3), 215–226, doi: 10.1177/1077800417704479

Nordstrom, S. (2019). Ensembles of life: Developing an affirmative and intensive concept in educational research. *Educational Research for Social Change*, 8(1), 14–40, doi: 10.17159/2221-4070/2018/v8i1a3

Palmer, H. (2014). *Deleuze and Futurism: A Manifesto for Nonsense*. London: Bloomsbury Academic.

Stengers, I. (2011). Relaying a war machine? In E. Alliez and A. Goffey (Eds.), *The Guattari Effect* (pp. 134–155). New York, NY: Continuum.

Stengers, I. and Despret, V. (2014). *Women Who Make a Fuss: The Unfaithful Daughters of Virginia Woolf* (Trans. A. Knutson). Minneapolis, MN: Univocal Publishing.

St. Pierre, E. A. (2001). Coming to theory: Finding Foucault and Deleuze. In K. Weiler (Ed.), *Feminist Engagements: Reading, Resisting, and Revisioning Male Theorists in Education and Cultural Studies* (pp. 141–163). New York, NY: Routledge.

The Faint. (2001). Agenda suicide. [Recorded by The Faint]. On *Danse Macabre* [CD]. Lincoln, NE: Saddle Creek Records.

Ulmer, J. (2017a). Writing slow ontology. *Qualitative Inquiry*, 23(3), 201–211, doi: 10.1177/1077800416643994

Ulmer, J. (2017b). Critical qualitative research is/as love. *Qualitative Inquiry*, 23(7), 543–544, doi: 10.1177/1077800417718298

Woolf, V. (1986). *Three guineas*. New York, NY: Harcourt, Inc.

18 Sex

A transdisciplinary concept

Stella Sandford

Introduction

What is sex?[1] Some feminists have harboured suspicions about this form of question, given its philosophical (or 'metaphysical'; Irigaray, 1985: 122) pedigree. But philosophy no longer has the disciplinary monopoly on it. Indeed, with regard to sex, the more interesting task today is to pose and to attempt to answer the question from within a transdisciplinary problematic. For the question requires a theoretical response capable of recognising that it concerns a cultural and political (and therefore neither a specifically philosophical nor a merely empirical) problem. It requires an account of sex which is theoretically satisfying while being both adequate to and critical of everyday experience; a critical-theoretical account capable of embracing the everyday experience of sex, its lived contradictions. This paper represents a first attempt to construct a transdisciplinary concept of sex to this end. It traces a line from Simone de Beauvoir's *The Second Sex* to some recent attempts to define 'sex' and various related but importantly different concepts, and ends by proposing an answer to the question 'What is sex?' that draws on the philosophy of Immanuel Kant. For our transdisciplinary efforts will of necessity spring from some specific discipline(s) while not remaining confined within them, and not allowing them to remained confined within themselves (which has been something of a problem for philosophy, historically).

With and without gender

Sex, *sexe*, *Geschlecht*, *sexo*, *sesso*, etc. Do these words all refer to the same thing? Presumptions about the obviousness of the meaning of sex might suggest that they do, but the least analysis reveals that the case is otherwise. For example, does 'sex' translate the French '*sexe*', or is it a false friend? We have reason to be cautious because of an English interloper: the concept of 'gender'. When, in the contemporary Anglophone context, we insist on the specificity of the concept of 'sex' we distinguish it from a range of related but distinct concepts: 'gender', 'sexuality' and (I would add) 'sexual difference'. Most importantly, the distinction between sex and gender, which emerged in the 1950s, in the published work and clinical practice of the American psychologist Robert Stoller, was seized upon in the following decades by feminists who immediately saw the direct political advantage of a vocabulary that allowed them to distinguish between what they saw as a biological reality (the functional distinction between male and female in reproduction: sex) and a socio-cultural system or demand (normative masculinity and femininity: gender). 'Gender' achieved a theoretical ascendancy in Anglophone feminist theory that it still holds today. In some other linguistic contexts seemingly straightforward translations of the sex/gender distinction were made; where this was not possible feminists also introduced the English 'gender' as a term of analysis into other languages.

In retrospect, it is possible to posit a conceptual distinction between sex and gender in the analyses of various thinkers before the distinction was marked in the technical vocabulary. So, for example, Mary Wollstonecraft's *A Vindication of the Rights of Woman* (1790) and John Stuart Mill's *On the Subjection of Women* (1869) both exposed the falsity of the presumption that the present state of women, deprived of education, was determined by nature; an achievement that can reasonably be seen as distinguishing between what is now called 'sex' and 'gender'. Indeed they laid some of the theoretical groundwork that later allowed the distinction to be made. Similarly, Anglophone feminists have tended to read the sex/gender distinction into Beauvoir's *Le deuxième sexe*, despite the terminology being absent. The famous claim that 'one is not born, but rather becomes, a woman' (Beauvoir, 1976 [1949]: 13) is for many the founding claim for the analytical priority of gender over sex in second wave feminism. I will return to Beauvoir later, to dispute this tendency. For now, the point to be emphasised is that where the originally English language sex/gender distinction operates, 'sex' is conceptually determined in its opposition to 'gender'.

Of course, many feminists who happen to be French have found the sex/gender distinction agreeable, and certainly it can be rendered in French. Nevertheless, the sex/gender distinction is decidedly foreign and indeed disagreeable to some of the major French feminist theorists of the twentieth and now twenty-first centuries. This has sometimes been an obstacle in the English language reception of these feminist theories from France, and not only because 'gender' is an alien concept when it comes to the interpretation of, for example, the meaning of '*le féminin*' for Luce Irigaray or of '*la différence sexuelle*' in various other psychoanalytical feminisms. If the English 'sex' is conceptually determined in its opposition to 'gender', but no such equivalent conceptual opposition animates these French feminist theories, there is reason to doubt even the ostensibly more plausible conceptual equivalence between 'sex' and '*sexe*'.

This leaves us with a two-way problem in the translation between French and English, which is precisely the topic of the entry for '*Sexe*', written by Geneviève Fraisse, in the *Vocabulaire européen des philosophies*. '*Sexe*', Fraisse writes, is only apparently a 'transnational' concept: 'The word "sex" in the English language essentially refers to the biological and the physical; in French, however, this word signifies "the sexual life" quite as much as "the sexed character of humanity"'. For Fraisse, it seems, 'sex' and 'sexual difference' are synonymous;

as are '*sexe*' and '*différence sexuelle*'. The English 'sex' and 'sexual difference' 'refer to the material reality of the human'; *la différence sexuelle* is the *presupposition* of a difference between the sexes defined in a certain way, whether biologically, as in the natural sciences, or philosophically, as in '*la pensée du féminin*', the thinking of 'the feminine' (Fraisse, 2004: 1115).[2] Most importantly, for Fraisse, '*Différence sexuelle*' coexists in French with '*différence des sexes*', from which it is distinguished to the extent that the latter 'implies the empirical recognition of the sexes without that leading to any definition of content' (ibid.).[3] '*Différence des sexes*', Fraisse writes elsewhere (1996: 44–45), is a 'philosopheme'.[4] To the extent that the French '*sexe*' includes '*différence des sexes*' within its meaning, as Fraisse effectively argues that it does,[5] it is already in some sense a theoretical concept, referring to something to be *thought* rather than a biological reality to be taken for granted. Without the philosopheme '*différence des sexes*', '*la différence sexuelle*' ('sexual difference', 'sex difference' or the English 'sex') is reduced to an empirical fact. According to Fraisse, American feminists, having only their limited (English) concept of sex, lacked any adequate linguistic tool with which to think *la différence des sexes*; they therefore 'invented' the concept of gender to make up for this lack.[6] But 'gender' is not a translation of '*différence des sexes*', which remains untranslatable into English. 'Gender', Fraisse writes (2004: 1156), has become a transnational term, but '*la différence des sexes*' is still, it seems, a French speciality.

Although Fraisse sees the invention of the concept of gender as a 'contemporary philosophical event' that acknowledges the necessity to think '*la différence des sexes*', the quickly achieved theoretical hegemony of 'gender' – which, it is true, for some decades almost entirely displaced any analysis of 'sex' in Anglophone feminist theory – is regrettable to the extent that it seems to efface 'sexe as sexuality' ['*le sexe comme sexualité*'] (Fraisse, 2004: 1155),[7] that is, what is included in the French concept of *sexe*, according to Fraisse. ('Gender', she puns, is a 'cache-sexe'. That doesn't translate well into English either.[8]) The Anglophone inability to think '*la différence des sexes*' with a concept of gender means that '*sexe*' is not *thought*; 'gender', that is, produces a philosophical deficit, ironically bolstering the old-fashioned view that '*la différence des sexes*' is not be counted among the starry array of philosophical objects, such that people will say, as Fraisse recalls in 1996 (6), 'How extraordinary! What an idea, to want to think the "*différence des sexes*"'! The consequences of this philosophical deficit are not just theoretical.

In the entry on 'Gender' in the *Vocabulaire*, written by Monique David-Ménard and Penelope Deutscher, it is argued that the Anglo-American distinction between biological sex and socially constructed gender identity rules out the possibility of thinking the primarily psychoanalytical concept of '*sexualité*' or '*la différence des sexes*' that these authors see as holding sway in French feminist thought. '*Sexualité*' or '*la différence des sexes*', they claim, is neither physiological nor psychical, but fantasmatic, to do with the drives [*pulsionelle*]. The social determinations of gender and the physiological givens of sex are just two of the materials by means of which fantasies and drives are forged.

(David-Ménard and Deutscher, 2004: 496-497) Clearly David-Ménard and Deutscher's *'différence des sexes'* is different to Fraisse's *'différence des sexes'*, but the authors make the same point for us here: the French and the Anglo-Americans do not think sex in the same way; indeed, the Anglophones do not *think* sex at all.

Pas de Beauvoir?

It is surprising, to say the least, that neither of the entries on *'Sexe'* and 'Gender' in the *Vocabulaire* mentions Beauvoir and *The Second Sex*. (Beauvoir, in fact, does not appear in the *Vocabulaire* at all. I just mention that.) How is this to be explained? Partly, of course, the absence is explained by the fact that Fraisse's account of the philosopheme *'différence des sexes'* is clearly the articulation of one particular position, not a general account of what is thought on the subject in French. David-Ménard and Deutscher's psychoanalytical concept of *'sexualité'* or *'la différence des sexes'*, which they are undoubtedly correct to contrast with a certain Anglophone concept of sex, is similarly specific. Overall, the main concern of both entries is to criticise the limitations of the concept of gender with regard to a French concept of *'sexe'* beyond the sex/gender distinction. Ironically, in the entry on *'sexe'*, this leaves us with precisely that philosophical deficit that its author ascribes to 'gender' – namely, a failure to *think 'sexe'*, since such a thinking would have to include what Anglophones call 'sex', too. Perhaps this is because the remit of the *Vocabulaire* extends only to *philosophical* concepts, and the English 'sex' does not count as such. But, first, the *Vocabulaire* is also allegedly about words; and, second, can philosophical concepts be cut off from the generalities of everyday usage? Especially when that concept is 'sex'? It is here that the question of a transdisciplinary, rather than a *narrowly* philosophical, concept is raised.

The concept of sex is not explicitly theorised in *The Second Sex*; nor does Beauvoir construct a concept of sex as a central theoretical element of her oeuvre. Nevertheless, *The Second Sex* opens the theoretical space that made this possible for her successors. Beauvoir tends to write of 'the sexes' (*'les sexes'*), 'the two sexes' (*'les deux sexes'*), and men and women's relation to their *'sexe'*, not of sex itself, and not of *'la différence des sexes'*. *'Sexe'* in *Le deuxième sexe* is not a theoretical construction but the site of a problem. When referring to the functional, biological concept of sex Beauvoir tends to write of the 'the division of the sexes' (*'la division des sexes'*),[9] but she begins her main discussion of this (in the first chapter of the First Volume, 'The Givens of Biology'), with a warning: 'it is necessary to say, from the beginning, that the very meaning of the *division* [*la section*] of species into two sexes is not clear' (Beauvoir, 1976: 36). The point of this chapter of *The Second Sex* is to demonstrate that biology cannot, on its own, supply an answer to the two main questions of the book: What is a woman? And why has woman been assigned or assumed the subordinate position of the Other in relation to man? If biology could answer the first of these woman's being would be reduced to her being-female. 'The fact is', Beauvoir writes, 'that she [woman] is a female' (Beavoir, 1976 [1949]: 36), but her sex or her being-sexed is not identical with this. When she writes that 'no woman can, without bad faith, claim to situate herself beyond her sex' she is not referring to 'her function as a female' ('*sa fonction de femelle*') (Beauvoir, 1976 [1949]: 13). The two sexes in *The Second Sex* are not just male and female but, more importantly, man and woman. It is sex in the sense of the sex of men and women, not of male and female, which is the topic of *The Second Sex*, and 'men' and 'women', unlike 'male' and 'female', are not biologically, but existentially defined.

Beauvoir describes the obviousness of the division of humanity into two sexes in the following way:

> It is enough to go for a walk with one's eyes open to be sure that humanity is divided into two categories of individuals, whose clothes, faces, bodies, smiles, gaits, interests and occupations are manifestly different. Perhaps these differences are superficial; perhaps they are destined to disappear. But what is certain is that, for now, they do most obviously exist.
> (Beauvoir, 1976 [1949]: 13)

As this is clearly not a list of biologically determined characteristics, many Anglophone readers have presumed that passages like this show that Beauvoir is really talking about gender, not sex. But granted that she is not talking about 'sex' in the sense determined by the sex/gender distinction this does not mean that she is not talking about sex in another sense. Refusing the reduction of sex to biology is the beginning of the opening out of the concept of sex for thought. That there is a need to emphasise the illegitimacy of this reduction shows that, as far as Beauvoir was concerned, there was *also* a concept of sex in French thought very similar to the Anglophone concept of sex determined in its opposition to gender. This takes us to the crux of the problem. In effectively refining and specifying the meaning of sex existentially, Beauvoir reminds us, precisely, that this effort of thought must pitch itself against the dominant popular concept of sex evident in the assumption, common in both lay discourse and in philosophy, that biological sex determines what it is to be a woman. ('What is a woman? "*Tota mulier in utero*: she is a womb", according to one'; Beauvoir, 1976 [1949]: 11)

We may call the popular, dominant concept of sex the modern 'natural-biological' concept of sex, not to commit it to a particular disciplinary-scientific origin or ontological status but because of the presumptions that constitute it. These presumptions are that there simply *is* sex duality (the exclusive division between male and female) and that that duality is naturally determined. As such, its referent is presumed to be a natural and not an historical object, and the possibility that the concept is precisely *modern* is hidden. I contend that this concept has no purely descriptive function in relation to human being, but the presumption in its use is, precisely, that it does. It has no purely descriptive function because the constitutive and exclusive duality of its terms – male and female – is empirically inadequate to the phenomena that it would allegedly encompass without remainder, meaning that its duality is in fact normative and prescriptive.[10] Further, the natural-biological concept of sex functions in relation to human being to refer to a natural foundation for existence, such that it offers itself as a naturalistic explanation for some aspects – sometimes even *all* aspects – of human psycho-social existence and behaviour. Thus the natural-biological concept of sex functions as something both naturally determined and naturally determining and it is effectively impossible to separate these two aspects. In allegedly describing a natural foundation for human existence, the natural-biological concept of sex prescribes a duality, the nature of which is taken to be more or less determining of aspects of that existence.

When the more sophisticated theoretical constructions of *sexualité* and *la différence des sexes* overwrite this popular conception, the palimpsest does not erase all trace of the natural-biological concept of sex; far from it. If this is not acknowledged, the concepts of sex as *sexualité* and *la différence des sexes* float free, with no critical or political purchase. This may be fine for psychoanalysis, but not for feminism. The recognition of this is the basis for another discourse on sex in French thought, the sociologically informed political determination of the concept of sex in Christine Delphy's work. Sex, for Delphy, is not a natural given but a social relation, enabling the identification and recognition of groups in a hierarchical relation of oppression and exploitation. Sex, in this sense, is a material and ideological condition for the reproduction of the means of existence in a particular social form. In common with Monique Wittig, Delphy's political concept of sex does not simply overwrite the 'English' popular natural-biological concept; rather it includes the latter as the – reified – form of appearance of the former.[11] There is a direct line from Beauvoir to Delphy and Wittig in this respect. Neither Delphy nor Wittig appear in the *Vocabulaire*, either.

The persistence of the popular natural-biological concept of sex is not merely a regrettable theoretical naivety that more sophisticated theorists can simply dismiss; *this persistence must itself be thought*. In her *Sexe, genre et sexualités* Elsa Dorlin insists on this. How can we explain, Dorlin asks, the contradiction between the medical sciences' acknowledgement that 'the complex process of sexuation is irreducible to the two categories of sex' and the medical practices – notably the medical management of intersex infants – which continue to accept, and indeed support, an unambiguous 'bicategorisation' as unquestioned fact? How to explain 'the persistence of a belief and a scientific practice which contradicts the rationality of the very theory of which it claims to be the application'? (Dorlin, 2008: 42–43) For Dorlin this contradiction amounts to a quasi-permanent scientific crisis, a crisis which remains unresolved because sexual bicategorisation is necessary to ensure the reproduction of the social relation of domination that we call 'gender' (even though, at the same time, science itself has revealed that sexual bicategorisation as social and historical norm, such that the social relation of 'gender' is in fact the ultimate basis for 'sex'):

> If the crisis in the natural foundation of sex (male/female) is what sustains gender relations, it is first of all the effect of a contradiction between scientific

theory and practice – a contradiction which is simultaneously both the effect of the crisis and its solution. The crisis is perpetuated as such. It is a scientific situation of the status quo which resolves a political problem, reifying the (political, not natural) categories of sex – bracketing, suspending the research into the natural foundation of sex, and employing a doxico-practical criterion (that is, gender) 'in the absence of anything better', 'while we wait'.

(Dorlin, 2008: 52)[12]

Thus the persistence of the modern natural-biological concept of sex must be thought, and not simply dismissed, because, its theoretical desubstantialisation notwithstanding, it still sustains the gender system and its compulsory heterosexuality (Dorlin, 2008: 55). Dorlin's analysis exhibits the contradiction between the two faces of sex – naturalised bicategorisation and denaturalised social-historical effect – and explains *why* the contradiction is sustained in terms of an ideological function. But is it possible to construct a single concept of sex for which this contradiction would be constitutive? And one, moreover, which explained *how* the contradiction is maintained?

'An object in the idea'

Any construction or philosophical determination of a concept of sex must in some way acknowledge the social reality or the effective actuality of the popular natural-biological concept of sex if it is to have any critical or political purchase. The construction of a critically adequate concept of sex is therefore the construction of a conceptual anamorphosis. In invoking anamorphoses I have in mind not Holbein's famous *memento mori*, but trinkets: the postcards, playing cards, bookmarks and so on that reveal one picture when turned this way, another when turned that. A single, transdisciplinary concept of sex – or at least a concept with pretensions to being such – would have to be similarly vacillant: encapsulating both a theoretically determined account of the functioning of the popular natural-biological concept *and* its criticism. The psychoanalytical concept of a fantasmatic complex, championed by David-Ménard and Deutscher, and Fraisse's philosophical concept of *la différence des sexes* do not do this precisely because of their disciplinary delimitations. I submit that this would be the case with any disciplinary concept of sex.

If there is already a path cut in the direction of a single, transdisciplinary concept of sex in feminist theory it runs from Beauvoir through Delphy and Wittig, but not much further. Judith Butler took the baton across the Atlantic but her *Gender Trouble*, brilliant though it is in many respects, effectively dismissed sex – it explained it away, rather than specifying it conceptually. (This is because, in *Gender Trouble*, Butler remained mortgaged to a presumptive natural-realist ontology, according to which sex could not be said to exist, coupled to an epistemological problematic, according to which the in itself of sex could not be known.[13]) But Butler, gender theorist par excellence, *did* see that the normative dimension of the popular natural-biological concept of sex was *politically* the force to be reckoned with; thus her criticism of 'sex'. In this respect, contra Fraisse, any *gender* theorist, precisely in their rejection of the popular natural-biological concept of sex and its normative dimension, thinks sex better than the psychoanalytical theorist or philosopher of *sexualité* and *la différence des sexes*, who remain aloof from it.

The task of constructing a critical concept of sex in its greatest generality requires, as we have said, a determination of the nature of the popular natural-biological concept of 'sex' which can account for its actual effects, its social existence. I suggest that we can find the means for this in Kant's philosophy.[14] In the *Critique of Pure Reason*, Kant, having discussed the *a priori* contribution to experience of the faculties of sensibility and understanding and the legitimate employment of the concepts of the understanding (limited to the realm of possible experience), famously introduced what he called the 'ideas' of pure reason, or 'transcendental ideas'.

The faculty of reason, according to Kant, itself generates, *a priori*, certain concepts (that is, ideas) and principles which, according to the 'demand of [speculative] reason ... to bring the understanding into thoroughgoing connection with itself', guide the use of the understanding, pointing it towards the absolute totality of the series of conditioned appearances, its unconditioned ground. The idea of 'freedom' is, according to Kant, an idea in this sense. The idea has no possible congruent object in experience, it does not determine any object for cognition (it has no 'objective validity', in Kant's specific sense of being valid for the determination of objects in general), but it 'serve[s] the understanding as a canon for its extended and self-consistent use' (Kant, 1998 [1781/1789]: 390, 403). This is for Kant the legitimate or proper 'regulative' use of the ideas of pure reason.

But the ideas of reason are also misused, or misapplied, in illegitimate 'constitutive' uses; that is, by mistaking their subjective necessity for objective validity, giving a purported objective reality to the object of the idea. This gives rise to what Kant calls 'dialectical' or 'transcendental' illusion, which is distinguished from both error and empirical and logical illusion in being 'natural', unavoidable and incorrigible – 'irremediably attached to human reason'. For even when the being-illusory of the transcendental illusion is revealed it does not cease to deceive us (Kant, 1998 [1781/1789]: 384–387). The unavoidable tendency to understand the necessity of the 'constant logical subject of thinking' (my being the 'absolute subject of all my possible judgements') as 'a real subject of inherence' (Kant, 1998 [1781/1789]: 416),[15] that is, a substance in the ontological sense, is just such a dialectical illusion, according to Kant.

If the trick of all transcendental illusion rests in 'the taking of a subjective condition of thinking for the cognition of an object', its necessity lies perhaps in reason's inability to think its idea 'in any other way than by giving its idea an object'. And in fact, Kant writes, the dialectical illusion of the substantiality of the soul, for example, expresses a proposition ('the soul is substance') that is perfectly valid *so long as we keep in mind* that nothing further can be deduced or inferred from this, 'that it signifies a substance only *in the idea* but not in reality'. This 'object in the idea' – this is the crucial phrase – is really only a 'schema for which no object is given' (Kant, 1998 [1781/1789]: 439, 417, 605, emphasis added).

The regulative principles of pure reason are called 'transcendental principles' to the extent that they *must* be presupposed for a coherent use of the understanding. For example, 'we simply have to presuppose the systematic unity of nature as objectively valid and necessary', according to Kant, in order to determine within the 'manifoldness of individual things' in nature the identity of species, genera, and families (Kant, 1998 [1781/1789]: 594–595). The mistake is to suppose that this unity, which is a mere idea, is to be encountered in nature itself.

Kant's example here of the specifications of species, genera and families pertains to the domain of what he elsewhere called the 'systematic description of nature' (Kant, 2001: 40, 39), distinguished from 'natural history'. But as Robert Bernasconi (2001a) has shown, the idea of reason also has a role to play in natural history, specifically – and this is of immense historical significance – in determining the concept of race.[16] As Bernasconi points out, the concept of race is not derived, for Kant, from nature; rather it is explicitly posited as a conceptual necessity for natural history. For Kant, as Bernasconi (2001a: 29) explains, 'in the present state of our knowledge the idea of race imposes itself', as regulative idea.

Clearly the idea of race provided an example, for Kant, of the legitimate, regulative employment of an idea of reason. Even if the legitimacy of this idea is now questioned politically, it remains true that the concept of race has no corresponding, scientifically identifiable, object in experience, although the lived experience of being-raced is undeniable. Does this mean that 'race' imposes itself as transcendental illusion? If it does, Kant's idea of transcendental illusion is now historicised.[17]

But what of the modern, natural-biological concept of sex? What grounds are there for thinking that sex might be an idea of reason and – in a sense yet to be determined – a transcendental illusion?

To recall, the presumptions internal to the modern, natural-biological concept of sex are that there simply is sex duality (the exclusive division into male and female) and that this duality is naturally determined. Further, in so far as 'sex' refers to a natural ground for human existence it is presumed to be something naturally determining. As the exclusive duality of its terms is empirically inadequate to the variety that it would allegedly encompass without remainder, the duality of sex is not descriptive, but prescriptive – quite literally prescriptive in the case of the intersexed infant who will be made to conform, more or less successfully, to one or other of its terms. Taken together, the constitutive presumptions and the prescriptive function of the modern natural-biological concept of sex contradict each other. As previously stated, the concept has no purely descriptive function in relation to human existence, but the presumption in its use is precisely that it does.

These two contradictory elements in the concept of sex may perhaps be understood as the difference between its uses as an abstract and a concrete noun: abstractly, the general term for the (presumed exclusive) duality of male and female; concretely, referring to particular instances of one of either of those two terms. The equivocation between these uses – a conceptual juddering so fast as to be invisible – accomplishes the same 'transcendental subreption' that Kant (1998 [1781/1789]: 577) identified in the representation of a formal regulative principle as constitutive, the result of which is hypostatisation. Or, just as, in the first paralogism of pure reason, the formal, transcendental unity of apperception is taken for the 'real subject of inherence' (substance understood ontologically), so too the formal principle of the exclusive division into male and female (the prescriptive or, in Kant's terminology, regulative, principle) is taken for the cognition of an objectively real object (for Kant, an object given in intuition).[18] The 'transcendental doctrine of the soul', or 'rational psychology', is the taking of the idea of the soul for a real object and the subsequent claims to be able to infer from this idea alone the essential attributes of the soul.[19] In the same way, we may say, the 'transcendental doctrine of sex', taking the idea of sex for a real object, claims to be able to derive from the idea of sex alone the essential attributes of men and women.

Is 'sex', then, a transcendental illusion? Sex is not a transcendental illusion on Kant's own definition, since this includes a reference to its a-historical inevitability, 'irremediably attache[d] to human reason'. Sex is *our* illusion; it was not Plato's, for example.[20] But to the extent that we are also required to account for the actual effects of the concept of sex – its real existence as a structuring component of human experience – there is, to use Kant's word, something 'unavoidable' about it. The idea of sex, like all ideas of reason according to Kant, is 'merely a creature of reason'; but the ideas 'nonetheless have their reality and are by no means merely figments of the brain'; 'we will by no means regard them as superfluous and nugatory' (1998 [1871/1889]: 386, 504–505, 396). Thus, we might say, sex is an objective *historical* illusion: an illusion that cannot be contrasted with reality because it *is* real to the extent that its effects are real. However, *given as object only in the idea* 'sex' (like the transcendental idea of the soul, for Kant) 'leads no further' (Kant, 1998 [1871/1889]: 417),[21] or its leading further is precisely the form of its ideological function.

What is the relation between this philosophical interpretation of the popular, natural-biological concept of sex as a regulative idea and the possibility of a single transdisciplinary concept of sex? For the moment, we can say this: there is already a kind of homology between them. The transdisciplinary problematic arises in the relation between conceptual generality, on the one hand, and everyday linguistic usage, experiences and practices on the other. The objective historical illusion of sex is, I have suggested, precisely the transcendental subreption of this relation or, in another vocabulary, the effective reification of the concept, at the highest level of its generality, empirically instantiated in almost every aspect of our lives. Avoiding the transcendental subreption is not merely a matter of theoretical vigilance; it is a political struggle at the level of everyday experience. The question of the meaning of sex is not a dispute to be settled by intellectuals or scholars; it is the lived contradiction of our sexed existence today.

Notes

1 This essay was first published in *Radical Philosophy* 165, January/February 2011. It is reprinted here with permission. It was part of a joint project (with Peter Osborne and Éric Alliez), later funded by the AHRC: 'Transdisciplinarity and the Humanities: Problems, Methods, Histories, Concepts' (AH/I004378/1). Some of the results of this project are published in Éric Alliez, Peter Osborne and Stella Sandford (Eds.) Special Issue of *Theory, Culture & Society. Transdisciplinary Problematics*, 32(5–6), September–November 2015 (Alliez, Osborne and Sandford, 2015). This includes Sandford, S. (2015), which focusses on the transdisciplinary concept of 'gender'.
2 See also Fraisse, 1996: 45: '"*Différence sexuelle*" is a philosophical presupposition [*un parti pris*] peculiar to French thought, notably that of Hélène Cixous or Luce Irigaray; *différence sexuelle* is already a definition of *la différence des sexes*, the ontological or psychological affirmation of a difference which is the starting point for a philosophy of the feminine'.
3 See also Fraisse, 1996: 46: 'The concept of "*différence des sexes*", such as one finds in Hegel, for example (*Encyclopedia*), has the advantage of leaving open the questions apparently resolved by the preceding concepts [of *différence sexuelle* and *gender*]'.
4 For example, Fraisse, 1996: 44–45.
5 Fraisse, 2004, 1156: 'The English language has at its disposal only *sexual difference* while French, can use, for nuance, *différence sexuelle, différence des sexes* and, indeed, *différence de sexe*'.
6
> It was decided that the necessity for thinking *la différence des sexes* would be symbolised by the concept of gender [*Il est décidé de symboliser, par le concept de genre, la nécessité de penser la* différence des sexes]. Thus the concentration of attention on this notion of *gender* is a contemporary philosophical event.
>
> (Fraisse, 2004: 1155)

7 '*La sexualité*', note, is also not the same as the English 'sexuality'.
8 Literally, in English, something that 'hides sex'; but also what we call in English, rather less elegantly, a 'g-string'.
9 For example: '*La division des sexes est en effet un donné biologique, non un moment de l'histoire humaine*' (Beauvoir, 1976 [1949]: 19).
10 On the empirical inadequacy of the duality of sex categories see Fausto-Sterling, 2000. See Dorlin, 2008, especially 'L'Historicité du sexe', pp. 33–54.
11 See, for example, Delphy, 1993; Wittig, 1992. On this political concept of sex see also Sandford, 2007.
12
> *Si la crise du fondement naturel du sexe (mâle/femelle) permet de maintenir le rapport de genre en état, elle est d'abord l'effet d'une distorsion entre théorie et practique scientifiques, qui est à la fois l'effet de la crise et la solution de cette dernière. La crise est maintenue comme telle. Elle est une situation scientifique de statu quo qui résout un problème politique, à savoir la réification des catégories, non pas naturelles mais politiques, de sexes: maintenir la recherce du fondement naturel du sexe en suspens, utiliser <<faute de mieux>> ou <<en attendant>> un critère doxico-practique – le genre.*

On the relative stability of this crisis and its function see also 2005.
13 For this argument see Sandford 1999. Nevertheless, the importance of *Gender Trouble* for the philosophy of sex is hard to overestimate.

14 The following argument is elaborated at greater length in the Coda to Sandford, 2010.
15 This is the first of the 'paralogisms of pure reason'.
16 Bernasconi's essay on race (2001a) has provided me with a model for part of the present discussion of sex.
17 Compare Michel Foucault's conception of the 'historical *a priori*':

> This a priori is what, in a given period, delimits in the totality of experience a field of knowledge, defines the mode of being of the objects that appear in that field, provides man's everyday perception with theoretical powers, and defines the conditions in which he can sustain a discourse about things that is recognized to be true.
>
> (Foucault, 1970: 158)

18 Which is not to say that the 'transcendental unity of apperception', qua (self-)consciousness of the spontaneous action of the understanding, does not itself harbour a metaphysics. But that is another matter.
19 Its substantiality, simplicity, and 'personality', that is, it's being a 'person', and the (problematic) ideality of external objects.
20 See Sandford, 2010.
21
> [O]ne can quite well allow the proposition. The soul is substance to be valid, if only one admits that this concept of ours leads no further, that it cannot teach us any of the usual conclusions of the rationalistic doctrine of the soul, such as, e.g., the everlasting duration of the soul through all alterations, even the human being's death, thus that it signifies a substance only in the idea but not in reality.

References

Alliez, É., Osborne, P. and Sandford, S. (Eds.) (2015). Special Issue of *Theory, Culture & Society. Transdisciplinary Problematics*, 32(5–6), September–November.
Beauvoir, S. de. (1976) [1949]. *Le deuxième sexe*, Vol. II. Paris: Gallimard
Bernasconi, R. (2001a). Who invented the concept of race? In Bernasconi, R. (Ed.) *Race*. Malden, MA, and Oxford: Blackwell.
Bernasconi, R. (Ed.) (2001b). *Race*. Malden, MA and Oxford: Blackwell.
Cassin, B. (Ed.) (2004). *Vocabulaire européen de philosophies: dictionnaire des intraduisibles*. Paris: Éditions du Seuil/Dictionnaires Le Robert. [Translated: Apter, E. et al. (Ed.) (2014). Dictionary of Untransltables: A Philosophical Lexicon. Princeton, NJ: Princeton University Press.]
David-Ménard, M. and Deutscher, P. (2004). Gender. In Cassin, B. (Ed.), *Vocabulaire européen de philosophies: dictionnaire des intraduisibles*. Paris: Éditions du Seuil/ Dictionnaires Le Robert.
Delphy, C. (1993). Rethinking sex and gender. Trans. D. Leonard. *Women's Studies International Forum*, 16(1):1–9.
Dorlin, E. (2005). Sexe, genre et intersexualité: la crise comme régime théoriqu'. *Raisons politiques*, 18, 117–137.
Dorlin, E. (2008). *Sexe, genre et sexualités*. Paris: PUF.
Fausto-Sterling, A. (2000). *Sexing the Body: Gender Politics and the Construction of Sexuality*. New York, NY: Basic Books.
Foucault, M. (1970). *The Order of Things: An Archeology of the Human Sciences*. London: Tavistock Publications.
Fraisse, G. (1996). *La différence des sexes*. Paris: Presses Universitaires de France.
Fraisse, G. (2004). Sexe. In Cassin, B. (Ed.), *Vocabulaire européen de philosophies: dictionnaire des intraduisibles*. Paris: Éditions du Seuil/Dictionnaires Le Robert.

Irigaray, L. (1985). *This Sex Which is Not One*. Trans. C. Porter. Ithaca, NY: Cornell University Press.
Kant, I. (1998) [1781/89]. *Critique of Pure Reason*. Trans. P. Guyer and A. W. Woo. Cambridge: Cambridge University Press.
Kant, I. (2001) [1788]. On the use of teleological principles in philosophy. In Bernasconi, R. (Ed.), *Race*. Malden, MA and Oxford: Blackwell.
Sandford, S. (1999). Contingent ontologies: Sex, gender and 'woman' in Simone de Beauvoir and Judith Butler. *Radical Philosophy*, 97, 18–29.
Sandford, S. (2007). Sexmat, Revisited. *Radical Philosophy*, 145, 28–35.
Sandford, S. (2010). *Plato and Sex*. Cambridge: Polity.
Sandford, S. (2015). Contradiction of terms: Feminist theory, philosophy and transdisciplinarity. Special Issue of *Theory, Culture & Society. Transdisciplinary Problematics*, 32 (5–6), 159–182.
Wittig, M. (2002). The category of sex. In *The Straight Mind and Other Essays*, Boston, MA: Beacon Press.

19 Conclusion
The rusty futures of transdisciplinary feminism

Jasmine B. Ulmer

Introduction

Transdisciplinary feminisms remain in motion. In moving across disciplines, they flow—fall—seep into different theories, methodologies, and practices. As the authors in this collection have expressed, there are many diverse and hopeful visions for how this can, and does, occur. Their writings are filled with rich endeavors that pose, perform, run away, live in the hyphens, inhabit spiritual dimensions, decolonize, and carefully—but willfully—intervene across varied global academic perspectives, genealogies, and histories. From art to ecology, education, history, sociology, critical theory, chemistry, and more, scholars are reshaping feminisms in ways that are at once inter-, multi-, post- and transdisciplinary. And as they convey with us here, many of these movements have not been uncontested. Even more to the point: feminisms continue to be contested across disciplines. The pasts of feminist work carry over into the work of the present, and likely will continue to do so in futures that have yet to be determined. By way of response, this last chapter considers transdisciplinary feminisms through rusty futures.

Rust is akin to feminist work: rust effectuates gradual, uneven changes over time in ways that can be all too easily dismissed or wiped away—but also in ways that can mark us all. Rust, moreover, is a chemical change—a change that occurs in metal after repeated exposures to water and moisture in the air. Sometimes the rates of change are so slow that they seem imperceptible, if not nearly impossible (such as when the World Economic Forum (2018) estimated that it will likely be *another 200 years* before women gain political and economic parity). At other times, rust emerges from more immediate changes that can be felt in the air, heard rumbling through the atmosphere, and seen across rapidly changing and precipitous weather conditions. Hashtags supporting movements such as #BelieveWomen, #MeToo, and #TimesUp follow this trajectory.

Rust might seem like an unusual place to begin, and perhaps it is. Yet, there is something involving rust, though—in this moment, here, now, today—that feels like it is something that should be addressed. Maybe it has something to do with the messiness of rust. Or, maybe it has something to do with the stories that rust can tell along the way. Perhaps it has something to do with ongoing commitments to listening, writing, and small, everyday activisms. I am not sure. What I am more confident of, however, is that we cannot think of our futures without also thinking of our pasts, and that there are times when, in order to move forward, we must first return to where we began. This doubled back-forth move is pertinent to rust: the 'rusty futures' of transdisciplinary feminisms carry across the ways in which we choose to read, write, tell our own feminist histories, pass them on to others, and further our generative and generationally overlapping feminist commitments along the way. In these regards, rusty weatherings are not only figurative and literal in scope—they are also everyday expressions of hope for transdisciplinary feminisms yet to come.

Anteriority and futurity

But first, a brief prefatory remark. Namely, this chapter is a writing story. It is my writing story (or, a small part of it, at least), and it is a writing story that includes some of the people who have mattered most along the way. It keeps with Laurel Richardson's approach to writing stories, which, for her, involve 'narratives that situate one's own writing in other parts of one's life such as disciplinary constraints, academic debates, departmental politics, social movements, community structures, research interests, familial ties, and personal history' (Richardson and St. Pierre, 2005: 965). Notably, many of the contributions to this collection do the same.

Listening to the progression of rust

I have been thinking about transdisciplinary feminisms through rust. This is easy to do in the City of Detroit, as rust is something that I am constantly surrounded by. Detroit is part of the Rust Belt, an area in the Midwest and Great Lakes region of the U.S. that has continued to experience deindustrialization in recent decades; depending on the vantage point, there are places where the term can be quite literal indeed. When I moved here several years ago, the effects of deindustrialization were beyond what I had anticipated. It quickly became apparent that research situated in the area would benefit from different, thoughtful, localized approaches. And from feminist approaches, too.

Unsure of how and where I should begin, I turned to listening as a feminist practice. Listening is something that I have long tried to do, especially when it had involved listening to the children in my elementary classroom before that. Oftentimes, I would be confused as to why a child had just done a particular thing, such as having a sudden, expletive-laced outburst during class, turning bright red from frustrations I could not see, stuffing their pockets with leftover chicken bones from lunch, or quietly folding inward without explanation. Although some would have said that I should have used classroom management and behavior management strategies to contain these situations, I usually chose to begin by listening, instead. I am glad that I did, for I was often humbled and surprised by what, when given the opportunity, the children had to say. Children are exposed to many things in life, including experiences far beyond their years. And what it made me wonder: if seven- and eight-year-old children carry so many burdens and traumas around with them on a day-to-day basis, then what must life be like for most adults? From my time listening both *to* and *with* children, I realized that we may never fully know what the others around us are carrying with them, but that, through empathetic listening, we can try. Had I known about what Bronwyn Davies (2016) describes as emergent listening, I would have tried to do just that.

But, not yet having taken graduate courses in feminist research methods, and not having yet become a feminist researcher myself, I did not yet have the language to refine how I thought, wrote, or chose to act. Therefore, it was only later on that listening became a holdover from graduate coursework in feminist research methods. Whether housed in programs of sociology, anthropology, women's studies, or education, the instructors I studied with often referred to Carol Gilligan and her impact on research. Beyond the book, *In a Different Voice: Psychological Theory and Women's Development* (Gilligan, 1982), course readings also addressed what she referred to as The Listening Guide (see, for example, Gilligan, 2015). In my university, at least, there seemed to be a resurgence of interest in her writings around that time. Although I can't report that I was faithful to the methods she carefully outlined, that I did traditional interviews, that I created I-poems, or that any of my work would be recognizable to those who are familiar with hers, The Listening Guide has stayed with me. I have continued to take seriously Gilligan's suggestion to begin research by formulating questions about voice and relationship. And I have appreciated how she keeps asking us to consider these questions (Gilligan, 2015: 69):

- Who is speaking and to whom?
- In what body or physical space?
- Telling what stories about which relationships?
- In what societal and cultural frameworks?

Though I have largely situated my writings within other feminist paradigms, Gilligan's questions are the ones that I have continued to ask myself, particularly during my first years in Detroit. From listening to conversations that street artists were initiating through graffiti, to similarly critical conversations happening through folk art in the neighborhoods nearby, to photographing all of the above, I spent much of my initial time here listening, even when that meant listening in unconventional ways. Ways that did not involve approaching a person or multiple persons, asking them for insight, recording and transcribing what they shared, only to then analyze their words by incorporating them into mine. Ways that did not involve traditional forms of interviewing, or even oral forms of speech. Rather, these were ways that involved listening to *how* people were already communicating with the world around them and listening to *what* they were already trying to say. This was a way, if you will, of listening to the progression of rust—listening to progression of slow, everyday change.

This became a practice, a technique that I hoped to hone within my own writing practice —one that was continuing to draw from embodied movements, choreography, and dance. Erin Manning's writings were influential along the way, and I returned to worn copies of her books often. I imagine I will always be swept away by the opening sections of *Relationscapes* (2009), in which she engages with the concepts of prearticulation, preacceleration, and relationality. After reading this text, I was no longer able to think without it, for Manning put into words many of the affects that I had not yet been able to articulate, especially when it came to feeling still, stuck, silent. As she writes, 'To move is to engage the potential inherent in the preacceleration that embodies you. Preaccelerated because there can be no beginning or end to movement. Movement is one with the world, not body/world, but body-worlding' (Manning, 2009: 15). Until reading *Relationscapes*, I had not realized that however much it may feel to the contrary, we are never actually fully stopped. I thought about this more the other day during yoga when the instructor echoed something similar: even when it appears otherwise and we seem stopped and still, we are still breathing.

All too often, both then and now, I find myself holding onto and moving with unnamable affects that take all too long to formulate into words. I am thankful to Manning for explaining why in a language I could understand. I am someone who isn't always able to locate words. At least not right away or on demand, however much I would prefer it to be otherwise. It takes time, patience, and a willingness to resist the unhealthy scholarly practices that many of us claim to be working against (while instead leaning further into that which we know we should avoid). I respect Manning's integrity in her commitment to writing, and I admire her courage in publishing *The Perfect Mango* (1994/2019) two and a half decades after it was written, as it was written then. I understand why she waited—sometimes texts aren't ready, and sometimes we, as authors, aren't ready to let some texts, some words, some thoughts, some events out into the world. There are times when we can feel that something isn't quite right, even if we don't know what it is. There are times when we are still prearticulating, still preaccelerating, still initiating the next movements. There are times when we are still waiting to remove the rust.

Rusty intra-actions

Listening had the potential to be a more-than-human endeavor, I realized, as I read more and more about how research methods could be situated within our vibrant world. Following the recommendations of kind thought leaders in the qualitative community, I read Karen Barad, Jane Bennett, Rosi Braidotti, Vicki Kirby, Susan Hekman, Diana Coole, Samantha Frost, Isabelle Stengers, Vincianne Despret. I read Sara Ahmed's (2017) *Living a Feminist Life*, that is, until it got too real—too recent—and I had to put it down. So, I picked back up worn copies of books by Kate Chopin, Virginia Woolf, and Toni Morrison, instead. I worked my way through writings by Maria Puig de la Bellacasa, bell hooks, Angela Davis, Gloria Anzaldúa, Catherine Malabou, Anna Tsing, Luce

Irigaray, Annemarie Mol, Stacey Alaimo, Aph and Sy Ko, Judith Butler, and I read and reread texts by these authors and others again and again. Along the way, one of the most interesting collections I encountered was *Posthuman Research Practices in Education*, edited by Carol Taylor and Christina Hughes (2016). I was surprised, but also honored and delighted, to later begin collaborating with these smart women, both within and beyond this collection on transdisciplinary feminism.

For instance, to explore the post-industrial cities in which we were living, it was in a subsequent project that Carol and I had taken up the idea of post-industrial methodologies for post-industrial cities (Taylor and Ulmer, 2020). She lived in Sheffield, U.K., at the time, and as we moved throughout our cities, we considered how elements such as air, water, and metal can come together in intra-active, diffractive ways (Barad, 2007). From there, we considered how *we* are intra-actively and diffractively constituted through, by, and within by those same elements. Since then, I have found myself continuing to sit with notions of rust, as it was this project and its quiet attentiveness to our cities that brought rust into sharper focus for me. Our project led me to more deeply consider where I live, and how the places we call home are always already positioned within broader historical, economic, political, and sociological contexts—it is just that we do not always pause to think about those factors in our daily life. It also prompted me to return to the archives of the photographs I had taken around Detroit. In going through the archives of what I already had been photographing (Figure 19.1), I was given occasion to think about how even though there may not always be immediate evidence of the intra-actions unfolding around us every day, when we do look for it, rust is something that we *can* see. Rust is a daily byproduct of our more-than-human world, as well as our entanglements within it.

Rust was also something that Susan Nordstrom and I had been talking about, specifically with regard to the public, intra-active, research-creation that Susan had assembled for Women's History Month. The university art museum promoted it as follows:

> *Disassembling Statement → Assembling Solidarity*: Introduction and demonstration of a feminist interpretation of Michelangelo Pistoletto's Sculpture for Strolling and Suzanne Lacy's untitled instruction by Susan Nordstrom (CEPR). After the opening ceremony, the community will be invited to visit the Rotunda in the McWherter Library and participate by contributing newspaper clippings on women's issues. This is an ongoing project and every Wednesday in March the gathered or contributed newspaper clippings will be used to form a sphere. The finished sphere will be walked from the McWherter Library to the closing ceremony of Women's History Month.
> (Art Museum at the University of Memphis, 2016, para. 1)

Several years after Susan told me about this interactive exhibition and the events surrounding it, I still have a vivid image in my mind related to the sculpture. I seem to remember that one day, after rolling the sculpture back into her

Figure 19.1 Rust.
Photo: J. Ulmer, Dec. 2015, Eastern Market, Detroit, MI.

office, she said that she wiped her hands on her legs, only to realize that because the sculpture was rusty, her pants were now rusty, too. Whether real or imagined, there has been something in that image that has stayed with me. The idea of rusty and streaky handprints reminds me of the difficult behind-the-scenes work that transdisciplinary feminist work entails, and it reminds me of the ways in which the work we do sticks with us (and even sometimes sticks *to* us, whether we want it to or not).

Another example of rust as a trope within research comes from one of the first pieces that I published with Mirka Koro-Ljungberg (Ulmer and Koro-Ljungberg, 2016). In it, her thinking was influenced by an author who thought about pictoral writing through the use of blood and tears as a form of ink. I can still hear her excited rush of thoughts as she conveyed what she read. The author's surname was Rust, and after reading Rust's (2013) piece myself, I've occasionally thought about what it might mean to write through blood and tears and rust since. For me, these have flowed together with notions of writing differently and flow back to

Mirka who encouraged me to write differently—and inquire differently—as a graduate student. In my dissertation I engaged policy praxis through a kaleidoscope of feminist theories: from the transitional spaces of Anzaldúa, to the plasticity of Malabou, to the entanglements and intra-actions of Barad, to thinking with theory more generally (Jackson and Mazzei, 2011), I appreciate how I had full rein to write a dissertation study that was steeped in feminist theory and practices, even if not always openly so. Sometimes it takes a little while for rust to become noticeable; the beginning can be easy to miss.

Transdisciplinary rustlings

For me, much of this work has not been particularly overt. This is, in part, because of how I have been situated within various universities and disciplines – where to have jumped up and shouted 'I am a feminist researcher' would have quickly meant that I no longer had the privilege to do research. In any event, I'm not one to draw attention to myself, much less shout. I am an introvert who is more interested in the work—in the everyday practices. I am, of course, interested in how feminist theories guide our inquiries and methodologies and research. But, I'm *more* interested in how we as feminist researchers in higher education can infuse feminist practices into everything we do. *How is this feminist?* is a question that I constantly ask myself.

And yes, as I write this, I hesitate. There are, of course, many feminisms, particularly across disciplines, and what the 'best' approach to feminism is and how 'feminist research' should be carried out is keenly disputed territory. Am I doing the 'right' kind of feminisms? Have I read enough? I certainly have not read all of the foundational texts, much less engaged with them deeply. I'm thinking, though, that maybe that's okay. Such thoughts bring to mind one of the books that I'm reading and thinking with now—Julietta Singh's *Unthinking Mastery: Dehumanism and Decolonial Engagements* (2017). Singh's observations on how we often remain tied to the structures that we claim to be working against particularly move me:

> Conceiving of ourselves as intellectual masters over those bodies of knowledge (broad or discrete) that we have tasked ourselves to engage connects us to historical practices of mastery that our work seeks to explore and redress. We must with increasing urgency revise the very idea (and the languages we use to describe) our work as intellectuals—with what resonances, and toward what possibilities.
>
> (Singh, 2017: 9)

In keeping with Singh, then, it *can* be acceptable to eschew notions of expertise, particularly within fields that are inwardly and outwardly contested. It can be acceptable to live with bodies of knowledge and respectfully bring them into our theories, methods, and practices. Approaching knowledge building differently (and our various roles in it) is not only acceptable, it is necessary.

I am reminded here, as perhaps you are too, of Audra Lorde's oft-quoted observation that *'the master's tools will never dismantle the master's house. They may allow us temporarily to beat him at his own game, but they will never enable us to bring about genuine change'* (2012: 112, emphasis in original). This raises questions, of course, regarding what to do next. For if we aren't able to dismantle inequitable structures with the same tools with which they were built, then where might we find alternatives? How might we do things differently, resonate differently, move toward possibilities that are actually new and different? We might do this by returning to the question of *How is this feminist?* Or, if the answer we come up with is that it's not feminist, then we might shift the question into *How might this become feminist?* We might ask this as an ongoing question of the many theories, methods, and practices we take up.

Rusty accounts

As I mentioned earlier, feminist work reminds me of rust. Rust is a sign of encounter, progression, expansion, continuation, weathered change. Rust emanates from changes over time, changes which are relational and slow-moving, even imperceptible. How might rust 'work' as a story—one in which it is possible to see ourselves in?

There is something involved in crafting research narratives of a successful academic life and career – the competitive processes of applying for grants and promotions; the individualism of obtaining tenure; the significance of individual bodies of work – that, to me, at least, seems antithetical to feminist work. While relationality may be one of the most important transdisciplinary concepts, *research narratives are often anything but relational*. When we are asked to write research narratives in this way, what we are being asked to do is ignore how we exist within a complex network of relations—how we read and write and think with others, even when it seems like we are doing the work of scholarship alone. This lends itself to creating the same false sense of individualism that transdisciplinary feminisms regularly work against.

What I realized in writing this chapter—in writing through the rust—is that *this* is the beginning of the research narrative that, in a more ideal and creatively-minded world, I would be able to write. That instead of writing *about* the concept of relationality and how I take it up in my work, I could write in ways that are *actually relational*, instead. I could write in ways that are authentic and accurate and tell the important parts of the research stories in real-time as they unfold. And I could include

- Reading lists of the feminist texts that have shaped and reshaped my thinking;
- Acknowledgements of the books that were recommended to me, and by whom;
- Excerpted passages from those books with close readings of their influence;
- Insights gained during conversations and collaborations with others; and
- General expressions of gratitude for everyone who has helped along the way.

Traditional research narratives simply don't leave much room for accounts of what has mattered most in our respective and collective research trajectories. Consequently, when our writings conform to tightly structured narratives and abbreviated word counts, much is lost. For instance, there isn't room to return to graduate texts encountered in feminist sociological and anthropological courses, and how I'm still wondering about questions Lila Abu-Lughod and Judith Stacey asked of feminist researchers nearly three decades ago. No, there's no room for that, because the trajectory of our work is supposed to be about us as individuals: what we did, what we achieved, what sorts of demonstrable, measurable impacts we've had along the way. There is little to no room, if any, to share the moments that have mattered most. Such as a) how conversations with Jessica Lester prompted me to consider our personal and professional commitments; b) how this work became alive in the world through collaborations with Carol Taylor and Susan Nordstrom; c) how I began to write and teach with gratitude after Brooke Hofsess and Shauna Caldwell told me how much they were enjoying *Braiding Sweetgrass* (Kimmerer, 2013; c.f. Ulmer, 2018a, 2018b); d) how others taught me to read, cite, and celebrate texts differently (e.g., Bridges-Rhoads, Hughes, and Van Cleave, 2018; Van Cleave and Bridges-Rhoads, 2017); and e), how after picking up *Unthinking Mastery* (Singh, 2017) on the recommendation of Candace Kuby and Becky Christ, I am now rethinking it all again. These are but too few of the many examples that I could share; there are countless more, and I am grateful for each and every one—because each one supports my sense of doing academia differently.

Traditional research narratives don't allow us to fully acknowledge the contributions others make to our work, especially with regard to those with whom we collaborate, converse, and read. Rather, they encourage us to perpetuate the myth of the lone, independent researcher as if that were a real thing, as if we spontaneously emerged into the world completely out of our own volition. In order to inflate our achievements and sense of scholarly worth, we are encouraged not only to erase our immediate friends and colleagues, but also the scholars who have influenced our work. Refusing to do that is, I suggest, a modest but important feminist task. I know (I believe) that the tiniest moments can be the most important, and there's no reason not to be grateful.

It's easy to get stuck in the process of scholarship, particularly when it hits close to home or the lives that we all live inevitably get in the way. There are times when we will experience extended patches of rust—encounter too much rust—and occasionally feel a bit rusty ourselves. There are times when we have to find our way through it, and there are times when we can help others do the same. These are times when we can set aside desires for mastery and dominance and expertise, credit others, and show where our best thinking is at any given moment in time, even though there is, of course, always more to learn, to read, to write, to think, to share. Put simply, there is always more to do: in life, in scholarship, with women and girls, and more. But perhaps, just perhaps, one of the tiny ways we can do this is further feminism as an everyday practice. Transdisciplinary feminisms offer to show the way how, in part by encouraging us to treat people as people, including our own selves.

For me, at least, making claims at feminist scholarly work includes writing in ways that are consistent with a feminist practice. Centering our work as if we did it all alone, thought it all alone, without the influence of others, in an unnaturally compressed amount of time and space is anything but feminist. Rather than squish narratives into a formulaic few pages, then, I'd much prefer to consider relational and reciprocal impact instead, which is the beginning of what I've attempted here. Feminism is a collaborative endeavor, and I could not do the feminist work that I have done without the opportunities I've had to think alongside so many feminist researchers, including the feminist scholars in this collection.

Conclusions to books can provide a natural occasion to think toward futures in general, and it is certainly easy to imagine futures with new, shiny finishes. This conclusion has not been that. To come to the conclusion of a book is one thing, to come to the conclusion of multiple species is another. We are living in the midst of mass extinctions in the Anthropocene, an epoch that is signaling futures of a different sort: *rusty futures* in which the decisions of the past will continue to contaminate what lies ahead for us all unless we begin to live relationally and in reciprocity with those around us. This is of concern to us all. I will choose, however, as I often do, to take comfort in the writings of Luce Irigaray (1991: 38), who observes that 'anything too rigid often breaks. And when the time of the thaw comes, it rusts away in the waters.'

References

Ahmed, S. (2017). *Living a Feminist Life*. Durham, NC: Duke University Press.

Art Museum at the University of Memphis. (2016). *Women's History Month*. Retrieved from www.memphis.edu/amum/do_it/womenshistorymonth.php

Barad, K. (2007). *Meeting the Universe Halfway: Quantum Physics and the Entanglement of Matter and Meaning*. Durham, NC: Duke University Press.

Bridges-Rhoads, S., Hughes, H. E. and Van Cleave, J. (2018). Readings that rock our worlds. *Qualitative Inquiry*, 24(10), 817–837.

Davies, B. (2016). Emergent listening. In N. K. Denzin and M. D. Giardina (Eds.), *Qualitative Inquiry Through a Critical Lens* (pp. 81–92). New York, NY: Routledge.

Gilligan, C. (1982). *In a Different Voice: Psychological Theory and Women's Development*. Cambridge, MA: Harvard University Press.

Gilligan, C. (2015). The Listening Guide method of psychological inquiry. *Qualitative Psychology*, 2(1), 69–77.

Irigaray, L. (1991). *Marine Lover of Friedrich Nietzsche*. Trans. G. C. Gill. New York, NY: Columbia Press.

Jackson, A. Y. and Mazzei, L. (2011). *Thinking with Theory in Qualitative Research: Viewing Data Across Multiple Perspectives*. New York, NY: Routledge.

Kimmerer, R. (2013). *Braiding Sweetgrass: Indigenous Wisdom, Scientific Teachings, and the Wisdom of Plants*. Minneapolis, MN: Milkweed Editions.

Lorde, A. (2012). *Sister Outsider: Essays and Speeches*. USA: Crossing Press.

Manning, E. (2009). *Relationscapes: Movement, Art, Philosophy*. Cambridge, MA: Massachusetts Institute of Technology Press.

Manning, E. (1994/2019). *The Perfect Mango*. Brooklyn, NY: Punctum.

Richardson, L. and St. Pierre, E. A. (2005). Writing: A method of inquiry. In N. K. Denzin and Y. S. Lincoln (Eds.), *The SAGE Handbook of Qualitative Research* (3rd Edition) (pp. 959–978). Thousand Oaks, CA: SAGE.

Rust, M. (2013). Blood and tears as ink: Writing the pictorial sense of the text. *The Chaucer Review*, 47, 390–415.

Singh, J. (2017). *Unthinking Mastery: Dehumanism and Decolonial Entanglements.* Durham, NC: Duke University Press.

Taylor, C. A. and C. Hughes. (2016). *Posthuman Research Practices in Education.* London: Palgrave Macmillan.

Taylor, C. A. and Ulmer, J. B. (2020). Post-industrial methodologies for post-industrial cities. *Somatechnics*, 10(1), 7–34.

Ulmer, J. B. (2018a). Pivots and pirouettes: Carefully turning traditions. *Qualitative Inquiry*, 0(00), 1–4, doi: 10.1177/1077800419829778

Ulmer, J. B. (2018b). Writing as gratitude. In Van Cleave, J., Bridges-Rhoads, S. and Hughes, H. (Eds.), Readings that rock our world. *Qualitative Inquiry*, 24(10), 819.

Ulmer, J. B. and Koro-Ljungberg, M. E. (2016). Writing visually through (methodological) events and cartography. *Qualitative Inquiry*, 21(2), 138–152.

Van Cleave, J. and Bridges-Rhoads, S. (2017). Writing data. In M. Koro-Ljungberg, T. Löytönen and M. Tesar (Eds.), *Disrupting Data in Qualitative Inquiry: Entanglements with the Post-Critical and Post-Anthropocentric* (pp. 105–116). New York, NY: Peter Lang.

World Economic Forum. (2018). Key findings: Global gender gap report 2018. Cologny/Geneva, CH: Author. Retrieved from http://reports.weforum.org/global-gender-gap-report-2018/key-findings/

Index

ableism, definition of 20
ableness, negations of 20
Aboriginal Dreamtime 142
absence, agency of 36–7
absenting, epistemological violence of 36
Abu-Lughod, Lila 245
academic: hegemony 200, 203; theories 59; workplace 43–58
access, problem of 19, 22
accommodation 25; principles and practices of 20, 22; restricting access to 23
activist-teachers-of-colours 163
Acuff, Joni 203
adjectival cosmopolitanisms 155
African National Congress 120
Afrocentric womanhood 205
agentic dis/orientation, productive mode of 10
Ahmed, Sara 8, 22, 30, 33, 240
Alexander, M. Jacqui 128, 132
American Africanism 36
Angharad, Jên 169, 171
anthropocene feminism 90
anthropocentric/ism 60, 63, 64, 71
anti-blackness 61, 64, 159, 161
anti-feminine (presenting)-queerness 148
Anwalt, Bradly 118
Anzaldúa, Gloria 127–9, 143, 154, 156
apparatus 13, 93, 97, 99, 218, 222
arts-based autoethnography 199, 202, 207
arts-based research: autoethnographic reflection 202; complicating feminist discourse 203–4; coping and forward movement 207; critical race feminism and intersectionality 205–6; on inspiration for art making 200; material feminist narratives 206–7; method of 213–14; passion and dissent 208–9; racialized and gendered identity in 199; textile and fiber arts 201; theory in the flesh 204–5, 207; transdisciplinary narrative 200; on women of color as thought/t.h.o.t leaders 201–2
Asher, Nina 104, 107
"as if," practice of 40–1
assemblage 2, 4, 17, 61, 95–7, 99, 142, 170, 179, 213, 219–21
austerity, politics of 172, 174–5
autoethnography: arts-based 207; 'I' of 213; sense of 104, 134, 199

Bakhtin, M.M. 143
Bal, Mieke 91; transdisciplinary concepts 92
Barad, Karen 4, 8, 12, 92–4, 97, 99, 142, 184–5, 188, 190, 194–5, 222, 240, 243
bathroom signage initiative 78
Belcourt, Christi 61, 73
#BelieveWomen movement 237
belonging, sense of 103, 195
Bergson, Alexandra 221
Bernasconi, Robert 232
Bettcher, Talia Mae 22, 79–80, 84–5
biological racism 120
biomateriality, of individual living bodies 79
biopolitical paradigm 20
Black bodies: dehumanization of 10; and production of whiteness 37
Black feminism 125, 146; within hip-hop culture 201
Black feminist theory 40
Black Lives Matter movement 134
Blackmore 12
blackness: reality of whiteness and 36; significance of 36
Black people 6, 33, 37, 158, 160

Index 249

black sand-water encounters 64–6
Blackwell, Kelsey 159
Black women 145; hair experiences of 204; identity and sexuality of 201; during slavery 35–6; spirituality of 128; *see also* woman of color (WoC)
body-at-home, 'neutral' description of 7
Braidotti, Rosi 10, 35, 37–8, 40–1, 240; figuration of the nomadic subject 35
Brennan, Joy 19
Bresler, Liora 144
British Journal of Sport Medicine (BJSM) 118
Brown feminism, within hip-hop culture 201
Burlein, Ann 22
Butler, Judith 230
Butler, Octavia 29, 34–5, 37, 40–1

ceremony 66–7, 241
Chac Mool (Carlos Fuentes) 214
Chand, Dutee 119–20
chemistry education: Barad's agential realism on 185; cogenerative dialogues 187–9; gendered nature of 184; intra-action with students 193–6; research on 185–6; 'scientific' practices in 185; snaplogs, use of 189–93; socio-cultural aspects of 184, 186; teaching, learning and research 184–5; transition state theory 186–7; use of material feminist theory in 184–5
Chen, Mel 19
Chicana/Latina feminism: Coyolxauhqui imperative 130; enfleshed praxis across disciplines and dimensions 125–6; healing colonial wounds through spiritualized methodologies 129; spiritual activism of 127–8; as spiritual facilitators 126–7; spirituality of 124–5, 127; spiritualized methodologies of 128–9; spiritual possibilities of 134–5; spiritual praxis of 130, 132–3; transdisciplinary feminist research 134–5; womanism and 126–7
child-educator watery relations 73
childhood pedagogies 2, 59, 64, 70–2
chromosome screening 116
cisgender feminism, political motivations of 81
cisgenderism 76, 84
clothing, policing of 45
Coahuiltecan people 67, 70–2
coalition-building, among trans and cis-people 85

Coast Salish forest (British Columbia) 60, 62, 69, 70–1
Coatlicue (goddess of creation and destruction) 130
cogenerative dialogues (cogens) 185, 187–9
cognitive learning 60
colonial dehumanisation 160
colonial educational systems 130
colonialism 5, 12–13, 61, 73, 126, 130, 133, 156, 157 commodification of education 91
community 24, 53, 57, 64, 67, 72, 76–7, 104, 127, 133–4, 170, 174, 178–80, 213, 240–1
community-based knowledges 59
community-building and alliances 81
confessing ignorance, act of 157
conocimiento 127
consciousness of the borderlands 107
constitutional equality 160
constructing a life, effects of 132
contamination-by-association 90
corporeal cosmopolitanism 154–6
cosmopolitics, formulation of 155
counter-diagnostic effects, conditions for 24
'counter-eugenic' relations and spaces 24
Coyolxauhqui imperative 130–1
Crenshaw, K. 199, 202, 204–5
critical cosmopolitanism 156
Critical Disability Studies: definition of ableism 20; false problem *see* false problems; knowledge-in-advance 17; problem of structure 22; as transdisciplinary 16, 23–5; transdisciplinary pluralism 21–3
critical race feminism: and intersectionality 205–6; processes of social categorization 205
critical trans politics, notion of 87
Critique of Pure Reason (Immanuel Kant) 231
curative 17–18, 20

Dakota Access Pipeline, on Great Sioux Nation territory 66
dance 95, 168–9, 172, 240
David-Ménard, Monique 226–7, 230
Davies, Bronwyn 239
Davis, Brent 144
Davis, Daryl 133–4
deadly fantasy, notion of 13
de Beauvoir, Simone 2, 224

250 *Index*

de Casanova, Erynn Masi 44–6
decolonial-queer feminism 153, 162; decolonial-Black-queer-feminisms 165
deep listening, notion of 139, 141
deficit, objectification of 20
Deleuze, Gilles 16, 21, 25, 168, 217; *Difference and Repetition* (1994) 22
Deleuze, Gilles and Guattari, Felix 6, 93, 97, 142, 213, 219
Delphy, Christine 229–30
Despret, Vincianne 212, 214, 221–2, 240
detoxification of the body 130
Deutscher, Penelope 226–7, 230
developmentalism 63
dialectical illusion 231
dialogic cosmopolitanism 155
dialogicity, politics of 154, 158–9
dialogues: body-based elements of 163; cogenerative 187–9; dialogue-in-practice 154
diaspora identities 107
diasporic, notion of 106
Differences of Sexual Development (DSD) regulations 116–17
differential consciousness 156, 158, 162
diffraction: in Barad and Haraway 190; for ecofeminist performance pedagogy 94–5; as metaphor 91–4; metaphor as 91–4; notion of 95; translation into dramaturgical form 98; workshop as pedagogy of 95–9
disabled bodyminds, status of 20
disciplinarity, fortress model of 2
disciplinary knowledge 1–3, 12, 77, 91, 217
(un)disciplined thinking: academic disciplines and 217; artifacts of 213; conditions for certain thoughts 216–20; demands of 220–2; method to examine 213–14; and power of transdisciplinary thought 222; sense-making apparatus 218–19; significance of 212–13; terrain of 214–16; transdisciplinary thinking 213
dismantling privilege 155–61
division of labour 90
Dolan, Jill 94, 99–100
Dorlin, Elsa 229–30
dramaturgy: effects of differentiation on 99; as experimental apparatus 97–9; practice of 95, 97; self-reflexive 99; translation of diffraction into 98
dress and clothing: dress codes, influence of 44–8; politics of 44

dress codes and sexism: about clothing appropriateness 45; in academy 44–8; appropriateness based on clothing choices and habits 45; appropriate to the job 44; attributed to women's clothing 47; and belief of natural belonging 45; in business workplace 44; Casanova's study on 44–6; Entwistle's view on 45, 48; in female-dominated spaces 47; judgements about women's clothing 45; Molloy's view on 49; policing of clothing 45; power dressing 51–6; rules of "dress for success" 51; "rules" or conventions of dressing the female body 45; sex discrimination in 46; sexual objectification 45; sociology of 48; uniforms and safety wear 44; in white-collar workspaces 47; women's negotiation of unequal dress rules 46
dress for success, rules of 49, 51
dressing for work, issues of 47

early childhood education 59; curriculum-making 63, 69; developmental watery pedagogies in 62–3; education training 63; water play in a toddler classroom 62; water revolution in 64, 73
ecofeminism 90; aspects of diffraction for 94–5
ecofeminist fabulations, in the university 99–101
education: chemistry education *see* chemistry education; colonial curriculums 131; colonialism in 130; in early childhood *see* early childhood education; higher education 44, 93; privatization of 130–1; reforms in 130
embodiment 76, 77, 79, 80, 84–6, 98, 121, 132, 139, 144, 155
e-motion 179
empathetic knowing, act of 157
energy work 129–31; as methodology 133–4
enforced cosmopolitanism 156
Enlightenment dualisms and paternalisms 142
ensemble of life 213–14, 220
Entwistle, Joanne 45, 48
Equity Services 77–8
Erickson, Fredrick 144
eSwatini 61–2
ethnic social networks 106
Euromerican liberal cosmopolitanisms 156
Euromerican political philosophy 156
Evans, Nicolas 177–8

faith-based practices, discriminating against 48
false problems 21, 24; of access 19; of cure and disciplinary fidelity 18–21; effect of 20; problem of 17
Fanon, Frantz 7, 164; safety, theory of 160; transformative violence, theory of 160
female athletes 116–21
female athleticism: feminine version of 116; medical intervention to lower testosterone levels 118; *see also* sportswomen's bodies, surveillance of
female embodiment 76, 80
female worker, semiotics of 50
feminism and trans activism 85
feminism, productivity of 81
feminist activism 43
Feminist Educators Against Sexism (#FEAS): on dress codes and sexism 44–8; Power Dressing project 44, 46–7, 56; purpose of 43; transdisciplinary feminist project 44
feminist indiscipline 4; walking as 11–13
feminist material-discursive-embodied engagements 60
feminist materiality, tenets of 184
feminist research 185, 189, 239, 243
feminist socio-political praxis 6
feminists of colours, activist-scholarship of 163–4
feminist theory–praxis 6
feminist transdisciplinarity 5, 32, 153, 237; agency of absence 36–7; anteriority and futurity of 238; becoming transdisciplinary feminist researcher 38–40; inquiry 80, 84–6; knowing/feeling across time 32–5; listening to the progression of rust 238–40; methodology of 32; nomadic subjectivity 35–6; prerequisites for 154; rusty accounts of 244–6; rusty intra-actions 240–3; subjectivity through gender and race 34; in surveillance of sportswomen's bodies 120–1; transdisciplinary rustlings 243–4; unlearning in the wake 37–8
feminist transdisciplinary scholarship 84
Fernandes, Leela 127, 129, 158
Five Mujeres, The 44
Flint River 63
folds of time and place: extensive and intensive pleats in/of movement 169–71; futures folds 179–81; gastric folds 176; gender unfolds 174–5; gut-cradling mannerism 175–8; Leibniz's concept of 168; more-than of methodology 171–2; movement (un)folds and becoming unstuck 178–9; staring with movement folds 168–9
'folk genetics' of Black athletic physicality 120
forced migration: of nomadism 35; of slavery 35
Fordham, Signithia 145
forest–water encounters 67–9
Foucault, Michel 25, 84, 217, 235n17
found poetry, notion of 105
Fraisse, Geneviève 225–7, 230–1
freedom, concept of 34, 231
Fritsch, Kelly 17
Fuentes, Carlos 214

gender: authenticity 76, 82; concept of 224; social determinations of 226; social relation of domination 229
gender democratization 79; in public spaces 87
gendered marginalization 204
gender essentialism 90
gender examinations 116
gender inequality 203
gender legitimacy 76, 82
gender policing 77, 80, 116; material consequences of 80; of women-only spaces 83
Gender Recognition Act (UK) 79
gender suspicion policy 116
Gender Trouble (Judith Butler) 230
gender verification policy 116
generated poetry, notion of 105
getting lost, concept of 104
Gilligan, Carol 239
Glissant, Édouard 141, 154, 161, 163
Global North 124, 126, 157, 164
Global South 120, 135, 155
glove-using economy 195
Goldacre, Ben 119
Gordon, Lewis 160
Gotman, Kélina 94
Grosz, Elizabeth 92–3
Guattari, Felix 170–1
Guerrilla Girls 44, 48
gut, thinking 168, 170, 180

Haraway, Donna 6, 13, 29, 92, 94, 99–100, 184, 190, 221–2
Harvey, David 155

Heldian cosmopolitanism 156
Herschel, Caroline 10
Higher Education (HE) teaching 44, 93, 154, 243; diffractive 'differencing' in 93
Hill, Lauryn 201, 203
hip-hop culture: Black/Brown feminism within 201–2; feminist theory of 202, 207; generationally specific 202; patriarchal power structures of 205
Hofman, Ana 141
Holbein's *memento mori* 230
Holmes, Barbara 128, 164
home 31–3, 38, 61, 70, 103, 105, 107, 108, 112–13, 193
Hominina 175, 179
hope 59, 64, 105, 154, 180, 202, 222, 238
Hull, Akasha Gloria 128
human–nonhuman: coalitions 6; relationality 10
human rights law, Ontario (Canada) 77
hybrid consciousness 107
hyperandrogenism regulations 116

identity: concept of 33, 48, 107, 112, 200–1; politics of 56, 78, 81, 156–7; race/gender and 8, 199–202
Imaginary Homelands (Salman Rushdie) 106
immigrant 103, 106
impossible paradox 46–7, 50, 52
inclusion, paradox of 19–20, 82
independence and uninterruptability, fiction of 19
Indigenous feminism/s: black sand–water encounters 64–6; forest–water encounters 67–9; knowledge-theory-practice 59–61; mastery and control as primary modes of knowing 64; ocean estrangements 61; *siwasho* medicine 61; Standing Rock Oceti Sakowin encounters 67; theories of change 60; on water as life 66; water pipes and racial capitalist abandonment 63–4; water revolution in early childhood education 73; watery pedagogies 62–3; Yana wana 69–72
Indigenous knowledges 59–60
Indigenous peoples 124–5, 158–9
Industrial Revolution 172
inheritance, relationalities of 7–8, 60, 66, 161, 163
interconnectivity 125, 132–4
interdisciplinary 16–17, 91, 193–4, 214

International Association Federation of Athletics Federation (IAAF) 116–17; policy on hyperandrogenism 118–19; use of testosterone evidence 119
International Olympics Committee (IOC) 116
interruptions, in transdisciplinary feminist work 153–5; privilege and accountability (first interruption) 155–8; radical healing (third interruption) 162–5; vigilance and refusal (second interruption) 158–62
intersectionality 25, 83, 119–20, 125, 157, 163; Crenshaw's theory of 202, 204; critical race feminism and 205–6; of racialized and gendered body 205
intra-action 93, 188–90; rusty intra-actions 240–3
Irigaray, Luce 140, 225, 246
Islamophobia 159

Jones, Alison 157, 159–61
justice-based praxis 154

Kafer, Alison 17, 20
Kantian cosmopolitanism 156
Kant, Immanuel 224, 232–3; *Critique of Pure Reason* 231; idea of transcendental illusion 232
Kindred (fiction novel) 29, 32; Kevin and Dana, story of 29–33; literary and cultural value of 34; notion of time 30; Octavia Butler's 29, 34–5, 37, 40–1; positioning of Black women during slavery 35–6; present-ness of slavery 33; reproduction of knowledge 30; rereading melancholic subjects 30; time-traveling experience 29; transdisciplinary feminist methodology 32
knowing/feeling across time, notion of 32–5
knowing in being, practice of 12
knowledge building 243
knowledge-creation and exchange, nature of 96
knowledge production 1, 31, 38, 48, 187, 202; modes of 77, 124; transdisciplinary feminist practice and 154
knowledge, reproduction of 30
Knowles, Solange 204
Kolata, Gina 118
Koopman, Colin 23
Koro-Ljungberg, Mirka 242
Ku Klux Klan (KKK) 133

LaBelle, Brandon 142
Lane, Cathy 139
Lang, Theresa 97
Lather, Patti 104
Leonardo, Zeus 160–1
'letting go/moving on' praxi 6
life: with disability 20; without disability 20
Limits of Cross-Cultural Dialogue, The (Alison Jones) 159
Listening Guide, The 239
lived experience 105; of feeling like a foreigner 103–5; of Indian diaspora 106; of minority community 104; sense of belonging 103
Liverpool 6–8, 10
living in-between, notion of 106–8
Lorde, Audra 162–3, 244
love 140, 158, 161, 164–5; radical love 155
Lugones, Maria 156–7, 162, 164–5
Luther, Rashmi 113
Lykke, Nina 93, 184, 194

McCartney, Andra 140–1
McRuer, Robert 16, 23
Mader, Mary Beth 21
'male' hormone *see* testosterone
mannerism, concept of 168–72, 174–5, 178, 180–1
Manning, Erin 16, 171, 179–80, 213, 240
Martin, Jane Roland 145
masculine and feminine energies 72
Massumi, Brian 97
material feminism 12, 185–7, 196; narratives on 206–7
materialist ethico-onto-epistemological endeavour 6
matter 4–6, 12, 93, 185–8, 193–6
Matthews, John 95–6
Mayan law of In Lak'ech 127
Mazzei, Lisa 12, 96
melancholic subjects, knowledge of 30–2
Merleau-Ponty's phenomenology 7
mestiza consciousness 107
#MeToo movement 47, 237
Mexican Revolution of 1910 214
Mingus, Mia 25; principle of creating collective access 25
Mitchell, David T. 23
Mol, Annemarie 21, 95
Molloy, John 49
Moraga, Cherrí 203
Morrison, Toni: on parasitical nature of white freedom 36; *Playing in the Dark* (1993) 36

Moten, Fred 142, 146
Muddying the Waters (Richa Nagar) 153

naked parades 116
Nash, June 214
Neimanis, Astrida 66, 95
nepantlera 127–8
new materialism 90, 142, 170
nomadism: 'as if' as nomadic resistance 40–1; becoming-nomadic 38–40; forced migration of 35; nomadic subjectivity 34, 35–8
non-transcendent knowledge 13
non-White 'others,' notion of 10
normalized settler atmospherics 64
North American Free Trade Agreement 215
Novotny, Helga 186

objects 7, 12, 13, 92, 130, 186, 212, 213, 216, 221, 226
ocean estrangements 61
Olympic Committee 120
ontological equality 160
ontological negation, effects of 32, 35
opacity, right to 161–2
oppression, theory of 85, 129–30, 134–5, 142–3, 158, 164, 202, 206, 209
'oppressor/being oppressed ↔ resisting' complex 156
Owens, Lama Rod 154, 162–6

Palmer, Helen 93
Pape, Madeline 119
parental/carer relationships 177
pedagogy 16, 90–100, 128, 130, 187–8; living pedagogy 104–5
peer review, practices of 17
people of color (PoC) 124, 159–61, 208; participation in 'dialogues' about race 161; violence against 208
Perfect Mango, The (1994/2019) 240
performance 48, 50, 92–4, 94, 99, 105, 118, 200; performance studies 91
Performing (with) Matter 93–4
personhood, extraction of 10, 33
Phelps, Michael 117
photography 48, 50
Pinto, Samantha 138, 148
placebo and nocebo effects, research on 18–19
Playing in the Dark (1993) 36
Poetics of Relation (Édouard Glissant) 154
Poitras, Violet 69

Index

political fictions 35
Porter, Ronald 160–1, 164
post-colonial 103–5
potentiality, concept of 21
power dressing 56; concept of 49; with women academics and students 51–6
Power Dressing project 44, 46–7; design and curation of 48–51; key intention of 52
powerful knowledge, concept of 12
power-laden binaries 59
power shoots 56
Price, Margaret 16, 20, 22
problem solving 17, 133
professionalism, notion of 47, 204
professional philosopher 19
property, afterlife of 32
public education, privatization of 130
public spaces, gender democratization in 78, 80, 87
public washrooms: regulation of 82; trans-inclusion in 82
Pulkkinen, Tuija 43
pure reason, ideas of 231–2
Pussy Riot 44

Qualitative Inquiry conference 207
queer feminism 147, 153, 155, 162
queer style 50
queer walking 5

race: hierarchies of 12, 34, 37; idea of 232
race–gender–class relations 10
racial stamina 8–9
racism 5, 73, 83, 120–1, 130, 157, 159–61
radical feminism 81, 83–4
radical healing, notion of 162–5
Ralston, Helen 103
rational psychology 233
Raymond, Janice 81, 86
Reconceptualizing Early Childhood Education Conference (RECE), Denmark 133
Records, Olivia 82–3
reflexivity, notion of 80, 99, 139, 141, 148
relationality, notion of 10, 60, 154–6, 158, 161–2, 164, 240, 244
Relationscapes (2009) 240
Research Excellence Framework, UK 90
Resilience and Triumph (Rashmi Luther) 113
respectability, politics of 202
rethinking "Self," process of 107
Richardson, Laurel 238
Riddell's vision of transinclusive feminism 86
Rudolph, Norma 12, 133–4
Rushdie, Salman 106

Sandoval, Chela 156
Sauer, Beverley 173
savarna (dominant/dominator castes) 157–9
scholars-of-colours 164
science education research group 188
science, gendered nature of 184
science learning 63, 188–9
scientific racism 120
Sedgwick, Eve Kosofsky 143
self-deception 157–8
self-identified gender identities 76
Semenya, Caster 2, 120; athletic record 116; battle for legitimacy 116–18; scrutiny of her physical appearance 117; testosterone regulations 117; 'unnatural' body 117
sensing–feeling–knowing activity 6
sentipensante (sensing/thinking) 128
serendipitous walking 5
settler colonialism 61, 73
sex: analytical priority of gender over 225; Anglophone feminist theory on 225, 227; categories of 230; concept of 2, 224, 228; contradictory elements in the concept of 232–3; de Beauvoir notion on 227–30; Delphy's concept of 229; discrimination 46; division of humanity 228; duality of 228; English theory on 226; exclusive division into male and female 233; French theory on 225–6; *la différence des sexes* 226–31; natural-biological concept of 228–33; natural foundation of 229; philosophical determination of 230; psychoanalytical concept of 226; *sexualité* 226, 227, 229, 231; and socially constructed gender identity 226; transcendental illusion of 233; transdisciplinary concept of 230; with and without gender 224–7
sex duality 228, 232–3
sex–gender binary 1
sex testing 2, 116
sexism 43, 44–8, 56–7, 86, 120–1, 126
sexual abuse 121
sexual difference 224–6
sexual objectification, at workplace 45
sexuation, process of 229
shadowing 185, 187, 193–6

Shahidi, Yara 206
Sharpe, Christina 31–2, 34, 38, 61, 64; theorization of the wake 35
silence 8, 10, 34, 37, 66, 105, 138, 139, 143–7, 161, 164, 165, 175
Simmons, Kristen 64
Simondon, Gilbert 173, 179
Singh, Julietta 243
situated knowledges, power of 1, 13, 43
siwasho (medicine) 61, 62
slam poetry 207
slavery: afterlife of 32–3; effects of ontological negation 32–3; forced migration of 35; positioning of Black women during 35–6; present-ness of 33; slaves as 'cargo' or 'pawns' 10; transatlantic slavery 33, 41; treatments of enslaved people 32; White participation in abolition of 10
slave trade 7, 10, 40–1
Smith, Linda Tuhiwai 72
Smith, Mark M. 142, 145
snaplogs, use of 189–93
Snyder, Sharon L. 23
social categorization, processes of 205
social codes, at workplace 47
social/ecological transformation 128
social hierarchies 30–1, 40
social justice 31, 142; purpose and goals of 131; spiritualized transdisciplinary models of 129, 131
social transformation 129, 131
sociology of dress 48
soul, substantiality of 231
sound feminisms: attunement 140–1; deep listening and 139, 141; perspectives on voice and silence 138; qualitative research on 138; reclaiming of 146; resonances, reverberations and reverb 141–3; significance of 138–47; social justice 142; sonic arts-based research 139; sonic color line 145; vibrational affects of 141–3; voice, silence and noise 143–7
sonic methodologies 138, 148
South African Sports Confederation 120
speculative 1, 4, 6, 12, 29, 40, 169, 170, 172, 231
spiritual activism 127–8, 130, 165
spiritualized methodologies 128–9, 131, 133, 135
spirituality, notion of 126
spiritual praxis, notion of 130, 132–3
spiritual transformations, of selfhoods 128

spiritual wellbeing 131
Sport's Court of Arbitration (CAS) 117
sportswomen's bodies, surveillance of 116–21; critical intersectional analysis of 119–20; feminine version of female athleticism 116; feminist transdisciplinary and 120–1; gender policing and 116; medical intervention to lower testosterone levels 118; racial difference in 120; regulatory practices in 116; testosterone, policy on 118; testosterone-suppressing medication 117; *see also* Semenya, Caster
Stacey, Judith 241, 245
Standing Rock Oceti Sakowin Camp 61, 66, 67, 72
Stanford, Stella 17, 23
Stenberg, Amandla 206
Stengers, Isabelle 24, 221–2, 240
Stoever, Jennifer 142, 145
Stoller, Robert 225
Stone, Sandy 83
Strathern, Marilyn 21
Sumara, Dennis 144
systemic gender disparities 43

technology of the self 49–50
tenure 81, 212, 213, 220, 244
testosterone 118; discourse of science and sport 118; IAAF policy on 119; impact on athletic performance 118; medication suppressing production of 117; misconceptions about 118; naturally-produced 118; public health issue regarding levels of 118–19
textile (and fiber) arts 48, 201, 206
Theatre and Performance Studies 91–2
theory in the flesh 202, 204–5, 207
theory-knowledge 60
theory-methodology-praxis 4, 6
Thich Nhat Hanh 154, 163, 165
This Bridge Called My Back: Writings by Radical Women of Color (1981) 203
Thompson, Marie 113, 145–6
time, notion of 30
time-travelling 29, 34
#TimesUp movement 47, 237
Titchkosky, Tanya 20
Tovar, Inez Hernandez 165
Traister, Rebecca 203
trans bodies: coalition-building with cis-people 85; dehumanization of 81; patriarchal colonization of 81
trans informed epistemologies 76, 84

256 Index

transcendental illusion 231–3
transdisciplinarity 21, 31; Bal's concept of 92; as boundary-negotiating practice 17; diffraction as metaphor 91–4; feminist *see* feminist transdisciplinarity; knowledge production 1; learning opportunity 99; metaphor as diffraction 91–4; notion of 17; problem solving using 17; promise of 23–5; unlearning in the wake 37–8
transdisciplinary discipline 43
transdisciplinary feminisms *see* feminist transdisciplinarity
transdisciplinary feminist research 124; role of pedagogy play in 90; spiritualized methodologies as 128–9
transdisciplinary pluralism 24; intuiting the virtual through 21–3
transdisciplinary rustlings 243–4
transdisciplinary 'transition state' 185
transdisciplinary traveller 38–40
trans-exclusionary radical feminist (TERF) 76; concerns to preserve women's-only safe spaces 81–2; contesting trans-exclusionary radical feminism 83–4; epistemological necessity of 84–6; historical backdrop to 81–3; on legitimacy of Nixon's claim to womanhood 82; radical feminism as 82; and trans informed accounts 81
transfeminism 84–6
Transfeminist Manifesto 84–5
transformative 'living pedagogy' 105
transformative violence, theory of 160
transgender washrooms 78
transinclusive feminism 85; Riddell's vision of 86
transition state 1, 184–97
trans-misogyny 86; oppression of 85
transphobia: charges of 80; definition of 84; notion of 84, 86; recognition of 82
Transsexual Empire, The (Janice Raymond) 81
transsexual women 81, 82; exclusion from 'the Land' in the Michigan Women's Music Festival 82–3; exclusion from women's spaces 82; integration into feminism 86; ontological legitimacy of 83, 86; rights to legally identify as women 79; self-identification policy 83
Trans Woman Manifesto (Serano) 85
traveler, becoming 38–40
Trinh, Minh ha 103–4, 6, 112, 113
Trishanku's curse 106–8

trust, notion of 82, 85
Tuck, Eve 60
Turtle Island 66, 72

Universal Credit 177
university institutional practices 11

Vancouver Rape Relief Centre, Canada 81–2
van der Tuin, Iris 92–3, 95–6, 99
violence against women: collaborative action against 85–6; in public spaces 80, 82
violence, vulnerability to 32
violent exclusion, practices of 23
virtuality, meaning of 21–2

Wake, the: theorization of 35–6; transdisciplinary unlearning in 37–8
walking: with buildings and sugar 6–11; as feminist indiscipline 11–13; as trans (disciplinary)mattering 4–6
wardrobe engineering 49
washroom inclusivity: bathroom signage initiative 78; and debates about who gets to count as a woman 77–81; and gender identity 78; gender policing 77; problem of access to public bathrooms 77; transgender people's access to 78; trans-inclusion in public washrooms 82; Western's policy on 77–81
Waterman, Ellen 141
water revolution, in earlychildhood education 73
watery pedagogies: Black-Indigenous feminist knowledge-theory-practice 59; black sand-water encounters 64–6; child-centered 60; developmental and anthropocentric 64; in early childhood education 62–3; Euro-Western colonial practices 64; forest–water encounters 67–9; Mní Wičhóni Nakíčižiŋ Owáyawa 66; ocean estrangements 61; possibilities for 59; Standing Rock Oceti Sakowin encounters 66, 67; troubling mastery and control 64; water pipes and racial capitalist abandonment 63–4; Western scientific modes of knowing water 64; Yana wana 69–72
Western Art Music notation 148
Western masculinism 10
Western modernity, Braidotti's notion of 10
White (privileged) body, notion of 10
white freedom, parasitical nature of 36

white nationalism 133
Whiteness: attending to 6–11; dependence on the production and reproduction of blackness 36; edifice of 8; as inheritance 7; institutionalization of 8; normalizing episteme of 11; production of 37; as unracialized identity or location 8
white racial domination 7
white supremacy 30, 38, 157; strategies of 11
Williams, Angel Kyodo 83, 154, 162–4
Wilson, Elizabeth 170–1, 176–7, 180
Womack, Anne-Marie 23
woman "as nature," domination of 91
woman, definition of 82; as adult human female 83
womanism, theory of 124–6, 128, 204, 205
woman of color (WoC) 48, 129, 200; artful and feminist modes of expression by 206; challenges for 203; fight for the equality 204; lived and spiritual experiences of 125; lived realities of 202; philosophies of 125; theory in the flesh 202, 204–5, 207; as thought/t.h.o.t leaders 201–2
women-born-women 81–2
Women: Dress for Success (Molloy) 49
'women only' spaces 80

Women's March, The 47
Woodson, Carter G. 146
Woolf, Virginia 216, 220
workplace clothing 46, 48, 50
workshop 168, 169, 171; as diffractive pedagogy 95–9
World Anti-Doping Association (WADA) 119
World Medical Association (WMA) 117
Wynter, Sylvia 10, 31, 142; argument about race 10

Yana wana (indigenous name for water in Texas) 69–72; early childhood pedagogies 70–2
Yemayá (Goddess of the living Ocean) 132
Yergeau, Melanie 18, 21, 23–4; on conditions for producing 'counter-diagnostic effects' 24; essay in Critical Disability Studies 18; problem/solution dyad 21
Young People and Place project 171

Zambrana, Rocío 17
Zapatista uprising 214
Zen Buddhism 158

Printed in Great Britain
by Amazon